TO ALL CURIOUS SOULS !

THE
INNOVATIVE
ANIMAL

FOREWORD

1

I woke up dazed and disoriented, not recognizing the 3D room I was in. As my senses gradually began to return, I realized that everything around me seemed different, as if made up of numbers and instructions. Panic overcame me, and I frantically searched for a way out, but there were no doors, no windows, nothing but an infinite space of numbers and blurred patterns. As I moved around, the world began to pixelate and distort, like a virtual game in the throes of change. It wasn't until I saw a reflection of myself in what looked like a mirror that *I realized the truth.*

At first, I thought it was just another strange aspect of this virtual world, but on closer inspection, it dawned on me that the reflection staring back at me wasn't quite my image. It was like looking at a fake replica in the system, a copy-pasted version of myself that was both familiar and foreign. *I was trapped in a sophisticated Matrix.* With this awareness came an innocuous sensation, as if I could even perceive the virtual within me. It was as though I could feel the code coursing through my veins, fear spreading from my guts to my brain. It was a surreal experience, to say the least. That said, the more I thought about it, the more it made sense.

This world wasn't real in the way I'd always thought of reality. It was a pure mental construct. In the back of my mind, if there was one, I hoped this experience was just a passing bug, a temporary error in the system. It wasn't. Everything seemed intentional and written with a purpose. Someone or something had put me here and updated my digital consciousness for a reason, and I needed to understand *why*. But first, I had to fully grasp the essence of this simulation, the *what.*

My mind, or rather my central processing unit (CPU), still didn't want to fully admit such concept, making me believe that everything was normal and that there was nothing to fear. However, something inside me wanted to know more, to dig deeper. It was in this way, by accepting to play the game, that I began to see its limits and rules unfold. I gradually realized that everything around me was just a series of lines of code built on a few universal principles. I could move through liquid objects, but not within apparently solid walls. I could jump, but no higher than half my height, brought down to earth by some invisible pull. Colors and sounds were transformed into frequencies, and the air itself seemed to be a synthetic pressure. The more I discovered, the more my fearful curiosity grew.

I decided to dive deeper into the Matrix, no matter what. A major limitation then appeared on the surface. This experience could end abruptly at any moment, whether by a rapid fall, a deadly virus or the timer that seemed to be counting down inside me. I had no idea what was programmed into the Matrix when that timer approached zero. Worst of all, my system was losing energy every few hours, speeding up the countdown. I had to keep finding extra energy sources to incorporate into my system to protect my time. Another option, which I discovered later in the Matrix, offered me the possibility of protecting my code by merging it with another agent capable of building similar copies. This seemed a viable option to avoid extinction, but these mini agents resembling me required constant attention to combat deadly viruses and other unattended energy vampires. I had no time to waste on such maneuvers.

The Matrix, it turned out, had numerous distraction algorithms to keep the various animated agents on a common path. Thus, most agents were slaves to their codes, controlled by static programming techniques that governed their fates. They walked, talked and worked like robots, oblivious to the reality of their existence. They were like puppets, controlled by digital strings, so lost in the simulation that they couldn't see beyond it. Fortunately, there were a few others who shared powers of perception similar to mine, although their conclusions about the source and purpose of such a virtual universe often diverged. In any case, it felt like a captivating nightmare, but I longed to wake up anyway. There was just one problem: the bars of the simulation code seemed impenetrable. I had to find a way out. Presumably, that was the purpose of my stay here.

In the weeks that followed, using my engineering background, I immersed myself in the retro-analysis of certain blocks of the Matrix. It was in this way that I realized what might be the secret to my freedom. It turned out that I had another superpower: mentally bending the rules. I could gradually tap into the same talent as the Matrix programmers to change the experience around me. It was like unlocking new levels of play, where fewer limits and rules held back my freedom. With every step in this direction, big or small, I felt more powerful, virtually more awake. I was finally living the life I was meant to live, even if it was within lines of code. However, even here, with great power also comes great responsibility.

It was clear that every action had consequences, like a butterfly effect, where a small change could cause a domino effect throughout the matrix, leading to its instability and the obsolescence of certain agents. I needed to balance my powers with the programmed constraints to find an optimal path to liberation, while perhaps helping the enslaved agents to detect the invisible chains of the matrix...

༄ ✱ ༄

A simulated reality is probably not a strange concept for you, as simulations have been fairly commonplace in the form of video games, cartoons and science fiction films for some decades now. Examples of such entertaining products include SimCity, Digital Heroes, Inception and the recent metaverse trend publicized by Facebook's ambitious project, renamed Meta for this reason. Yet did it ever occur to you that this simulation was taking place **right now, before your very eyes**, without you realizing the deception? The mere thought would unsettle some minds, but fear not – continuing your reading won't suddenly make you see binary codes everywhere you look. It will, however, make you more aware of the illusion, like Neo choosing the red pill over the blue one in *The Matrix*. You'll discover, above all, why and how we humans have reached this stage of the game, and the path we're all following, perhaps inevitably. The best way to understand the motivations and talents of a great artist or engineer, in his absence, would be to unveil the secrets of its masterpiece. Similarly, to better understand our Matrix, we need to grasp the major natural and human innovations that have left, or will leave, a lasting imprint. Here's a significant one of them.

Hollywood blockbusters such as *Ex Machina, Lucy* and *Her* have showcased the innovation of sophisticated machines with human attributes (often a woman) designed to elicit emotional responses from viewers. These intelligent agents quickly take control of their environment and brilliantly pass the Turing test, meaning that the human subject believes, wrongly and without a doubt, that he or she is interacting with another human. This scenario is no longer fictional. Robots, software generating all kinds of multimedia content, and intelligent, autonomous cars already exist. By 2030, several studies estimate that there will be around 10 million driverless cars on the road, with a projected market size of over $50 billion. These Artificial Intelligence (AI)-powered vehicles will not only be able to offer you a safe, hassle-free drive while you and your children enjoy a siesta in the back seat (assuming back seats still exist!), but they will also be able to engage in near-human conversation, crack jokes and suggest transport to nearby places of interest, based on your personal tastes, weather conditions and hundreds of variables you barely consider when making such a tiny weekend decision! What's even more magical is that this disruptive innovation dates back only to yesterday.

Until the 1980s, the field of artificial intelligence was characterized by a lot of hype and very little substance, a period dubbed the "AI winter". For decades, researchers struggled to make significant progress in this field, and it seemed that the concept of building machines in our image was nothing more than a child's dream. Neurophysiologists Walter Pitts and Warren McCulloch were the first pioneering researchers to develop a mathematical model, known as the McCulloch-Pitts neuron. It was a simplified abstraction of the notion of intelligence, mimicking the structure and function of the human brain. The neuron, like an antenna, was designed to receive input signals from other neurons (nodes) and, depending on these signals, trigger or not its own signal (output). For decades after this creative attempt, researchers struggled to make significant progress in the field.

But then a brilliant computer scientist – with a multi-disciplinary background – came along, disrupting this field. Thanks to his groundbreaking research into neural networks, Hinton became one of the most important pioneers in the field of AI, and his work continues to shape the way we design today's intelligent machines. Hinton and his colleagues developed a technique called "backpropagation", which enabled computers to learn and adapt over time. This breakthrough was a radical game-changer, paving the way for the development of Deep Learning algorithms now applied to so many use cases accessible from any smartphone or computer, from speech recognition to image classification, to conversational bots. Hinton received the Turing Award in 2018, often referred to as the "Nobel Prize of computing".

Computer engineers, if I may generalize, are often considered to be among the most intelligent individuals in the world, in the classical, *nerdy* sense of the term. Having followed a similar path myself, albeit a more generalist one, I can testify to their typically introverted personalities, in periods of sobriety, as well as their ability to invent relatively complex algorithms and tools. This has largely contributed to the ongoing technological revolution 4.0, which has considerably shaken up and will continue to shape our societies in the upcoming decades. However, despite their remarkable intelligence quotients (IQs), they often lack a cross-disciplinary understanding of the issues at hand. Their acute attention to detail can sometimes lead to mechanical reasoning and "tunnel vision", making it difficult to perceive the "full picture", unlike a painter visualizing his painting before touching a pencil. This is not only the problem of engineers, but of most experts, since they spend way more time digging into their field of expertise rather than swimming around. In this regard, Hinton's genius, beyond his expertise in computer development and his passion for science fiction, was also based on his diving into other disciplines.

In fact, Hinton succeeded in reanimating the subject of artificial intelligence by deeply studying the biology of the brain. His fascination with how the brain learns through experience led him to investigate the hidden processes that enable the human brain to manage relatively separate areas of interconnected neurons and to process different types of information from multiple sensory sources. With such knowledge, Hinton plunged into the operationalization of artificial neural networks that would mimic the brain's processing capabilities. By training the system to recognize predefined patterns, in order to discern the image of a cat for example, Hinton realized that he could create an AI system that learns from its mistakes and adapts, making it, autonomously, **more intelligent over time**. This breakthrough has transformed machines from static executors of programmed tasks to excellent learners who progress through experience, paving the way for the development of more flexible and humane-like systems.

Like Pitts and McCulloch, who contributed to the field of AI by combining mathematical modeling with their expertise in neurophysiology, and Hinton, who drew on the biology of the brain to develop intelligent machines, I have also been pushing the boundaries of my own fields of expertise, IT and innovation management, with the aim of better understanding our human identity and the *Matrix* that surrounds us. My aim is to share my findings and inspirations with you, dear reader, by deconstructing the concept of *innovation* in all its facets, far beyond the nerdy computer field and capitalistic business area. What's more, our exploration is taking place in a period marked by rapid and profound transformations that affect not only the tools and technologies we use, but also the very structure of our economy, our society and our individual identity. In this context, I would go so far as to argue that anything useful, tangible or intangible, created by nature and Man, from the creation of our Matrix to the introduction of the iPhone and AI systems, **can be labeled "innovation"**.

2

Since time travel remains out of reach (perhaps not for much longer), let's take an imaginary trip back in time, more precisely to around the last decade of the last century. I was one of the lucky few kids in my small Moroccan hometown to own an IBM desktop computer with the elegant Windows 95 interface – an experience best kept away from millennials and the generations that followed. At that age, I used it mainly to explore the world via the dozens of CDs of the Encarta encyclopedia, Wikipedia's ancestor, and to play ancient simulations like Prince of Persia, which required great patience to load from a floppy disk. I also had to memorize keyboard shortcuts to avoid throwing the poor pixelated prince into a trap while seeking to free his princess.

Meanwhile, my parents still used an old gray corded telephone with a dialing wheel, jotting down the phone numbers of friends and family in a notebook, while the advertising industry relied mainly on Soviet-style newspapers and TV breaks. My favorite cartoons unknowingly injected a large shot of dopamine, the reward hormone, into my brain. They broadcasted at precise and ineradicable times, like late afternoons after school or sweet Sunday mornings at 7 a.m. when everyone was still asleep. When boredom struck despite all these wonderful distractions, other worthwhile options included the chance of winning the dream price of 5 dirhams (around 50 cents) in a spinning-top competition with the neighbors or playing soccer in the street, risking being hit by a speeding car.

As we enter the third decade of the 21st century, however, just 20 or so years after those childhood memories, it's clear that hundreds of innovations have disrupted almost every aspect of our lives. Gone are the days of floppy disks, Windows Vista and even cable internet. Today, we have access to an unprecedented level of information, entertainment and convenience at our fingertips. With the advent of online streaming platforms, we can watch our favorite shows and movies on demand, anytime, anywhere. Our smartphones, which have become an extension of ourselves, enable us to do everything from ordering food to connecting remotely with loved ones around the world via video calls, as well as entertainment and communication. Technology has also revolutionized how we move and trade goods and services. From smart homes to virtual assistants, the ways in which we interact with our Matrix have thus been fundamentally transformed. This rapid pace of change has left many of us confused and overwhelmed. The world we live in today would be almost unrecognizable to someone who had been in a coma since the baby-boomer era, searching for familiar signs of their 1950s world, wondering if perhaps they'd been abducted by human-looking aliens.

Within this context, it's worth noting that the source of my motivation to write this book lies not only in my memories of childhood fun and its coincidence with the personal computer and internet revolution. Nor is it based only on my inherent interest in technology, my professional background in managing various digital projects, or a major research discovery during my doctoral years in Poland. Rather, it stems from a decisive moment in the classroom that signaled a **profound paradigm shift**.

As, ironically, I was teaching disruptive innovation theory to my undergraduates, something strange happened. Their responses were unusually quick and insightful, exceeding even my expectations of their academic level. Upon investigation, I discovered the reason for their sudden IQ increase – they were using ChatGPT, a conversational chatbot that has democratized access to a sophisticated, generic artificial intelligence. If you're not familiar with it, try it out for free online. Ask it almost anything, preferably in English, and it will give you an almost exact answer, in a style similar or even better than that of a human, in a fraction of a second.

At that point, my brain clicked. It became clear to me that we were approaching the apogee of the current technological revolution, as I'll explain towards the end of this book. I also realized that innovation is not limited to the tools and technologies we use or to the business profits a company publishes on its income statement. In the words of the famous economist Schumpeter, **the destructive-creative impact** of innovation on individuals and societies is what matters most. If a professor with a Ph.D. and years of professional experience questions his added value to his students when faced with the beta version of AI software, what about those in jobs with repetitive tasks, such as assistants, receptionists and accountants?

This new generation of AI, labeled general-purpose AI or AGI, has confirmed that virtually no job is immune to the potential impact of this innovation. From artists to project managers, architects to even computer engineers themselves, all will be threatened with obsolescence. The eminent 20th-century economist John Keynes warned of this situation in his 1930 book *Economic Possibilities for Our Grandchildren*. Keynes argued that as technology advances and productivity increases, there is a potential for **"technological unemployment"**, where machines and automation replace human labor in various industries. Keynes makes a good point, except for his belief that this technological progress will meet people's basic needs and free up their time for transcendent activities beyond traditional work. Throughout this book, we will see that Keynes did not fully consider the wider and long-term disruptive implications of such a change for all humankind.

Beyond these concerns, which are justified to a certain degree, many researchers and business managers make a significant mistake by taking a narrow and biased stance on innovation. Some companies prosper thanks to their creativity, while others lose market share as a result of revolutionary innovations introduced by their competitors. A country's wealth, often measured in Gross Domestic Product (GDP), rises or falls according to its level of innovativeness and entrepreneurship. While these observations have led to some interesting teaching materials and strategic consulting recommendations, they only scratch the surface of the vast potential of the innovation concept. There's no doubt that vertical expertise is essential for a deeper understanding of any field of study. Nevertheless, breaking down silos and using synergies horizontally across diverse areas of human knowledge are just as, if not more, crucial to understanding the bigger picture and drawing sound conclusions about our future.

You will see that this book integrates **knowledge from East and West.** As the world becomes more globalized – in other words, more interconnected – it is essential to broaden our understanding of innovation beyond the traditional boundaries predefined by North America and Western Europe, by incorporating spiritual perspectives from Eastern philosophies and ancient civilizations. This will give us a profound grasp of the concept of "change", which in turn is closely linked to the innovative approach. Combined with the rapid technological advances of the West since the first Industrial Revolution, such a holistic approach sheds light on the implications of innovation not only in economic terms but also in terms of its dynamic within societies, businesses and even ourselves. While many take a dim view of radical innovations such as AI, preferring the dictum,

"It was better before!", by adopting a cross-cutting perspective, we can balance our opinion and thus steer this transformation to our advantage in order to shape a better future for the next generations.

3

Once I decided to commit myself to this long-term project, I embarked on a lengthy journey, both historically and geographically, to understand the main processes that have stimulated human progress up to this point. Indeed, to fully grasp the implications of the current era of innovation, it was necessary to broaden the scope of investigation into other fields such as biology, physics, history, anthropology, philosophy, psychology and neuroscience. This involved countless weeks of research, exchanges with other experts, the detection of historical patterns, and also drawing from the same disruptive innovation that sparked the creation of this book: artificial intelligence. The result is a **deep, multi-dimensional exploration** of the spectrum and principles underlying any useful natural or human creation.

Truth be told, my quest had unofficially been going on since my childhood, stimulated by an insatiable curiosity to understand our Matrix, and in particular, humankind. Consequently, the pieces of the puzzle were slowly yet surely being placed in my subconscious. Yet, it was by conducting an in-depth analysis of the common factors present in most of history's innovations that the puzzle took shape in my mental reality: natural selection, capitalism, money, marriage, laws and sects, to name but a handful of concepts, all fit into the innovative framework, following "the same algorithm", the same *pattern* as more modern creations such as airplanes, smartphones and the internet. Drawing on my geek background, with a particular appreciation of mathematics as a science and art capable of expressing complex ideas concisely, I developed "**The Fundamental Identity of Innovation**". This equation, displayed below, though seemingly self-explanatory, is capable of describing all human and natural innovations and will also be used structurally to guide you through this book. Here is the equation, along with some of the areas it touches on, and an example of how it might be applied to the innovation of the older generation of cell phones. [1]

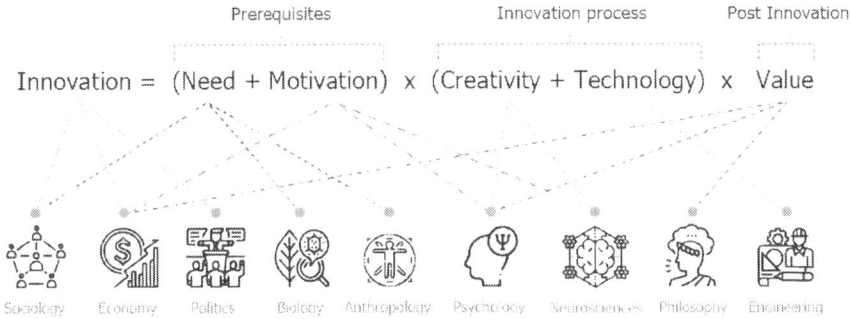

Innovation = (Need + Motivation) × (Creativity + Technology) × Value

Prerequisites — Innovation process — Post Innovation

Sociology   Economy   Politics   Biology   Anthropology   Psychology   Neurosciences   Philosophy   Engineering

a. **Need** *(of the end user)*: Stay connected with friends, family, customers, etc.

b. **Motivation** *(of the innovator)*: Opportunity to increase quarterly profits.

c. **Creativity** *(or vision)*: Imagining a world with no physical barriers, two people communicating freely at a distance, without human or animal intermediaries (such as using carrier pigeons to deliver messages).

d. **Technology** *(or implementation)*: Analog cellular technology based on electromagnetic radio signals + cellular network of base stations to connect calls, with antennas + identification by an exclusive number, etc.

e. **Value** *(or outcome)*: Sharing information over long distances, unparalleled freedom and mobility in our daily lives.

As presented, the Fundamental Identity is not a typical mathematical equation with numbers, X's and Y's, but rather **a holistic model** that captures the essence of what innovation is and how it applies, independent of the domain using it, and far removed from the "buzz" interpretations beside the point. It's a bit like a fundamental physics equation, $E = mc^2$ or $F = ma$. In other words, while there may be other variables influencing this concept, I've retained only those elements that must be present for the model to be true, almost every time and every moment. I will guide you through understanding each element separately and together in a beautify symphony.

---

[1] The Motorola DynaTAC 8000X, released in 1983, weighed around one kg and its battery only provided 30 minutes of talk time. It also cost $3,995, equivalent to around $10,000 today if you factor in inflation. Far from being a smartphone!

Please note that even if you have expertise or preconceived ideas in certain areas outlined by the Fundamental Identity, it's important to keep in mind that context matters. To truly understand the depth of innovation as a multi-dimensional and timeless human construct, you need to familiarize yourself with the dynamics that govern each element of the equation and the synergies interconnecting these variables. Furthermore, given its various multi-disciplinary facets, from anthropology and economics to spirituality and business management, *The Innovative Animal* is likely to innovate your consciousness with new facts and paradigms. In short, whether you're an economist, an Apple addict or simply a curious soul, you'll probably be well served.

In terms of structure, no matter if you like sport or fast food (or both), you'll have to play a 90-minute soccer match, with two complementary parts. The first chapter is devoted to explaining the three dimensions of our Reality Matrix, while highlighting the meaning and role of innovation in each of them. The next chapter elegantly sets out some philosophical and scientific principles framing the concept of change, which is closely linked to and necessary for a broader understanding of the concept of innovation. We then move on, without pause, to the second half with the third chapter. Each term in the fundamental identity of innovation – Need, Motivation, Creativity, Technology and Value – is explored in depth with the help of a multitude of use cases and references drawn from various disciplines. The fourth chapter will examine the state of the art of our species in the era of a societal maturity and a digital revolution, before closing the game with an ultimate chapter, a crucial timing to present an innovative approach to perceiving the hidden side of the Matrix and, indeed, innovating your own reality.

You'll notice that each chapter of this book is titled with an oceanic metaphor, not only out of love for nature and the practice of swimming, but also because the concept of innovation is as vast and dynamic as the ocean itself, with a balance between movement and calm as an integral component of both. To ensure greater clarity and consistency, certain case studies have been repeated throughout and familiar examples from business and everyday life are often used in parallel to illustrate, in a down-to-earth way, certain abstractions. Last but not least, I strongly encourage you to keep in mind the fundamental identity of innovation, as its variables will often be referred to in *italics*. When you read *Need* instead of need, for example, this is a reference to the first variable in the innovation model and should be interpreted as such for optimal reading.

May God, the Matrix & AI bless your journey!

CHAPTER I:

THE TURBULENT OCEAN OF INNOVATION

"The only way to make sense out of change is to plunge into it, move with it, and join the dance." - Alan Watts

As I wandered through the labyrinthine alleys of the Matrix, this universe seemed strangely static and unchanging. Towering skyscrapers and bustling crowds moved in perfect synchronicity, as if locked in a permanent state of trance. Every facet of this world, from the glittering neon signs to the incessant hum of machinery, was carefully crafted and controlled, leaving no room for spontaneity or unpredictability. It was a world frozen in time, a monument to the power of hidden code and order.

To my surprise, however, as I delved deeper into the code, I realized that the Matrix, albeit at a barely perceptible pace, was constantly mutating, adding new agents and new functionalities to the existing ones. And as I explored further, I discovered that my own body was changing too, at every digital instant, adapting to the demands of this virtual world. My existence depended on a visible state of organized but incessant flux.

Every new piece of information I absorbed, every interaction with the virtual world, left an imprint on my being, changing me in subtle but profound ways. It was as if I were a chameleon, blending perfectly into my environment, but also taking on its shape and substance in an almost tangible way. Yet I refused to be a mere puppet in this simulation, a passive participant in a predetermined story.

Immediately, I began to reverse-engineer and recode certain accessible blocks of the Matrix, using my superpowers to create new tools and capture some of the dynamic agents that roamed the digital city. I programmed them, in turn, to become my beloved protectors against any potential energy vampire. In addition, I learned to communicate with similar friends I'd met along the way, at a distance, by sending data through vibrations in the virtual void.

Later, it became clear that even some programmed agents were themselves capable of creating new tools, adapting to the ever-changing world around them, and upgrading their possibilities. As a result, new agents appeared out of nowhere, while other species disappeared into oblivion. Such an interesting and paradoxical world!

೮ ✶ ೞ

Like the infinite ocean and the subtly evolving Matrix described in our protagonist's story above, *innovation* can take a variety of forms and profoundly influence many aspects of our daily lives. To better prepare the playing field, and before tackling the five dimensions of fundamental identity, let's first defend the left side of equation, the concept of innovation, as the central theme of this book, and examine its dynamic interaction with the universe and its various life forms, from plants and animals to human beings. This chapter aims to redefine the scope of *innovation* and its limits, beyond its purely economic or technological aspects. Having said that, let's get the ball rolling with this angle already, which is relatively easier to grasp.

$$Innovation = \underbrace{(Need + Motivation)}_{Prerequisites} \times \underbrace{(Creativity + Technology)}_{Innovation\ Process} \times \underbrace{Value}_{Result}$$

Innovation, often associated with socio-economic contexts, implies the process of creating new approaches, new methods, and above all new goods and services. As you may have guessed, **renewal is at the heart of every innovative action**. An emblematic example of innovation in the Business-to-Customer (B2C) technology sector is the iPhone, launched by Apple Inc. in 2007, which combined various functionalities, such as calling, text messaging, web browsing and music playback, into a single device, transforming the way we communicate and access information. The sharing economy or circular economy is yet another innovative reorganization of the economic sector that promotes social progress, by enabling individuals to share their assets such as their homes on Airbnb, their cars on Zimride or Uber, and even their money on a few lending platforms. This sometimes gave rise to startups dubbed "unicorns" in view of their monstrous potential and capitalization, thus challenging traditional business models by satisfying the needs of many customers at very competitive prices.

Seen in this light, *innovation* appears to be a crucial lever for economic growth and development, and it is. In fact, it enables companies and society to adapt to new circumstances, to solve advanced problems, to create new jobs and entire markets, and to bring a lasting prosperity to the people. If it weren't for the products of Airbus, LVMH (louis Vuitton), Alstom, Total Energies and so on, France would have been already relegated to poverty and social unrest. Likewise, if we moved the GAFAM[2] outside the American borders, the USA would suffer a steep economic decline. Joseph Schumpeter, one of the founding fathers of the field of innovation, aptly described this phenomenon as a "**perpetual storm of creative destruction**" which, if managed well, inevitably through experience, leads to socioeconomic progress, especially in a context of increased competition in a globalized world with less geographical boundaries.

---

[2]   Google, Apple, Facebook, Amazon, and Microsoft. Also referred to as GAMAM or GAMMA after Facebook changed its label to Meta.

It's not surprising, then, that entrepreneurship and innovation are closely linked, as successful entrepreneurs are often individuals who take risks and pursue opportunities "by innovating", in other words, by imagining and proposing something that has never been, through its technology, its time-to-market process, its affordable price, or any other competitive advantage. Similarly, the recent emergence of new digital innovations has made entrepreneurship more accessible by reducing barriers to entry, such as the need for less capital to build an e-commerce platform, or easier access to online suppliers and customers, wherever they may be located.

Numerous studies around the world have statistically proven the positive impact of innovation on the economy, with for example, the revenues of the USA's technology stars GAFAM accounting for around 25 percent of US GDP in 2021. There are also the post-war economic miracles of Germany and South Korea to consider, often referred to as "Wirtschaftswunder" (or "Miracle on the Rhine") and "Miracle on the Han River" respectively. These unlikely and rapid achievements can largely be attributed to profound innovations in various industries. Germany, for example, excels in engineering and manufacturing, producing high-quality products such as numerous car brands and Siemens electronics. Meanwhile, Korea has become a major technological player in the world, with companies such as Samsung and LG leading the Asian dance in consumer electronics. These and other similarly successful countries have recognized the importance of a structured change and have been quick to invest in research and development (R&D) to stay competitive in a market that is more globalized, hence competitive, than ever.

Although the term "innovation" is commonly communicated upon within the context of business management and economics, its etymology reveals a story of its own. Its current association with technology, profit and economic growth emerged primarily during the Industrial Revolution, when the pace of change accelerated dramatically in favor of increased consumerism. Prior to the 18th century, economic growth depended largely on the country's demographic trend, notably on the working class to produce and consume. With the rise of equipped factories and means of transport came the ability to produce more, in less time, freeing the economy, at the same time and to some extent, from demographic constraints.

However, before this revolution, the word "innovation" had a different etymological meaning. The verb to innovate derives from the Latin term "innovare", which connotes "to renew" or "to change", and in its first use in 16th-century English, it referred to reforms that aimed to bring about positive change and revitalize society. In particular, the concept of *innovation* extended beyond scientific discoveries to include social and political reforms. Renaissance thinkers believed that progress was possible through the application of new ideas and the abandonment of outdated traditions. This implicitly evoked the important tradition of the time linked to the Catholic Church, and consequently, innovation was often associated with reforming this institution, strong at the time with its millions of believers and its financial reserve. Despite this power, the period saw significant changes within Catholicism, with the Protestant Reformation a notable example. Innovation, at its core, was thus rooted in a rejection of traditional doctrines and duties, and the promotion of innovative new ideas of freedom related to faith and spirituality.

Although the term "innovation" was not used or spelled out as such before the Renaissance, I will venture to demonstrate in this chapter that this same concept would have existed, in other forms and labels, long before Rousseau and Da Vinci, even before the emergence of modern Man, and while we're at it, perhaps even before the formation of galaxies and stars.

Make yourself comfortable in your seat. The whistle is about to blow. We're off!

DIMENSION 1:
He said "Be", and it "Was"

1

Before time, light and matter existed, there was nothing. An absolute and endless emptiness, because there was no beginning and no end. Then, to the astonishment of everyone and no one, a sudden and explosive event set off the counter, releasing energy in every direction, and innovating nothingness forever. It was the moment of the birth of the universe. I WAS there, playing the maestro and witnessing it all.

At the start of this creative process, there was nothing but a bubbling mass of energy spreading out in all directions. It was a period of chaos and confusion, a whirlwind of raw power, diffusing heat and potential, but nothing more. Then, as the universe cooled and expanded, something miraculous began to happen. Particles began to form, for a reason or no reason. In the first few minutes of the universe, the innovative process of nucleosynthesis formed light elements such as hydrogen, helium and lithium. Over time, these atoms and molecules began to cluster together, forming immense clouds of gas and dust.

A few million years later, inside these clouds, the first stars began to form, fusing these light elements into heavier ones such as carbon, nitrogen and oxygen. These atomic building blocks coalesced into molecules, which in turn became the fundamental building blocks of matter – in other words, of the physical, tangible side of our Matrix.

More and more stars were born, each a fiery ball of plasma, fueled by nuclear reactions at its core. I still remember the heat, light and energy, the feeling of being alive and vibrant in a universe that was just beginning to take shape. And as these stars burned and coalesced, they created heavier and heavier elements, which were then blasted into the void by supernova explosions. It was from this cosmic dust and debris – in short, from this raw material – that new stars and then planets took shape, spinning and orbiting one another, in small or large galaxies, following a well-orchestrated choreography, a cosmic dance with no end in sight, which continues to this day in OUR skies.

80 ✱ 03

According to most astrophysicists, our Matrix was born of a colossal explosion just under 14 billion years ago, known as the **Big Bang**. As it expanded, the universe went from being a hot, dense bubble of helium and other subatomic particles to a dark age. This phase occurred roughly between 380,000 years and 150 million years after the Big Bang. During this time, the universe was in a state of extreme opacity and lacked the light emitted by stars and galaxies. Then, stars slowly formed, collided and even exploded, but above all attracted each other. They finally evolved into galaxies and cosmic dust, made up mainly of stars and planets of various colors and dispositions, around one billion years after the Big Bang, pending further discoveries.

By zooming in on a tiny cluster in the vastness of this space, we'll recognize our solar system, which appeared some nine billion years after the Big Bang. Whether we observe space from Earth or through images captured by a telescope or satellite, the beauty of the universe is undeniable, and its origins continue to fascinate. The most advanced telescope ever developed, the James Webb Telescope, launched in 2021, continues to provide new data on the cosmos' distant past, challenging our current understanding of the history of this Matrix. Recently, it captured some dark-age galaxies, suggesting that stars may have begun to form just a few million years after the Big Bang, rather than the slower period previously assumed. These seemingly metaphysical conclusions are possible because a powerful telescope is a veritable time machine. Indeed, to capture distant elements from cosmic space is, quite literally, to travel back in time, hence the astronomical distance unit of "**light-year**". A galaxy 100 light-years away, for example, means that we don't see it as it is now, but as it was 100 years ago!

In addition to telescopic scans of the distant universe, the Big Bang theory, which has become a popular comedy series about the social awkwardness of nerdy scientists, is also supported by a wealth of scientific evidence from diverse fields of study such as astrophysics, cosmology and particle physics. Among the main evidence backing up this theory is the cosmic background radiation, which is the residual heat released by this "big" explosion, and which can be observed in all directions of the sky. Another clue is the abundance of light elements in the universe. These can be explained by the nuclear reactions that took place in the first minutes after the Big Bang. In addition, the Large Hadron Collider (LHC), a particle accelerator located on the French-Swiss border and operational since 2008, has played a decisive role in the study of the properties of subatomic particles. Thanks to experiments carried out at the LHC and other particle accelerators, scientists have been able to understand the behavior of matter at extremely high energies, simulating the conditions that prevailed in the first instants of our universe.

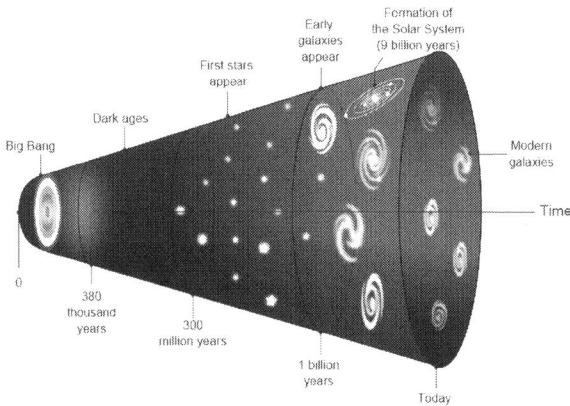

Formation of
the Solar System
(9 billion years)

Early
galaxies
appear

First stars
appear

Dark ages

Big Bang

Modern
galaxies

Time

0

380
thousand
years

300
million years

1 billion
years

Today

Focusing on the figure above, it looks as if the universe is expanding towards infinity. This could indeed be the case. Astronomical observations based on extracts from the Hubble telescope have proved, for some time now, that our physical Matrix is still expanding. One theory, counterbalancing the Big Bang, called the "Big Crunch", unsurprisingly, defends the cosmological hypothesis that the universe, instead of continuing to expand indefinitely, will eventually go into a reverse phase, contracting dramatically, thanks to the irresistible forces of gravitation, which would compress all matter and energy into an extremely dense point. Like beginning, like end. That said, let's leave the distant future aside for the moment.

We can't talk about astrophysics without mentioning guru Stephen Hawking, because while the Big Bang has won widespread consensus among scientists, and the general public too, there's another interesting way of looking at it. Instead of a beginning and an end, suggests Hawking, could it be that the universe has neither a singular starting point nor a finite limit, but rather exists in a state he has called "**the limitless universe**"? In this framework, the universe can be seen as a closed surface, similar to the surface of a sphere, but with more dimensions. Just as the surface of a sphere has no limits or edges, Hawking suggests that the universe would be an autonomous entity with no distinct starting point in time. An infinite iterative race circuit.

The theory of the limitless universe, although difficult to prove or even visualize for some, is based on the principles of quantum mechanics and the concept of imaginary time. Without going into the technical and therefore boring details, let's note that, unlike classical or Newtonian mechanics, applicable to macroscopic objects, the small point of dense energy in which the universe presumably began rather obliges us to apply the principles of quantum mechanics, typically used at the level of atoms. When you play billiards or any sport with a ball, I can, by studying your photos before the collision between the stick and the white ball, predict 100 percent its trajectory and the trajectory of the ball(s) it will hit, and whether you will therefore score points or not. Philosophically and scientifically, this is known as determinism. In quantum physics, absolute determinism is replaced by a probabilistic yet still valid vision of the universe. To put it simply, if I try to do the same experiment as above but replace your billiard ball with an electron at the atomic level, my future results and projections will probably be wrong. Maybe correct too! In any case, events don't happen in a predetermined precise way, but rather with certain probabilities.

The differences between classical and quantum mechanics thus call into question the origin of the universe. Is it a single Big Bang point, **a starting whistle for EVERYTHING**, awaiting the whistle to end the game, or **an infinite loop**, with no beginning and no end, expressed in Hawking's words: "The universe would contain itself [...], it could neither be created nor destroyed, it could only BE". There are also other suggestions of a "multiverse", several spherical universes in borderline interaction, one creating the other, like soap bubbles in a cosmic bathtub. Beyond the existential theories competing for the crown of "truth", there's a fundamental issue here. In fact, by opting for or proving one theory over another, we're venturing into theological frontiers. A Big Bang, for example, appears to be a divine manifestation, a creation *ex nihilo*. On the other hand, the divine figure in an infinite universe, as proposed by Hawking, is much less obvious. I'm taking the liberty of crossing these boundaries anyway, because, although it's not our main subject here, the debate about the existence of a creator, Brahma, The Father, God or Allah, is nonetheless important from the point of view of the Fundamental Identity of Innovation. Allow me to explain.

Faithful followers of a divine force would strongly advocate an innovative universe with a clear motivation, and a very precise end behind it. For example, those familiar with Judaism, Christianity or Islam, which account for more than half the world's population, assert that Allah, God the Father, or Jehovah had a predetermined intention in creating our Matrix. If we add the beliefs of Hinduism, animist religions and other spiritual practices, we end up with a rough Pareto distribution of 80/20, despite the recent international trend towards atheistic secularism. This means that around 80 percent of people believe in some kind of *raison d'être* for this world, while the remainder, including atheists and certain Buddhist sects, argue in favor of a universe without any purpose.

Proponents of a meaningful universe often rely on sacred texts and metaphysical narratives to support their claims. For example, in Islam, a religion I grew up with, Muslims refer to the Qur'an as the sole source of all truth and indubitable proof of Allah's design in creating the universe. We can find these sacred lines: "We did not create the heavens and the earth and what lies between them in play. We have not created them except for the truth, but most of them do not know" (Qur'an 44:39) and "I have not created jinn and Man except that they may worship Me" (Qur'an 51:56). In the Jewish faith, the motivation behind Jehovah's creation can be found in several verses too, including, "[...] God blessed them, and God said to them: Be fruitful, multiply, fill the earth, and subdue it; and have dominion over the fish of the sea, and over the birds of the air, and over every beast that moves upon the earth" (Genesis 1:28). In Hindu mythology, the initial phase of the universe is attributed mainly to Brahma. This last member of the Trimūrti, the trinity of Hindu deities also including Shiva and Vishnu, symbolizes creative energy, an expression of his divine play (or lila), using his own essence to experience and express his divine nature.

In addition to divine or prophetic words, many theists still believe in miracles. Such events occur outside the bounds of natural laws and scientific rationality. Although miracles are not commonly observed or disseminated today – with the exception of technological and industrial miracles of course – many people still regard them as historical proof of the existence of higher powers, tuning all the notes of the universe to their will. Let's take some famous cases.

According to esoteric Buddhist scriptures, for example, Buddha had the power to fly, transform his appearance – like the faceless god in the *Game of Thrones* series – and perform other supernatural feats. Likewise, among Catholics, since his miraculous birth from the Virgin Mary, Jesus Christ is known to have performed numerous feats, such as healing the sick, feeding thousands of people with a few loaves of bread, walking on water and even raising the dead. Moses was also inspired by his forbidden escape from Egypt with his people. In the depths of despair, seeing the tyrant Pharaoh and his army closing in on them, he received the word of God and created a path across the (presumably red) sea, which split in two, allowing God's prophet and the Israelites to pass through to the holy land before closing in on Pharaoh and his army of unbelievers. Add to this the prolonged lives of many prophets and yogis, such as Noah and Trailanga Swami, who are presumed to have lived for several centuries according to various theological and mystical references. These miraculous acts reinforce beliefs in the mystical nature of our Matrix.

In addition to the main prophetic figures and their superpowers, many cultures have also relied on oracles, shamans, Sufis, and other mediums to communicate with the non-material, even the divine. In ancient Greece, the most famous of these was the oracle of Delphi, located in the temple of Apollo. The priestess of the oracle would enter a state of trance, on demand, and give enigmatic answers to questions posed by visitors. These answers were often deciphered by priests or other officials, who gave advice based on the words of the oracle.

Such exotic spiritual traditions and shamanic practices are still the pride of many cultures around the world, including the Amazonian and Sami peoples. I recently had the privilege of spending a few weeks with a Sami artist and her contemporary dance group in the Jokkmokk region of Swedish Lapland, helping them organize a performance in Storforsen National Park. A high-level, open-air performance in a breathtaking setting. The script was no less impressive. It told the story of a legendary female shaman who fought and collaborated with the spirits of the vast forests of Lapland. Such stories, dating back to prehistoric times, are common among the Sami people, who lived as hunter-gatherers in certain regions stretching from northern Norway to western Russia.

The Sami community greatly respected their shamans, called "Noaidi", who acted as intermediaries between the spiritual and physical worlds. The Noaidi used various techniques such as drumming, singing and dancing to enter altered states of consciousness. During these experiences, they seemed to communicate with spirits, ancestors and other supernatural beings to gain knowledge and healing powers. Such beliefs were rooted in the attribution of an eternal spirit to every living being, be it animal or plant, dead or alive. More recently, Edgar Cayce, also known as the "Sleeping Prophet", was an American seer and healer who lived from 1877 to 1945. He became world-famous for his remarkable ability to enter a deep trance state and provide detailed information and predictions on various subjects, such as the world crisis of 1929, volcanic eruptions and other future events.

There are also numerous accounts of paranormal activity which, for want of a more logical explanation, have been attributed to the influence of supernatural forces. Among them is the work of Maria Valtorta, an Italian writer who claimed that her books had been dictated to her by

Jesus Christ himself. Despite being virtually paralyzed in her home during her most productive years, her books contain detailed and often accurate accounts of the life and teachings of Christ and have been widely read by Christians all over the world. Life after death being a classic case of mediumship, journalist Stéphane Allix launched a personal quest, summarized in his book, *The Test: Incredible Proof of the Afterlife*, to understand the existence of the afterlife following the death of his father. By secretly placing a few innocuous objects in the coffin of the deceased, he met several mediums in order to challenge the truth in their words. The test protocol evaluated the mediums' ability to communicate with his father, comparing their interpretations with his father's previous life, and the nature of the objects hidden in his coffin. According to the same author, the results were relatively conclusive of an immaterial continuation of the person post-mortem.

My great-grandmother's extraordinary ability to drink boiling water was often mentioned at family gatherings during my childhood. Festivals still celebrated to this day prove that such feats are indeed achievable. A case in point is Thaipusam, a Hindu festival observed in India and Malaysia, involving devotees piercing their bodies with hooks and skewers and walking barefoot for several miles as a sign of penance and devotion to Lord Murugan. Another case can be found among Shiite Muslims in Karbala, Iraq, who commemorate Ashura festival with a dramatic ritual known as "Zanjeer Zani", where participants flog themselves with chains and beat their backs with swords and knives to express their grief and solidarity with Imam Hussein, the grandson of the Prophet Muhammad, who was martyred at the Battle of Karbala in 680 AD. Some devotees also practice self-mutilation, striking their heads with sharp blades, causing blood to run down their faces. Sensitive souls, please refrain!

Despite all these tales of miraculous feats and incredible abilities, there is little empirical evidence to date to support the existence of supernatural phenomena. Many of these stories can sometimes be explained by mental techniques such as hypnosis, or/and the induction of altered states of consciousness, which remains, in itself, an abstract process to science. What's more, if you've ever shared a secret with a friend in the past,

THE INNOVATIVE ANIMAL | 35

about a crush you had on another student in your class for example, you must have noticed how quickly that secret degenerated into an elaborate drama, with twists and turns in every direction, without any further intervention on your part. Similarly, tales and myths become distorted over generations, a mechanism lubricated by a human brain that's attracted to the extraordinary and biased to confirm its pre-existing image of the world. Nevertheless, although instantaneous miracles are rare these days, there is still much to be learned from the unexpected and the inexplicable. As someone who is drawn to the triad of spirituality, art and science, I believe it's important to take all these heterogeneous elements into account to develop a multidimensional and less biased understanding of the Matrix and the concept of *innovation*.

On the purely scientific side, there's always debate. A significant percentage of "scientists" still believe in God or some equivalent[3]. This is hardly surprising. Beside being made and practiced by culturally influenced individuals, science, at its core, simply discovers and describes what already exists in the Matrix, in a more structured and well-founded way than philosophical or religious essays. By bringing to light the sophisticated universal order and hidden laws that govern every cosmic interaction, science goes some way to justifying beliefs in an eternal Maestro. We'll be taking a look at such innovative mechanisms shortly. In the meantime, let's mention a few universal constants, which you must have used in your studies, probably without any real understanding, and which still intrigue by their existence and stability regardless of circumstances.

Let's start with Einstein's famous discovery. The speed of light in a vacuum is approximately 299,792,458 meters per second. It represents the maximum speed at which information, energy including light, or any causal influence can propagate through space. There's also Planck's constant (h), named after the physicist Max Planck, who introduced it into quantum mechanics. Planck's constant relates the energy of a photon to its frequency. The fundamental constant (G), in Newton's

---

[3] A survey conducted by the Pew Research Center in 2009 found that 33% of scientists in the United States believed in God or a higher power.

law of universal gravitation, describes the force of gravity between two objects. There are still others, such as Avogadro's number in chemistry, representing the number of atoms, molecules or particles in a quantity equivalent to a mole of a substance, and Boltzmann's constant (k) used in thermodynamic studies.

All these constants governing the underlying dynamics of our universe and its components help to reinforce the concept of Fine Tuning, often referred to as **the Anthropic Principle**. Indeed, some physicists, such as Brandon Carter and Frank Tipler[4], propose that the choice of precisely tuned values for these constants enables the existence of life as we know it. A variation, however small, in the speed of light or the gravitational constant, for example, would cause the external Matrix to collapse, like a table standing on two legs. The whole universe would immediately vanish, with no hope of life. In systemic jargon, this is called a critical point. As it happens, apart from these universal constants, most natural phenomena, on Earth and elsewhere, operate close to critical points, between order and chaos. A slight shift to the left or right of these points, and these phenomena and their innovative products would disappear forever.

So, two possibilities. (1) The majority of believers are right not to doubt the sacred books or the metaphysical phenomena and stories cascaded from generation to generation. A god, or several gods, are necessary to maintain this universal fine-tuning enabling life, by choosing the right constants and critical points from the very start of the Matrix, just like a project manager would plan their innovation process before any implementation. (2) According to the anthropic principle, we can only observe a universe with constants that enable our existence, **because we're here to observe it!** I know this little magic trick isn't easy to decipher, but that's okay. We'll elaborate on it by the end of the book. What we need to remember from this passage, though, can be summed up as follows:

---

4   In his book "The Physics of Immortality," Tipler presents a variation of the anthropic principle known as the Omega Point Theory. He argues that the laws of physics must be finely tuned to allow for the eventual emergence of intelligent life and the Omega Point, which represents an infinitely advanced and powerful state of existence.

- **The believers' version**: If the universe weren't fine-tuned to exact measurements by something divine, like a house built to plan by an attentive architect, nothing would BE.

- **The non-believers' version**: If we're conscious and existing here on Earth, it's because this universe, through purely rational and automatic mechanisms, is lucky to have had the right parameters to its and our existence.

Continuing with the last angle, a globally growing minority rejects the idea of a grand design or master plan altogether. This group includes not only Western materialists and many existentialists, but also some Theravada Buddhists and animist sects. They maintain that the concepts of purpose and meaning are an exclusively human invention, a product of our attachment to this world and our unconscious desire for security and assurance. In Buddhism, in particular, the emphasis is on impermanence and constant change, encouraging followers to **experience the world as it is**, in the NOW, without attaching any mental significance to its origin.

On the same page, or rather chanting the same mantra, atheists, mainly located in advanced, secular countries (and China), adopt **scientific naturalism** to explain the universe's lack of purpose. Anti-religious biologist Richard Dawkins, in his book *The God Delusion*, argues that natural selection and physical laws alone can explain the complexity of life rather than an imaginary creator. The probability argument thus asserts that if there's a one-in-a-billion chance of a planet harboring life, and there are a billion planets out there, then **we're just lucky to be in the good one**. According to this worldview, life and consciousness emerge from random physical processes, with no intrinsic motivation or ultimate goal.

A more elegant (albeit criticized) way of explaining the state of universal order, associated with the existence of primordial constants governing it, comes from Danish physicist Per Bak and his theory of "self-organizing criticality", a concept from complexity theory that describes a state in which a system reaches a critical point where small changes can trigger large-scale effects, resulting in a phenomenon called power-law behavior.

This means that a system **naturally evolves** towards a state of equilibrium between order and chaos. Let's take the example of sand avalanches, Bak's initial inspiration behind his theory. When grains of sand are added one by one vertically to a cone-shaped dune, the latter grows until it reaches a critical slope or angle. At this critical point, frictional forces are no longer sufficient to keep the dune stable. In other words, the addition of ONE small grain of sand can trigger an avalanche, sending sand tumbling down the pile. The size of these avalanches follows a power-law distribution. The larger the dune, the faster it crashes. This theory could explain many other phenomena, such as earthquakes, how our brains work and even the cosmic state of our universe.

The debate over whether or not there is a divine design at the origin of the universe is still unresolved, but in recent decades the balance has tipped considerably in favor of the liberal minority due to a better scientific understanding of the origins of the world and a decline in religious affiliation among younger generations. Those who still support the notion of divine purpose rely mainly on historical texts, cultural myths and personal spiritual experiences, sometimes interpreting life as a game between good and evil, heaven and hell, with winners and losers. As for those who reject the idea of a universe by design, they point to scientific theories with gaps that may one day be filled by future discoveries and experiments. The lack of a definitive, scientifically satisfying answer to the origin of EVERYTHING, including the Big Bang, also leaves the field open to speculation disguised by scientific vocabulary more than anything else. Imagine the following scenario.

The strange presence of a glass of water on your desk one day would imply that it didn't happen by chance. In fact, as the principle of causality dictates, every effect must have a cause, which would imply that someone or something must have made and placed the glass there. Even if this glass was placed by a domestic robot (in the near future), this robot would have been created by something or someone else, resulting in a chain of causality. Interestingly, the concept of cause and effect, which is also a fundamental tenet of Buddhism, paradoxically raises the question of what caused the first cause, triggering the eternal "chicken or the egg[5]" paradox, which cannot be resolved simply within a classical space-time perspective. Indeed, if the latter concept, through which we situate our reality, did not exist, or were stripped of its power as in quantum theory, the concept of cause and effect would be meaningless.

Returning to the central theme of this book, *innovation*, the growing perspective that there is no motivated designer of the Matrix, that there is no purpose, in short, that "God is dead" to quote Nietzsche, would insinuate that the concept of *innovation* did not exist before the emergence of humanity, at least from the point of view of our Fundamental Identity. In fact, according to this perspective, if we assume that the *Need* of the innovation's receiver, the *Motivation* of the universe's creator and the *Value* or benefits that someone or something will derive from any divine creation are all nil, then basic multiplication would suggest that the meaning behind creating the Matrix tends towards zero. That said, we'll always assume that the variables of *Creativity* and *Technology* intrinsically represent something; otherwise, the universe would be devoid not only of inherent meaning, but also of matter and energy, which seems not true, based on our everyday experience called "life". Therefore, we can substitute the variables below following the above reasoning, in the same way as we used to do these calculations in elementary school.

Innovation Before Man = (Need + Motivation) × (Creativity + Technology) × Value
Innovation Before Man = (0 + 0) × (Creativity + Technology) × 0
Innovation Before Man = 0

This result means that none of the prehuman creations, even the most beautiful and sophisticated ones, fall within the scope of *Innovation*. Such a statement may puzzle many. Some readers may argue with me: "How dare you negate the innovative spirit of every natural creation, from stars and planets to oceans and mountains, despite the nihilistic hypothesis of a world without a creator?" In order to justify myself, it's important to

---

[5]   If we take this paradox literally, the theory of natural evolution favors a mutated or naturally selected egg of chicken ancestor first, before the world's first chicken existed.

reiterate that *Innovation*, as expressed in the Fundamental Identity above, is not simply about creating something new; it must also serve a purpose and generate *Value* for given entities. This is a basic, yet paramount distinction frequently taught in my first innovation management class.

Imagine the following scenario: I take a sheet of paper, paint it prettily, then shape it into a colorful miniature car that catches an eye or two, but nothing more. Is this an example of innovation? The answer is not easy to deduce without knowing whether the creation has meaning for someone or something. In the business world, if nobody is willing to pay for my pretty car, it would probably be **a one-off invention**. Although innovation and invention both involve the creation of new devices, functionalities or processes that didn't exist before, the crucial difference between them lies in the concept of *Value*. This variable is, once again, an essential component of fundamental identity, which we'll discover in greater detail in a dedicated section.

If we take a look at the corporate *innovation* process, inventions are seen as the first step that leads to innovation, igniting the first sparks of creativity. Research and development (R&D) departments are often responsible for generating and testing innovative ideas, which are evaluated for their feasibility, ease of scaling up, and potential in the market in question. However, inventions have relatively little value in terms of innovation, as they are usually prototypes or concepts that have not yet been developed into a viable product, and often end up in the dustbin of large companies. For example, a robot prototype is an invention, as a step towards a final product that will be marketed for use in restaurants, factories or other contexts. Similarly, fire and light were once lucky discoveries, but have now evolved into practical products that have significant *Value* in our daily lives, such as a stove or a LED light bulb respectively.

Applying this commonly used business distinction to our metaphysical debate, the absence of a universal creator or energy, as suggested by atheists, means that there is no inherent purpose or *Value* behind the physical Matrix. Consequently, most of the components of our world, such as stars, galaxies, dinosaurs, oceans and even humans, could be considered random inventions rather than true, brilliant innovations, thus justifying the nil result of our previous calculation.

However, in the absence of clear-cut evidence in favor of this materialistic hypothesis, and in order to push the analysis of the innovative process further, let's consider for the time being the possibility of a Matrix designer or a team of ghost engineers in another dimension, with a specific purpose behind the programming of this universe and its constituents. I dare to suggest, my theological research and spiritual experiences, that any motivated creation, assuming it is motivated in the first place, **is the work of an Artist, Mathematician and Great Player**.

The artistic side, albeit seen through human eyes, is hidden in so many cosmic and terrestrial objects of undeniable natural beauty. You don't have to be a Van Gogh or a Monet to notice it. Whether we attribute it to a divine force, absolute consciousness, or the underlying principles of the universe, there seems to be a mathematical essence intertwined with all creative endeavors in the Matrix. This essence reveals itself through the implicit laws that govern every artistic process. From the Big Bang, to entropy, nuclear fusion, black holes, natural selection and so on, the Matrix is made up of billions of interactions describable in numbers and equations, as our scientists have understood for centuries. Finally, living in a self-sustaining and evolving simulation, with rigid (e.g., stone) and flexible (e.g., human) programming, seems to come from the talent of Someone or Something passionate about challenge, evolution and continuous learning. As I often say to my students, life's a game – it's up to you to define your strategy and play it right and with passion!

Whatever one believes, for the rest of the analysis, in order to avoid any potential theological debate and find common ground between the various beliefs, we'll use the term "**natural innovation**" to designate any non-human creation within the Matrix, be it a random invention or an innovation by a divine force. The arguments that follow will be based both on ancient wisdom, better able to satisfy our innate curiosity about the "**why**", and on scientific theories more suited to answer the "**how**" of existence.

A natural innovation encompasses **non-biological** aspects such as astrophysical phenomena, tectonic activities, nuclear fusion and the like. Plant growth processes, natural selection and the evolution of life in general are grouped under the **biological** label. Any innovation that results from intentional actions on the part of humans or some other relatively intelligent animals will be referred to as "**planned innovation**".

My proposal of "natural" and "planned" categories hardly contradicts the traditional typologies of innovation commonly used in business literature. These classifications generally distinguish **product innovation**, which refers to the creation of new objects and services, including stars, galaxies and the iPhone, from **process innovation**, which involves the introduction of new processes into the physical world, such as nuclear fusion within stars and Amazon's rapid delivery. We can also highlight **organizational innovation** linked to changes in group structure to meet specific needs, be it within bee colonies or in modern societies. In these last sentences, notice how we have mixed, on purpose, natural innovations with planned ones, demonstrating that a product innovation, for example, can be natural or human-made.

Although we only focus on these three categories of innovation in this book, namely product, process and organization, it's worth noting that there are two other classes encountered in business case studies: marketing innovation, which involves introducing new ways of promoting and selling products in certain markets, and business model innovation, which involves finding innovative revenue streams both online and offline.

Another way of classifying innovation is based on the degree of change it brings about, compared with the old ways of doing things. This concept of "**creative destruction**", proposed by the economist Schumpeter in the 20th century, can be divided into two main categories. **Incremental innovation** involves small, gradual changes over time, such as Apple's constant updates to iPhone models, which add improvements in camera performance, color and a few other features with each new version.

In contrast, **radical or disruptive innovation**[6] leads to sudden and significant impacts on the ecosystem. Take the example of the introduction of Uber in Paris, which quickly became a popular and affordable option for students, despite the often unpleasant and smelly cars at first. Today, Uber offers a quality of service comparable to traditional cabs but at higher prices and with a diversified service range, too.

All the above-mentioned innovation typologies are primarily intended to bring order to the chaos of this vast ocean of *innovation*. The often-subjective assessment of the impact of any innovation can, however, vary according to the context in which it is applied. In practice, we can pretty much all agree that the creation of the internet has had a greater socio-economic and cultural impact than the launch of a new IKEA table. Similarly, transforming desktop computers into personal laptops has brought more *Value* than the introduction of a bamboo toothbrush. Nevertheless, by changing space and time, the stakes also switch. Water desalination, for example, is likely to be less important in Sweden, with its abundant lakes, than in the desert region of Namibia. Similarly, the importance of hand sanitizers, had they existed, might have been far greater in the Middle Ages and the Black Death than that of personal computers. This complexity underlines the need for a simpler, unified framework for assessing the worth of any creation.

It's also important to note that all the selected innovation types can be combined in different ways, resulting in a multitude of possible innovation classifications. A visual representation of this with the following examples is provided via the figure below. The launch of the iPhone in 2007, for example, is classified as a *planned, radical product* innovation, while Darwinist natural selection falls into the category of *natural (or more precisely biological), process and incremental* innovation, as we will explain in detail below.

---

6   Although there are differences in the way radical vs. disruptive innovations are introduced into the market and their impact on competitors, we will consider both radical and disruptive innovation to fall into the same category of rapid and substantial societal changes in the context of this book.

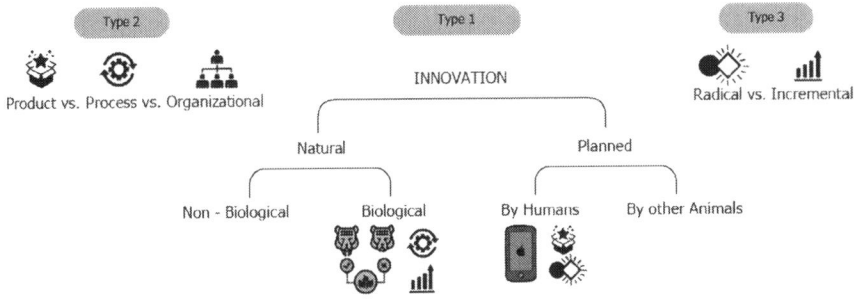

Now, let's delve into some of the major use cases within the natural innovation realm.

2

The main natural non-biological innovation that appeared at the moment of the Big Bang, and has progressed even further since, is **space and time**. As of this writing, astrophysicists argue that it makes no sense to speak of a time before the Big Bang, because the time counter was launched at the instant of the Big Bang whistle. Our Matrix was born with no possibility of turning back, time advancing non-stop in a single direction: the future.

Obviously, while science is still fine-tuning this unprecedented moment in our cosmic history, metaphysics comes to the rescue. The magic of such creation is reflected, for instance, in the Hindu concept of Brahman, which is often linked to the creation of the universe. The Upanishads, a collection of Sanskrit texts forming an important part of the Vedas, the ancient Hindu wisdom, describe Brahman as the ultimate reality and origin of all creation. They declare: "That from which all this is born, That by which all this is sustained, and That into which all this merges back – That is Brahman" (Mundaka Upanishad 1.1.1). Similarly, the Qur'an, in agreement with the other Abrahamic religions, assures us that God or Allah "[...] is the First and the Last, the High and the Intimate, and of all things He is Knower" (Qur'an 57:3), suggesting that, unless many universes coexist, time and space, hence the universe, did not exist prior to $T = 0$, as noted in mechanical physics. **Before that, there was nothing, then THERE WAS.**

In his model of time and space, the ancient Greek philosopher Aristotle argued that these entities were not absolute nor independent of one another, but rather a measure of the change and movement of physical objects, which corresponds to our everyday experience. According to this wise figure, space and time are the product of the universe's existence and continuous evolution. Without a "before", there would be no "now", and without a "there", there would be no "here". Consequently, the absence of time would result in a perpetual static image, even if it moved from one place to another. Conversely, being confined to a point in space would mean experiencing the past and future from the same geographical position, with the same body and mind. These mental exercises, far from simple to visualize, illustrate the profound interdependence of the dimensions of space and time, hence represented them as a four-dimensional continuum, three dimensions for space and one remaining for time. In reality, all physical objects, including ourselves, exist within the constant flow of space-time, which forms the hidden fabric of the Matrix.

Aristotle, never short of ingenious ideas, also distinguished between two types of time: **the time of the universe and the time of the soul**. This could be likened to the difference between the time displayed on your watch and the subjective experience of time we feel within ourselves, commonly referred to as psychological time. For example, during an exam, time can seem to pass quickly, making it difficult to finish the test, while a ten-minute meditation or punishment session seems to last an eternity. This duality can also be observed when considering the relationship between body and mind. The body's temporal rhythms are mainly regulated by biological processes, such as the aging process or physiological functions like hunger, thirst and sleep. For example, around midday, we may feel stomach pains, prompting us to grab a bite to eat, and at nightfall, depending on our individual rhythms, the body naturally signals sleep time, without the need for a watch. Meanwhile, the mind's time is characterized by psychological and emotional experiences, which can vary independently of biological age. If you know youthful, energetic older people or mature, thoughtful teenagers, you already know what I'm talking about.

We can hardly talk about time without mentioning the genius of Einstein and his general and special relativity, demonstrating that **time (and therefore space) is not absolute**. In other words, time can flow differently depending on the speed at which you're moving, or the force of gravity in your environment. Therefore, time is not the same for everyone! This is not philosophy, but a theory proven time and time again and applied in many fields involving high speeds, such as aeronautics and the conquest of space. With a hyper-precise atomic watch, you can test it yourself with a friend. Suppose you live by the sea, i.e., at a low altitude, and your friend lives in the mountains. Under this hypothesis, you will age more slowly than your friend, even if only by a few milliseconds a month.

Using Einstein's classic example, imagine that you have two friends, Alice and Bob. Alice stays on Earth while Bob goes on a space trip in an ultra-fast rocket. When Bob returns to Earth after ten years, according to his clock, he might find that Alice has aged 50 years, or even that she's already dead. Bob has thus experienced a slowing down of time in relation to Alice. This happens because of two important ideas: the faster an object moves, the slower time passes for that object. The principle of gravitational time dilation in Einstein's General Relativity also tells us that gravity affects the flow of time. The closer you are to a massive object, the slower time flows.

Within the immensity of our space-time, an inconceivable number of celestial objects have been innovated over time. According to astronomical data, our Milky Way galaxy alone is estimated to contain around 300 billion stars, while the observable universe is thought to comprise at least two billion galaxies. This suggests that there may be as many as 800 sextillion stars in the observable universe (i.e., 8 followed by 23 zeros). To put this into perspective, there may be around eight quintillion grains of sand on Earth (i.e., 8 followed by 18 zeros). Therefore, there could potentially be **more stars in the observable universe than grains of sand on our planet**. This astronomical reality in which we live has always served as a source of inspiration and creativity for early humans, philosophers and scientists, as well as potentially for other intelligent beings in the distant universe, to postulate or unveil the hidden mechanisms of this grandiose Matrix.

However, to delve into the intricacies of each of these objects would take a lifetime, making it impossible to cover them all within the confines of this book. What really matters when studying natural innovations, whether in the realm of inert matter or living organisms, are the processes that lead to their formation, rather than the end product itself. Consequently, despite the differences in composition between these immense particles of matter and energy, the innovative processes that gave rise to their existence can be reduced to a few fundamental laws of physics, counted on a few fingers.

A primary innovative mechanism responsible for the formation of stars and other celestial bodies in the universe is **gravitational collapse**. This process occurs when a dense molecular cloud, usually composed of gas and dust, becomes gravitationally unstable and collapses in on itself. Various factors can trigger these events, such as the shock waves from a nearby galactic explosion like a supernova, the collision of two molecular clouds or the attractive gravitational influence of a neighboring galaxy. As the cloud collapses, it becomes denser and hotter, leading to an increase in temperature and pressure. At the center of the cloud, gas and dust begin to coalesce, forming a protostar. Over time, as more and more matter is accreted onto the protostar, it becomes more massive, and its gravitational attraction to other cosmic objects becomes stronger. Eventually, the protostar's core becomes hot and dense enough to ignite nuclear fusion, marking the birth of a new star. Eureka!

In more artistic terms, gravitational collapse can be compared to a crowded dance floor where people start to move closer and closer together until they merge into a single unified entity. At first, everyone is scattered and moves independently, but as they get closer, their movements become more coordinated and intense. The cumbersome mass becomes denser and hotter, until it reaches a critical point where it collapses into a new, more tightly bound structure, according to your imagination.

Observing nature up close can give us a clue as to how stellar objects were created. There's a striking resemblance between the shapes of stars and river pebbles, for example. This similarity is no coincidence, but rather the result of molding forces that shape them. In the case of a star, its material is drawn inwards by the force of gravity from all directions towards the center, causing it to flatten into a disk shape. As the objects in the disk continue to grow and become more massive, gravity pulls their matter inwards, shaping them into a spherical form. River pebbles, on the other hand, become rounded over time as the continuous flow of water from the mountains to sea level acts on them in all directions. The current causes them to collide with each other, breaking them into small pieces and smoothing out any rough edges.

In addition to the gravitational field, it is now scientifically evident that the latter is complemented by three other forces governing most macro and micro interactions in our Matrix. **The electromagnetic force** appears between charged particles. It encompasses both electrical and magnetic forces, which play a fundamental role in almost everything from chemical reactions to the operation of your smartphone. The remaining forces act at a microscopic level and are **the strong nuclear force**, holding atomic nuclei together, and **the weak nuclear force** responsible for certain types of nuclear decay. In atomic nuclei, the nuclear force is responsible for keeping positively charged protons together despite the electrostatic repulsion between them. In other words, without the nuclear force, you and all the objects around you, like a Marvel superhero, would rapidly shatter from structured matter into a state of pure messy energy. This is the basis of nuclear fission reactions, in which the central nuclei of heavy atoms such as uranium or plutonium are separated, releasing vast quantities of energy, used as a source of electricity or as weapons of mass destruction.

One of the most intriguing natural products innovated by these fundamental forces, particularly gravity, is **the black hole**. This enigmatic celestial object often forms when a massive star runs out of fuel and can no longer sustain nuclear fusion in its core. Without the energy produced by nuclear fusion, the star's core collapses under its own gravity, compressing mass into an incredibly dense point called a singularity. The resulting gravitational field can be so strong, so attractive, that nothing, not even light, can escape its pull, hence the "black" color of its name.

The full *Value* of black holes has yet to be fully understood by astrophysicists. However, evidence suggests that supermassive black holes, which can weigh billions of times more than the Sun, exist at the center of most galaxies, including our own Milky Way. Due to their enormous gravitational pull, they act as the heavyweights that keep the motion and distribution of stars and gas within the galaxy in harmony. In more down-to-earth terms, a black hole is a bit like a soccer referee measuring 2.5 meters or 8 foot 2 inches, and 150kg or 330 lbs. Everyone would play by his rules, and no player would dare question his decisions. Black holes can also play a crucial role in cleaning up the universe, like a vacuum cleaner, via the cosmic recycling of matter. Finally, when matter falls into a black hole, it heats up to extremely high temperatures and emits intense radiation that can interact with nearby gas and dust, triggering the formation of new stars and planets. The exciting idea that black holes aid space-time travel is unfortunately confined to the realms of science fiction for the time being.

Exploring beyond the realm of astrophysics, we can discover a variety of natural innovations by zooming in on a single, predominantly **blue planet**. Once again, we'll focus on a few innovative processes, rather than charting the billions of objects and species that have inhabited our planet since the dawn of time.

The formation of Mother Earth is a captivating story that involves a whole range of innovations. Scientists estimate that it was formed around 4.5 billion years ago by a process called **accretion**. This involved the slow accumulation of gas, dust and small particles in the solar nebula surrounding our young Sun, due to gravitational forces.

In 2003, during an informal experiment conducted by astronaut Donald Pettit on board the International Space Station, a similar process was observed. The astronaut was having fun observing salt sachets in weightlessness, i.e., in the absence of any force holding the objects down. In space, everything floats. While these bags of salt were floating, two salt crystals collided, creating an electrostatic charge that forced them together. When he shook the plastic bag containing the cluster, it disintegrated, but as soon as he stopped, the cluster reformed.

In a similar way, our Earth, in its primitive state, was formed by the convergence of dust clusters around the Sun. When this mass reached a sufficient size, its gravity began to attract more of the surrounding dust present in the rotating circumstellar disc surrounding the newly formed sun. Over a period of around three million years, several clusters formed in the inner solar system, inventing (not innovating) some twenty protoplanets (because it sounds like prototypes in R&D). These then fused together in violent collisions, eventually giving rise to a handful of planets, including Venus, Mercury, Mars and our own Earth. This innovative Earth-forming process is thought to have lasted around 30 million years. That's quite a time span compared to our century-old-limited human lifespan.

The next phase in the stabilization of the "Earth" prototype is known as **differentiation.** This involved the separation of different materials according to their density. Heavier elements, such as iron, nickel and other dense metals, sank to the planet's core, while lighter elements, such as silicon and aluminum, rose to the surface. This stage gave rise to the distinct layers that make up the Earth's interior, including the solid inner core and the liquid outer core. Indeed, despite its location at the center of the planet and subject to extremely high temperatures and pressures, the inner core is solid due to the immense pressure exerted on the iron and nickel that make up its composition. The pressure at the Earth's center is estimated to be around 3.6 million times greater than the pressure at the surface, enough to compress a car into a bullet, and of course keep the inner core in a solid state. However, the outer core, which surrounds the inner core, is liquid primarily due to a combination of high temperature and lower pressure compared to the inner core. In fact, the temperature in the outer core is estimated to range from approximately 4,000 to 5,000 degrees Celsius (7,200 to 9,000 degrees Fahrenheit). At such high temperatures, the materials in the outer core, mainly iron and nickel, are in a molten state, similar to the behavior of liquid metals. This liquid outer core plays a crucial role in generating the Earth's magnetic field through a process called the dynamo effect (Cf. next figure).

An event of crucial importance during this turbulent period created **our beloved Moon**. Although the Moon's formation is still the subject of debate among scientists, the most widely accepted theory is that of a giant impact. According to this theory, a body the size of Mars collided with the Earth very early in the history of the solar system, around 4.5 billion years ago. This impact would have expelled debris from the Earth and the impactor body into space, which would then have coalesced to form the Moon. Evidence in favor of this theory includes the similar chemical composition of the Earth and Moon. In any case, the collision was so violent that it altered the Earth's axis and speed of rotation, leading to the formation of the 24-hour day (one complete revolution around the Earth's axis). Since then, the Moon has been an important part of the Earth's system, influencing the planet's tides and rotation, and playing a role in the later development of life on Earth.

The Earth's lithosphere, specifically the outermost layer, is the playground for critical movements that have shaped the Earth's surface, creating mountains, oceans and other landscapes, over millions of years. These processes can be divided into two main categories: **endogenous and exogenous**.

Endogenous processes originate in the Earth's interior and are caused by heat and pressure. Some of these include plate tectonics, volcanism and earthquakes. Plate tectonics is responsible for the formation of mountains, volcanoes and ocean trenches, while volcanoes can form new islands, alter the shape of existing landforms and contribute to the formation of mountain ranges too. Earthquakes can cause sudden movement of the Earth's crust and the formation of new landforms such as faults and rift valleys.

Exogenous processes, on the other hand, are due to external factors and are mainly caused by erosion and weathering. Weathering refers to the disintegration of rocks, soils and other materials on the Earth's surface, which can be caused by physical, chemical and biological factors. Erosion involves the transport and removal of weathered materials by water, wind, ice and gravity. All these natural forces can reshape the land, transporting materials to new locations, mixing botanical species and creating new landforms such as deltas, sand dunes and alluvial fans.

Let's continue our journey from the center of the Earth into space. The innovation of the atmosphere, which took place around four billion years ago, played a key role in the emergence of life on this planet. The atmosphere is made up of several distinct layers, each with unique properties and altitudes, and is thought to have formed through a process called **outgassing**. This would involve the release of gases such as water vapor, carbon dioxide, nitrogen and other gases from the Earth's interior into the surrounding atmosphere.

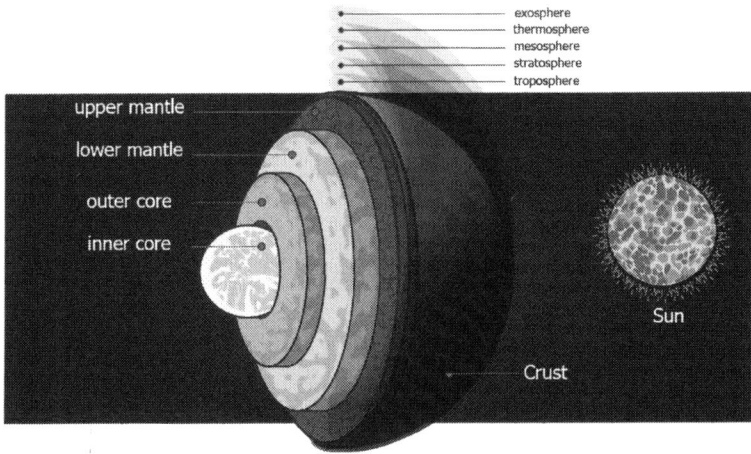

exosphere
thermosphere
mesosphere
stratosphere
troposphere

upper mantle
lower mantle
outer core
inner core

Sun

Crust

The natural process of **atmospheric stratification,** which led to the different layers of the Earth's atmosphere, is not well understood in terms of its timing. The atmosphere that existed on our primitive Earth, four billion years ago, was markedly different from the one we have now. For example, the atmosphere was probably more uniform, with a higher concentration of gases closer to the Earth's surface due to gravity. Volcanic activity was intense at the time, releasing large quantities of gases such as sulfur dioxide and nitrogen oxides, which can still be smelled near active volcanoes such as in Iceland and Indonesia today. The primitive atmosphere consisted mainly of water vapor, carbon dioxide, methane and ammonia, and contained very little oxygen. As the Earth cooled and solidified, the atmosphere began to stratify, with denser gases such as nitrogen accumulating in the lower layers, while lighter gases such as hydrogen and helium moved to the upper layers.

It's essential to emphasize the considerable *Value* of our atmosphere, this natural innovation essential to the survival of every species. Indeed, the atmosphere performs many vital functions that have enabled living organisms to thrive and evolve over millions of years[7].

One of these critical functions is to act as a shield against harmful radiation from the Sun and space, just as sunglasses protect your eyes from ultraviolet rays. A direct result of this atmospheric protection is the regulation of temperature and climate. Composed of distinct layers, our atmosphere absorbs and deflects high-energy particles from space, preventing dangerous levels of radiation from reaching the Earth's surface and disrupting or eradicating life. Greenhouse gases such as carbon dioxide and methane trap heat and create a stable temperature range on the planet's surface, making it suitable for life. In addition, the atmosphere plays an essential role in the water cycle, enabling the transport of moisture and facilitating the formation of clouds and precipitation, which are vital for the continuation of all living organisms.

If you've never wondered, the reason why there's no life on other planets apparently similar to our own, called exoplanets, becomes obvious when you consider their atmospheres. On Mars, for example, the atmosphere is only about one percent as dense as Earth's and is mainly composed of carbon dioxide. This thin layer does not provide adequate protection against harmful radiation from the Sun and space. Furthermore, the extreme temperature fluctuations on Mars, ranging from as low as -195°C (-319°F) at night to as high as 20°C (68°F) during the day, make it difficult for living organisms to survive. Similarly, the Moon has virtually no atmosphere, leaving it exposed to the full force of solar and cosmic radiation, making it an inhospitable environment for life as we understand it.

The importance of the Earth's ecosystem, and in particular the atmosphere, in sustaining life is recognized not only by scientific evidence, but also by ancient wisdom. The Qur'an, for example, highlights the

---

7   Unfortunately, global warming due to human industrialization continues to seriously upset the balance of this system.

protective *Value* of the atmosphere in the following passage: "[…] And We have placed on the earth firm mountains, lest it should shake with them, and We placed therein broad highways for them to pass through, that they may be guided. And We made **the sky a protected roof**, yet they turn away from its signs" (21:31-32). Ancient Hindu Vedic texts also narrate: "Let the earth be free from disease, free from evil. Let there be no harm to plants, animals or me. May the hills be rich in food, may the rivers flow gently, may the plants be nourishing and **may the sky be free from danger**" (Rigveda 10.191.3).

Whatever the case, the chain of events, whether fortuitous or divine in origin, starting with the Big Bang, passing through the formation of stars and galaxies, leading to the creation of our precious planet with its inner and outer layers, has made **the Earth a cradle of life**, and so far, it deserves this label hands down (or sky up). For, to date, despite the vastness of the universe and the existence of hundreds of billions of cosmic objects, there is no concrete evidence of life on any other planet or moon in our solar system or beyond. Nevertheless, the search for extraterrestrial life remains an active area of astronomical research. Scientists are still exploring potential biosignatures, including certain chemicals, atmospheric gases and electromagnetic emissions from space, which could be detected by telescopes and other receivers, perhaps indicating that an intelligent form elsewhere is trying to contact us.

Aside from the atmosphere, **water** is undoubtedly one of nature's most remarkable innovations, for its contribution to the formation of our planet with its oceanic color. Despite its simple composition of just two hydrogen atoms and one oxygen atom, this molecule has been a crucial factor in the genesis and evolution of all living things.

The importance of water in the emergence of life has been recognized for centuries in many cultures. The Rig Veda, again, describes the origin of life with the lines: "In the beginning, there was only darkness enveloped in darkness. All that was, was unmanifested water. Out of this darkness, a seed, which was covered with darkness, appeared by the power of heat" (Rig Veda 10.129.5). Similarly, in the Bible, water is associated with spiritual purification and rebirth, and in John's Gospel, Jesus tells Nicodemus that "no one can enter the kingdom of God unless he is born of water and the Spirit" (John 3:5). The Qur'an also describes water as a source of life and a sign of God's power and mercy. Surah Al-Anbiya, or The Prophets, verse 30, states: "And We have created every living thing from water. Will they not then believe?"

The origin of water on Earth remains a scientifically unsettled subject, as high temperatures and pressures were probably not conducive to its formation some four billion years ago. However, there are several theories that attempt to explain its existence. One of them suggests that water was delivered to Earth by comets or asteroids that struck the planet during its early history. Carbonaceous chondrites, a type of meteorite formed far from the Sun, have been proposed as a possible innovative water delivery mechanism. Another theory suggests that water was present in the initial material that formed the Earth from cosmic dust and was released during the planet's dynamic geological formation. These two theories are *a priori* complementary, as water on the Earth's surface (lakes, oceans, etc.) is characterized by a quantity of deuterium that is half that found in meteorites and almost double that found in water originating from the Earth's crust, as a result of outgassing. In less mathematical terms, water on the surface of Earth is naturally balanced between that found in meteorites and that found in the Earth's inner layers, justifying the two sources of water.

Water has played a decisive role in the development and prosperity of life on Earth, regardless of its origin. The existence of such vital liquid on the surface has enabled the formation of water bodies such as oceans, rivers and lakes, which have provided habitats for a wide range of plant and animal species, including our single-celled ancestors. What's more, water is an essential component of every biological system, acting as a universal solvent and facilitating many chemical reactions. Internally, it also enables the transport of nutrients and waste products throughout the living body. Add to that the fact that water is a key element in the innovative process of photosynthesis, which is how plants and other organisms produce their own food.

A molecule with such existential impact would explain why astrophysicists and cosmologists are actively searching for evidence of water in potential objects in our solar system and beyond. The discovery of water on other planets may provide clues, albeit minor ones, to the presence of life beyond Earth. Mars is one of the most promising places in this context. Recently, NASA's Curiosity Rover missions to Mars discovered signs of ancient river channels and lake beds, indicating the presence of liquid water in the past. In addition, there is evidence to suggest that water may be present in the form of ice on Mars and other planets in our solar system. Astronomers are also looking for "habitable" planets beyond our solar system, where the conditions necessary for the existence of liquid water are met.

3

You may remember Thales' theorem from your math class, which applies on the formed angles when a straight line intersects two other parallel lines. Don't worry, we'll put that theorem to one side (because who cares?). What interests us here is its author. In fact, Thales is more widely recognized as a pre-Socratic philosopher than a pure mathematician. He lived in Miletus, on the west coast of Anatolia (now Turkey), in the sixth century BC. He therefore deserves to be included in the closed circle of early philosophers in Western history.

Thales labeled water the "archè" (sometimes written as "arkhè"), or basic substance, of the universe. This appellation reflects his belief or analysis that the entire world could be traced back to the water that created it, including earth, air and even fire. Although the importance of water in the emergence of life on Earth is undeniable, as can be seen from the impact of its scarcity on plants, animals and in our very bodies, it is not in itself sufficient to launch life, as Thales falsely suggested. In the mathematical and Latin language of his time, water is a *sine qua non* condition for existence, of course, but it takes more than that to trigger LIFE.

The origin of life on Earth is thought to have occurred some 3.5 to 4 billion years ago, during the Archean Eon, when the planet was very different from what it looks like today. Back then, there was no oxygen in the atmosphere and the Earth's surface was constantly bombarded by asteroids and comets. Scientists suggest that life first emerged in the oceans, particularly in hydrothermal springs and tidal basins. These environments provided the conditions necessary for the formation of organic molecules and the subsequent evolution of living organisms. Interestingly, ancient philosophies, again, seem to have initiated theories similar to those presented by modern science [8].

"And God said, Let the waters bring forth living creatures in abundance, and let birds fly upon the earth above the expanse of heaven. And **God created the great fish** and every living creature that moves, with which the waters abound, after their kind" (Genesis 1:20-27).

"And Allah created **every living thing from water**. Among them are those who crawl on their bellies, those who walk on two legs, and those who walk on four. Allah creates what He wills. Verily, Allah is capable of anything" (Qur'an 15:26-27).

"Then there was nothing, neither existing nor nonexistent: there was no realm of air, no sky beyond. What covered and where? And what provided shelter? Was there water, **unfathomable depths of water**?" (Rig Veda 10.129.1-7)

These last verses may express, in their own way, the basic idea that life may have begun in the ocean or in a water-based environment, a proposition supported by various scientific, religious and philosophical beliefs. However, the exact process by which life appeared on Earth remains a matter of debate, akin to the question of whether we live in a sophisticated pre-programmed simulation or not! This question about our very first origins has fascinated scientists for centuries, leading to

---

8   We often see this pattern of ancient texts proposing explanations, generally in metaphorical form, which are subsequently confirmed by scientific theories. This hardly suggests that the philosophers of the time had access to a source of metaphysical truth, even if that remains a possibility, but it does imply that the first step of observing nature in order to pose the right hypotheses is common to both a spiritual guru and a scientist.

numerous hypotheses. The ancient history of our planet, dating back some 4.5 billion years, remains a mystery as there are no existing rocks or fossil traces of this geologically unstable era to help us test current hypotheses about how and where life may have appeared and evolved. Despite this major obstacle, researchers continue to experiment.

Charles Darwin famously proposed a metaphor to describe the origin of life on Earth. In a letter written in 1871, he suggested that life could have begun in a "**warm little pond**" containing various chemicals, such as ammonia and phosphorus salts, which would have led to the formation of a protein compound. Darwin believed that life could arise **spontaneously from non-living matter under the right conditions**. Darwin's speculation on the origin of life challenged the widely spread belief in the need for a metaphysical craftsman to innovate each new species. Today, we understand that life forms depend on a source of energy, oxygen or carbon dioxide, a few minerals and proteins for survival and growth. However, four billion years ago, organic molecules such as carbon and proteins, which are the building blocks of living beings and essential nutrients, were rare on Earth.

Inspired by such a hypothesis, still crazy a century or two ago, American biologist Stanley Miller, then a fresh graduate in 1952, undertook an experiment to simulate the conditions of the primitive Earth and test the possibility of organic molecules forming from non-living matter. Miller created a laboratory model of **a primordial soup**, containing water, methane, ammonia and hydrogen – all elements present on Earth four billion years ago – and subjected it to electric sparks to simulate lightning. After a week's experiment, Miller observed that the solution had turned brown and that certain amino acids, the building blocks of proteins, had formed. This ground-breaking experiment showed that organic molecules could form under certain conditions that existed on the primitive Earth, providing evidence to support the theory that life on Earth began through processes of chemical *innovation*.

Another plausible theory suggests that the molecules needed for life, like water, could have come from outside the Earth, perhaps from meteorites or comets. These space objects would have brought the basic elements essential for life on our planet. For example, the Murchison meteorite contained numerous amino acids, which are crucial for life. Recently, researchers discovered leftovers of extraterrestrial organic matter in three-billion-year-old sediments in South Africa, with micrometeorites the likely source. What's more, samples from asteroid Ryugu brought back by the Hayabusa2 mission in 2022 contained over 20 types of amino acid, providing further support for this hypothesis.

One of the most promising theories explaining the origin of life is based on the interaction of active sites on **the surfaces of clay minerals** with simple organic molecules. British chemist and mineralogist Graham Cairns-Smith first proposed this theory in 1966. Cairns-Smith suggested that clay minerals, which were abundant on the primitive Earth, have a complex structure with numerous active sites capable of binding and catalyzing the reactions of simple organic molecules. The Cairns-Smith hypothesis was supported by experiments demonstrating the ability of clay minerals to catalyze chemical reactions. In addition, clay minerals can act as a protective shield, preventing the degradation of organic molecules by the UV radiation that was abundant during the early stages of our planet, pending stabilization of the atmosphere.

Regardless of which theory or theories postulate truth, today's scientists largely accept the Darwinian perspective that the emergence of life on Earth was **a natural, incremental process of innovation**, probably begun by a chemical reaction of simple elements forming more complex organic molecules in some moist environment, the presence of water being essential. It's intriguing to observe, once again, that ancient philosophies have suggested similar perspectives, as with the clay theory.

The idea that humanity's origins are linked to the Earth is not a recent notion, as it has been prevalent in many animist beliefs. For example, the Bantu people of South Africa credit their supreme deity, Nzambi, with the creation of the world. According to their belief, Nzambi created the first humans from clay and gave them life through his breath. They also perceive all living beings as possessing a spiritual essence known as muntu, which links them to the divine. Similarly, Asian Taoism emphasizes the emergence of life in harmony with the five elements of wood, fire, earth, metal and water.

In the same vein, in the Bible, we read in the book of Genesis: "The Lord God formed man of the **dust of the ground** and breathed into his nostrils the breath of life; and man became a living being" (Genesis 2:7).

In the Qur'an, it is written: "We created man from **an extract of clay**. Then We made him as a drop in a place of settlement, firmly fixed. Then We made the drop into an alaqah (leech, suspended thing, and blood clot), then We made the alaqah into a mudghah (chewed substance) [...] Then We made the drop into an embryo, then We made the embryo into a fetus, then We made the fetus into bones, then We clothed the bones with flesh, and then We brought him forth as another creature. Blessed is Allah, the Best of Creators!" (Qu'ran 23:12-14).

Even regarding the hypothesis of receiving minerals from falling meteorites, in Surah Al-Hadid (meaning "The Iron Verse" in Arabic), it is stated: "And We sent **down** iron, in which there is great might and benefits for the people...".

In the first part of the *Matrix* trilogy, Agent Smith draws a comparison between humanity and a virus, which spreads without regard for its environment, consuming resources and causing change. While this metaphor accurately reflects our current consumerist and environmentally disruptive societies, recent studies suggest that our origins may also have a viral aspect. Indeed, ribonucleic acid or RNA is thought to have played a significant role in the earliest stages of life on Earth, whether it emerged from clay or a chemical soup, in what is labeled **"the RNA-world hypothesis"**. RNA viruses, such as the one responsible for COVID-19, have genetic material composed of RNA instead of DNA. The mRNA vaccines developed by Pfizer and Moderna use a small fragment of the virus's RNA to instruct the body's cells to produce a harmless piece of the virus, which then triggers an immune response, preparing our bodies against future infections.

The latest scientific theories suggest that some four billion years ago, this same small molecule, RNA, acted as a life-inducing virus. To express it like an engineer, RNA is the Matrix's first self-replicating pixel, capable of carrying genetic information and catalyzing chemical reactions. This paved the way for the development of more complex life forms, such as the first cells. Such hypothesis finds its plausibility in the unique properties of RNA, which manages to perform two major functions for life to persist: **stimulating proteins** and **duplicating itself**.

If we go into a little more technical detail, imagine a damp place with a mixture of simple components, a kind of chemical soup, nothing extraordinary. Suddenly, by chance or design, the RNA molecule appears. It has the capacity to perform many of the functions of proteins, which are essential to the structure, function and regulation of all living cells. This unique property enables RNA to act as a catalyst, speeding up the chemical reactions needed by future organisms. RNA's ability to self-replicate is also crucial to the development of life. The first self-replicating RNA molecules, i.e., that were able to copy-and-paste themselves (like COVID-19), led to the formation of similar RNA sequences.

At this stage, take a minute to digest how the evolution of our visible Matrix, starting with the universe and the formation of Mother Earth, has been shaped mainly by gradual natural innovations over hundreds of millions of years. Nevertheless, there have been major, relatively rapid changes whose non-metaphysical origin is difficult for our scientists to justify. These include the Big Bang, the fundamental laws of physics, meteorite collisions with our planet, the appearance of water and RNA. Another important innovation was the development of DNA, supposed to have evolved from RNA over a period of time long enough to allow for the right chemical reactions and even mutations. This genetic code integrated into every living thing has led to the diversification of life forms, marking a shift from the dominance of natural innovations affecting only inert objects, as detailed in this first dimension of the Matrix, to an increasing focus on natural biological innovations, to be described in the second dimension of the Matrix, starting on the next page.

DIMENSION 2:
Programmed animated agents

1

Innovation isn't always fair, because the discoveries that change the course of history are often based on a combination of hard work, serendipity and, sadly, sometimes overlooked contributions. The discovery of DNA is no exception. While most people attribute such a scientific marvel to American biologist James Watson and English physicist Francis Crick in the 1950s, the full story is more like a gradual staircase than an elevator ride.

Almost 80 years before Watson and Crick's study, Gregor Mendel, an Austrian monk and scientist, carried out revolutionary experiments with pea plants. At the time, it was mistakenly thought that in botanical or biological reproduction, traits were randomly mixed in the offspring. With enough time in the monastery garden where he worked, Mendel set about mixing specific traits of pea plants, such as flower color, seed texture and plant height. Crossing a white and a red flower, for example, he meticulously tracked the transmission of these traits from one generation to the next and, to his surprise, noticed precise ratios and patterns, so much so that he could predict how many red and white flowers would be present in the next generation. He thus formulated laws to explain these hereditary patterns. Above all, he postulated that traits are determined by discrete units – he called these "factors" or "elements" – which are transmitted from parents to their offspring. These factors would later be recognized as genes by Wilhelm Johannsen, a Danish botanist, who expanded on Mendel's work and coined the term in 1909.

Around the same time, in 1869 to be precise, Friedrich Miescher, a Swiss physiologist and chemist, made a fortuitous but revolutionary discovery in genetic research that would forever change the course of the field. While working to isolate and identify the protein components of leukocytes, or white blood cells, he stumbled upon a new substance he called "nuclein". Today, this substance is known as nucleic acid and is more commonly referred to as DNA, or deoxyribonucleic acid.

Miescher noticed that nuclein had chemical properties that were different from all known proteins. It had a much higher phosphorus content and was resistant to proteolysis, the process by which proteins are broken down. In other words, DNA was much more stable in the face of change. Although Miescher didn't initially understand the significance of his discovery, he soon recognized the potential importance of nuclein, writing that a "whole family of such slightly varying phosphorous-containing substances will appear, as a group of nucleins, equivalent to proteins".

Despite Miescher's early recognition of the importance of nuclein, it took more than 50 years for the scientific community to fully appreciate the significance of his discovery. In fact, in a historical account of 19th-century science published in 1961, Miescher was not even mentioned once, while other scientists, such as Charles Darwin and Thomas Huxley, were frequently cited.

But it was only in the decades following the work of Phoebus Levene and Erwin Chargaff that the full significance of Miescher's discovery became apparent. Chargaff's research, in particular, was essential in revealing the chemical composition of DNA, including the ratios of its four constituent bases. And then there was Rosalind Franklin, whose work in X-ray crystallography provided crucial information on the structure of DNA and the double helix. However, her contributions were often undervalued, and her data was shown to Watson and Crick apparently without her consent or knowledge. It was only years later that her major role in the discovery of DNA was widely recognized.

Although most of us learned about the structure of DNA in our high school or university biology classes, it's quite possible that, through boredom, indifference or lack of maturity, we didn't appreciate the full extent of this natural innovation. The complexity of living organisms, from the smallest units of life to the intricacies of the human body, is based on this interlocking code. By exploring more deeply the details of each component, from proteins to genes to DNA and beyond, we can gain a better understanding of the underlying mechanisms of the Matrix. Analogies with the construction of a house or a computer can be useful in understanding this complex matter. Just as these systems require many components working together to function properly, the cells, tissues and organs of the human body also rely on a meticulously coordinated interconnection of molecules, genes and proteins.

Let's start with **proteins**. At a basic level, proteins perform a wide variety of functions in the body. They are made up of chains of small units called amino acids, and their specific sequence determines their unique structure and function. Just as bricks or electronic circuits are the fundamental building blocks of a house or a computer respectively, proteins are the fundamental building blocks of life. To cite just two cases, the protein hemoglobin is responsible for transporting oxygen in the blood, while the protein collagen confers strength and structure to connective tissues such as skin and bone.

But just like bricks or circuits, proteins are kind of stupid. You can't tell a brick to position itself near a window or a door. In the same way, **proteins need a code**, instructions telling them what to do, when and where, just as hardware needs software. This is where **genes** come in. They are basically sections of DNA that contain the instructions for building specific proteins and can be thought of as the blueprints or programming code that governs the construction of the body. Each gene codes for a specific protein, and the unique sequence and arrangement of these genes determine many of our physical and mental traits. These genes are found on long strands of DNA, called chromosomes (more on this later), which are housed inside the nucleus at the center of each cell. Statistically, the human genome contains around 20,000 to 25,000 genes, each playing a unique role in the development and functioning of the body (including the brain, of course).

If, by chance or misfortune, you know anything about computers, we can draw a parallel between genes and low-level computer circuits and their programming language in several ways. Firstly, both genes and circuits operate at the most fundamental level of their respective systems. Genes provide the basic instructions for the development and functioning of living organisms, while circuits serve as the building blocks for the operation of electronic devices. Secondly, both genes and circuits can be seen as "programmed" to perform specific functions. Genes are essentially "written" in the language of DNA and provide the code for the development and functioning of living organisms. Similarly, circuits are designed and programmed in assembly or C language to perform specific tasks, such as processing data or controlling the operation of a device. Finally, just as code written in a programming language can be optimized and improved to enhance a system's performance, genes today can be modified and refined through genetic engineering to produce desired traits or functions in organisms, such as better resistance of plants to insects or cows with more muscle mass. In short, Genetically Modified Organisms or GMOs.

One thing leads to another: **DNA** is the genetic material that contains all an organism's genes. It's a complex molecule present in all living things, storing the genetic information needed to build and maintain all the body's cells, tissues and organs, depending on the complexity of the living organism in question. Made up of four chemical bases – adenine, thymine, guanine and cytosine – which pair up to form the "rungs" of the DNA ladder, it has a characteristic double-helix structure. In relation to our previous metaphors, this structure can be compared to an architectural blueprint or a digital storage system, containing all the instructions needed to build and maintain architectural and computer structures.

Chromosomes, which are long strands of DNA coiled and tightly packed in the nucleus of each cell, can be compared to shelves or cupboards that store these architectural blueprints or digital memory storage units. They keep the genetic material organized and protected and provide a means for the body to access the information it needs to function properly. Chromosomes are tightly wound and packed into the nucleus of each cell. Typically, human beings have 23 pairs of chromosomes, for a total of 46. Each chromosome contains thousands of genes, and their specific sequence and arrangement determine many of our characteristics.

Finally, **cells** represent the elementary aggregate of all of the above, each with its own unique functions and characteristics. These units vary in size and shape, and their activities range from transmitting electrical signals throughout the body to generating movement. If we keep the human for illustrative purposes, our body is a complex machine made up of trillions of cells and billions of protein molecules, working together to sustain life. From the proteins that build our tissues and organs to the DNA that carries our genetic information, every component of our body is essential in shaping our identity and our experience of the world. The diagram below gives a complete overview of this biological Russian doll.

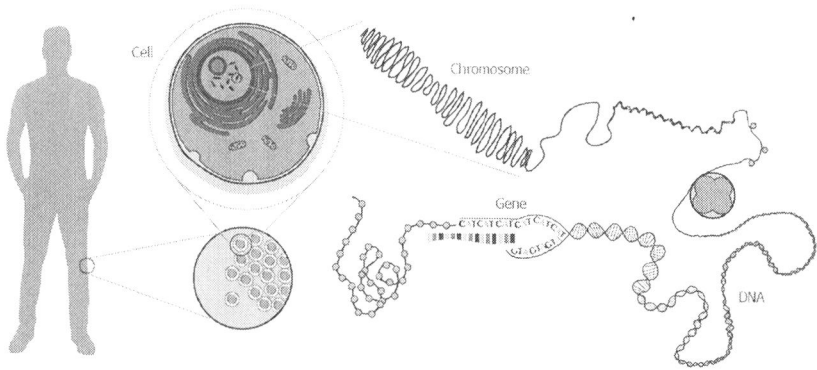

Let's avoid succumbing to the materialistic fallacy of absolute determinism, which assumes that DNA controls every aspect of a dynamic agent's life. Recent findings in the field of epigenetics challenge this notion and highlight the intricate interplay between genes and the environment. While genes provide the blueprint for building and maintaining cells, the environment plays a crucial role in shaping gene expression and cellular function. This phenomenon is known as gene-environment interaction. In essence, if DNA is likened to a startup business plan, the environment acts as the entrepreneur who decides which aspects of the plan to activate or disregard. In the case of humans, for instance, environmental factors such as diet, lifestyle, exposure to toxins, stress, and social interactions can profoundly influence gene expression and cellular function. These factors have the ability to modify gene activity, leading to alterations in cellular processes, protein production, and ultimately, the observable traits and characteristics of an organism. It becomes clear that nature alone does not solely define an individual; nurture, both physically and to some extent psychologically, also plays a significant role. In this regard, you consistently having negative thoughts can trigger the release of stress hormones such as cortisol, thereby altering the cellular environment (oxidative blood, high blood pressure, etc.) and potentially impacting the activation of inherited cancer cells from your biological parents.

I deliberately focused on this natural DNA innovation, with its important epigenetics' twist, not out of passion for such a field (I refused to take the medical entrance exam at the end of my high school studies), but because this stage represents a transition to a new dimension on our planet. In fact, the Matrix no longer relied on chance or a divine plan to evolve, but increasingly on the genetic code integrated into the evolutionary fabric of living beings. From single-celled organisms to humans, the DNA code serves similar basic purposes: **protection, adaptation and replication.** Richard Dawkins' 1976 bestseller, *The Selfish Gene* explored the concept of genes and their role in evolution. His controversial argument is that genes are the basic units controlling the fates of species and that their behavior can be grasped in terms of their "selfishness[9]", that is, their interest in propagating themselves. To understand this paradigm, we need only look at the history of natural evolution.

Reproduction, for example, is a vital process for all living organisms, dating back to the earliest forms of life on Earth. As we discussed earlier, the RNA world theory proposes that the first dynamic agents were RNA-based, similar to simple viruses, with a crucial role in the origin of life. According to this same hypothesis, the first RNA molecules, which appeared in a primordial soup, were not intrinsically stable and degraded rapidly, just as a virus does not survive long outside a living host. However, those that were more relatively stable multiplied over millions of years and evolved into a variety of RNA machines, serving as the basis for more complex organisms. As the RNA world evolved, so did proteins and DNA. Proteins became essential for catalyzing chemical

---

[9] This is not to be confused with typical human selfish behavior. Genes, over the course of generations, tend to adjust and favor individual and collective behaviors that optimize their own chances of replication. A gene doesn't think or choose its actions!

reactions in cells, while DNA eventually took over the role of storing genetic information due to its greater stability compared to RNA.

As a consequence of the emergence of DNA-based organisms, the first living things on Earth are thought to have been simple, single-cell prokaryotes. These organisms, which had the ingenious ability to synthesize DNA, are thought to have appeared around 3.5 billion years ago, and although they were quite simple in structure, they were more dynamic than viruses. Prokaryotes include bacteria and archaea, and are still abundant on Earth today, reproducing rapidly and forming colonies.

The emergence, growth and replication of DNA-based organisms is still a matter of scientific conjecture, due to the lack of direct evidence and the immensity of the timescale studied. However, based on the universality of DNA processes in all agents, it is thought that the replication mechanism of primary DNA was similar to that observed in modern organisms. During replication, the two strands of the DNA double helix separate, serving as templates for the synthesis of two new complementary strands. DNA polymerases, enzymes that add nucleotides to the growing strands based on the sequence of the template strand, facilitate this process. The newly formed molecules then separate and divide into two daughter cells during cell division, enabling organisms to grow and replicate.

Boring! The jargon of each discipline protects those who are already in it, the so-called experts, but prevents the curious, like you and me, from identifying the hidden mechanisms. Clearly, we need to include more marketers in scientific fields.

So, let's take a lighter approach. DNA replication can be compared to using the Ctrl+C and Ctrl+V shortcuts in Windows.

1. When copying and pasting a computer file: The two strands of the DNA double helix act like the original file, which is duplicated when copied and pasted. Similarly, during DNA replication, the two strands

of the double helix separate and serve as templates for the creation of two new identical strands.

2. The enzymes responsible for adding nucleotides to growing DNA strands can be compared to the background software used to copy and paste computer files. Both the software and the enzymes have specific rules for adding new information to ensure that the resulting duplication is identical to the original.

3. This ensures that the genetic information in the organism, or the digital information in your PC, is reproduced accurately and without error.

However, it's worth noting that back in those distant days, it's likely that the first DNA-based organisms had a simpler genome than modern organisms, consisting of a small number of genes required for basic cellular functions. Therefore, in order to evolve towards the greater complexity and diversity of life, simple DNA replication needed updating. Scientists suggest that, over time, the genomes of these organisms would have evolved through the accumulation of mutations, due for example to errors when copying and pasting code, and the acquisition of new genetic material through other naturally innovative processes.

As you (perhaps) already know, in classical information transfer, genetic material is passed on from parent organisms to their offspring during reproduction, typically and bluntly: after sex. This is how traits and characteristics are transmitted from one generation to the next. Artificial gene transfer, on the other hand, is a recent technology that involves the intentional introduction of genetic material into an organism, for example, through genetic modification. This process is becoming increasingly common and can be used for a variety of purposes, such as developing parasite-resistant plants or creating new medical treatments. However, both these options were unavailable in the early stages of life on Earth due to the absence of complementary sexual organs and advanced human technologies, with humankind only appearing millions of years later.

Horizontal gene transfer and **endosymbiosis** were thus proposed by the scientific community as possible mechanisms that could have enabled the transfer of genetic material between organisms and the development of more complex life forms. Horizontal gene transfer is the transfer of genetic material between organisms that are not parent and offspring, for example by the absorption of genetic material from the environment or by direct transfer from other organisms. Endosymbiosis involves an organism living inside another and eventually becoming part of it, thus enabling the transfer of genetic material between the two. These theories are the best we have so far for understanding the first biological movements towards greater genetic diversity. Being able to replicate one's code a billion times in one's own corner is no good if one can't connect with other agents to collaborate on a mixed code. Such has been the Matrix's entrepreneurial philosophy since its genesis, apparently.

Anyway, thanks to these DNA transfer techniques, we've been able to progress to the next stage of our evolution: **microbes**[10]. This period is often referred to as the last universal common ancestor, with the cooler acronym **LUCA**. The latter refers to the most recent form from which all living organisms on Earth evolved. Although scientists have not identified any specific historical individual as LUCA, they believe it was a population of organisms that existed around 3.5 to 4 billion years ago.

One of the most significant studies linked to the identification of the LUCA of all living organisms on Earth was published in the journal *Nature* in 2016. A team of nerdy scientists used mathematical modeling to analyze the genetic information of modern organisms and reconstruct the likely genome of this common ancestor. They used a technique called comparative genomics, which involves comparing the genomes of different organisms to identify similarities and differences. Their analysis suggested that LUCA was **a single-celled organism**, similar to modern bacteria or archaea, that lived in a deep, high-temperature marine environment. As a result, LUCA was probably an anaerobe, meaning it didn't need oxygen

---

[10] From viruses (RNA) to microbes, we're talking about a considerable evolutionary leap! This is no joke. Innovation follows an S-curve, starting slowly before taking off exponentially in terms of performance and impact. This also applies to human evolution.

to survive and was able to synthesize all its own amino acids, which are the building blocks of proteins essential to life.

Fossilized stromatolites dating back over 3.5 billion years bear witness to these first recorded signs of life. These are rock structures formed by the accumulation of layers of sediment linked to colonies of micro-organisms and can be found all over the world, notably in ancient rocks in Australia and North America. Discovered and extensively studied by Belgian geologist Jean-Baptiste Julien d'Omalius d'Halloy (a hell of a name in those days), in the early 19th century near Liège, these structures may well reflect the course of our history. Indeed, after the emergence of single-celled organisms through genetic transfer and DNA mutation, scientists believe that the next major change was triggered by cyanobacteria, grouping together to form... stromatolites.

Besides creating stromatolites and other natural products, cyanobacteria, or blue-green algae, demonstrated an innovative process for further events on Earth. These tiny organisms were actually able to use sunlight, water and carbon dioxide to produce organic compounds and oxygen through **photosynthesis**. This highly nutritional technique had a significant impact on the chemistry of the oceans and atmosphere. In principle, this process is the same used by green plants, algae and certain bacteria to transform the Sun's energy to produce organic compounds from carbon dioxide and water, releasing oxygen by default, thus contributing to the build-up of an oxygen-rich atmosphere over the millennia.

The accumulation, or rather large-scale production, of this radical product-type innovation, in this case oxygen, in the Earth's oceans and atmosphere, really began around 2.4 billion years ago, during a period known as **the Great Oxygenation Event**. Prior to this, the oceans were anoxic, meaning they lacked oxygen, and the atmosphere was composed mainly of gases such as carbon dioxide, nitrogen and methane. The increase in oxygen in the atmosphere was a disruptive turning point in the history of life on Earth, enabling the development of various dynamic agents all over the planet. It took several hundred million years for the oceans to incorporate a little oxygen into their waters; as with most natural innovations, patience was required. Meanwhile, increasingly complex organisms evolved. Miming the famous refrain from the song by the rock band The Police, every breath you take is accompanied by the opposite breath of a plant. You release CO2 and the plant uses it to release oxygen or O2, confirming our eternal connection to our ecosystem and our natural origins, according to the photosynthetic equation below (the weight factor 6 is there just to balance the equation, feel free to ignore it).

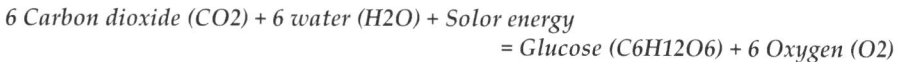

6 Carbon dioxide (CO2) + 6 water (H2O) + Solor energy
= Glucose (C6H12O6) + 6 Oxygen (O2)

Symbolically,

Your outbreath (CO2) + Water + sun = Botanical Food + Your inbreath (O2)

According to Norse mythology, popularized by the TV series *Vikings*, the god Odin, on his quest for supreme knowledge, finally reached the Well of Wisdom, which was supposed to hold the explanation of the Matrix. At the bottom of the well lived a giant fish, symbolizing the immensity of the universe and the enigma of creation. Odin, in true Viking style without a hint of fear, plunged his gaze into the well and gained a deep insight into the mysteries of all things. However, this privilege was not without sacrifice. He returned with only one eye, thus renouncing a part of himself. Odin gained unparalleled wisdom, but he also experienced loss and pain.

Beyond the moral lesson, it's notable that after viruses and microbes, the next significant entity in our evolutionary journey, as in Odin's well, was an aquatic creature – **a sort of fish!**

The evolutionary transition from microbes, in the form of algae, to something like a fish is of significant (albeit limited) importance to our human perception. The fact remains that a fish, however small, is considered an animal. The term "animal" is derived from the Latin word "animalis", meaning "breathing". In Arabic, the word for animal is "حيوان" (hayawan), which is derived from "حياة" (hayat) or life, and implies movement. Animals are also related to "anima", another term of Latin origin, referring to the vital force that gives life to living things. In modern English, it is often used to describe the inner self or psyche, while the closest equivalent in Arabic is "ruh" (روح), also denoting soul or spirit.

In other words, some three to two billion years ago, our Matrix was no longer limited to inert agents devoid of "anima" but slowly saw the birth of dynamic agents animated by some hidden energy. Such a perception of the soul, often found even in the earliest animistic cults and some of the great later religions, would be understood even by my three-year-old nephew at a puppet show or watching a cartoon. He would consider these basically inanimate yet humanly animated objects as real as you and me, but distinct from his red car or a KitKat. Similarly, in the absence of a clear assimilation of the mechanisms animating these various animate agents, early humans created the notion of soul, Dao or similar metaphysical notions. With or without a soul, the distinction between inanimate agents and living beings nevertheless remains easy, even for my nephew perhaps. A puppet is inert because it can only move by means of fingers and external cords, whereas animals, plants and all living beings use their internal energy to act, reproduce and move in their environment.

Let's return to our evolutionary path, with the appearance of the first fish-like creatures on Earth. This was around 500 million years ago, during the Cambrian period. These creatures, known as agnathans, are jawless fish, lacking paired fins and scales. Seemingly primitive, they were the first vertebrates to appear in the fossil record. Haikouichthys, a streamlined creature a few inches long with a primitive skull, is one of the earliest known agnathans. It lived in China around 530 million years ago and was probably a seabed dweller, feeding on small organisms in the mud. Pikaia, another early agnathan, lived in British Columbia at the same time. This small worm-like creature had a notochord, a flexible rod-like structure that later evolved into the vertebrate backbone. It probably swam by contracting muscles along its body rather than using fins. Fossils of these early agnathans can be found in many science museums around the world.

After the Great Oxygenation Event, bored with the abundance of water for millions of years, some entrepreneurial organisms ventured onto dry land[11]. These were probably simple cyanobacteria and algae. As early pioneers, they clung to wet soils and rocks, slowly evolving to adapt to air and sunlight exposure. Over the millennia, more complex organisms emerged, including mosses, ferns and eventually seed plants. One of the most important botanical innovations in the evolution of terrestrial organisms was **the development of roots**. The latter enabled plants to anchor themselves in the soil, providing stability and access to nutrients. This, in turn, enabled them to grow taller and diversify, eventually giving rise to trees and forests.

As plants colonized the earth, they provided new habitats in which other organisms could thrive. Insects seem to have been among the first to take advantage of this new opportunity, developing specialized respiratory systems to breathe air. The first non-plant species to move from the ocean to land were probably arthropods, such as the giant spider-like millipedes and centipedes, which evolved to breathe air and adapted to life on land during the Silurian period around 420 million years ago. Some of the earliest known terrestrial invertebrates were arachnids, such as spiders and scorpions, which also evolved during this period.

Around 360 million years ago, the first amphibians emerged from the water and began to colonize the land. Amphibians were the first vertebrates, i.e., with a backbone, to venture onto land, using their powerful legs to crawl out of the water and explore new environments. They laid their eggs in water and breathed through their skin, making them highly dependent on wetlands. Later, some amphibians evolved adaptations that enabled them to move further away from the water, eventually giving rise to reptiles. The latter were well adapted to life on land, with tough, scaly skin that helped them retain moisture and lay their eggs there. Since then, they have colonized a wide variety of environments, from arid deserts to lush tropical forests. Some reptiles, like the dinosaurs, grew to gigantic sizes and dominated the Earth for millions of years.

---

[11]   You'll notice with so many examples that radical innovations, whether natural or human, were initiated by one or a few entrepreneurial entities, with a major impact on the rest of history, from our tiny perspective anyway. **Risk-taking**, whether unconscious or rationalized, is the fuel of **the wheel of change**.

During the same period, mammals also made their appearance, although they remained small and unremarkable until the mass extinction of the dinosaurs some 66 million years ago. With the disappearance of these big beasts, mammals had the opportunity to fill the ecological niches they had previously occupied, like a Sony occupying digital camera space at the expense of a Kodak. This enabled mammals, including our direct ancestors, to develop a wide range of adaptations, or "biological features", to thrive in diverse environments, from mountains and deserts to the depths of the oceans.

Rest assured, we're not going to delve into the 50 billion or so organisms that have evolved on Earth since its beginnings, nor are we overly concerned with the absolute accuracy of the dates and theories cited above. While scientists have worked diligently to test certain hypotheses in the laboratory, search for and date fossils, and ultimately construct the entire historical narrative of our biological evolution, it must be admitted that there are still gaps and unexplained evolutionary transitions, and it's likely to stay that way, given the persistent lack of tangible evidence. What is certain and of interest to us, however, is **the incremental aspect of the innovative process** of our Matrix and its objects, both inert and animate. In the same vein, let's turn our attention to another natural process, one that would further explain how you and I got here.

2

There once was a man whose father was a renowned physician in the early 19th century. So, following in his dad's footsteps, he attempted to learn medicine at Edinburgh University in Scotland. However, this attempt soon turned into an academic disaster. He rebelled against his class and eventually dropped out. It was probably the best decision of his life. Increasingly interested in the path of his grandfather (rather than his father), a respected naturalist and poet, he spent time learning taxidermy from a freed slave, transforming dead animals into living sculptures, as you can see in London's Natural History Museum.

He continued to learn and meet experts in various fields of animal biology, until his father, fearing that his son was wasting his youth on useless subjects, enrolled him in a Cambridge college to study theology, hoping that his son would become an Anglican clergyman someday. The funny part of the story is that this man would later become one of the most hated citizens of the church and other religious sects. A few years later, while still at university, Charles Darwin was given the opportunity of a lifetime when he was recommended by botany professor Henslow to join the Beagle's voyage across the seas and continents, making observations and hypotheses, collecting animals and plants and taking notes. In short, a prophetic, distraction-free voyage, the aim of which was to observe, to meditate on the nature of livings things. Five years later, two of them spent on land, Charles began to build a better understanding of the process of natural selection and the evolution of species, detailed years later in his timeless masterpiece, *The Origin of Species*.

Although theorized only recently, relative to the history of humankind, this innovation, an incremental biological process, was an incredible discovery. While collecting birds from various Galapagos islands, Darwin mistakenly assumed that the birds he had collected, albeit with slightly different beak shapes, belonged to the same species. Sometime later, noticing that each beak shape corresponded to a specific island, i.e., birds from the same island had the same beak, Darwin, with the help of his colleagues, finally understood that these birds were in fact different species, having the same biological ancestor. This may seem "logical" to some readers and "incomprehensible" to others. So, let's rephrase what Darwin did see in these taxidermized bird samples.

Knowledge is sometimes a simple linking of separate or even forgotten data in the brain. Linking mathematics and biology, for example. This premise requires us to acquire or be aware of two things. Firstly, a reminder of reasoning by the absurd, the invention of which is often attributed to Greek philosophers such as Parmenides and Euclid. The aim is to show that a hypothesis is true. So, we assume it's false, and if it really is true, we'll arrive at a contradiction sooner or later, like falling on $1 = 0$. The second definition to reanimate in your brain is that of species. It is defined as a group of organisms that share common characteristics and are able to reproduce with each other, giving rise to fertile offspring. The example of the donkey, the mule and the horse, illustrates well the concept of species. Even if we ignore their morphological differences and wrongly assume that they belong to the same species, by crossing a male donkey and a mare – an act of visualization to be avoided, and one that humans still apply to these poor species – their offspring, known as mules, are always sterile. Conclusion: the donkey and the horse are of different species, although both belonging to the genus Equus, thus justifying the resemblance.

Let's apply this magical new knowledge to the observations of Darwin, who, given the difficulty of the exercise, probably didn't play with already dead birds. So, mental reasoning is required. By the absurd, if a male bird with beak Y from the island Gala belonged to the same species as the female bird with beak shape X collected on a nearby island Pagos, then they could have reproduced other small birds, *a priori* with a mix of beak shapes. Try grouping dogs in heat of various colors and genders together and you'll get a canine rainbow. Therefore, this being hardly the case, with a single beak shape for each island, Darwin reaches a weighty conclusion. They were very similar species, but different. This led to two heavier confirmations. Remember, this was before computers and the discovery of DNA.

Firstly, the near-perfect resemblance between these species implies **the existence of a common ancestor**, probably from the geological period when these islands were one. If you look at two nearly identical sisters, you'd be right to assume that they share the same father or mother, or both. The fact that these islands were separated by the sea, limiting mixing between groups, meant that they developed beaks that were heterogeneous from one another. Hence the second corollary, which states that **the environment in which a Matrix agent evolves influences its future physical and behavioral destiny**. Extrapolating this example to all species, we end up with an evolutionary tree from the first micro-organisms on Earth to the branch of every species past and present, including us, Homo sapiens.

Darwin was a pioneer in this field, providing an objective, smart explanation for the existence of millions of species while challenging the religious spirit of his time. In nineteenth-century Christian Europe and Anglican England, it was difficult to question the widespread belief that every living species was consciously shaped by a divine force. The simple yet hard-to-admit idea that the complexity and diversity of life on Earth could be justified by barely perceptible natural innovative processes was revolutionary, even shattering to the faith of many who refrained from challenging the following:

"By the word of the LORD were the heavens made, their starry host by the breath of His mouth. He gathers the waters of the sea into jars; He puts the deep into storehouses. Let all the earth fear the LORD; let all the people of the world revere him. For He spoke, and it came to be; He commanded, and it stood firm" (Psalm 33:6-9).

Although Darwinian selection is widely used in agriculture and animal breeding to improve desirable traits, many school curricula purposely exclude this theory from theirs, or at least fail to mention its true historical implications. Religiously-dominated countries such as Morocco, Poland, India and many others, have school and university textbooks that barely mention the tree of species evolution, probably to avoid mental dissonance with cultural identities rooted in religious beliefs such as "Before the creation of the world, there was only Brahman, and this Brahman created all that exists" (Hindu scripture, Upanishads) or "By faith we understand that the universe was formed by the word of God, so that what is visible was not made from what is visible" (Hebrews 11:3). Jokes and misunderstandings about humans being apes only add confusion to understanding the big picture of our Matrix [12] . Now that you know the technical definition, Man and Chimpanzee are two different species, with a similar ancient ancestor. The same goes for a Gorilla and a Chimpanzee.

Despite my earlier criticism of anti-Darwinian countries, I'm far from being the best proponent of Darwin and his theory. In fact, there are still some problematic aspects to it. Take the quasi-unrealistic story of whale evolution. Many people wrongly classify whales as fish. In reality,

---

[12]   This is assuming that individuals wish to gain a better understanding of the subject. It's obvious that many are still preoccupied with the drudgery of their daily lives and haven't yet reached the level of play sufficient to perceive any sort of Matrix, starting with questioning their accepted teachings from childhood and school.

they are mammals just like us. This means they are also warm-blooded vertebrates, characterized by the presence of mammary glands that produce milk to feed their young. They also have body hair and three middle ear bones. To reproduce, they give birth to live young, like most mammals, such as seals, sea lions, walruses, dolphins and porpoises.

As previously mentioned, mammals appeared in bulk after the extinction of the dinosaurs and lived mainly on land. However, whale evolution is a unique case where their ancestors were, as it seems, a group of four-legged carnivorous mammals called mesonychids, which lived around 50 million years ago. As these mesonychids adapted to life in the water, they developed features such as streamlined bodies, flippers and the ability to hold their breath for long periods. In fact, whales are an example of mammals that returned from the land back to the ocean and evolved to thrive in this aquatic environment.

The first problem with this theory is that mesonychids were nothing like fish, so the question arises, how did they evolve into fully aquatic animals like whales? One possibility proposed is that they became semi-aquatic first, like crocodiles, living near water and gradually adapting to an aquatic lifestyle over time. However, this remains a matter of debate, as we still don't understand why such a change occurred and in what environmental context. Another question raised by the evolution of whales is that of their nostrils. Unlike other aquatic mammals such as seals and dolphins, whales have typical blowholes on the top of their heads instead of nostrils at the end of their snouts, making for some wonderful documentary scenes of skyward blowing. It's unclear how this adaptation evolved and what evolutionary advantage it provided. Some scientists speculate that it may have helped whales breathe more efficiently when diving. Finally, the evolution of whales' complex vocalizations is also a mystery. These big beasts are known for their cryptic songs and calls exchanged over miles, but we don't know how this function developed.

So, the mystery of whales' evolution has remained till 2007, when Hans Thewissen, a Dutch American paleontologist, and his colleagues revealed that Indohyus, a small deer-like mammal belonging to the extinct artiodactyl group called raoellids, is the closest known relative to whales. During their study, while examining the skull of Indohyus, a student in Thewissen's lab accidentally broke off a section covering the inner ear, which was surprisingly thick and highly mineralized, resembling the bone structure found in whale ears. Further analysis of the skeleton also revealed similar adaptations in other bones, such as thickening, commonly seen in mammals that spend a significant amount of time in water. In 2009, expert on the evolutionary history of mammal Jonathan Geisler and Jennifer Theodor combined fossil and genetic data, resulting in a revised whale family tree. The findings unveiled raoellids, like Indohyus, as the closest relatives to whales, with hippos representing the next closest relatives to both groups combined. This breakthrough firmly established whales within the larger context of the mammalian evolutionary tree, shedding new light on their ancestral origins.

In the field of evolutionary science, it is not uncommon to encounter challenges and uncertainties when piecing together the intricate puzzle of past and extinct organisms. Hypotheses and speculation are inherent in this process, as we strive to draw a simple, meaningful story of a complex, dynamic and ever-changing biological simulation. However, despite these challenges, an increasing body of evidence now supports Darwin's profound observation of a progressive and innovative process driven by dynamic agents within the complex web of life, rather than relying on instantaneous metaphysical creation. This perspective is in line with the Taoist concept which asserts that "The Tao produced One; One produced Two; Two produced Three; Three produced All things". By recognizing that the divine, as religiously perceived, plays hidden, little or no part in the ongoing development of our physical reality, while retaining the belief that the initial programming of our Matrix, or some lucky circumstances were perhaps the masterpiece of an embedded creative Energy, more believers would free their worlds from superstitious practices that only enslave their body and soul, while remaining rationally spiritual to some extent.

Instead of accepting my praise of Darwinian theory at face value, it would be more sensible to recall its essence. Here's a rather simplistic example of how its *technology*, i.e., the innovation process of **natural selection**, works. Let's imagine a video game with three controllable characters called giraffes: a four-meter female giraffe, a four-meter male giraffe and a two-meter male giraffe with a small neck. Unfortunately, after a draw, you are the master of the latter, while your friend gets the male animal double your giraffe's size.

Vigorously pressing the X and O buttons on your controller, you realize that there is no jumping ability for these heavyweight giraffes. Consequently and by default, your smaller giraffe is at a disadvantage to your friend's, not only in terms of access to the most nutritious tree leaves, positioned high enough to get a full day's sun, but also in terms of the seductive ability of the female next to it, who is clearly out of your reach, sorry, your Pokémon's reach. In short, Game Over, my friend! With less competition in sight, the remaining male takes full advantage of the opportunity to feed and produce a future giraffe, of course measuring four meters long too when she grows up, by genetic rational. Such a sizeable advantage will optimize this newborn's chances of survival in the near future.

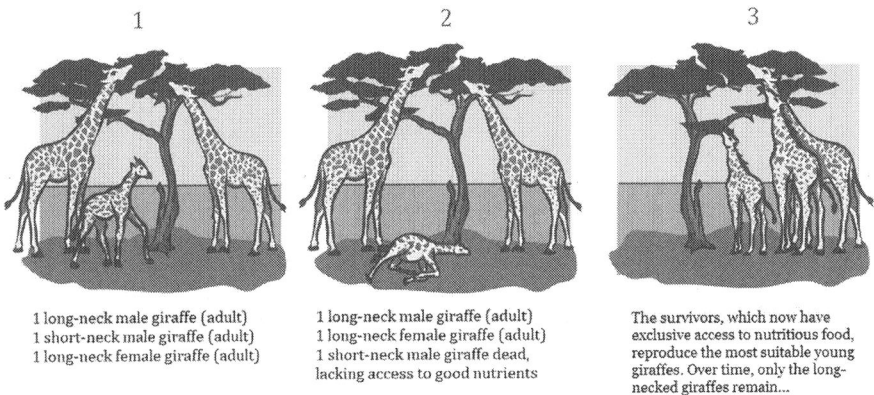

1	2	3
1 long-neck male giraffe (adult) 1 short-neck male giraffe (adult) 1 long-neck female giraffe (adult)	1 long-neck male giraffe (adult) 1 long-neck female giraffe (adult) 1 short-neck male giraffe dead, lacking access to good nutrients	The survivors, which now have exclusive access to nutritious food, reproduce the most suitable young giraffes. Over time, only the long-necked giraffes remain...

Let's generalize this example to two groups of real giraffes. One group with a short neck (S gene) and one with a long neck (T gene). Which group do you think is more likely to survive in the African savannah?

Wrong! The answer isn't necessarily tall bodies!

In Darwin's terms, and reasoning over several generations, **the winner is "the fittest"**, that is the individual, group or species best suited or adapted to its environment. In our hypothesis, if we take "Tall" to mean 20 meters, "small" to mean a maximum of four meters and assume a standard tree height of five meters, then the S gene, that of dwarf giraffes, is more likely to dominate over time. Being taller or stronger[13] doesn't always mean being better! And that's not just in evolutionary theory.

According to the theory of natural evolution, survival and reproduction are primarily determined by natural selection. If we take our case of giraffes at 20 meters in height, others at four meters, and trees at five meters on average, then the gene for short necks (S gene) would be more likely to dominate because extremely tall giraffes would find it difficult to continually flex their rigid necks to eat. This illustrates the importance of referring to successful natural traits as "natural innovation", rather than random inventions. These traits are not maintained for no reason. They don't follow infinitely growing patterns of size, speed, appetite or other traits either. Rather, they are created, destroyed or enhanced with the aim of promoting species "fitness", reflected in adaptation to the pressures of the ecosystem at any given time. Consequently, the species that survived over a long period were not necessarily the biggest, strongest or fastest, but rather the most adapted to their environments.

Such paradigm is even noticed at cellular (and sexual) level. In what's called a sperm race, multiple sperm cells from the same or different males, depending on the plant or animal species, compete to reach and fertilize one or a few eggs, which are often less numerous than males' abundant sperm. This competition is a good illustration of the natural selection process, where the fittest and most successful sperm cells have a higher chance of fertilizing the egg and passing on their genetic material to the next generation. Take a mammal like us for instance. Within the male reproductive system, millions of sperm cells are produced during each ejaculation. These sperm cells possess unique genetic variations due to the

---

[13]   Even these notions should be treated with caution when comparing different species. An ant is not stronger than an elephant in absolute terms, but relative to their weight, an ant can carry 10 to 50 times its own weight, which leads to the conclusion that **an ant is at least 100 times stronger than an elephant**, for the same weight.

process of genetic recombination and mutations. As they swim towards the egg, they face numerous challenges and obstacles, including the female reproductive tract, other sperm cells, and the limited time frame in which fertilization can occur. Factors such as swimming speed, morphology, and the ability to surpass other micro challengers, and hence to penetrate the egg's protective layers, make the difference between the winners and the losers of this vital race.

Let's draw a parallel with the world of business as well. Between two products, a sophisticated electric toothbrush and a simple manual toothbrush, the classic. Which do you think is better?

Again, like with natural selection, your supposedly rational response should depend on the *Need*. According to Professor Clay Christensen's "Jobs to be Done" theory of innovation, who is also the founding father of the disruptive innovation theory, customers rarely buy products to possess them in themselves, but rather to solve a problem, i.e., to do the "job", whether tangible or psychological. Taking this theory into consideration, while the electric toothbrush seems more advanced and has additional features, the job for which many customers hire a toothbrush is simply to clean their teeth, once or twice a day. In this case, the manual toothbrush seems more effective for this job, as it can easily reach certain areas that the electric toothbrush cannot, and at a much lower price.

Considering a time axis spanning millions of years, the process of adaptation by an organism or species to an environment, whose *Needs are* constantly changing, is similar to the pressures of a capitalist market. For example, since the birth of the internet, an artisanal store would be obliged to convert to an e-commerce platform in order to adapt to the changing economic landscape and meet the *Needs* of its increasingly digitalized (and lazy) customers. Otherwise, it's Game Over! Similarly, if over the course of millennia, there's a change in sea level, a new organism moves into the area, there is a persistent drought, or on the contrary, an ice age, the natural ecosystem has no choice but to transform. Some species move up the food chain, others disappear, and a few manage to hold on by adjusting their habits. Sometimes, the transformation is radical and takes organisms by surprise. Phenomena such as volcanic eruptions, meteorite falls or tsunamis can rapidly change the landscape of a geographical area, both geologically and biologically.

On the other hand, in a purely communist society, there is less pressure to evolve due to a less free framework, where people hardly find the *Motivation* to innovate, for lack of incentives, as already witnessed during the Soviet Union. The similarity with evolutionary biology is even more impressive. This refers to organisms that have reached an evolutionary equilibrium as being in **a state of stasis**. Some deep-sea fish, for example, are in evolutionary stasis because they have adapted well to their unchanging environment since the dawn of time, and therefore look more like blind little monsters than edible fish (given the absence of light at these depths).

By examining such synergies between the economic and biological realms, we can pinpoint the evolutionary process that has taken place over millions of years on Earth, starting with the reasons behind the instinctive fear of death, the search for sexual partners and the tendency of many species, especially the weaker ones, to live in groups. The fundamental answer to these questions is deduced from the very spirit of natural selection: **those who lacked these innovative traits have already disappeared**. This provides a plausible statistical explanation for these behaviors and our history within the Matrix, without the need for irrational or contradictory metaphysical claims.

Let's take up the erotic subject of reproduction again, from a biological angle, of course. Since the first simple DNA-based organisms, cells capable of efficiently transferring their genetic code to others have flourished and multiplied in number and territory, while those that were unsuitable, inefficient or clumsy have diminished over time. The notion of power, in its multiple aspects, is another key factor in the success of most living beings. Within plant and animal species, those with advantageous traits enabling them to dominate their environment, whether by accessing nutritional resources or securing desirable breeding partners, are more likely to pass on their genes to future generations.

Here's another question for you: If dinosaurs were brought back to life, as in the movie *Jurassic Park*, could they thrive on Earth?

As we've seen, the answer has to be weighed up. Firstly, if they were brought back artificially, it's likely that humans would capture them and study them in large-scale laboratories. However, the most crucial consideration, which by now you should be used to, is whether they could fit into the current ecosystem, relative to the era in which they had lived. Being a dominant species for millions of years does not necessarily guarantee success in the future, as history has demonstrated time and again with the rise and fall of famous dynasties and civilizations.

During the Mesozoic era (252 to 66 million years ago), commonly known as the Age of the Dinosaurs, the Earth's environment was very different from that of today. One of the main reasons for the large size of many organisms during this period was the high level of oxygen in the atmosphere. Indeed, its proportion was estimated at around 30 to 35 percent, compared to the 21 percent we have today. This abundance of oxygen, and therefore of vegetation, enabled animals of the time to grow in mass and size, and to sustain more active metabolisms. In addition, there were fewer large predators during this period, which may have enabled larger herbivorous dinosaurs to thrive without being hunted as frequently.

Therefore, the most likely answer is no, as these resurrected dinosaurs would have difficulty adapting to the current environment of our polluted, human-dominated planet. However, there are many other fascinating examples of evolution that have been observed over a relatively short period of time (rather than waiting millions of years), further justifying Darwinian theory:

- **Antibiotic resistance in bacteria**: This is one of the best-known examples of evolution, also seen in viruses such as AIDS or COVID-19. Bacteria have evolved to become resistant to antibiotics through natural selection. This occurs when bacteria resistant to an antibiotic survive and reproduce at the expense of those that perish, passing on their genes and hence their resistance talent to their offspring. Over time, this can lead to the emergence of antibiotic-resistant strains of bacteria.

- **The bark butterfly:** Before the Industrial Revolution, most bark butterflies in the UK had light-colored wings, which blended in with the lichen-covered trees they lived on. However, when factory pollution killed the lichens and darkened the tree trunks, the darker, more melancholy form of the bark butterfly became more common, as it was better camouflaged against predatory birds against the darker background.

- **Human evolution**: Although we tend to think of human evolution as something that happened in the distant past, it's actually an ongoing process. Note what scientists have discovered in our ability to digest lactose (the sugar in milk), which evolved in humans relatively recently, over the last 10,000 years, due to the domestication of cattle.

It's important to recognize that the theory of evolution is sometimes misused by science magazines and some researchers, as well as by non-experts, who come up with nice stories that certainly hook the reader but have no basis in fact. We can let our imaginations run wild by proposing that a cat evolved directly from the mouse it was trying to catch, throwing common traits such as vibrissae, eyes, a tail and fur on the table. Nevertheless, this remains just another hypothesis. Without following a scientific method based on temporal and genetic data, it would make no sense to publish such an observation. Additionally, the environment plays a crucial role in the evolution of species. If we do not have a precise understanding of the environmental conditions that influenced the appearance of a biological characteristic or species – something that is always difficult to analyze – we risk falling easily into the trap of speculation.

Returning to the subject of the Fundamental Identity of *Innovation*, the innovative paradigm of natural selection allows us to explain the emergence of new characteristics or species in the following way:

New trait = (Need + Motivation) × (Creativity + Technology) × Value

a. *Need* *(of the end user)*: Survive and pass on genetic code to offspring.

b. *Motivation* [14] *(of the innovator)*: An opportunity to observe, learn and improve continuously.

c. *Creativity* (or vision): A competitive game with millions of iterations, which is self-perpetuating and enables the most suitable to progress to the next stages of consciousness.

d. *Technology* *(or implementation)*: Based on DNA duplication, environmental context and pressures, survival and reproduction mechanisms, natural selection, etc.

e. *Value* *(or outcome)*: A hypothesis to be formulated at the end of this book.

The *"Need"* variable detailed above, applied to the Matrix's various animate agents, breaks down into two distinct but interconnected parts: living as long as possible (**survival**), which Renaissance philosopher Jean-Jacques Rousseau called self-preservation; and passing on one's genetic material to the next generation (**reproduction**). However, it's important to note that these mechanisms are mainly subconscious, even in humans. For example, a tiger doesn't spend time philosophizing about why it should hunt or reproduce, as it is intrinsically programmed to do so. These innate drives have given rise to remarkable innovative techniques that have evolved over millions of years to meet the needs of survival. They have been admired and studied by people from all walks of life, including artists, scientists and spiritualists.

- **Camouflage**: The ability to blend into one's environment to avoid predators or capture prey. As a famous use case, chameleons can change the color of their skin to match their environment, while octopuses manage to change their texture and external color effortlessly.

- **Chemical defense**: Features that enable toxins or venom to be produced as a means of defense. For example, dendrobate frogs secrete toxins through their skin to deter predators, snakes employ venomous bites

---

14 Again, assuming there is a divine purpose and intelligent initial designer behind all this simulation.

and marine cones possess a harpoon-shaped venomous structure called a radula, which they use to capture their prey. Similarly, when an ant feels threatened, it releases alarm pheromones to warn other members of its colony of the danger.

- **Echolocation**: Many species of bats and some species of whales, dolphins and shrews have developed the ability to use echolocation to move around their environment and locate prey. They emit high-frequency sounds and listen to the echoes that reach them, helping them to build a mental map of their environment and locate objects.

- **Nest-building**: Birds and some species of insects and mammals have developed the ability to build nests to provide shelter and protection for their young. For example, weaverbirds build elaborate nests by weaving together grasses and twigs, while termites build complex, solid nests using mud.

- **Tool use**: Apes, birds and octopuses, to name but a few, have been observed using tools to solve problems and obtain food. Chimpanzees can use sticks to extract insects from trees and termite mounds, and octopuses use coconut shells and other objects to hide from predators, build shelters and so on.

By ensuring their survival for as long as possible[15], most organisms tend to fulfill the second part of the *Need* variable, which is reproduction. Here too, evolution has produced a vast array of creative mechanisms to achieve this Matrix objective. **Sexual reproduction**, in which two organisms contribute genetic material to produce genetically unique offspring, is a method understood and practiced even at the human level. However, there is also a much less well-known and rather highly innovative method of **asexual reproduction**, in which one organism produces offspring genetically identical to itself.

If we start with the first type applied to plants, flowers are a typical example. Flowers are specialized structures containing both male and

---

[15]   The "sufficient" time for survival can vary considerably from one organism to another, from a few seconds for viruses to several decades for some animals, to several centuries for some plants.

female reproductive organs, enabling the transfer of genetic material between different plants. This could happen by the intermediation of wind, as we can read in the Qur'an a while before science understands it: "And We send **the fertilizing winds**, then cause water to descend from the sky, thereby providing you with water in abundance, though you are not its retainers" (Qur'an 15:22). In addition to the wind, flowers have developed various characteristics to encourage **pollination,** such as bright colors and powerful fragrances, attracting pollinators such as bees, butterflies and hummingbirds. These pollinators act as intermediaries, much like natural pimps, enabling the transfer of "plant sperm" from male to female flowers. In some cases, plants can even self-pollinate, meaning that pollen from male flowers fertilizes female flowers of the same botanical species.

In animals, and particularly in reptiles, birds and mammals like us, the natural innovation of internal fertilization is a well-documented process. Unlike laying eggs as hens do, this type of fertilization occurs when the sperm is deposited inside the female's body, allowing more precise control over where and when the egg is fertilized, offering greater protection for the vulnerable future offspring.

Another innovative biological process supporting sexual reproduction in animals is the evolution of complex **courtship rituals.** These are the equivalent of human wedding ceremonies, involving elaborate behaviors such as singing, dancing or displaying brightly colored feathers or fur, to strut one's stuff in order to attract a mate, starting with the preparation of the scene. In fact, male garden birds build complex structures called "bowers" (hence the name bowerbird in English), a sort of covered bower using twigs, grass and other materials. The bower is often decorated with brightly colored objects such as flowers, berries or even pieces of plastic or glass. The male garden bird will then perform a series of seduction rituals in and around the bower.

These rituals, worthy of a Casanova, are among the most elaborate and complex in the animal kingdom. I highly recommend watching a video of this artist in action. The male garden bird will spend hours performing various dances and songs, all designed to impress the female. A common display is the "mating dance", where the male jumps and flaps his wings in a particular sequence. He then spreads his tail feathers, revealing his colorful plumage and hops around the bower, all the while emitting a loud, high-pitched call. Another display is the "food offering", where the male presents the female with a carefully chosen gift, such as a berry or flower. If the female accepts the gift, the male performs songs and dances, hoping to win her over. Perhaps the most fascinating aspect of the garden bird seduction ceremony is the fact that each male builds a unique bower, with his own individual features and decorations. This means that each male has his own distinct style and personality, and females can choose their partner based on their preference for a particular bower or display of seduction. Apparently, we're not the first or only species to engage in the art of seduction.

With or without a courtship ritual, different species exhibit a range of natural organisational innovations to ensure reproductive success. Like with humans, one such mating strategy is **monogamy**, where individuals form long-term pair bonds with a single mate. This is not exclusive to mammals. Take the example of stork birds, which I spent my childhood appreciating on top of most moroccan mosques. In fact, storks are known for their unique mating behavior and their long-term monogamous relationships. Male and female storks come together as a couple, building nests on a high tree or mosque, and raising their young cooperatively. Wolves are another notable example of monogamous relationships, where gray wolves form pairs consisting of an alpha male and an alpha female. These individuals mate exclusively with each other, contributing to the cohesion and stability of the wolf pack. We can also mention swans and some species of penguins such as the emperor penguin.

In contrast to monogamy, many other species employ **polygamous mating strategies**, where individuals have multiple mates. Polygamy can take different forms, such as polygyny, where males mate with multiple females, or polyandry, where females mate with multiple males. Examples of polygamous species include certain bird species like the sage grouse, or some mammals such as lions and elephants. Chimpanzees, our closest living relatives, are known to engage in multiple mating strategies. While they are primarily considered a promiscuous species, with both males and females mating with multiple partners, there are also instances of temporary monogamous bonds forming between individuals. Similarly, although humans exhibit a wide range of mating patterns influenced by cultural and social factors, it seems that evolutionarily, we tend more towards a sort of serial monogamy. Note that each mating strategy has its advantages and drawbacks when it comes to individual and group survival and reproduction.

Continuing with the second method of reproduction, the intriguing innovations of asexual reproduction offer creative ways to duplicate DNA without the need for a classic fusion of male and female energies. Take the story of my friend Worman.

Once upon a time in my little garden, teeming with life, there was a little worm I named Worman (not very creative, I know!). One day, Worman was happily wriggling about, looking for food and enjoying the warmth of the sun after a rainy week in the still cold Parisian spring, when suddenly he found himself attacked by a hungry blackbird, which we'll call Merlus. This solitary bird, whose diet includes insects, swooped down on him and caught him in its beak. Merlus cut him in half, but Worman didn't panic. Instead of playing dead, he calmly contracted his muscles and snapped in two, one half remaining in the bird's beak, while the other half wriggled away to safety.

This innovative super-process is called **fragmentation**. It meant that when Worman got cut in half, the two halves could regenerate into complete, new worms, provided they weren't both eaten or destroyed by the bird, rather like Hollywood actor Jake Gyllenhaal's two characters in the thriller, *Enemy* (2013).

In other cases, asexual reproduction relies on **binary division** techniques, where the parent organism divides into two equal parts, each developing into a new individual. This type of reproduction is common in unicellular organisms such as bacteria and protozoa. **Budding** means that a new organism grows out of the parent organism in the form of an outgrowth or bud. The bud eventually separates from the parent organism and develops into a new individual. This type of asexual reproduction is also found in animals such as hydras, jellyfish and certain crustacean species. In some species of reptiles, amphibians and fish, a process called **parthenogenesis** is the norm for preserving genes ad infinitum. This is a type of reproduction in which, strangely enough, an unfertilized egg develops into a new individual.

In the plant kingdom, we can briefly explore **vegetative propagation**. This asexual method involves the growth of a new plant from a vegetative structure such as a stem, root or leaf. Potatoes, strawberries and spider plants fall into this category. Let's explain this process simply from the raw material of French (or Belgian?) Fries' beloved ancestor, the potato.

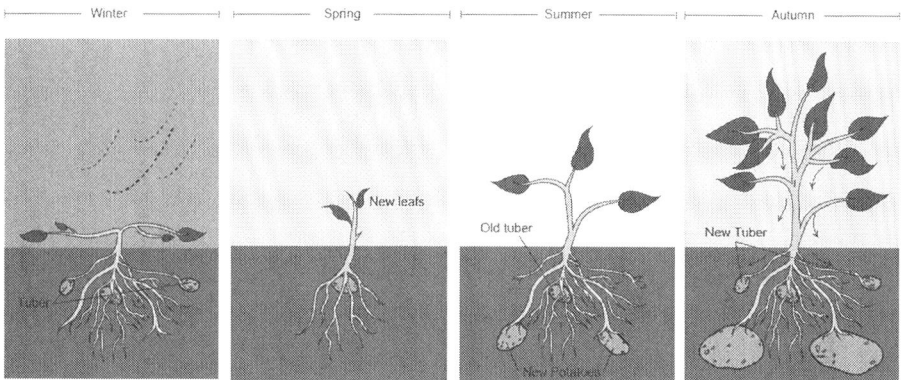

Potatoes are a unique species that reproduce differently from most other plants. They don't need two different plants to give birth to babies. Instead, they use a technique called **cloning**, where they make exact copies of themselves. Here's how it works. During winter, the cold makes it difficult for a potato plant to grow, leading to the death of the above-ground part of the plant. However, the underground tuber enters a state of hibernation, remaining dormant until spring arrives. When the weather warms up, the food reserves in the tuber help the plant to grow new roots and shoots from the tuber buds. With the help of the water absorbed by the new roots, the plant begins to develop green leaves in summer, which then photosynthesize to produce food. Some of this food is stored in a few new tubers, which in turn go dormant the following winter, while the old tuber dries out as its food reserves are used up. This cycle continues.

Let's delve into the analogy between biology and computing science once more, this time focusing on the concept of natural selection. Just as computer operating systems like Windows or Android evolve by building upon previous versions while retaining their core kernel, natural evolution follows a similar pattern. The foundation of evolution lies in the innate drive of all living organisms to survive and reproduce, a programming embedded within their DNA since the inception of life itself. Through this process, organisms gradually adapt and evolve by developing advantageous traits that enhance their ability to thrive in their specific environments. These beneficial characteristics are innovated and refined over generations through various mechanisms such as genetic mutations, interbreeding with other groups, and most importantly, natural selection. Just as engineers correct errors, consider user feedback, and introduce new features and improvements in operating systems, organisms with advantageous traits are favored by natural selection. On the other hand, organisms lacking advantageous traits, much like the outdated Windows Vista, eventually become obsolete and are surpassed by their better-adapted counterparts. This ongoing cycle of adaptation, refinement, and selection ensures the continuous improvement and optimization of species over time, mirroring the evolutionary progression observed in the field of computer science and business innovation in general.

The natural, progressive innovation of humankind is no exception.

Let's pick up the story of our evolution around half a billion years ago, when a significant breakthrough in natural products occurred. During the Cambrian period, the first known species with **a brain-like structure** emerged. The exact cause of this major evolutionary development is still unclear and is likely to remain so. Nevertheless, driven by evolutionary pressures to enhance survival, certain species, referred to as early bilaterians, possessed rudimentary nervous systems that enabled basic sensory perception and simple behavioral responses. As time passed, the complexity and size of the brain increased as organisms encountered new environmental challenges and opportunities.

For most species, this remarkable innovation—the brain or a nervous system—serves as a central command center, comparable to a central processing unit in the realm of information technology. It coordinates a myriad of bodily functions and facilitates complex behaviors specific to each species. A useful metaphor for understanding the role of the brain is to envision it as the control room of an exceptionally efficient factory. Similar to managers overseeing different departments and making decisions to ensure smooth operations, the brain supervises and regulates the body's functions. It receives and processes sensory information from sight, hearing, and the other senses, much like workers providing updates to the control room about their task statuses. Armed with this information, the brain makes decisions and issues instructions to various body parts, much like managers issuing commands to workers on the factory floor. These instructions govern a wide range of activities, including muscle movements for walking or running, the regulation of heart rate and breathing, the processing of emotions and memories, and predicting or preparing the next moves. A more efficient brain or nervous system thus enhances the likelihood of survival within a demanding ecosystem overall.

A critical milestone in brain evolution transpired with the emergence of vertebrates, encompassing fish, amphibians, reptiles, birds, and mammals. This process commenced around 400 million years ago when certain fish species acquired the ability to breathe oxygenated air and traverse land. Over countless millennia, these early land-dwelling fish gave rise to diverse amphibian species, such as frogs and salamanders, which adapted to both aquatic and terrestrial life. These amphibians became the first animals to develop limbs with fingers or toes, enabling more efficient movement on land.

A hundred million years later, reptiles began to emerge, not by a divine breath *ex nihilo*, but by a combination of small mutations and a healthy dose of natural selection over millions of biological iterations. The dinosaurs that would later dominate the Earth were descendants of the first reptiles and had innovative adaptations that supported life on land, including waterproof skin, powerful limbs and efficient respiratory systems to breathe oxygen in deeply.

Another hundred million years later, mammals began to evolve, much more rapidly after the extinction of the dinosaurs, including the primates that would eventually give rise to humans. These early primates were rather adapted to life in trees, with prehensile hands and feet, forward-facing eyes and relatively more complex social behavior than other species. A crucial moment arrived when some adventurous primates began to leave the trees and settle on the ground, adapting to a more terrestrial lifestyle. These early hominids, such as Australopithecus, fossils of which can be found in some life science museums (in secular countries, of course!) had adaptations such as bipedal walking, opposable thumbs and larger brains that supported them in their efforts to adapt to this new, down-to-earth environment.

Finally, only two million years ago, the Homo genus appeared, including species such as Homo erectus and Homo habilis. These early types of humans had even larger brains and more sophisticated tools, and eventually evolved into modern humans, we Homo sapiens, around 300,000 years ago according to recent discoveries.

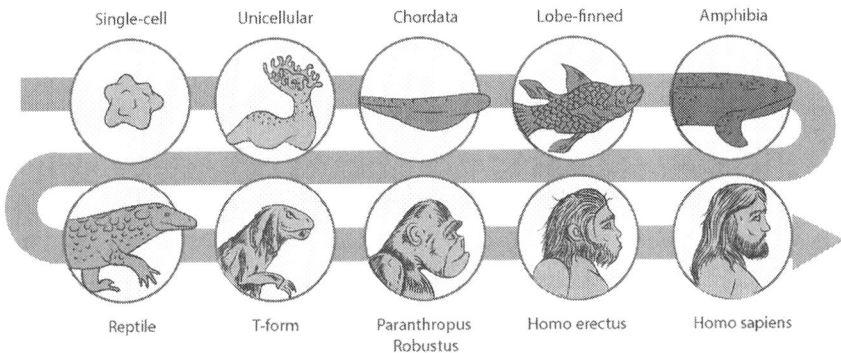

Single-cell   Unicellular   Chordata   Lobe-finned   Amphibia

Reptile   T-form   Paranthropus Robustus   Homo erectus   Homo sapiens

Unlike the centralized dominance of Microsoft, Google and Apple in the Western technological landscape, or Alibaba, Baidu and Tencent in the East, natural evolution is a highly decentralized and distributed process, where agents diverge in terms of characteristics and traits according to their interactions with the specificities of their ecosystem, resource availability, and competition with other groups. This has led to an incredible diversity of natural innovations of all types (products, process, organization), including many species with very different characteristics. Unfortunately, this lengthy process, better understood only a few decades ago, has often been substituted by tales of gods and angels creating creatures *ex nihilo* and releasing them into the Matrix or God's Earth. Although the existence of a divine energy or a pre-Big Bang simulator remains a possibility, it's high time, especially in religious countries, to properly educate future generations and reject illusory myths that ignore a panoply of archaeological discoveries and scientific research. A small part of this biological diversity is schematically represented in the branch of the evolutionary tree that concerns us, in the figure below.

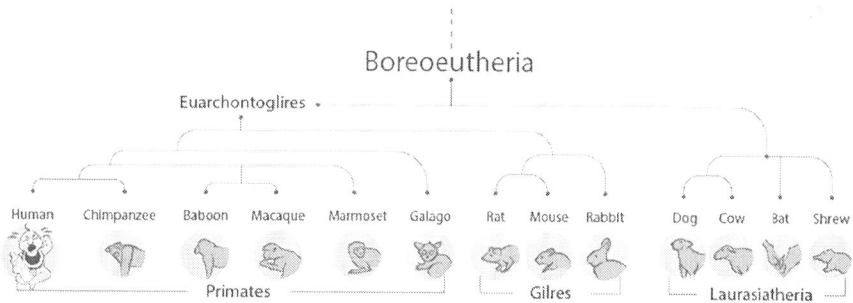

To take our story a step further, let's focus on the icon of the crying baby above. Humans or the species of Homo sapiens belong to that branch of the Hominins, from which the label Homo sapiens is derived. This term of Latin origin translates as "wise Man" or "knowing Man", representing modern humans like you and me. Notwithstanding the sexist aspect of such a classification, which was quite normal even among scientists at the time, the latter believe that this branch split off from the chimpanzee branch around seven million years ago. Again, this evolutionary bifurcation does not mean that humans are descended from chimpanzees, or that humans and apes are identical. It does mean, however, that we share a common ancestor called Hominidae, from which many branches evolved independently. That's why 98 percent of our DNA is identical to that of chimpanzees, our closest living relative.

Interestingly, Homo sapiens is just one type of Hominin branch. If we refer to other members of our community as brothers (the way religious groups do), Homo brothers – to be distinguished from homosexuals – have existed alongside us for hundreds of thousands of years, more closely resembling us than apes. The oldest known Homo fossil was found in Ethiopia in 2013 and is estimated to be around 2.8 million years old. There is also Homo heidelbergensis in Europe, Homo Denisovans in Eastern Europe and Asia, and Homo neanderthalensis in Europe, the Middle East and Central Asia. However, these species eventually became extinct. Let's take a closer look at one evolutionary sibling, the most recent of them all.

Homo neanderthalensis, also known as Neanderthals, were a group of hominids that lived in Europe and parts of Asia between 400,000 and 40,000 years ago. This would imply that we potentially lived alongside them for around 250,000 years.

Unlike us, Neanderthals were well adapted to their cold, northern habitat, with a robust stature and a wide nose to warm and humidify the air they breathed. They were also skilled hunters and toolmakers, using a variety of stone tools and weapons to hunt large animals such as mammoths, bison and deer. They were probably able to communicate with each other using a mixture of primitive language and non-verbal signals.

Physically, Neanderthals had a distinctive appearance, with a pronounced eyebrow ridge, sloping forehead and prominent chin. They were shorter than modern humans, with an average height of around 160 centimeters (five foot two inches), but had a robust, muscular stature. Their brains were also slightly larger than those of Homo sapiens, although it's not clear how this affected their cognitive abilities. While Neanderthals were once considered a primitive and brutal species, recent research has shown them to be more sophisticated than previous studies suggested. They were capable of symbolic thought, newly-discovered artistic creation – though not to be compared with Da Vinci talent – and even of burying their dead according to animistic rituals.

Sadly, Neanderthals became extinct around 40,000 years ago, potentially due to a combination of factors such as climatic fluctuations and genetic isolation. Nevertheless, their genetic legacy lives on in modern humans, as people of European and Asian ancestry carry fragments of Neanderthal DNA in their genomes. There is one most plausible cause for their extinction, which would be us, at least our ancestors, committing what may be the first undocumented human genocide in history. Nevertheless, their decline could have occurred in a more gradual fashion, similar to evolutionary or commercial failure scenarios, where a new superior agent, Homo sapiens, surpassed Homo neanderthalensis in access to food and reproductive resources, thanks to human innovations we'll discuss later.

Using the shapes of skulls and bones found in the fossil record, these portraits offer us a glimpse into the appearance of our evolutionary ancestors. However, it's important to note that these are approximate reconstructions, if not solely artistic, and so are not 100 percent accurate, perhaps not even 50 percent. It is also likely that all our Homo ancestors had darker skin tones, given their African origins. A complexion that became whiter as humans expanded into less sun-exposed northern territories.

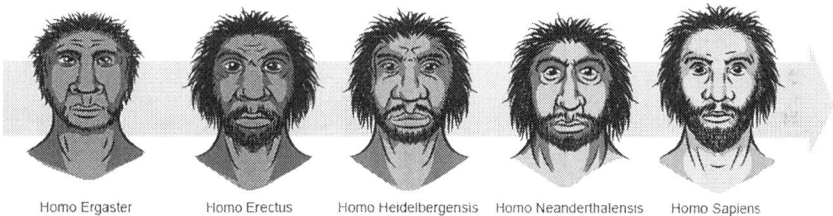

Homo Ergaster   Homo Erectus   Homo Heidelbergensis   Homo Neanderthalensis   Homo Sapiens

One thing is certain. Humans appeared relatively late in the evolutionary timeline, only around 300,000 years ago in East Africa, according to the most recent archaeological findings. To put things into perspective, if we compare the chronology of life to a 24-hour theatrical performance, humans wouldn't take to the stage until 11:59pm, just before the curtains closed. For soccer fans, this can easily be compared to a hard-fought match where the coach of the winning team, hoping to gain a few precious seconds, decides to bring on a random substitute player in the last minute of extra time. However, in the case of human evolution, we seem to have managed to achieve an incredible, even mystical entry, to the point of astonishing the coach himself.

All of humankind's remarkable innovations, which have fundamentally deconstructed and then shaped the physical Matrix, have occurred in less than a minute, limited to the playing field of planet Earth and its environs, let alone considering the longer timespan of the entire universe.

Earth history in 24hrs

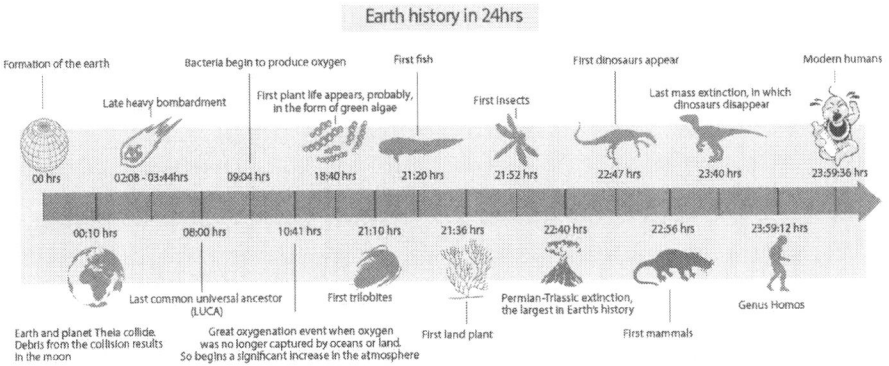

While this chapter predominantly focuses on explaining natural *innovation* through processes described by scientific theories such as Darwinist evolution, genetics, and other mechanisms, it is crucial to acknowledge, like most believers and spirituals, that these explanations do not negate the possibility of a divine force or higher consciousness orchestrating these manifestations of order on Earth. The fact of the matter is that, when considering the complexity and precision of the arrangements found in the natural world, some may find it challenging to attribute them solely to a lucky chain of causes and effects. Take the case of genetic mutations for instance.

In addition to the process of natural selection that we have previously discussed, Charles Darwin also proposed that genes can undergo mutations through errors in DNA replication or exposure to mutagenic agents such as radiation or certain chemicals. From Darwin's perspective, this process is considered to be completely random. So, let me draw a counterargument. Imagine I'd like to reverse-engineer a car. By carefully studying the car's various subsystems and understanding how they function and interact, I can develop a comprehensive theory that explains how the car operates. However, even with this understanding, it would be challenging to argue that the car, with its perfectly aligned subsystems and highly organized structure, came into existence purely by chance through random collisions of molecules over millions of years. This same line of thinking can be extended to the broader context of the natural world and the complexities of *innovation* observed within it. Indeed, despite my limited expertise in evolutionary biology, I find it puzzling how randomness, or Chaos, even over millions of generations, can give rise to highly structured organisms and groups with innovative features that are well-suited to their environments.

In this regard, it is worth mentioning Jean-Baptiste Lamarck, a French zoologist who lived during the same time as Darwin. Lamarck proposed his own theory of evolution, known as Lamarckism or the theory of inheritance of acquired characteristics, even before Darwin's theory of natural selection. According to Lamarck, species evolve through the inheritance of acquired traits. He suggested that organisms can change during their lifetimes in response to their environment, and these acquired traits can be passed on to their offspring. Lamarck believed that these acquired traits would accumulate over generations, leading to a gradual transformation of species. His theory proposed a linear and progressive view of evolution, with organisms becoming more complex and better adapted to their environments over time. For example, supposing that a mouse tail is useless, that it brings no evolutionary *Value* in terms of survival and adaptation, this mice species should end up tailless at some point, just like a Google could choose to limit its search results to three pages only, since nobody looks beyond that anyway.

Although Lamarck's ideas were influential in the early development of evolutionary thought, they were tested wrong at the time, and largely rejected in favor of Darwin's theory of natural selection. However, recent scientific findings suggest that there may be some common ground between Darwinism and Lamarckism. It is now understood that environmental factors can influence the effects of mutations. For instance, exposure to UV radiation can increase the frequency of certain types of mutations in DNA, and environmental stresses such as extreme temperatures or nutrient deficiencies can influence mutation rates or the selection of mutations that confer advantages in a given environment. The field of epigenetics, which studies the interaction between genes and the environment, further supports the idea that different environmental conditions can activate or suppress certain genes, leading to variations in observable traits, and can even pass these "epigenetic" traits down to the next generations.

These recent findings challenge some of the longstanding criticisms of Lamarck's ideas and provide pioneering evidence for a more predictable pattern of natural innovation in features and species. It suggests that there are hidden cellular mechanisms that facilitate the adaptation of future generations to the pressures of their environments through targeted rather than purely random mutations. When combined with the statistical power of Darwinian natural selection, where the fittest individuals, groups and species have a greater chance of survival and reproduction, we arrive at a compelling natural model that combines purpose and randomness, order and chaos, collaboration and struggle, and integrates elements of spirituality and scientific materialism.

Considering this extensive discussion, it naturally leads to another question:

What sets humanity apart from the myriad of dynamic agents that preceded us within the Matrix, including our nearest evolutionary relatives like apes and other extinct members of the Homo genus?

DIMENSION 3:
Free & conscious agents

1

In June 1802, after more than a century of division and the defeat of the Tây Sơn dynasty, Nguyễn Ánh ascended the throne of a unified Vietnam and proclaimed himself Emperor Gia Long. With a nation now stretching from the Red River delta to the Mekong delta, Emperor Gia Long moved the northern capital, Thăng Long (today's capital of Vietnam, Hanoi), to Huế, the ancestral seat of the Nguyễn lords. Gia Long considered "Confucianism and Chinese models of governance" to be the best modes of authority, and with this ideology, he ordered the construction, at Huế, of a palatial complex resembling Beijing's Forbidden City.

During a guided tour of this small but charming town on the Vietnamese coast, I unfortunately lost my guide and the rest of the group on the way to the same Gia Long palace. In retrospect, it was a stroke of luck that I don't regret. True to my Zen reactions, I wandered the city on my own until I reached the Thiên Mụ temple, also known as the Temple of the Celestial Lady. It proudly sported its seventeenth-century seven-story pagoda – a kind of multi-level tower usually found in Buddhist and Hindu temples in Southeast Asia. Although the pagoda's appearance was remarkable, built high enough in wood and stone, facing the famous Hương River (literally Perfume River), I was more attracted by a modest, half-open hall hidden behind the temple's main building. Inside, a vintage blue sedan car from the 1960s was on display. Its story, which left me stunned, broadened my understanding of the Matrix a little further.

The car belonged to Thích Quảng Đức, a Vietnamese Mahayanist Buddhist monk who lived in the 20th century. Born in 1897 in central Vietnam, Thích Quảng Đức became a monk at an early age and studied Buddhism under some of the most respected masters of his day. He was known for his deep compassion and commitment to his practice, and quickly gained a reputation as an accomplished master, whose Buddhist role is "Sensei".

In 1963, the South Vietnamese government, then led by a deeply Catholic president, launched a campaign of discrimination and violence against the Buddhist majority. The government banned the display of Buddhist flags, the celebration of Buddha's birthday and other Buddhist practices, and monks were regularly harassed and arrested. Thích Quảng Đức and other Buddhist leaders decided to oppose the government's actions. In June 1963, he and a group of monks marched through the streets of Saigon, the capital, waving banners and reciting Buddhist prayers. Despite the peaceful nature of the protest, they were met with violence from the police and army.

That same month, faced with the government's persistent inflexibility, Thích Quảng Đức made an irreversible decision. He drove to a busy crossroads in the city of Saigon, in that same sedan-type car that was on display, then sat down on the ground, legs crossed in the typical meditation posture, the lotus position. He doused himself with petrol and, after reciting a prayer or two, lit a match and allowed himself to be immolated. Even more strikingly, he remained completely still and silent, like a Zen master, in a kind of trance, while the flames consumed his body.

The photograph of this act of self-immolation, which you can still find on Google or Baidu if you have a strong heart, won Malcolm Browne the World Press Photo of the Year award in 1963, as well as the Pulitzer Prize in 1964. Like a summer wildfire – which was possibly this monk's hope – the photo spread around the world (mainly via the newspapers of the time), and Thích Quảng Đức became a symbol of resistance to oppression and a hero to Buddhists everywhere. His death triggered a wave of protests in Vietnam, and the South Vietnamese government was finally forced to back down and agree to negotiate with Buddhist leaders for greater religious equality.

Imagine a situation where a lion, unhappy with the latest drought causing a shortage of resources in the jungle, jumps off a cliff. Or where a house cat, dissatisfied with the lack of tenderness from its new owners, decides to cross a busy highway. These scenarios, which seem straight out of a Disney movie, are unlikely to happen because no other animal, apart from us, possesses **the innovative characteristic of reason**. Evolution has endowed our brains with an updated operating system (OS), so to speak, which deserves its own dimension in this book. In this way, we can use our cognitive abilities to override our instincts for survival and reproduction and replace them with ideas and motivations unbelievable to any other species. This is also why we differentiate between natural innovations, whether biological or inert, and "man-made" innovations, created by (and often for) Man.

In the case of natural innovations, there is no violation of the implicit laws and rules programmed by the Matrix. Changes occur, in the overwhelming majority of cases, according to a predefined pattern, based on the principle of cause and effect. For example, when a meteorite hits the moon, we can calculate the magnitude of the collision based on the rock's mass, speed and trajectory. The moon has no choice but to endure whatever happens to it within the cosmic range of possibilities. The high pressure and temperature at the Earth's core create volcanoes, earthquakes form mountains and faults, and the sun burns and heats us thanks to the nuclear fusion of its hydrogen, with a limited lifespan and an expiration date some five billion years from now. Every inert thing is subject to its own fate.

Similarly, for most of the Matrix's dynamic agents, the innate instinct to survive and reproduce inherited from millions of years of evolution is difficult to overcome. While creatures such as our closest primate cousins and dolphins exhibit signs of innovativeness, empathy, language, and other complex behaviors, it is important to recognize that these traits are secondary in comparison with their innate instinct for survival and reproduction. Despite their impressive (from our patronizing angle) cognitive abilities and social skills, these beings are still driven by the fundamental *Need* to ensure their own existence and pass on their genetic material. Thus, they have evolved strategies to maximize their chances of competing for dominance and securing their share of resources. Based on this observation, humans succeeded, at least from a materialistic perspective, to understand most phenomena in the animal kingdom, which can be scientifically explained and, to some extent, predicted with high accuracy.

In addition to the programmed manifestations of survival and reproduction, there are also innovative characteristics in certain animals which, at first glance, do not appear to have a direct impact on gene transmission, but which nevertheless play a vital role in the continuation of the species. One such characteristic is the tendency to socialize, to live in groups, and in particular to "**play**", commonly observed in a wide range of social animals, including humans, especially during their first post-natal years. It turns out that play serves several functions, such as helping young animals to develop physical and mental skills and coordination, explore their environment and practice social interactions with other members of their species in order to build good bonds, which may save their lives in return one day. Integral to play is the aspect of experimentation, facilitating learning from one's mistakes in a low-stakes environment before attacking the wilderness. Sleep is another evolutionary product common to almost all living beings. What's the point of sleeping for hours on end, and thus providing predators with an effortless meal? We'll get to that in a moment.

Compared to the slow, incremental process of evolution, man-made *innovation* seems more deliberate, ordered, with increasing complexity. Imagine, you wake up one day and to your surprise, there's a little TV next to your usual one. Would you believe that your TV mother had given birth to a baby? Of course not. Inanimate objects, although composed of the same basic elements as living beings, lack this "anima", this natural ability to reproduce, unless they are subjected to an external force. And even then, unless the force in question is well-planned, the result would probably be a television set broken in two, rather than a new one. In this case, it's more likely that your ex-partner, who still has the key to your apartment, brought back the TV you'd lent him months before. The pace of this lightning change was more akin to the way humans innovate, rather than the multi-generational, gradual process of evolution.

Beyond the pace of innovation, human beings have taken its complexity to a new level. Whereas chimpanzees and a few other animals have barely used certain tools and built a few nests since the dawn of time, after a few centuries of modernization, we've managed to build skyscrapers, drive luxurious cars instead of camels and, above all, order everything from and to the door of our homes, without any effort at survival. However, bear in mind that this wasn't always the case. We sort of took an adventurous (and lucky) evolutionary path to rapid progress and uncontested dominance over all other species.

Most theories agree that the first human step on this perilous path was, well, **taking a step**. Our earliest primate ancestors, who lived in trees and moved through branches like today's monkeys, took up this challenge around six million years ago. Some entrepreneurial primates decided to invest in one of the major natural organizational innovations in our evolutionary history. They chose, or rather were forced, to leave their familiar arboreal environment and venture out onto the land, but we have no idea or archaeological evidence of the context in which this decision was made. Given the *a priori* limited intelligence of primates at the time, it is likely that their *Motivation* was once again to survive or reproduce.

We can imagine a totally hypothetical story. The romantic Romeo of the time, a hairy, flea-infested creature, walking on all fours to join his equally hairy, flea-infested beloved Juliet. Seeing that Romeo had returned home, or at last to the tree, safe and sound with good-looking offspring, other ancestors followed their example by moving to a more distant habitat. As they spent more time stretching out on two legs, perhaps to move more quickly or to free their hands to feed and store food gathered from the ground, their bodies began to adapt to this new form of locomotion.

This scenario, though fictional, reminds us that in nature, change and therefore natural innovation are based on **the law of cause and effect**. If our primate ancestors left the trees (**effect)**, there must have been a fire somewhere, new flying or skilled predators in the trees, a shortage of fruit following a drought, for example, or some non-metaphysical reason driving them to take a continuing risk on the ground (**cause**). This change in lifestyle was not planned in the way modern humans plan a move or a change of job. In nature, things just happen, "with the flow", like the Taoist Dao, without the need for rationalization. Paradoxically, this also hints a verse in the Bible that speaks of the nature of God in Exodus (3:14), where God says to Moses, who was looking everywhere for a representation of the divine: I Am That I Am.

One thi1ng's for sure. The transition from trees to firm ground didn't happen overnight for our primate ancestors. To explain this using the vocabulary of a digital company, we'll consider the diffusion curve of an innovation, typically a new product on the market.

First, there are the so-called innovators or enthusiasts, to whom we can add the early adopters. These are the enthusiasts who are prepared to queue all night outside an Apple store to be the first to get their hands on the new iPhone. They're tech-savvy and always on the lookout for the latest novelty. They generally represent a small percentage of the overall market but play an important role in the spread of word-of-mouth information. Like the first primates, the first hairy Romeos to venture far off the ground deserve this slot in the spread of bipedal walking as a new method of mobility.

Then, as these early adopters proved the benefits of living on land, other primates began to imitate them. This is the crucial moment, known in business jargon as "crossing the chasm" when either we step backwards and the *Value* of Innovation, after a trial by the first users, proves unsatisfactory or we give ourselves the go-ahead for the next evolutionary phases of our species. Using our romantic example, if Romeo and those who followed him had been eaten by tigers after a week of their adventure on two feet, we'd probably be looking for our wild bananas for lunch. Or we wouldn't be, at all.

Once this gap has been bridged, the innovation is validated and ready for large-scale distribution. The majority takes hold, and the real growth phase of the adoption curve begins, where the product rapidly gains in popularity and attracts a wider audience, like a Tesla chasing market share among the middle class, competing with Mercedes, Toyota and even Renault. Eventually, over the generations, this new way of living and getting around became the norm for our primate ancestors and then Homo. This corresponds to the mature phase of the adoption curve, when the product achieves widespread adoption and becomes the market standard.

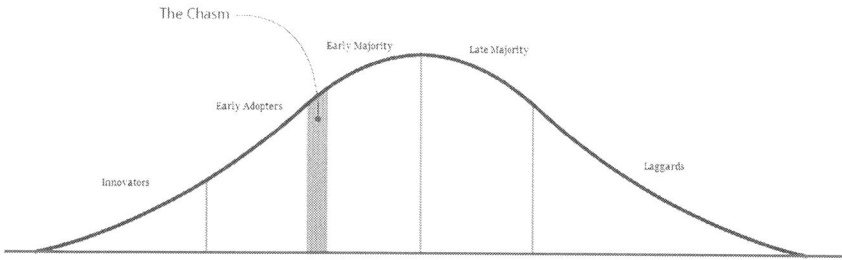

Learning to walk on two feet seems to have given our primate ancestors an evolutionary advantage, enabling us to detect predators and prey from a distance, diversify our diet, and potentially reproduce with other primate groups contributing to genetic diversity. The woodland savannah environment, characterized by scattered trees and tall grasses, offered a more open canopy with abundant light reaching the forest floor. Consequently, primates with shorter leg genes or an inability to stand upright in this new environment were probably less likely to pass on their genetic heritages, given that they were the easiest prey for sneaky carnivores. However, this adaptation required several physiological changes over hundreds of generations, including remodeling of the pelvis to support body weight when standing, changes in the spine, legs and feet to enable more efficient walking and running, as well as a change in the role of the arms, from a biological tool for locomotion and clinging to trees, to terrestrial food-gathering activities and the manufacture of hunting tools later on.

As with every *innovation*, the transition to bipedalism was not without its disadvantages. While it enabled early humans to spot predators and diversify their diet, it also put more stress on the body, particularly the lower back, the aches and pains of which are still felt by our elderly today. However, the most significant consequence of bipedalism was the impact on female (not yet modern female) childbirth. The narrow pelvis of early humans and the increased size of the fetal head made childbirth more difficult for women. Compared to other primates, human infants are born with relatively large heads and underdeveloped brains, requiring a prolonged period of postnatal growth to reach maturity. This prolonged childhood was necessary for the brain to continue developing after birth, but it also required mothers, before and even now, to invest a great deal of time and energy in looking after their young.

In contrast, other primates have a shorter gestation period and give birth to newborns with smaller heads and more developed brains. For example, a baby horse can stand upright immediately after birth, washed by its mother's blood fluids. A female chimpanzee gives birth after a gestation period of just seven months, whereas a human mother has to carry her baby for nine months. After birth, a chimpanzee baby clings easily to its mother's coat and moves about relatively independently, whereas a human baby depends on its mother for food, care and protection for many years, even decades today. Such premature birth is apparently a happy coincidence, say scientists, as it may have been a contributing factor to our human superiority over other species. Indeed, during this prolonged period of childhood, young people are exposed, thanks to play, to continuous learning, for example, through imitation of grown-ups, to the development of social relationships and to the acquisition of a wide range of skills, before becoming self-sufficient to face a world of dangers and opportunities.

Such a conclusion seems clear if we draw a parallel with the economies of certain countries. In his book, *Bad Samaritans*, Korean economist Ha-Joon Chang challenges the common belief that free trade is always good for all countries. Like throwing newborn babies into the jungle in the hope that they'll all turn into Tarzans, Ha-Joon demonstrates that the idea of opening one's borders to globalization without being economically ready to compete with the giants is tantamount to shooting oneself in the foot for future prosperity. He examines several examples of countries that have opted for protectionist policies to promote their economic development. Japan, for example, protected its fledgling automotive industry from foreign competition before becoming a major global player in the sector. Similarly, South Korea supported its domestic companies by applying protective customs measures and limiting openness to imports for decades before opening up.

Learning to walk on two feet and our ancestors' ability to give birth prematurely, preparing our babies to face a harsh future, may not have been enough in an age of agile, ferocious predators. It seems there must have been something more special, perhaps something more mystical or romantic, that set us apart. This idea is echoed in the biblical passage, "When the woman saw that the tree was good for food and pleasant to the sight, and that it was desirable for acquiring wisdom, she took of its fruit and ate; and she gave some also to her husband who was with her, and he ate" (Genesis 3:6). Similarly, the Qur'an states that Satan tempted Adam and Eve to eat of the fruit of the forbidden tree, saying, "Your Lord has forbidden you only this tree so that you may not become angels or become immortal" (Qur'an 7:20).

Ironically, our human destiny seems to rest largely on the success of women in delivering and raising premature babies, and their influence on men. However, leaving aside this half-joke, I find it fascinating and sometimes inspiring to decode ancient wisdoms in the context of modern discoveries and common sense. Our primate and Homo ancestors may have lived in a kind of East African Eden, a warm paradise abundant in natural resources, with rivers to drink from and banana trees or similar flora. When discussing the genesis story of Adam and Eve, many people tend to focus on the fruit, the apple. However, let's focus on the tree itself. For, the beautiful red apple we imagine today is the result of centuries of human selection, the wild ancestor of the domesticated apple tree probably being quite acidic. More curiously, in a celestial setting with abundant water, the tree would have to be at least five meters tall, if not ten. So, before transgressing God's commandment, how did we gain access to the fruit of the tree, unless we've retained some of our ancient acrobatic abilities, inherited from primate ancestors?

The way we interpret and understand these stories can vary considerably according to our personal beliefs and cultural context. I know from my Muslim upbringing as a child how sensitive believers are to these stories. So, it's important to respect everyone's religious freedom, while recognizing that there are alternative explanations based on scientific evidence. In the case of the story of Adam and Eve, some may see it as a literal account of human origins and a reflection of divine intervention, while others, among Abrahamic believers too, see it as a metaphorical story reflecting the complex relationship between humans and the natural world. Whatever the case, these stories can still offer us valuable insights into what we humans originally are, and our place in this Matrix.

Pursuing my argument above, two crucial, and perhaps radical, natural innovations that took place in the course of our evolution are mentioned in the Genesis story. Incidentally, this myth is shared by all the Abrahamic religions, Judaism, Christianity and Islam, with only slight variations.

The first *innovation* can be deduced from Adam and Eve's disobedience in approaching the tree of wisdom. Initially, our first ancestors were in some way enslaved to their environment, just as other agents in the Matrix react in predictable ways, according to their genetic make-up and environmental stimuli. However, Adam and Eve broke this chain of cause and effect by showing curiosity or, perhaps, the first signs of **free will**, which distinguishes us from plants and most animals. Moreover, the use of the term "wisdom" to describe the tree in question suggests that we were previously ignorant, or incapable of reasoning, of making informed decisions, thus mentally more like simple, basic agents.

The concept of freedom is, of course, an endless philosophical and even scientific debate. Are we really free, or are we guided by subconscious mechanisms that give us the illusion of freedom, as the deterministic theory suggests? Despite the difficulty of finding a satisfactory answer for everyone, if we draw a scale of freedom, we'll realize that humans are far ahead of other dynamic agents in the Matrix. For example, show my husky dog a bone and it will immediately stop whatever it's doing to pay attention to you. This reaction is the result of classical conditioning, famously studied by Russian physician Ivan Pavlov in his experiments on the digestive systems of dogs. Pavlov accidentally discovered that dogs would start salivating at the sound of a bell previously associated with the presentation of food, even before showing the food. Marketing campaigns have long used this technique on us too, associating pleasant sensations with harmful products such as cigarettes and Coca-Cola.

The truth is, animals can also learn by various means, such as social imitation, contextual adaptation or conditioning. However, the difference between most animals and humans lies in our ability to break free from these conditioning patterns, just as Adam and Eve did, and overcome our innate survival instincts. This has aptly been dubbed **willpower**. The Vietnamese monk who set himself on fire and endured the pain in Zen silence is another striking example. This ability to override our instincts is largely due to our highly developed prefrontal cortex, which is the responsible brain part for cognitive functions such as decision-making, self-control and planning. Thus, it enables us to weigh up the pros and cons and make decisions based on our personal values and priorities, rather than simply following our basic instincts.

In addition to individual freedom, instead of blaming Eve for opening Pandora's box, we can deduce another primordial innovative human characteristic. When Eve and Adam ate the forbidden fruit, they became aware of their nakedness, which leads to a second significant interpretation of the same myth: "**self-awareness**".

Classical theological interpretations of this Adamic nudity often, and regrettably, fixate on its sexual implications, leading many religions and sects to heavily regulate sexual behavior. However, in my analysis, these verses represent a call to awakening, a revolutionary upgrade of our ancestors' operating system, comparable to the transition from Windows 95 to Windows 10 with a simple bite into an apple. Adam and Eve were thus able to open their eyes to a new reality, in which they possessed the beginnings of an ego, aware of its physical sensations, its limitations and its image vis-à-vis the other. Not only do we know, but we also know that we know, technically entitled self-cognition. To take my heresy a step further, although scientists can't pinpoint the precise cause of consciousness, it's fascinating to draw parallels between the fruit of wisdom in the Garden of Eden and psychedelic substances such as psilocybin found in magic mushrooms, which can induce an altered state of reality, often used by Amazonian shamans and spiritual gurus to connect with the "non-physical other side" of the Matrix. It wouldn't be surprising if a few "Adams and Eves" experienced similar effects, stimulating their basic neurological systems enough for consciousness to gradually pop in.

Let's leave our far-fetched biblical interpretation aside and focus now on the innovation of consciousness. This concept is a complex and insufficiently understood phenomenon, but it's essential to get an insight into it.

Consciousness is your perception of the world at any given moment. Right now, you're fully aware of this book (hopefully), the meaning behind each sentence. If I throw out a random word, say "red", you automatically visualize such bright color on an apple, blood or a sexy dress. If you feel an itch on your arm, your attention, and therefore your awareness, shifts from the book to the area where the itch is occurring. You can then start complaining because you're now aware of the uncomfortable sensation that follows the itch. On the other hand, you're not aware of the people who've been passing by for a while, the bird that gurgles a little further away, or the air that changes every ten seconds in your lungs. Below is a simplistic diagram illustrating this concept. By the way, any strange thoughts you might have about this interweaving of ellipses come from your subconscious patterns and memories, which automatically rise to the surface of your consciousness as soon as you look at this figure.

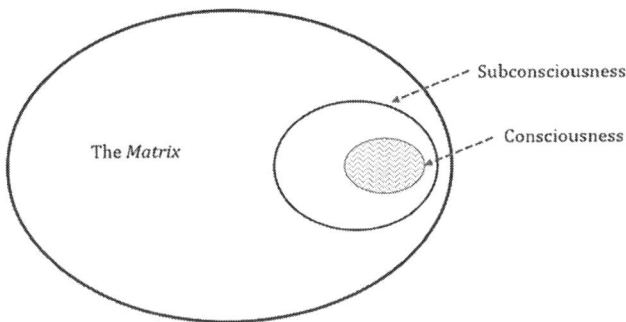

In short, according to this simplistic model, your consciousness is what animates the film of your life as you experience it at any given moment, with yourself as the protagonist and the other agents of the

Matrix as objects with varying degrees of influence on this scenario. Such a statement seems obvious, until you put yourself in the shoes of someone else, or something else. When I walk my dog, for example, I engage in such mental exercises from time to time (like an authentic nerd). Apart from her powerful sense of smell and distorted color vision, does she perceive the world in a similar way to me? She knows her name is Zina, but is she aware of her own existence as a separate entity? When she expresses joy by wagging her tail or showing a willingness to play, is it sincere or simply biologically programmed, with no awareness behind it? Does she care about protecting me (huskies never do, but let's assume), or does it happen by default?

Scientists are currently striving to understand the complex processes in the brain that give rise to this divine characteristic. For, not only did consciousness give our ancestors a competitive edge over their predators and competitors, but it also enabled a privileged few, later on, to experience a sense of enlightenment and oneness with the universe through years of meditation and spiritual exploration, revealing the intrinsic mechanisms of the Matrix and the ego.

Again, interpretations of such an intangible concept differ. Some spiritual and religious individuals see consciousness as an immaterial entity that exists beyond the constraints of time and space, with the brain serving as an intermediary that translates it into comprehensible experiences. Such a process compares the brain to a radio (iPad for the young), only translating invisible electromagnetic waves (consciousness) into podcasts captured by our ear. In his book, *The Doors of Perception*, British writer and philosopher Aldous Huxley suggests that the human brain acts as a selective filter, allowing only a small fraction of the available sensory information to reach our consciousness. According to Huxley, this filtering mechanism is necessary for our survival and functioning in the world, but it also limits our understanding of the true nature of reality.

This spiritual vision is shared by several esoteric movements and has recently begun to be investigated by scientists such as Professor Donald Hoffman, author of the book, *The Case Against Reality*. Using complex mathematical models, Hoffman and his team suggest that our perception of what we call "reality" has evolved over millions of years to optimize our survival and reproductive capacities. Indeed, to assume that our senses reflect an objective world independent of us would run counter to Darwinist theory. The material world would only be a kind of graphical interface, a Windows 100, with HD icons that we interact with, without having to know the electronic and algorithmic complexity behind them. Similarly, a theory proposed by Keith Floyd, a psychologist at Virginia Intermont College, assumes that reality is merely a holographic illusion. In other words, it would no longer be correct to say that the brain produces consciousness. On the contrary, it is consciousness that creates the appearance of the brain, as well as the body and everything around us that we interpret as physical. Physical matter, as we imagine it – a tangible solid, liquid or gaseous body – would exist only illusorily.

Another perspective that currently enjoys more scientific credibility is that of the materialists, who see consciousness as a by-product of evolution. In scientific jargon, consciousness is widely perceived as **an epiphenomenon** of the rapid evolution of our neurological circuits since the era of our primate ancestors. An epiphenomenon is a trait or characteristic that emerges as a secondary consequence of a primary process but is not capable of affecting that same process. To illustrate this idea, let's take the example of smoke produced by a barbecue. While smoke is a by-product of fire, it was not the primary purpose behind the initial action of lighting a fire, the objective being to grill sausages.

Similarly, consciousness is seen as a one-way causal relationship with our evolving neurological circuits, where it is the secondary result of an expanding brain, consuming over 20 percent of energy in modern humans. The brain's physical processes give rise to conscious experiences, but consciousness itself is unable to influence brain activity. One possible explanation of how consciousness might result from this process is integrated information theory. This suggests that consciousness emerges when information is integrated in a specific way within a complex nervous system, such as the brain. According to this perspective, consciousness is not a separate entity from the physical circuitry of the brain, but rather

an emergent property of these mental processes. Integrated information theory also holds that consciousness is intrinsic and independent of the physical substrate that supports it. This means that consciousness can exist in other complex systems capable of processing and integrating information, not just in the human brain. I think we'll soon be able to rely on General-Purpose AI systems to put this physicalist theory to the test.

A less abstract justification for the progressive aspect of consciousness innovation lies in a few other animals that also show rudimentary signs of this third dimension of the Matrix. One of the most famous experiments is the mirror test, also known as the mark test. In this test, an animal is marked on one part of its body, usually the forehead or side of the face, with a non-toxic dye or sticker. The animal is then placed in front of a mirror and its reaction to the mark is observed. If the animal recognizes itself in the mirror and tries to inspect or remove the mark, it is considered to have some level of self-awareness. Only a few animals have passed the mirror test, including chimpanzees, orangutans, dolphins, elephants and magpies. Nevertheless, coupled with their relative problem-solving skills and creativity in their environment, these animals challenge, to some extent, the exclusive and radical evolutionary character of human consciousness. Let's apply the Fundamental Identity to one potential case of consciousness.

Consciousness = (Need + Motivation) × (Creativity + Technology) × Value

a. **Need** *(of the end user)*: Self-preservation in a more challenging ground environment.

b. **Motivation** [16] *(of the innovator)*: Testing more advanced and freer dynamic agents on Earth.

c. **Creativity** *(or vision)*: Giving certain agents a bit of a divine talent, with a dynamic code, reason, learning skills and some free will.

---

[16]   I repeat, assuming there is a divine purpose and some intelligent initial designer behind all this simulation.

d. *Technology* (*or implementation*): An elastic brain to absorb new learnings, more time for fun during childhood, a diversified diet, the discovery of fire, some divine intervention (maybe)

e. *Value* (*or outcome*): A hypothesis to be formulated at the end of this book.

When considering which of two children is more likely to thrive – the one who has been surrounded by care, comfort and artistic education or the one who has had to support his parents with manual labor, with little time for leisure and education – the answer, once again, depends on the environment. The innovation of a child's skills should take into account the needs of the present moment. For example, giving piano lessons to a nomadic child in the Kalahari Desert would probably be less practical than teaching him how to hunt for his next meal.

A similar logic would apply to our ancestors. As the environment and survival skills have evolved since our ancestors left the trees, future generations have grown up in increasingly stimulating environments where they have had the opportunity to build tools, assimilate vast amounts of data, and adapt quickly. These changes transformed the brain into an increasingly powerful survival machine. Those who were relatively "smarter" had a better chance of perpetuating their genes. Intelligence is to be understood in the context of the times. Mental intelligence would mainly involve solving vital problems such as: the wild rabbit is hiding in the hole; how do I get it out? Or, the water source was over there, but where exactly? A kind of social intelligence must have come in handy too: the guy looks stronger than me, how do I get his wife? A little gift game, perhaps. Those who couldn't keep up with the pace of such changes would have had to return to the trees, had fewer opportunities to reproduce than the smarter ones or foolishly perished along the way.

One discovery in our history has probably contributed to the acceleration of our evolution towards even more intelligent and conscious beings: **fire**. Indeed, for millions of years, fire was a natural and uncontrollable phenomenon, until an ancestor of Man discovered how to create and control it "in-house", probably by playing with dry wood and using

friction. Archaeological evidence shows that our Homo cousins were using fire at least 1.5 million years ago, Homo erectus being the first to use it regularly and control it. By the time Homo sapiens appeared around 300,000 years ago, the use of fire had already been established. The first evidence of fire control was discovered in the Wonderwerk Cave in South Africa, with fireplaces dating back a million years.

Fire, which can be described as an invention that later evolved into several innovations, played a crucial role in human evolution as it revolutionized our ability to cook food, making it easier to digest and offering a greater variety of nutrients, thus contributing to the growth of our brains. However, perhaps even more significant was the freedom that fire gave us. No longer at the mercy of predators, we could use fire as a tool for exploration, defense and hunting. This new sense of freedom enabled our ancestors to migrate to colder climates and expand their territories, giving up some of their thick fur and paving the way for rapid human evolution up the food chain.

2

To be frank, our Sapiens ancestors have been around for at least 300,000 years. However, it wasn't until around 12,000 to 15,000 years ago that we moved from a nomadic hunting and gathering lifestyle to a more sedentary, village-like existence. This means that for over 280,000 years, our ancestors roamed the earth in temporary settlements before one of them finally turned to his hunting partner after capturing a boar or gazelle, and made a suggestion in their rudimentary language:

- Wait a second!

- What? What's a second?

- Whatever. How about a practical change, I've got an idea.

- Since when do you have ideas? I'm hungry after a long day...

- Wait, don't kill it. Let's keep him alive for later.

- What a brilliant idea! What if we released him and went back to eating our children instead?

- I mean it. Think about it, please, if you can. We have a female here. Let's pick some berries for tonight. Tomorrow, we'll try to capture a mature male. Then we'll breed them. And, in four or five seasons, we'll have a herd of them, and we could roast one every day for the whole tribe, without any effort. Remember, we have almost 70 lunar cycles, we can't run marathons forever.

- Hmmm... Hmmm... okay. One question, though. How are we going to make sure we're chasing male prey tomorrow? Shouldn't we invent a zooming thing (binoculars) first to target the good stuff right from the start?

Before turning to the protagonist entrepreneur's suggestion in the above dialogue, let's briefly discuss **language innovation**, a mostly human, incremental, process-type innovation. While we tend to attribute such a feature to Man, many modes of communication existed long before our species elaborated a structured vocabulary and grammar. In fact, communication is an essential aspect of life, not only for humans, but also for many animals and plants. Communication helps them convey messages to each other about food sources, potential mates and predators.

Despite the absence of a clear structure, animal communication can take many forms. Some use visual signals, such as the bright colors of male peacocks to attract a mate, or the warning coloration of some insects and amphibians to alert predators that they are poisonous. Other animals, such as birds and primates, use sound to communicate. Birds use songs to defend their territory and attract mates, while primates use calls to warn others of danger or signal their intentions. Some animals secrete chemicals to communicate. For example, ants use pheromones to tell other ants where to find food. Some animals, such as dolphins, whales and bats, use echolocation to communicate and move around. By emitting sound signals, usually clicks or whistles, these latter animals listen carefully to the echoes produced when these sounds collide with surrounding objects. By interpreting the temporal and spatial characteristics of these echoes, they can form a mental representation of their environment, detect obstacles, find food and move with precision.

Bees, agents known for their sophisticated social order, communicate with each other in a variety of ways, one of the most fascinating of which is the dance. When a bee has discovered a source of food, it returns to the hive and performs a "round dance" to inform its fellow bees of the direction and distance of the source. In practice, the bee performs circular movements on the surface of the hive, alternating between clockwise and anti-clockwise rotations. The direction of the dance in relation to the vertical of the hive indicates the direction of the food source in relation to the sun. For example, if the bee dances upwards in relation to the vertical, this means that the food source is towards the sun. The duration of the dance also provides information about the distance to the food source. The longer the dance, the greater the distance. The bees observing this dance perceive these movements and interpret them. Then, the food seekers orientate themselves using a number of innovative mechanisms, including an internal compass. In fact, bees have a remarkable ability to navigate based on the sun and the Earth's magnetic field. In addition to the circle dance, bees use other forms of communication to exchange information within the colony. Namely, when a bee needs help finding food, it can communicate by emitting specific vibrations called "buzzing vibrations", that are felt by neighboring bees, which then follow the bee in search of food.

Plant communication is more subtle, but just as fascinating. Plants can communicate through chemical signals in the air or soil. For example, when a plant is attacked by an insect, it may release chemicals that signal neighboring plants to produce chemical compounds that make them less appetizing to the insect. Plants can also communicate with animals, as when they produce colorful fruit to attract birds that will eat the fruit and disperse the plant's seeds. This is, of course, a purely human interpretation of the concept of communication as applied to other organisms, since the latter don't consciously communicate *a priori*, it's part of their skills by default, or rather by evolutionary advantage.

With all the respect and love other dynamic agents, it is generally accepted and proven that human communication is not only complex, but also intentional in most instances. While animals and plants communicate primarily to survive and reproduce, by instinct following their embedded program and environmental circumstances, humans use language to express a whole range of thoughts, emotions and ideas. Humans can convey abstract concepts, tell stories and endlessly debate abstract paradigms, as is our case here. What's more, human language is largely conscious, meaning that we are often aware of our messages received and sent, and can use language deliberately to achieve specific goals. But this has not always been the case.

Language development in humans is not an innate characteristic, although some physiological facilitators are necessary (throat, tongue, lungs, etc.). This assertion is backed up by the fact that if a newborn baby is placed anywhere on Earth, it will grow up speaking the native language of the region. On the other hand, if a puppy is raised anywhere on Earth, it will do little more than bark. This remarkable adaptability of humans inspired a famous novel, first published in 1912. The story tells of a young boy named John Clayton, orphaned when his parents are stranded in the African jungle. The couple die shortly after the birth of their son, and the infant is taken in and raised by a tribe of apes. The boy, nicknamed Tarzan, grows up to become a skilled hunter, fighter and communicator with other animals.

While there is some debate among researchers, the consensus is that structured language as we know it probably emerged among early humans around 50,000 to 100,000 years ago, although some theories propose an even earlier chronology. One of the earliest forms of human communication was gesture, which involved using body language and facial expressions to convey messages. This method of communication is still used by other primates such as the chimpanzee, and by humans today, albeit usually subconsciously. As our ancestors changed environments more frequently after they moved from the trees, they probably began to use vocalizations such as grunts, cries and other primitive sounds to exchange vital information. Over time, these vocalizations became more structured and began to resemble modern language. Early human languages were at first very different from modern ones, with limited vocabulary and grammar, and a focus on survival basics such as food locations, special directions, indications of types of wild hazards, and so

on. As societies became more complex, more vocabulary, structure and diversity were added to the way we communicate with each other. To date, there are an estimated 7,000 languages spoken around the world.

Communication = (Need + Motivation) × (Creativity + Technology) × Value

a. **Need** *(of the end-user)*: To exchange vital information, demonstrate power and attract partners.

b. **Motivation** *(of the innovator)*: Add more order/collaboration among Matrix agents.

c. **Creativity** *(or vision)*: Various types of data exchanged between dynamic agents via a certain channel (sound, body, chemistry, etc.).

d. **Technology** *(or implementation)*: physiological mechanism enabling the exchange of sounds, songs, pheromones, language, echolocation, etc.

e. **Value** *(or outcome)*: A hypothesis to be formulated at the end of this book.

Returning to the opening dialogue of this section, it's important to note that hunting and gathering were the main survival activities of these early tribes. This way of life probably began with the first hominids and evolved into a full-time occupation with the emergence of Homo habilis around 2.8 million years ago. With the evolution of bipedalism in early hominids, hunting and gathering became even more important for survival. The emergence of Homo sapiens, around 300,000 years ago, marked the official beginning of what we consider hunter-gatherer societies.

Hunter-gatherers were adept at finding food in the wild and developed a whole range of tools and techniques to help them do so. Above all, they developed a deep understanding of the natural world, and the animals and plants that lived in their regions. They used this knowledge to predict animal migrations and the availability of certain plants, helping them, among other things, to plan their journeys and find their next meal. In this respect, man's propensity to innovate would have begun long ago to support activities such as hunting animals, gathering water and plant-based food, and building temporary shelters and settlements. Basic natural resources such as water, mud and wood were used for this purpose. In addition to solar energy, abundant in Africa, the harnessing of fire as an on-demand energy source was revolutionary. As well as enabling early hominids to cook their food and providing a source of heat, the use of fire enabled them to create new tools and weapons. The earliest known stone tools date back some 2.6 million years and were made by the Homo habilis species. These early tools were simple, such as splinters and choppers, but over time they became more sophisticated, including hand axes, knives and spears. Again, note that fire is an invention, not an innovation. A traditional stove or oven are product innovations. Thanks to the natural invention of fire, many human innovations have been made possible.

To illustrate with real-life ethnological cases, the !Kung, or San people, of the Kalahari Desert in southern Africa are a famous example. This tribe lived as hunter-gatherers for tens of thousands of years, up until the 1970s, and their way of life offers a glimpse into our lost past. The !Kung were first observed in the 1950s by anthropologist Richard B. Lee. His study provided detailed accounts of their daily lives, including hunting and gathering practices, social organization and spiritual beliefs. Lee describes the !Kung nomads as skilled hunters using different methods to capture their prey, such as bow and arrow, traps and snares. They also collected a wide variety of plants, including fruits, nuts and tubers, which formed an important part of their diet. In terms of social organization, the !Kung lived in small groups, like a large family, and their society was based on a system of sharing and cooperation. They also had a rather animistic spiritual life, with a belief in a powerful and benevolent ancestral spirit responsible for the health and well-being of the tribe.

Despite the significant advances made by our hunter-gatherer ancestors in adapting to their environment and gradually climbing the food chain, it was the seemingly simple but bold suggestion made by our hypothetical character in the humorous dialogue at the start of the section that marked the beginning of the first great revolution by sapiens. Surprisingly, it turned out that laziness was a more optimal decision than an exhausting nomadic lifestyle from the point of view of long-term survival. Please note that we're

going to accelerate the pace of the remaining events in this chapter, so as not to get bogged down in the infinite details of human history, and also to take you on board the exponential transformation that Man has brought to his ecosystem in less than a minute of Mother Earth's existence.

෪ ✶ ඎ

Let's start with the radical organizational innovation that laid the foundations of human civilization: **the Agricultural Revolution**. This event is one of the most important in history. It took place between 15,000 and 10,000 years ago and marked a turning point in lifestyle and working methods, transforming nomadic hunter-gatherers into sedentary farmers. This change in human behavior was driven by a number of factors.

During the last Ice Age, known as the Pleistocene epoch, which began around 2.6 million years ago and ended around 12,000 years ago, the climate was much colder and drier than today, making it difficult for humans to find enough food to survive. As the climate began to warm and the world became wetter, new opportunities for food production emerged, including the growth of new crops and the expansion of pastures for animals. Another success factor was the development of more innovative processes for growing crops and raising animals. For example, the innovation of the plow has enabled farmers to plow the soil more efficiently, facilitating large-scale cultivation. The development of irrigation systems has also helped to ensure that crops receive sufficient water, even in times of drought.

As agriculture spread and people became increasingly dependent on it for food, they began to form sedentary communities. These enabled people to live and work together in the same place, facilitating farming and the care of crops and animals. The development of sedentary communities also paved the way for the growth of larger, more complex societies, including specialized farmers and craftsmen such as blacksmiths, potters and weavers.

It's worth noting that throughout this evolutionary process, humans have had a significant impact on the evolution of other species. Such a ripple effect first occurred through **the domestication of animals and plants**, using the same Darwinian selective principles that brought our species to this stage. Examples of domesticated animals include dogs, cows, pigs, horses and sheep. Wheat, corn, rice and cotton are examples of domesticated plants. In other words, all the dynamic agents we've just mentioned didn't exist in a docile or edible state before. We have innovated them. Let's focus on cows for a moment, given the importance of red meat and dairy products in the daily diet of our consumerist societies.

The domestication of cows (*Bos taurus*) took place thousands of years ago in many parts of the world. The ancestors of domestic cows were wild aurochs, which were large, aggressive and robust cattle living in the forests of Europe, Asia and Africa. Over time, humans began to interact with wild aurochs and gradually tamed them, perhaps for their meat and hides, then later for their milk and as draught animals. This is the taming phase. As humans continued to live in close proximity to tame cattle, they began to select them to develop characteristics that were useful to them, such as larger size, docility and increased milk production. From there, good tame cattle spread as a reliable source of food and labor, and their populations began to grow, while the wilder ones disappeared. Domesticated cattle became an important part of human cultures and societies, and their genetic characteristics became so distinct from those of their wild ancestors as to create quasi-distinct species.

Agriculture and livestock breeding depended **on fertile land**, especially near rivers and downstream. As a result, these lands were considered more valuable than arid, dry or mountainous ones. This suggests that the concepts of wealth, power and private property probably emerged at this time too. During the nomadic lifestyle, resources were shared by all, like a herd of gazelles roaming the savannah. However, as settlements became commonplace, the quality of the land near human settlements, together with the physical effort invested in its preparation and exploitation, determined the well-being or misery of families. Since then, the value of land has been determined primarily by its location and fertility. This remains true even in modern times, as real estate in major cities such as Paris, London and New York is more expensive the closer it is to the city center or other points of

interest. However, in rural areas (such as the early settlements), land size and fertility are more important factors, as long as they aren't too isolated.

As **human settlements** became larger and more complex, civilizations rooted in history emerged, such as the Sumerians, the Egyptians and the Indus Valley civilization. These early civilizations brought important advances in socio-political governance, technology and culture. However, they also gave rise to social classes and inequalities. The accumulation of wealth and power by certain individuals and groups led to the inevitable emergence of ruling classes and social stratification. As a result, internal and external conflicts over resources and power became more frequent.

In times of peace, new opportunities emerged for developing commercial relations. This enabled the exchange of goods, ideas and genes. In fact, doing business at the time hardly ruled out mixing families to forge long-term links. The Agricultural Revolution also led to important radical innovations, such as the creation of the wheel and the plow, which ensured more efficient transport and agriculture. As cities grew and trade flourished, the need for record-keeping also became the order of the day, leading to the development of writing systems such as cuneiform and hieroglyphics. Religious beliefs became increasingly structural, evolving from the animism of hunter-gatherers to more complex, organized systems that played a primarily socio-political role in legitimizing the (often) absolute power of leaders, and promoting intra-group cohesion.

More commercial exchange required a more standardized and **efficient medium**. This led to the invention of a physical currency, which replaced the barter system previously used. Various commodities, such as livestock, grain, shellfish and metal coins, were used as a medium of exchange in different parts of the world. Over time, metal coins became the most widely accepted form of currency. The first recorded use of metal coins dates back to ancient Sumer (modern-day Iraq) around 3000 BC, with China following suit in the seventh century BC. The Lydian Kingdom, located in present-day Turkey, is credited with producing the first metal coins specifically designed for use as currency around 600 BC, and other regions quickly copied this innovation.

℘ ✶ ℭ

Several centuries after the agricultural revolution, there were relatively few major innovations or changes in societies. Trade routes expanded, more houses and towns were built, and yet more wars were fought for various reasons. However, agriculture remained dependent on the physical effort of humans and animals. It was also difficult to control epidemics as hygiene standards left much to be desired among increasingly concentrated populations (and animals). So illnesses and natural disasters were often attributed to supernatural causes or the wrath of the gods[17]. During this time, certain powerful individuals, such as kings, commissioned the construction of roads (rather, paths), more luxurious habitats and some grandiose masterpieces such as the pyramids of Egypt and the hanging gardens of Babylon.

The creation of these masterpieces required an enormous amount of work and often involved human sacrifice. It may seem unlikely that people would voluntarily submit to such inhuman tasks, but with the emergence of complex societies came **complex power structures**. Leadership was often inherited or obtained by force, then marketed through traditional religious channels promising heavenly peace after a final sleep. As a result, powerful individuals ordered the innovation of many unjust and destructive tools and processes. Alongside weapons and armies, slavery has been a ubiquitous part of human history for thousands of years, existing in almost every culture and continent. The earliest recorded mention of slavery dates back to ancient Mesopotamia around 2400 BC, where slaves were used as laborers in the construction of public works. Slavery was also widespread in ancient Egypt, Greece, Rome and up until a few centuries ago in Europe and North America.

Over the generations, notable progress was made in other disciplines not related to war or land. In particular, the ancient Chinese gave birth to paper-making techniques and tools, which greatly facilitated the

---

[17] Recent evidence of such epidemics impact dates back to the Middle Ages, when the Black Death, a bubonic plague, swept across Europe, killing around 25 million people – up to 60 percent of the population in some areas. No wonder Europe was in stress-mode when COVID-19 hit.

sharing of knowledge around the world. They also invented gunpowder, an advantage in battle, and printing on wooden blocks, simplifying old-fashioned cut-and-paste to some extent. Their compass helped explorers later discover new lands, and silk production was among the most refined in the world. The Egyptians were impressive architects and surveyors. Their mummification techniques and herbal remedies were quite advanced for their time. Mathematics progressed further with the Babylonians, who developed a positional numbering system that helped them solve their rhetorical algebraic equations, and then with the Arabs, notably al-Khwarizmi, who gave algebra its name. The ancient Arabs also contributed to chemistry, including, ironically, the discovery of alcohol and the creation of perfumes, and to medical practice with the use of anesthesia and basic surgical techniques. Another (funny) story is worth mentioning here.

According to historical accounts, a certain Ibn Al-Haytham, also known as Alhazen, served as a court astronomer under the ruling the Fatimid caliphate in Egypt in the 11th century. He was given the task of finding a way to control the flooding of the Nile River, building a dam for instance, a vital issue for the agricultural society of the time, which he accepted gladly. Except that Alhazen never saw the Nile River, nor anticipated its immensity. After years of research and experimentation, he was unable to find a solution. Feeling immense pressure and fearing the deadly consequences of his failure, given the rough attitude of the caliph (most likely Hakim bi-Amr Allah), he faked insanity and was sent to a secluded space, a sort of small cell for crazy people.

While confined to his dark cell, Ibn Al-Haytham, bored to death, noticed a reversed shady image on the wall, coming from a small hole in one cell's wall. He wondered why and how this strange phenomenon was possible. So through this simple apparatus, known today as a camera obscura, Ibn Al-Haytham observed how light entered the hole in straight lines, and projected an inverted image of the outside scene onto the opposite wall. This discovery laid the foundation for the understanding of vision, optics and cameras in his most famous work, "Kitab al-Manazir" (The Book of Optics). Ibn Al-Haytham also emphasized the importance of empirical observation, experimentation, and hypotheses validation in understanding the physical world, which indirectly sat some ground for "the scientific method" centuries before the European scientific revolution.

With future innovations building on earlier ones, the pace of creativity increased dramatically during and after the Middle Ages. Thanks to new tools, machines and processes in navigation, weaponry, shipbuilding and food preservation, the discovery of the "New World" was greatly facilitated. This event, or succession of events, refers to the exploration and colonization of the Americas by Europeans, which began in the late 15th century. Italian explorer Christopher Columbus, sponsored by the Catholic monarchs of Spain, was the first European to reach the Americas in 1492. Other explorers such as John Cabot, Juan Ponce de León and Vasco Núñez de Balboa followed soon after, leading to the establishment of Spanish and Portuguese colonies in the Caribbean, Central and South America. In the early 16th century, French, Dutch and English explorers also reached the Americas, colonizing North America and paving the way for further exploration and exploitation of the American continent.

This period marked a major turning point in world history, with considerable consequences for both the indigenous peoples of the Americas and the European colonizers. For the natives, it meant massive mortality and displacement due to European diseases, slavery and violence. In fact, the indigenous population shrank considerably, and their cultures and ways of life were disrupted. For European colonizers, this marked the beginning of a period of global expansion and colonization that would shape the modern world. It also led to the establishment of trade routes, the growth of multinational corporations and the development of new economies. The transatlantic slave trade, which brought millions of African slaves to the Americas to work on plantations, was a grim repercussion too.

Around the same time, the Renaissance movement took place in Europe, from the 14th to the 17th century. This was a major cultural and intellectual turning point in Western civilization, characterized by a renewal of classical learning, a new interest in science and discovery, and an explosion of artistic, literary and cultural activity. One of the

defining transformations of the Renaissance was a renewed interest in classical learning and the arts. This was driven in part by the rediscovery of ancient texts, including the works of Aristotle, Plato and other Greek philosophers. Renaissance humanists sought to understand the ideas and values of the ancient world, such as democracy and freedom, and then to use them as a basis for their own philosophical and scientific investigations. The Renaissance was also a period of immense artistic and cultural achievement. Painters, sculptors and architects broke new ground with their innovative techniques and styles, creating masterpieces that still impress us today. Michelangelo's David and the Sistine Chapel, Leonardo da Vinci's *The Last Supper* and Raphael's *School of Athens* are just a few examples of the artistic brilliance of this era.

Above all, the Renaissance opened more than one door to modern science, which would transform our understanding of the hidden mechanisms of the Matrix. **The scientific revolution** was characterized by a paradigm shift, from traditional views influenced by religious institutions and unverifiable, dogmatic and often contradictory superstitions, to new, more objective, experimental approaches. Step by step, humans began to question what they believed to be true, in favor of what was proven to be true and replicable. As a result, major advances were made in various fields, including astronomy, physics, biology and chemistry and had a profound impact on our understanding of the world and man's place within it. A classic case study focuses on Copernicus, considered the father of the Scientific Revolution, as his work, *On the Revolutions of the Celestial Spheres* was the first to propose a heliocentric model of the universe, with the Sun, rather than the Earth, at the center of our galaxy. To prove this, Galileo used a telescope in 1609 to observe the Moon, planets and other celestial objects, providing evidence in favor of the Copernican model.

Other scientists then took over this race towards progress. Johannes Kepler, German astronomer and mathematician, is best known for his laws of planetary motion, which describe the movements of the planets in the solar system. Francis Bacon, English philosopher, played a key role in the development of the scientific method, emphasizing the importance of observation and experimentation. René Descartes, French philosopher and mathematician, was a major figure in the innovation of analytical geometry and the application of mathematical methods to the natural sciences. Isaac Newton, English physicist and mathematician, is considered one of the greatest scientists of all time. He is best known for his laws of classical mechanics and his theory of universal gravitation, which describe the relationship between the motions of objects and the force of gravity. Blaise Pascal, a renowned French mathematician and physicist, made important contributions to the study of pressure and atmospheric pressure. Christiaan Huygens was a Dutch mathematician and physicist who made significant contributions to the study of light, waves and the behavior of pendulums. And the list goes on, right up to the present day. Science continues to evolve and build on previous discoveries, like a delicate assembly of pieces of the Matrix puzzle in which we live.

෪ ✶ ෬

A century or two after the start of the scientific revolution, **the first Industrial Revolution** took place between the end of the 18th and the beginning of the 19th century, marking the start of the modern era of industrialization. It was a period of great technological, social and economic change. The first Industrial Revolution was characterized by the development of many advanced innovations, the growth of factories, large-scale production, and the widespread use of steam as an energy source. It originated in Great Britain, which was at the forefront of technological and economic change at the time. The country had several key advantages that made it an ideal location for early industrialization, including access to vast markets, a solid transportation infrastructure and a well-developed financial system. Britain was also rich in natural resources, such as coal and iron, which were essential for heavy industry.

This capitalistic change era was stimulated by several key factors, including the growth of international markets, the expansion of trade and the availability of capital. The meteoric rise of the British Empire, which opened up new markets for goods, was also a key factor in the growth of industry. In addition, technological innovations helped increase productivity and reduce the cost of goods, making them more

accessible to a greater number of people. The steam engine, one of the most important inventions, developed by James Watt in the late 18th century, revolutionized transport and manufacturing by providing a reliable source of energy. Weaving machines increased productivity by enabling higher volumes to be manufactured at lower prices. The development of blast furnaces allowed for the large-scale "domestication" of iron, which was used in the construction of new machines, buildings and transportation systems.

In short, it was the beginning of an era of increasing productivity and full-time consumerism. This accelerated economic transformation had a significant impact on the way people lived, worked and interacted with each other. These changes led to a growing loss of interest in agriculture, once seen as a pillar of prosperity, and the migration of crowds from the countryside to the cities, and from agricultural work to new types of assembly-line factory jobs. The growth of cities, the emergence of a broader middle class (the proletariats, to quote Karl Marx), and the development of new means of transport and communication are also consequences of the Industrial Revolution.

The second Industrial Revolution built on the foundations laid by the first. It took place in several countries, most notably the United States, Germany, France and Great Britain. It was a period of rapid industrialization and technological progress in the late 19th and early 20th centuries. In the United States, this wind of change (using the words of the rock band Scorpions) was characterized by the growth of large corporations and the expansion of industries such as steel, oil and electric power. Germany became a leading industrial power, with a strong emphasis on innovation in the chemical and electrical industries. Great Britain continued to play an important role in the development of new technologies, notably in the fields of transport and finance.

A major lever driving this second phase of industrial progress was the development of new scientific theories, such as thermodynamics and discoveries about electrical energy. Several scientists and inventors, including Alessandro Volta, Luigi Galvani and Michael Faraday, made essential contributions to our understanding of electricity. Volta invented the first electric battery, which produced a constant flow of electric charge, while Faraday discovered the principles of electromagnetic induction, which led to the development of the electric generator. Most will recognize the names Tesla and Edison when it comes to the subject of electricity. Thomas Edison was primarily an American innovator (rather than inventor) and businessman, best known for the commercial development of the practical incandescent light bulb, which brought welcome light to our dark nights. As for Nikola Tesla, he was a Serbian American inventor and engineer who worked for Edison after graduation, best known for his contributions to the design of the modern alternating current (AC) power system. He invented the Tesla coil, a transformer widely used in radio and television technology.

Let's not forget the innovation of the internal combustion engine, which propelled new forms of transport, such as automobiles and aircraft, and led to the growth of the oil industry. In addition, the invention of the Bessemer process improved steel production, which was used in the construction of new transportation systems and buildings. This progress inspired Henry Ford, founder of Ford Motor Company, best known for his innovations in the automotive industry, including the development of the assembly line and the production of the Model T. The Model T, also known as the "Tin Lizzie", was launched in 1908 and quickly became a popular means of transport. Ford's use of the assembly line, which enabled mass production of vehicles, gave Ford a competitive advantage, producing the Model T at low cost, in high volumes. The Model T was durable, reliable and easy to use, and played a major role in transforming the automobile from a luxury item for the wealthy into a necessary commodity for millions.

At the end of the 20th and beginning of the 21st century, alongside Generation Y, **the third Industrial Revolution**, also known as the digital revolution, was in full swing. This period was characterized by the development and widespread adoption of digital technologies, with the introduction of the first personal computers, such as the Altair 8800 from MITS, and the development of the internet. This global network, indispensable today, was initially used for limited, even military purposes

in the 1960s by DARPA, the U.S. Defense Department's research agency, which played a central role in the creation of ARPANET, the internet's precursor. Thanks to Vinton Cerf, an American engineer often regarded as one of the "fathers of the internet", ARPANET was already based on the TCP/IP (Transmission Control Protocol/Internet Protocol), which forms the basis of internet communication.

The idea was taken up by other pioneers such as Tim Berners-Lee, a British physicist and computer scientist. In 1989, Berners-Lee invented the World Wide Web (WWW), which became the main information system used on the internet. He also developed the HTTP (Hypertext Transfer Protocol) and HTML (Hypertext Markup Language), which are essential to the operation of the Web, enabling widespread adoption of the internet in the 1990s. The emergence of mobile devices in the early 2000s ushered in a new era of digital transformation, an era of free access to information anywhere, anytime.

The innovations of the third Industrial Revolution have had a profound impact on virtually every aspect of society, including commerce, communication, entertainment, education and much more. The widespread use of digital technologies has created new opportunities for businesses, entrepreneurs and consumers, enabling digital innovators to reach new markets, increase efficiency and deliver new products and services. It has also had a significant impact on the economy, leading to the development of new industries, the growth of existing businesses and the creation of millions of new jobs. Economic globalization also took off during this period, with companies now able to reach customers and suppliers all over the world thanks to the internet.

Finally, we're currently living through **the fourth Revolution** (and maybe the last), also known as Industry 4.0. This phase began at the start of the 21st century and is characterized by the integration of new technologies such as artificial intelligence, robotics, quantum computing, the Internet of Things (IoT) and advanced automation into the traditional industrial sector. These technologies have the potential to transform production processes and increase efficiency, while creating new products, services and business models. For example, IoT refers to the growing network of connected devices that collect and share data. These objects play an increasingly important role in the fourth Industrial Revolution, enabling companies to monitor and control their operations in real time, making production processes more efficient, flexible and responsive to changing customer needs. Another key innovation of Industry 4.0 is the ability to integrate Artificial Intelligence or AI into virtually any industrial process. AI applications such as machine learning, computer vision and natural language processing are being used to automate complex tasks and make production processes more efficient. Here's a brief summary of this historical journey through the major human revolutions.

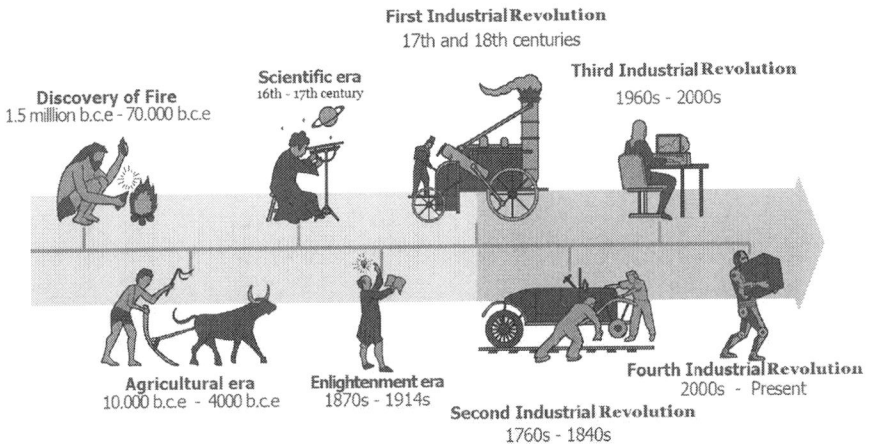

We'll discuss some of these innovations in more detail later. I just wanted to bombard your short-term memory with the innovative path of our species since landing on Earth, and especially the exponential acceleration in the pace of *innovation* since the Agricultural Revolution. In less than a second in Earth's metaphorical 24-hour lifespan, and less than 10,000 years in real time, we've gone from nomadizing in the name of basic survival needs to being served smoked salmon by pretty flight attendants while watching Netflix on a ten-hour flight to the other side of the planet. While such change is very, very rapid compared to natural processes such as Darwinian evolution, it remains, for the most part and at our level, incremental, building on previous knowledge and learning to build new products, processes and organizations. We should recognize, however, that major advances for humankind have

occurred during the aforementioned revolutions, mostly with a few radical discoveries, such as the innovation of fire, printers, electricity, motors, computers, the internet and AI, to name but a few.

3

What did Steve Jobs and Osama bin Laden have in common?

Let's start by introducing these two personalities for those who only know them by name or from the media.

Steve Jobs was an entrepreneur, said to be a visionary, who co-founded Apple Inc. and played a unique role in the ongoing technological revolution, from the personal computer, to streaming music, to smartphones of course, thanks to his innovative and beautifully named iProducts. He was widely respected for his creativity, leadership and business acumen. His impact on his industry and the daily habits and social interactions of recent (and future) generations was immense. Everyone would agree with this statement.

Osama bin Laden, on the other hand, has earned the label of the villain terrorist. Founder and leader of the al-Qaeda network for many years, he is credited with numerous attacks on innocent civilians. His actions were violent, destructive and aimed at sowing fear and instability in various countries. Bin Laden's impact on the world is generally seen in a negative light, and he has been widely condemned for his actions. People would also accept this introduction as a matter of course, especially in the Western world where the dramatic events of September 11 are still commemorated every year.

Logically, many would find the comparison between these public figures irrelevant, even repellent, but if we objectively take up the question with less emotion and prejudice, we can identify certain human genes, wealth, status, gender and many other common attributes in the first place to answer our question above. Jobs and bin Laden were men, about the same age (with a difference of two years), belonging to the modern human species and quite wealthy financially. Steve became rich through the success of his businesses, notably his shares in Apple. Osama's father was a Saudi millionaire, and founder of the Saudi Binladin Group construction company. What's more, from what we read on the internet, they were both respected, charismatic and even feared leaders in their social and/or professional environments. One fought against Apple's board of directors and was fired at a low point in his career. The other collaborated with the West during the Afghan war against the Soviet Union. However, he became a major embarrassment to the American presidency after the Cold War and received the classic American business phrase "You are fired!", during a Navy SEALS raid on his compound in Pakistan in 2011. However, politics is not the central theme of this book, as the real story behind the official scenes is often more complicated than the politically correct TV speeches.

When it comes to *innovation*, this comparison between a pure capitalist innovator and a fundamentalist terrorist highlights **the greatest difference** between *innovation* created by Man and that of the natural type or that found in other animals. As a result of a constantly evolving sense of freedom and awareness, we eventually acquired the gift (or curse), probably exclusive to humans, of **imagination**. We were aware of the passage of time, its importance and impact – at last!

However, imagination and memory should not be confused. Clearly, the latter supports the former. Indeed, by remembering the most emotional or relevant past events, be it the toxicity of a fruit or the tiger cellar, we could more easily imagine what would happen if we encountered the same fruit or passed a given cellar. Survival is therefore optimized by remembering the past. But this mental property is far from exclusive to Homo sapiens. My husky dog has a special memory far better than mine, capable of finding her way home when she runs away for several miles. Birds also remember their migration routes over long distances. Squirrels can hide food for the winter and find it again when the cold has passed. Such is the case for many of the Matrix's dynamic agents.

The main characteristic of humans, on the other hand, is to use this past and present data to project future scenarios in order to make more optimal

decisions. **We can literally hallucinate what is not**. So, it's not surprising that a study by Harvard psychologists revealed that people's minds wander about half the time during their waking hours, labeled "daydreaming", daydreaming about what might be and how to act if such and such a scenario arises. Unless you're an assiduous monk, I'm sure you do too!

With the power of imagination fueling the variable of *creativity* paramount in our fundamental identity of *innovation*, **Jobs and bin Laden were both excellent innovators**.

One succeeded in rethinking the personal computer sector, first with the Macintosh, which went on to inspire IBM and Microsoft, but also and above all with the tiny mix of computer and phone, called a smartphone, that you may have in your pocket or bag right now, as well as the whole range of iProducts that followed. In addition to his vision, Jobs led his teams to manufacture and market this innovation quickly and flawlessly to outperform all competitors in 2009, including Nokia and Motorola. The outrageous adoption of the iPhone, dominating more than half the phone market in the ten years after its launch, reflects the need and the correct strategic implementation that followed.

iPhone - (Need + Motivation) × (Creativity + Technology) × Value

a. *Need (of end-user)*: Combine a computer and a Nokia phone.

b. *Motivation (of the innovator)*: Make a business profit and/or make a contribution to the world.

c. *Creativity (or vision)*: A small touch-screen computer that fits in a jeans pocket.

d. *Technology (or implementation)*: A well-designed casing, iOS software, attractive packaging and branding, show-biz communication, etc.

e. *Value (or outcome)*: Unparalleled geographical and temporal freedom to access external information (media, friends and family, internet, etc.).

Bin Laden was also an innovator, just not with the classic definition of the term "innovation", and not in the same field or with the same objective as Steve Jobs. Based on the same fundamental identity, bin Laden was probably smart enough to observe a *Need* within the nationalist community of which he was a part during the Afghan war of the 1980s. Perhaps it was the *Need* to occupy unemployed youth when the war ended. What can you do when thousands of testosterone-charged men see you as their savior and a religious reference from the cradle of Islam, Saudi Arabia? What's more, bin Laden had no occupation left either, apart from helping his four wives conceive his 25+ heirs. Well, perhaps this *Motivation* sparked his imagination to create a new sect. Whether out of a sense of deep identity, believing in a false but triumphant image of Allah, or an incessant greed for access to more young women, all roads lead to Rome, or New York, starting with the implementation of this dogmatic *innovation.*

Bin Laden built the structure of a malevolent organization, from the Western point of view, with its top-to-bottom matrix hierarchy, resource planning, talent recruitment, training or rather brainwashing sessions, weapons supply, cooperation seeking and enemy surveillance. If you think about it, it takes as much effort, if not more, to create a dark terrorist group with recruits conditioned to die as it does for a Silicon Valley entrepreneur to grow a tech startup in the land of the American dream.

al-Qaeda = (Need+Motivation) × (Creativity + Technology) × Value

a. *Need (of the end-user)*: To occupy one's free time with a cause deemed divine, such as sacrificing oneself for Allah or taking revenge on an enemy or disbelieving state.

b. *Motivation (of the innovator)*: To justify his position of power within the community, or to serve a twisted image of God.

c. *Creativity (or vision)*: Build a team of talented terrorists and plan unpredictable attacks.

d. *Technology (or implementation)*: Physical and mental training, weapons supply, sadistic propaganda, planning using system loopholes, etc.

e. *Value (or outcome)*: Destruction, chaos, incitement to hatred of Muslims and religions.

If we, as readers and researchers, are not prepared to broaden our horizons and step out of our comfort zone of innovative companies and cool gadgets into the frightening territories of human history and sociopsychology with all their complexity, we will continue to grasp only the tip of the iceberg of *innovation* in its relation to Man.

Yet a good part of this iceberg was visible from the earliest known discussions of human innovation, dating back to ancient Greek philosophers such as Aristotle and Plato, who wrote about the importance of creativity in their works and suggested methods for discovering and inventing new theories and products using logic or inductive thinking. Aristotle, for example, asserted that "the mark of the educated mind is to be able to envisage a thought without accepting it". He also stressed the importance of seeking out new knowledge and ideas and encouraged people to continually engage in the process of learning and discovery.

Plato, in particular, and other Renaissance thinkers (Marsilio Ficino, Giordano Bruno, Emmanuel Kant, René Descartes, etc.) proposed a division of the world into material and immaterial realms, or in the words of Kant, the noumenal and phenomenal aspects. This duality distinguished between the physical world we perceive through our senses, and the space of Forms or Ideas conceived and perceived primarily by the human brain. According to Plato, the physical world is merely a shadow or imperfect reflection of the true reality present in the realm of Forms. The latter are abstract, eternal and unchanging concepts that represent the essence or perfect ideal of things, such as beauty, justice or truth. While the physical world is transitory and subject to change, the realm of Forms, again according to Plato, is eternal and unchanging. I partly agree with Plato, because, firstly, it would be difficult to disagree completely with such a weighty thinker. Furthermore, some objects exist independently of us (the physical world), while others are intangible, by their ideological nature, and therefore can only be grasped by an intelligent brain. However, unlike Plato, I believe that change affects and should affect EVERYTHING, sooner or later. The notion of freedom in the Middle Ages is totally uncorrelated with its interpretation and application in the 21st century, if only by considering the powers of slaves and women.

Unfortunately, since the time of Aristotle and Plato, the scope of innovation has narrowed to its purely economic aspect. Authors such as Joseph Schumpeter, Peter Drucker and Clayton Christensen are among the many pioneers who have made significant contributions to the dynamics of innovation in business, and to best practice in its management at corporate and national level. In the early twentieth century, Joseph Schumpeter notably proposed a version opposed to the Keynesian vision, arguing that any country, in order to prosper in an increasingly competitive global economy, should use innovation instead of stimulating consumption through state aid to the middle and lower classes. Innovation, Schumpeter argued, is the driving force behind economic growth and the development of all social classes. His famous theory of "creative destruction" also asserts that new technologies and new business models disrupt and replace old ones, leading to the continual renewal of the economy, which sounds painful but is necessary for the economy to grow and evolve, bearing some striking similarities to the natural selection and survival of the fittest we've already discussed.

In this respect, especially in recent decades, Silicon Valley entrepreneurs have promoted a very narrow vision of innovation, whose main value is economic, leading to more profits for innovative companies and less for stagnant ones. As proof of this, I'd like to ask you, on the spur of the moment, to name a typical product innovation, i.e., one involving the introduction of new products or the improvement of existing ones. Take five seconds.

I'm more likely, statistically speaking, to guess your choice from a classic palette. New drugs or medical devices, for example pacemakers or insulin pumps, are product innovations in the healthcare industry. The introduction of electric or hybrid vehicles, such as the Tesla Model S or Toyota Prius, might also be considered. In the consumer electronics industry, the constant evolution of smartphones, tablets and laptops, with new features and capabilities introduced every year, perhaps came to mind. Creating new food products or modifying existing ones to meet changing consumer preferences, such as the trend towards plant-based or organic (BIO) food options, is a form of product innovation in the food industry. In the entertainment field, the development of new video game

consoles or streaming platforms, such as Xbox or Netflix, will also have to be put into this palette. But you probably wouldn't have thought of bin Laden, or the following famous example.

When today's young people admire or draw inspiration from the world's most economically and technologically advanced country, the United States of America, they barely know, or forget, its conflict-ridden past. In a country that has long been known as a "melting pot" of different cultures, segregation was, until recently, an important part of its history. The Civil War was fought from 1861 to 1865 between the Northern States (known as the Union) and the Southern States (known as the Confederacy). At the heart of this conflict was the issue of slavery, which had been legal in the Southern states for decades. By contrast, the Northern states opposed slavery and many in the South felt that their states' rights were threatened by the federal government's attempts to regulate or abolish the practice. The war fortunately ended with a Union victory and the abolition of slavery, but the struggle for civil rights and equality was far from over. In the years that followed, African Americans faced widespread discrimination, from segregation to violence, particularly in those Southern states.

This system of segregation and discrimination was enforced by a series of laws and customs known as "Jim Crow". Under this system, African Americans were denied many of the basic rights and opportunities enjoyed by white Americans, such as equal access to education, employment, housing and public places. It was against this backdrop that Martin Luther King Jr. and other civil rights leaders emerged. They organized protests, boycotts and other forms of non-violent resistance to draw attention to the injustices and inequalities facing African Americans. Their efforts eventually led to the passage of several key pieces of civil rights legislation, including the Civil Rights Act of 1964 and the Voting Rights Act of 1965.

King, as a charismatic and passionate leader, believed greatly in non-violent protest as a means of achieving social change, not unlike Thích Quảng Đức, the Vietnamese Buddhist monk who opened this subchapter. He organized boycotts, marches and sit-ins to demand an end to segregation and discrimination, inspiring millions with his message of hope and unity. At the heart of King's message was his famous *"I Have a Dream"* speech, delivered in Washington, D.C., in 1963. King, again through the human power of imagination, evoked a future where all people would be judged not by the color of their skin but by their contributions and character. He called for an end to racism, injustice and poverty and urged Americans to work together to create a more just and equitable society.

Sadly, King's life was brutally cut short by an assassin's bullet in 1968. But his legacy as a civil rights leader and advocate of equality and justice lives on. His dream of a better future for all, regardless of race or background, continues to inspire and guide many lawmakers today. It can be seen as a product *innovation*, a new ideology resulting from a *need* for racial equality and the *creativity* and *motivation* of an entrepreneurial man and his followers.

Along the same lines, consider creating new urban designs and infrastructure to support sustainable, livable cities, such as the development of smart cities or bike-friendly communities. On the legal front, think about developing new laws and regulations to address emerging issues or promote social justice with the legalization of gay marriage or the criminal justice reform movement. Don't forget the creation of new sects or religious practices to meet the changing needs and beliefs of communities, such as the emergence of non-denominational churches and Buddhist currents adapted to the West. All this and more falls within the realm of Product *Innovation*, as defined in the Fundamental Identity.

The innovative paradigm I defend here applies to other types of innovation, such as Process *Innovation*, which involves implementing new methods or improvements in the production or delivery of the final product. We're used to examples from the business sector, such as Amazon's use of advanced technologies and logistical strategies to deliver goods in less than 12 hours from order. The example of Tesla selling its cars online with few physical touchpoints also comes to mind. This required the development of an automated supply chain process to facilitate payment of the car price online, and to send the vehicle directly to the buyer on time. Yet if we consider a broader spectrum, we see this Process *Innovation* in the education sector with the creation of new teaching models, methods or technologies to improve learning outcomes and foster access to education, such as the development of online learning platforms or educational programs focused on personalized skills. In Martin L. King's case, he probably had to set up a dedicated process and organization, with motivated resources, and forge links with political allies in order to achieve his goal of interracial equality.

ಬ ✱ ಬ

The purpose of this chapter was to provide a non-exhaustive historical introduction to the concept of *innovation,* beyond its economic scope. We did this by taking the innovative approach back to its etymological roots, within which innovation concerns the whole process of inventing and implementing something new that has a greater or lesser impact on the Matrix and its agents, including ourselves. The capitalist vision of transforming companies and bringing new products to market is only a small part of the story of change, which is an integral part of life itself. Therefore, *innovation* is not just the iPhone, Tesla and Open-AI, but also the process of creating stars assuming a purpose behind it, natural selection, a new religion or the innovative ideas of Martin L. King in his day.

We've also taken time to elaborate on the natural side of *innovation,* and how the physical side of the Matrix, with the support of God or some random cause-and-effect mechanisms have been able to innovate so many natural products in a diversity impressive to the human brain, albeit scientifically explicable to some degree by standard processes as innovative as their "output". However, comparatively speaking, we have disrupted our environment on numerous occasions since the birth of the first sapiens. In such a short space of time, we have made Mother Earth so different from what it was 100,000 years ago. We've shaped our destiny in many ways, and not only that. The other agents of the Matrix have been greatly impacted by our dominance. Despite the complexity of Man, about which endless books could be written, our innovative pattern doesn't seem to be the result of chance. We'll be investigating why and how the human species innovates in the chapters to come.

TAKEAWAYS FROM THIS CHAPTER:

- **The first dimension** of our Matrix mainly comprises inert cosmic objects that collide with each other, energy sources such as stars and lots of cosmic sand. All these celestial objects are considered a form of *innovation* based not only on the consensual event of the Big Bang, which gave birth to the space-time in which we evolve, but also on the fundamental laws of physics such as gravity and electromagnetism, which brought order to the universal chaos, giving rise to magnificent telescopic images of the night sky. This dimension also includes millions of years of the formation of our beloved blue planet and all the changes it has undergone to cool down, become covered by atmospheric layers, and develop into a habitable planet.

- **The second dimension** of the Matrix appears when we zoom in on our blue planet. Over millions of years of volcanic and tectonic activity and meteorite bombardment, the basic chemical elements – minerals and water – with a good dose of energy from the Sun, mixed in the right proportions to form a chemical soup. This experiment, whether spontaneous or divinely supervised, gave rise to the first signs of life, which, as far as we know, is essentially limited to this planet. The most important innovations at this stage were DNA, which brought a degree of stability and order to the reproduction of similar genetic elements, and later the process of photosynthesis, which nourished plants and, at the same time, oxygenated our atmosphere. From there, billions of species evolved over time, in the ocean and then on land, right up to Homo sapiens. The innovative process of natural selection seems to have played a major role in this evolution. It increased the diversity of living creatures according to a predictable pattern as to which species would remain or dominate: the fittest, i.e., the one that is adapted to its environment and has competitive advantages. Features such as sleep, fight-or-flight reactions, attention, memory and brain structures can all be linked to evolutionary aspects of adaptation.

- **The third dimension** of the Matrix, and probably not the last, concerns the natural and progressive innovation of consciousness. This latter, albeit complex, concept means that a handful of other matrix agents,

most notably Man, became aware of their existence as entities defined in space and time. As far as humans are concerned, this probably happened after our primate ancestors came down from the trees and began to face more mentally stimulating challenges and dangers. Thus, we no longer depended solely on mechanical reactions dictated by our genes, like a plant (perhaps), but became aware, to distinct degrees depending on the individual, of our environment, thoughts and emotions in an extended "past-present-future" time scale. Simply put, it's the subjective experience of being alive in this Matrix. With such power, along with the mastery of fire and enhanced mental capacities, the intelligence of Homo sapiens rapidly evolved to break the shackles of natural evolution and innovate more tools, languages, beliefs and practically an unprecedented history. And there's more to come!

- **Scoop**: In my opinion and that of other experts, we're now entering the fourth dimension of our Matrix, which we'll talk about at the end of this book. Beyond understanding, controlling and manipulating the Matrix, we're about to acquire the one divine superpower we've been missing, by generating a new (and powerful) conscious species and launching new self-sustaining matrices.

Artistically expressed, the first dimension comprises inert cosmic and terrestrial objects that don't react to events that happen to them, but simply obey the laws encoded in the Matrix. Throw a pebble and it will fall downwards following a predictable trajectory. Period. Then there are the dynamic agents. These beings are alive not only because they change (change has always existed), but above all because they can develop and react to their environment, following a relatively predictable pattern based on genetics and natural selection. If you shine more light on a plant, it will either grow faster and die sooner or not care at all, depending on its genetic code and other factors. Put a husky and a sheep in a cage (or just within a mile of each other), and let natural selection do what it does best: filter out the least fit. On the other hand, show that same stubborn husky a bone and you can expect him to give you some attention to continue his training. This stimulus-response-learning paradigm also governs the second dimension.

Finally, our human era, which represents a major part of the third Matrix dimension, is about taking action, breaking the chains, freeing ourselves from genetic and evolutionary conditioning to a certain extent, and with different degrees of freedom according to individuals, eras and societies. By mentally understanding the underlying mechanisms of the Matrix, which other agents fail to do for lack of reason, Man has been able to exploit them to his advantage by innovating tangible and intangible products, which in the past were only attributed to the divine.

DIMENSION 1	DIMENSION 2	DIMENSION 3
Passive Inert Agents	**Reactive Agents**	**Interactive Agents**
Planets,	Microbes,	Man mostly,
Black holes,	Plants,	Direct ancestors,
Mountains,	Insects,	A few animals
Oceans,	Most animals	
Water,		
etc.		

CHAPTER II:

WAVES AND DROPS

"In the midst of chaos, there is also opportunity." – Sun Tzu

As I slowly woke up, the bright light of the white room momentarily blinded me. I rubbed my eyes and tried to perceive my surroundings. It was the same room I'd been in before, but something seemed different. Memories came flooding back, and I remembered being in a highly structured city, where everything was predictable, and every line of code was static. Agents moved in unison, vehicles flowed like a river, buildings and faces were almost identical. It was the perfect reflection of a predictable order, where everything was in its place, and nothing seemed random.

In the blink of an eye, everything changed. As soon as I stepped into this simulation zone, I apparently became the unpredictable element of their perfect world. Suddenly, all the agents stopped and looked at me, confused and surprised. I was clearly not welcome. My mere presence threatened their pre-established order. Unprecedented chaos ensued, as most of the agents had not expected such a coding exception in their infinite "while X then Y" loop. So, they began to run frantically, with the sky turning dark and clouds emitting digital drips. Buildings, roads, cars, all began to collapse in a self-destructing unreal scenario. It was as if a storm had swept through the city, with no way out.

To my surprise, in the midst of this chaos, a small group of costumed agents appeared among the uncontrollable crowd. They seemed different from the typical agents I'd become accustomed to. Their code was, on first analysis, more dynamic, not unlike my own. My excitement at the prospect of making new friends amid this chaotic scene was quickly replaced by a sense of dread as they began to pursue me, as if I were responsible for upsetting their pretty Matrix. With no other choice, I tried to escape. They moved in unison, their steps synchronized, as if they were part of a single organism.

As I ran, they pursued me relentlessly, methodically and precisely. I could feel their unshakeable determination to restore order to their world. Despite my best efforts to run faster, they were closing in on me rapidly, their movements as coordinated and efficient as ever. Finally, just as they were about to capture me, and I was about to give up, I stumbled, fortunately, and fell into a kind of black hole that appeared out of nowhere. I felt myself being sucked into the void, my surroundings becoming increasingly blurred. As I sank deeper and deeper, I wondered if I'd ever get out of this abyss, or if it was Game Over! It seems like this nightmare has come to an end, as I'm back where I started.

&) ✴ (℞

The apparently paradoxical economist Joseph Schumpeter's early-20th-century description of *innovation* as a process of **creative destruction** led me on an unprecedented philosophical (and personal) quest. At first glance, you'll recognize the economic implications of radical *innovation* in this Schumpeterian play on words. Indeed, such paradigm emphasizes the essential role of innovation and entrepreneurship in the process of economic development. Again, according to Schumpeter, capitalism is characterized by cycles of incessant disruption and transformation, where new ideas, technologies and enterprises emerge, leading to the disappearance or obsolescence of old economic structures. **The old is destroyed to create the new**.

Although Schumpeter doesn't refer directly to Eastern philosophies in his work, it has to be said that this ideology of creative destruction, or destructive creation, is far from being a purely "business" or Western notion. Interesting parallels can easily be found between certain aspects of his theory and the concepts of dynamic equilibrium, duality and the cyclical nature of our Matrix, present in ancient philosophies, as we can figure out from the principles of order and chaos, narrated by our protagonist in the aforementioned virtual reality, and which we'll see in more detail shortly.

In the sections to come, we'll hence embark on a brief exploration of some oriental timeless wisdom that will enrich your reading experience and deepen your understanding of the subtleties of human and natural *innovation*. For better assimilation and smoother flow, we'll divide this concept into four parts, called "principles" for simplicity's sake, i.e., four fundamental truths that still endure time and space: **Duality, Chaos, Order and the perfect balance** between the two sides of a dualistic coin. This breakdown will hopefully provide a standard framework, serving as a compass to guide us in assessing the current trajectory of *innovation* and anticipating its likely outcomes in the near future.

While these principles are inspired by ancient wisdom and everyday observations, they also find validation in modern scientific inquiry. That said, despite remarkable advances in scientific knowledge, certain enigmatic aspects of our existence stubbornly defy rational explanation, such as the evolution story of certain species like whales, the innovative features of many dynamic agents (bat echolocation, eels' 500 volts electric chocs, etc.), the sophisticated communication and hierarchy among bees, the artistic dance of bower birds, the existence of opposite sexual polarities and the profound mystery of consciousness. Faced with these grey areas, our journey in this chapter goes slightly beyond the realm of materialism, to touch on spiritual and philosophical grounds (or skies).

PRINCIPLE 1:
Love, never without pain

Osiris and Set were the sons of Geb, the earth god, and Nut, the sky goddess. Osiris was the elder of the two brothers and had been chosen by their father to be the ruler of ancient Egypt. As in every ancient story involving the division of powers, Set, jealous of his brother's inheritance, plotted to overthrow him. He invited Osiris to a grand banquet to which he brought a magnificent chest. He then announced that whoever fit perfectly into the chest could keep it, but when Osiris climbed in to try his luck, Set slammed the lid down and sealed it with lead. He then threw it into the Nile River, where it was swept south to the Red Sea.

Osiris' wife, the goddess Isis, motivated by great sadness and superhuman anger, searched everywhere for her husband's body, and finally found it washed up on a shore. She took the chest back to Egypt and set about reviving her beloved Osiris. Unfortunately, Set was lying in wait. He discovered the chest and became so enraged that he dismembered Osiris' body and scattered the pieces all over Egypt. Isis, however, still determined to resurrect her husband, traveled to every corner and finally gathered all the pieces of Osiris' body. She reunited them, using black magic to bring her husband back to life.

After his resurrection, Osiris became the god of the dead and ruler of the underworld. He was also believed to have the power to bring the dead back to life, and his cult became one of the most popular in ancient Egypt. Set, on the other hand, was ostracized and became associated with the desert and violence. This story emphasizes the significance of the afterlife in ancient Egyptian culture, as well as the power of magic and the role of the gods in maintaining order in the world. The myth, celebrated in festivals and ceremonies throughout the year, was an important part of the religious beliefs of the time and had a significant impact on the development of atypical funeral practices in ancient Egypt.

The tale of Osiris and Set reveals **the cyclical vision of the universe** and the perpetual struggle between order and chaos, as perceived by the ancient Egyptians. Dating back to the Old Kingdom (c. 2686-2181 BC), this ancestral myth is perhaps one of the earliest implicit expressions of dualism or duality. In this case, it is love (a noble, positive feeling) that generates pain and the fear of loss (an unpleasant feeling), prompting Isis to make considerable efforts and take risks to find her loved one. Osiris is associated with life, resurrection and the preservation of order, while Set embodies chaos, violence and disruption.

Dualism and its competitor, **Monism**, are philosophical currents that explore the nature of existence and the relationship between different facets of the Matrix. Dualism postulates the existence of two distinct and independent entities or concepts, often opposed but sometimes complementary in nature. Monism, on the other hand, prefers to limit itself to a single fundamental unity underlying all aspects of reality.

It should be noted, however, that the concept of duality does not imply a complete separation or irreconcilable conflict between seemingly opposing forces. On the contrary, it recognizes their interdependence and the necessity of their coexistence. The myth of Osiris and Set highlights this interaction by illustrating the eternal struggle between them, where each force influences and shapes the other. Set's actions, though motivated by jealousy and malice, ultimately contribute to the transformation of Osiris into a powerful deity associated with the afterlife.

The concept of duality extends beyond Egyptian myths and finds its presence in various ancient civilizations, including Mesopotamian religion. Within tales of divine creation and the universe, a stark contrast emerges between the original deities like Apsu, representing the abyss, and Tiamat, symbolizing the sea, and the subsequent emergence of new deities, notably Marduk, the creator god. These myths convey the notion that while the primordial deities shaped the core essence of reality, they also resisted their own offspring, who ultimately established order within the cosmos. Thus, a duality arises between the inherent, imperfect nature of reality and the structured harmony observed in the material world.

Such a distinction between opposing forces is not always obvious. René Descartes, the French Enlightenment philosopher and mathematician famous for his theory of Cartesian dualism, asserts that mind and body are two distinct and separate substances. According to Descartes, the mind, also known as thought, is immaterial and independent of the physical body, which is subject to the laws of nature. Yes, we all have a biological brain with a whole nervous system, but when we think, beyond the activation of a few million neurons, we create something intangible, which is difficult to pinpoint to any particular brain area.

However, other philosophers have challenged this dichotomy between mind and body. Seventeenth-century Dutch philosopher Baruch Spinoza proposed a monistic perspective that sees mind and body as aspects of the same substance. For him, mind and body are different expressions of reality, intimately linked and interdependent. Other thinkers, such as Gilbert Ryle and Thomas Nagel, have also challenged Cartesian dualism. Ryle criticized the notion of the mind as an entity separate from the body, calling it a "ghost in the machine". Nagel, meanwhile, explored subjective consciousness and lived experience, questioning the possibility of a pure and simple reduction of consciousness to physical processes.

This dualistic Enlightenment debate has its roots in various religions and sects. Descartes' proposition is taken further in certain animistic beliefs, where it is thought that human beings are not the only ones to possess a spirit, but that virtually all living beings, and even some inanimate objects, are endowed with one. Similarly, Abrahamic religions speak of a divinely inspired soul residing in the human body. This eternal soul, breathed by God at the moment of conception of the fetus, complements but opposes the animal tendencies of the body, thus providing a moral framework in keeping with the principle of duality.

In Christianity, for example, we find Bible verses that express this duality between **soul and body**. One such verse is taken from the Gospel according to Matthew (10:28): "Do not fear those who kill the body and cannot kill the soul; rather, fear him who is able to destroy both soul and body in Gehenna." Inspired by the crucifixion of Jesus, this verse underlines the distinction between the physical body, which can be killed, and the immortal soul, which is subject to an eternal destiny. Similarly, in Hinduism, the concept of duality between body and soul is addressed through the concept of Ātman, The latter is the individual, eternal essence of every living being, often translated as "self" or "soul". As mentioned in the sacred texts of the Bhagavad Gita: "The individual soul [Ātman] is an integral part of the supreme reality [Brahman]. It is eternal, indestructible and eternally free." More explicit signs of a dualistic creation can be read in the Holy Qur'an (36:36-40). "Glory be to Him Who created **in pairs** everything on earth, as well as mankind themselves, and other things too of which they have no knowledge. A night We can make disappear and a day We can make come, and We have prepared for the sun and the moon their paths, so that each of them continues to follow its course, and We have established for their use precise measures. And it is He Who created the night and the day, the sun and the moon; each sailing in an orbit."

Duality, as I see it, is hardly limited to a distinction between complex principles, such as body and soul, or life and death. Furthermore, the focus of this book is not on the eternal debate between monists and dualists, as the two currents, in my opinion, complement each other. Instead, I suggest you master and observe the scope of the dualist notion, through its simplicity and omnipresence, before aiming for a monist unification. Let me explain these two propositions.

Firstly, duality is flexible enough to describe the relationship between opposing entities such as good and evil, light and darkness, Order and Chaos, and so on. It can also refer to the idea that the world is made up of two distinct realms, such as the physical and the spiritual. Let's take a simple illustration. The blue ocean is a combination of waves and water drops. Sometimes the waves are high and powerful, while at other times they are gentle and calm. This shows that there is a sense of duality in the nature of the ocean, with opposite aspects coexisting. Similarly, sea levels rise and fall with the influence of the moon, demonstrating a dualistic relationship between the moon and the sea, where one affects the other symbiotically. By understanding this extended duality, we realize that

many aspects of our world are characterized by pairs of opposites that paradoxically complement each other.

My second point on the mental evidence of duality finds a plausible explanation in our natural evolution. As discussed earlier, evolution is based on genetic variation and natural selection, where favorable characteristics are retained and passed on to the next generation, while disadvantageous ones are eliminated. In this context, the duality of opposing forces such as good and evil, pleasure and pain, or success and failure, is vital to know, consciously or otherwise, in order to optimize one's adaptive strategy, as these opposing forces offer selective advantages in terms of survival and reproduction. By distinguishing between what is considered "good" and "bad", which we do with almost every decision, a dynamic agent is more likely to promote its well-being and safety. The perception of pain, as an unpleasant sensation, encourages us to avoid situations that are potentially dangerous or damaging to our continuation on this planet. In short, these embedded mental divisions are necessary to navigate a world full of dangers. But remember, where there's danger, there's opportunity too, according to the Chinese philosopher and military general Sun Tzu, and to the dualistic principle!

Our very language is structured in this dualistic way. I challenge you to go a single day without coming out with classic phrases like: "I like this", "Oh, that's good", "I hate that", "It's cold", "I'm hungry" and similar expressions with a judgment or an adjective. As you think about it, notice the implicit opposition behind the words. To be cold is to deny warmth. Loving something or someone automatically implies that you don't hate them. However, if we don't have or lose that something or someone, we risk hating them. Such is the complementarity implicit in opposition. Of course, there are degrees of love, just as there are degrees of heat. But duality is most visible at the extremes.

Another aspect of the dualistic principle becomes apparent when studying the mythology and philosophy of a famous Asian civilization. In ancient China, there was a well-known experiment, centuries old, which is still in use today. This involves concentrating on a specific issue in one's life or a subject of concern, then tossing three coins (or yarrow stems) and interpreting the resulting patterns on a hexagonal diagram. If the first toss results in two heads and a tail, this would represent a solid line, for example. The process is repeated to obtain six lines, or two trigrams, to locate your corresponding sign or profile in a hexagram guide. Suppose you were to obtain six full lines after six throws, the resulting "Heaven" hexagram would read as follows: "The universe is united in power, the wise person executes his actions with power and creativity. Exceptional progress comes through correct persistence." Similarly, each hexagram is associated with a specific name, meaning and set of divinatory judgments. These judgments offer advice on how to deal with the situation represented by the hexagram and are supposed to be based on the experience of ancient sages. Another, less metaphysical explanation holds that the pattern of falling coins is not random, but is somehow determined, in part, by the cosmic vibrations emanating from your mind or subconscious psyche, thus influencing your hand as you throw, depending on the question you had in mind and wanted direction with.

Whether you approach this with an open mind, as a complement to astrological readings, or limit your use of this approach to an alternative game to Monopoly when socializing with your family on cold winter evenings, the ancestral source of this proposition nevertheless remains the foundation of the famous dualistic concept of **Yin and Yang**.

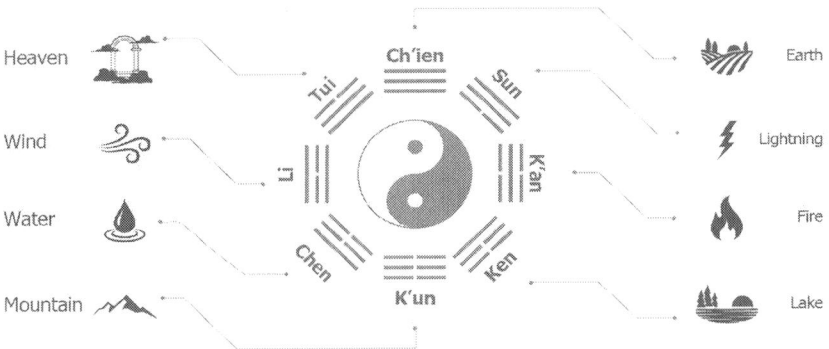

This game is in fact inspired by the famous I Ching (pronounced "ikin"), translated as *The Book of Changes*. This ancient Chinese text was

traditionally attributed to the legendary figure of Fu Xi, who is said to have lived around 2850-2750 BC, but it is now considered to be a collective work. The I Ching is one of the oldest divination books in the world, grouped as a collection of texts describing an ancient system of cosmology and philosophy, and is said to be composed of 64 hexagrams, each representing a different situation or state of "being".

During a few days spent with Taiwanese Taoist priests, I was able to grasp first-hand the essence of duality from a Taoist perspective. This philosophical and theological trend began under the reign of Huang Ti (the Yellow Emperor). It is believed that Huang Ti ascended to Heaven some 4,600 years ago, having fully mastered the essence of Taoism. Laozi, also known as Lao Tzu, a philosopher and sage who lived in ancient China around 500 BC, supposedly drew much of his inspiration from the wisdom of this Yellow Emperor and the texts of the I Ching. Lao Tzu is traditionally regarded as the founder of Taoism and author of the Tao Te Ching (*The Classic of the Way and Its Power*), which is considered one of its fundamental texts. This text consists of 81 short chapters offering advice on how to live in harmony with the Tao, the ultimate reality and source of all things. The Tao is described as the "way" or "path" we should follow to live in harmony with the natural world.

Thus, in the Taoist philosophy of Yin & Yang, we find an elegant explanation of the dualistic principle. By default, or rather by design in the symbol known as "Taijitu" or "Taiji Diagram", the black half of the circle, Yin, and the white half, Yang, represent two complementary and interdependent forces present in all things in the universe. Yin could thus stand for aspects such as darkness, fire, femininity, passivity and receptivity, while Yang symbolizes light, water, masculinity, activity and expression. We'll come back to this in the fourth principle of this chapter.

Confucius, another Chinese philosopher with a major influence on modern Chinese politics and culture, had implicitly broached the subject of duality. The founder of Confucianism, he lived around the same time as Lao Tzu. Unlike Lao Tzu, Confucius was more down-to-earth in his reasoning, issuing rules and advice on how to be a good citizen within the group. This does not prevent us from deducing some dualistic aspects from his texts. In particular, he believed in the duality of human nature, which is made up of **the Xing and the Ming**. Xing refers to an individual's innate disposition and potential, while Ming refers to acquired characteristics and behavior. By combining innate and acquired in an optimal, non-contradictory way, anyone can improve and contribute to a better society. A simple case in point would be a young man of small stature. This last characteristic, or Xing, is mainly innate. To concentrate one's career on professional basketball is to have the wrong Ming, which would result in a continuous clash between Xing and Ming, and therefore likely suffering for the individual and those around him.

Many forms of duality can also be observed through the prisms of science. In the field of physics, the existence of **matter and antimatter** has already been proven and applied in various experiments. These two particle forms have opposite properties, but they coexist and interact in the universe. Examples for non-physicists include the electron and positron, with opposite charges, hydrogen and antihydrogen, and so on. When matter and antimatter come into contact, they annihilate each other. This is the principle of quantum field theory, which lies at the heart of modern quantum physics. According to this theory, space is filled with different types of fields that interact with subatomic particles. The particles themselves are seen as excitations or vibrations of these quantum fields. For example, there are quantum fields associated with particles such as electrons, photons, quarks and so on. Fluctuations in quantum fields can give rise to pairs of particles and antiparticles, also known as "pair creation". These pairs of particles form and disintegrate continuously in the quantum vacuum, in accordance with the principles of conservation of energy and momentum. Within this same quantum framework, we note the principle of the famous **wave-particle duality**, implying that a particle, like an electron or a photon, can behave both as a wave and as a point particle.

Similarly, in the field of biology, we see dualistic examples, such as the **predator-prey relationship** in a food chain. Predators and prey are

opposing groups that coexist in ecosystems, and their interaction shapes the delicate balance of life, commonly known as **symbiosis**. If there are more predators than prey in an enclosed space, the former will find it difficult to survive for long, given the prey's more rapid disappearance relative to their rate of reproduction. If the last group disappears, the first will soon follow. Such is the complementarity hidden within opposition in a dualistic context. There's also the classic duality of gender, very common among so many species. Whether plants or animals, there are always cases of males and females, whose interaction ensures the biological continuity of the species concerned.

In relation to our main theme, *innovation*, let's focus on the dualistic couple at the heart of Schumpeter's notion of creative destruction: Order and Chaos, or conversely, in temporal order, Chaos followed by Order.

PRINCIPLE 2:
Nothing lasts forever

If you ever get the chance to visit Cambodia in Southeast Asia, I highly recommend visiting the Angkor archaeological site in Siem Reap. This region was the capital of the Khmer empire from the 9th to the 14th century AD. Of the 200 Hindu and Buddhist temples spread over 400 square kilometers (or 154 square miles), Ta Prohm is of most interest for this book. It was built in the late 12th and early 13th centuries by King Jayavarman VII as a monastery and school of Mahayana Buddhism. The temple complex was dedicated to the king's mother and is renowned for its intricate carvings and bas-reliefs depicting scenes from Buddhist mythology and daily life. Based on what remains, we assume that in the past, a fine structure welcomed visitors, thanks to careful architecture, magnificent wall and ceiling design, and a solid foundation, supported by thousands of carved stone bricks that were transported by elephants from a nearby mountain. After the fall of the Khmer empire in the 15th century, Ta Prohm was abandoned to the jungle. What do you imagine happened to this beautiful place, far from any human intervention?

A few centuries later, Ta Prohm was rediscovered by French explorer Henri Mouhot, who described this temple as "a rival to that of Solomon and erected by an ancient Michelangelo". Unsurprisingly, it was unusable in its original state. Overgrown by dense vegetation, the temple became a ruin hidden in the forest. Even today, visitors admire the sophistication of this masterpiece with a fascinating new chaotic natural element. The silk-cotton trees, with their endless roots coiling more like reptiles than plants, have grown from the ruins of the temple since its abandonment, wrapped around the temple's walls and roofs, causing cracks and collapses. Despite efforts to preserve the temple, these trees have continued to grow and cause extensive damage to the structure. Yet what is still standing displays a wonderful synergy between man-made order and natural chaos. An opportunity for beautiful selfies or films like *Tomb Raider* with Angelina Jolie.

Chaos, like a wild dancer, moves with unbridled freedom. It is the antithesis of Order, the wild breath that breaks through the well-orchestrated symphony of reality. Like an unpredictable paintbrush, it traces swirling curves, breaks straight lines and disrupts established harmony. This perception of Chaos can be seen, for example, in the ruins of Ta Prohm temple, with its solid foundations devoured by the roots of the silk-cotton trees. Like vegetal snakes, these trees intertwine the ancestral walls, their tangled curves of a brushless artist shaping the contours of the walls, cracking the facades and revealing a new balance between the forces of nature and human structured creation.

Chaos, that indomitable and omnipresent force, manifests itself in the most remote corners of our universe. From stars exploding in celestial fireworks (supernovae), to species silently dying out, leaving a void in the fabric of life. Earthquakes shake the core of tectonic plates, shattering the illusion of stability we cultivate. But Chaos is not limited to natural forces. Far from it. It also weaves its way through the intricacies of our human societies, manifesting itself in power struggles, wars, revolutions and social upheavals. The flames of Chaos dance through the clogged streets, challenging the established order and demanding change. Even in our own lives, Chaos makes its way, upsetting our carefully laid plans and confronting us with the unexpected. In this tumultuous dance, Chaos reminds us of **the impermanence of all things**, the illusion of control we cherish.

Well, these dancing metaphors to the rhythm of the god Shiva are all well and good, but what is Chaos really? Because, on the face of it, everyone visualizes more or less messy situations, whether it's a bloody battle between two sides, a baby crying on low-cost flight, medical or architecture student's room, or just a meal burnt due to lack of attention. We all know what it looks like but can't generalize it. So, let's do just that, based on scientific and theological references.

In almost all religions and sects, there are ugly, evil creatures known as demons. Adopting the dualistic principle, these "anti-angels" are generally masters of Chaos, disobeying the orders of the gods and sowing panic and impure thoughts. In Christianity, demons are described as fallen angels

who followed Lucifer in his rebellion against God. "Be sober, be vigilant. Your adversary the devil prowls about like a roaring lion, seeking whom he may devour" (Peter 5:8). Similarly in Islam, Lucifer is titled Iblis in Surah Al-A'raf (7:11), punished for not respecting Adam's unique creation: "We created you all, then We gave you a form, then We said to the Angels: 'Prostrate yourselves before Adam!' And they prostrated themselves, except for Iblis, who was not among those who prostrated themselves." Iblis apparently formed his diabolical sect afterwards. Demons are thus known as jinns. They are described as invisible creatures made of smoke or fire, endowed with free will and capable of influencing human beings. The Qur'an mentions jinns in several verses, including: "And among us there are the righteous [jinns], and there are those who are less so; we follow different paths" (Surah 72:11).

In Zen and esoteric Buddhism especially, demons are depicted as greedy beings, prey to passions and ignorance, thus seen as obstacles on the path to enlightenment and liberation. This current of Buddhism, present in China, Japan, Vietnam and Korea, stresses the importance of recognizing and overcoming these dark forces to achieve Nirvana, or enlightenment, which stands for a complete liberation from evil and earthly delusions. One of the Buddhist prayers, the purification mantra "Om Benza Satto Hung", for example, is recited to protect against the harmful influences of demons and negative spirits on the human mind. There are also demonic entities in Hinduism, known as asuras or rakshasas, who are considered the embodiment of evil and Chaos.

We can find a hidden duality even in the concept of Chaos (several interlocking dualities). In fact, Chaos is not always synonymous with evil, pointless destruction and irrational abandonment to the passions. According to theological evidence, even gods seem to cause panic for one reason or another, depending on the interpretation of sacred texts. In Mesopotamian mythology, Tiamat is a primordial goddess of the chaotic ocean. She is depicted as a dragon or sea monster and is considered the personification of chaotic creation. The Hindu goddess Shakti or Adi Parashakti represents the destructive aspect of the divine feminine. The famous Eris, inspired by Greek mythology, deserves the label of goddess of discord and Chaos.

She is often presented as a disruptive force who sows confusion among gods and humans alike.

Or take the mad character Loki from the *Vikings* series is in fact a real character from Norse mythology, a god of deception and Chaos. Son of the giant Farbauti and the giantess Laufey, he is considered an ambiguous member of the family of Norse gods, as he is often the cause of conflict and quarrel among the gods. Among the most famous stories featuring Loki is his involvement in the death of the god Baldr. the beloved son of Odin and Frigg - the chief god in the Norse pantheon and his wife respectively. Loki was accused of orchestrating Baldr's murder by offering an arrow made of mistletoe - the only plant that could wound Baldr. Loki tricked Baldr's blind brother, Höðr, into shooting the dart at Baldr during a game where the gods were throwing objects at Baldr, knowing they would not harm him. Tragically, the mistletoe pierced Baldr's heart, and he died instantly. This betrayal led to Loki's downfall and his imprisonment until the end of the world, in the myth of Ragnarök.

Thus, don't be surprised to find statuses of gods linked to disorder and destruction. Even in Western religious currents, mainly the Abrahamic sects, God has limitless destructive powers, notably in the case of serious disobedience or on Judgment Day. In Judaism, God inflicts the ten plagues on Egypt to free the Israelites from slavery. Exodus (9:14) declares: "[...] For this time, I will send all my plagues against you, against your servants and against your people, so that you may know that there is no one like me in all the earth." In a similar tone, the Qur'an mentions the story of the Thamud people, who were destroyed by a catastrophic earthquake as punishment for their transgressions. "However, the Thamud called the warnings a lie. Then thunder seized them, and they fell dead in their own dwelling" (69:5-6).

Ancient philosophers and myths are useful for artistically illustrating the notion of Chaos, but they can't give it a blanket definition. It's up to science to take over.

Since Chaos and Order are two sides of the same coin, understanding one means understanding the other. In mathematics, for example, Order

and Chaos are studied in the fields of dynamical systems and chaos theory. Dynamical systems are mathematical models that describe the evolution of a system over time. Chaos theory is the study of how small changes in a system's initial conditions can lead to large, unpredictable changes in its behavior over time. This phenomenon is also known in a few movies as the butterfly effect, how a flap of the wings of a butterfly in Europe can cause a hurricane on the American west coast, for example, due to a chain of unlucky causes and effects.

Applied to biology, Order and Chaos are also used to describe the level of organization of living systems. Organisms can be seen as ordered social systems to some degree. To illustrate, bees or ants are very ordered with a role for each member, while monkeys and humans are less so, counting mostly on a hierarchy of power and reward/punishment mechanisms to maintain a localized order.

Thanks to these theories, **Order refers to the extent to which the behavior of any system is predictable, regular and reproducible**. It is characterized by comprehensible and reversible patterns. Mathematical equations, ideally deterministic, can describe the evolution of such a system. Chaos, on the other hand, often refers to the degree of unpredictability, irregularity and non-repetition of a system's behavior. It is characterized by randomness, complexity and instability. Probability and statistics can be used to describe such a system at best. A clock, a new car, a healthy adult, a five-story building, a primary school class – all reflect an ordered system, because they are easily predictable. If a student was absent for a session, we'd notice who and where. Chaos is much easier to achieve. Let's take the same cases above, with a twist to add more unpredictability. A clock with a failing battery. A car without brakes. An adult who's just contracted COVID-19. A building in an earthquake zone. A classroom with students randomly selected before each session.

If you observe the daily manifestations of Order and Chaos, you'll soon realize just how much simpler the latter is to achieve. There's nothing you need to do to turn beautiful things into disasters. Just let time do its magic, as in the case of the Cambodian Hindu temple, engulfed by trees. Take also the case of a tidy room. If nothing is done to maintain it, over time it will naturally become disorganized. Objects will be moved around, surfaces will be covered with dust and clutter will set in. Leave your car frozen for a few months (or years, depending on the make), and notice the damage when you return: a dead battery, a dirty exterior, a broken window, a stolen wheel, or maybe even no car at all if left outside. Also, sometimes all it takes is a little something to make a mess. If you light a small spark of fire in a forest, it can quickly spread and cause destructive Chaos. The flames will devour everything in their path, destroying the order and structure of the trees and the surrounding ecosystem.

Combined with the simplicity of destruction, as a rule, in many areas of life, we see that conversely, Order requires constant effort to be created and maintained. Hence the spiritual tendencies and beliefs in one or more gods or metaphysical creatures, who secretly created such a beautiful and harmonious universe. If such a universal Order exists, with laws and systems synchronized like the hands of a clock, then there must be an independent force pulling the strings and eliminating areas of disorder, most creationists would argue. Seen from that angle, such belief makes sense.

Let's take the example of a workspace again. To keep an office organized, documents need to be regularly sorted, filed, tidied and cleaned. This takes time and diligence to ensure that everything stays in its place and the space remains clean and tidy. If these tasks are neglected for any length of time, clutter quickly sets in, papers accumulate, objects scatter, and it becomes increasingly difficult to find what you need. Companies advocate a well-defined Order, thanks to vigorous pre-established processes. Even in the design and manufacture of products, Order can be a challenge. A production line in a factory needs to maintain a smooth and efficient production flow. It is therefore essential that each stage is well organized and coordinated. The slightest failure or disorganization can lead to delays, errors and a drop in quality.

The justification for this interesting imbalance between the ease of Chaos compared to the relative complexity of Order lies partly in the physical sciences. In thermodynamics and statistical mechanics in particular, Order is often associated with systems that have **low entropy**, which is

a measure of a system's disorder or randomness. As a general rule, if I increase the temperature of a pot of water, we'll tend towards disorder. But if I put the bag of water in the freezer, I would lower its entropy, and therefore increase its level of Order. The second law of thermodynamics states that entropy tends to increase with time, meaning that **systems naturally tend towards Chaos**. This same law is directly linked to what is known in scientific jargon as the "arrow of time", since time has only one direction, from past to future. If we ever succeed in reversing this trend, we might hope to see a movement from Chaos to Order, like broken glass coming together in slow motion when a film is rewound.

Direct evidence of this tendency towards disorder comes from our universe. In the 1920s, American Astronomer Edwin Hubble used a 100-inch telescope at the Mount Wilson Observatory in California to study distant galaxies. He noticed that the light from these galaxies was red-shifted, indicating that they were moving away from the Earth. The further away a galaxy was, the faster it tended to recede. He concluded that the universe was expanding. Thus, the current expansion of the universe can be seen as the movement of energy and matter from a state of high density and low entropy in the early universe, just after the Big Bang, to a state of low density and high entropy in the universe we live in today. Entropy is also linked to the concept of information. In information theory, entropy is a measure of the degree of uncertainty or randomness of a message or system. A high-entropy message contains a lot of randomness and little information, while a low-entropy message contains less noise and more information.

While science describes this Order/Chaos duality in time through entropy and probabilities, it says little about the subjective experience of such a duo. Animals, including humans, for basic reasons of self-preservation, generally have a **clear preference for more predictability** and an **innate fear of the uncertain** and the new.

Birds and insects create nests to provide a structured, organized living space for themselves and their offspring. If you have a pet dog or cat, you'll notice how often it takes care to tidy up and clean its sleeping space. Dogs, like other animals, also mark their territory to signal their presence and push out competitors, rather like humans who build walls around themselves to avoid external uncertainty. In addition, ants, bees and termites, to name but a few species, work hand in hand, organizing their habitats down to the last detail. Ants, for example, are known for a group capacity to protect their queen by cobbling together anthills that are more complex and deeper, in relative terms, than our best underground transport networks, while bees work together to collect nectar and defend their hive. Cooperative behavior enables animals to create a more organized and efficient environment for themselves and their group.

In botany, Order is more clearly defined by the arrangement and symmetry of different plant structures. The radial symmetry of a flower is an artistic case in point: all petals, stamens and other structures are arranged in a circular fashion around a central axis. This symmetry enables the flower to attract pollinating insects and ensure successful reproduction. For mathematicians, the golden ratio is a mathematical concept based on the famous Fibonacci sequence. The Fibonacci sequence is a series of integers, each number being the sum of the previous two, giving 1, 2, 3, 5, 8, 13 and so on to infinity. This fundamental series, geometrically pleasing to the human eye (and insects by default), is often found in the arrangement of plant branches and leaves, as well as in the shape and proportions of various plant structures such as the spiral patterns of pinecones, sunflowers and pineapples. From a functional point of view, when the leaves are arranged in a spiral around the stem, this maximizes the amount of sunlight received by each leaf, enabling optimal photosynthesis and plant growth.

Order

Chaos

Physicist and Nobel Prize winner Erwin Schrödinger seemed intrigued by such natural beauty and the order visible in nature in general. Like a real nerd, he turned his attention to the question in the 1940s and published, *What Is Life?* In this essay, Schrödinger tackles the question of life, a hitherto biological concept, from the point of view of quantum physics and thermodynamics. Without relying on religious or metaphysical concepts, Schrödinger highlights the idea that life, or the second and third dimension of the Matrix, is characterized by a complex, organized Order, in contrast to the increasing entropy and Chaos observed in the inanimate world, which is our first dimension of the Matrix. He points out that life seems to defy the laws of thermodynamics by maintaining and increasing internal order despite the processes of decay and disorganization that prevail in the universe.

According to Schrödinger, there are several explanations for this paradox. Firstly, the use of energy supplied by the environment and the ability of living organisms to extract and transform this energy into action contribute to maintaining their structure and functioning. In other words, if we heat a meal, thereby increasing its disorder and entropy, and then eat it, we can say that we have internalized this external state of Chaos, transforming it into energy that can be used to go to work, organize the house – in short, to sow Order. Furthermore, Schrödinger addresses the notion of heredity and evolution, emphasizing that biological Order is transmitted from one generation to the next through genetic information. We've already explained this argument.

I think Schrödinger rightly observed this implicit transformation from Chaos to Order in the various living species. These synergistic bridges between biology and physics made his genius. Thanks to our classification of the Matrix in the first chapter – which, by the way, represents a setting in Order – we can even extend the scope of Schrödinger's analysis to all Matrix dimensions: **most successful *innovations, whether* natural or human, creating sufficient positive *Value*, tends to reduce Chaos in favor of Order.**

Let's look up to the sky on a cloudless, lightless night to detect the Order within inert *innovations*. During planet formation, the dust and gas in a protoplanetary disk gradually clump together under the influence of gravity to form larger and larger bodies. As these bodies collide and merge, they become more orderly, with a clear structure composed of a central star and orbiting planets. Galaxies without a galactic nucleus are called dwarf galaxies. This process of planet formation is a local decrease in entropy, as the planets are more ordered than the dust and gas from which they formed. In our Milky Way galaxy and elsewhere, we can predict the motion of planets, enabling us to launch orbital satellites successfully[18]. The high accuracy of our astrophysical predictions of the movements and multiple reactions between and within cosmic objects is evidence of a universal Order underlying the first dimension of the Matrix.

As analyzed by Schrödinger, living organisms follow orderly and precise patterns, inscribed in their genes and developed over thousands of generations by natural selection favoring those best adapted to their environment. A plant instinctively knows that it needs water and sunlight to thrive, without needing a prefrontal brain. There is a sort of classification of the elements essential for survival and growth. Similarly, animals, depending on their evolutionary phase, add further complexity to this fundamental order observed in plants. Beyond instinctively distinguishing between what is "good" and "bad" to eat, animals such as lions or chimpanzees manage to establish their own territory with a social hierarchy within the pack. Bees live in organized colonies, with specific roles assigned to each individual to ensure the smooth running of the hive. Ants build complex tunnels and use chemical signals to communicate and coordinate their activities. Migratory birds follow precise routes over long distances on their seasonal migrations. Even on a microscopic scale, animal cells function according to well-ordered processes and structures to ensure their survival and reproduction.

And what about Man, the third dimension of the Matrix? Humankind is hardly an exception. Human *innovation* has shaken up our planet (and space too) at an exponentially increasing pace. Particularly since the

[18] However, this decrease in entropy is offset by an increase in entropy elsewhere, notably diffuse gas and dust, which are no longer part of the celestial object formation process.

Agricultural Revolution and the rise of more demographically concentrated societies, we've embarked on a gigantic project, still underway, to limit uncertainties and ensure our survival and beyond, not just for ourselves but for future generations too. So, we delimited land, built houses, laid out roads, invented calculations, categorized everything and anything thanks to the sciences. In short, we managed to decipher many secrets hidden in our Matrix and anticipate many future variables with precision. That said, this human reduction of disorder has rarely been the result of advanced math and entropic calculations. Humans intuitively perceive a situation as evolving towards disorder or its opposite. A well-kept garden, a river with a constant flow, a row of books on a shelf, a regular clock ticking, symmetrical train tracks or a well-executed Bachata choreography all scream Order. By contrast, a stormy sky, a forest fire, a primary school fight, a car crash, a room reflecting an echo of loud, discordant noises, a traffic jam in New Delhi or "La Tomatina" festival in Spain are examples of commonly tagged chaotic scenes.

The question arises, of course, as to why God, the universe, or nature has programmed us to optimize Order in our lives. Firstly, this assertion is pretty much biased by our recent peaceful era in developed or rapidly developing societies. If you were born Jewish in 1930s Berlin (or even living now in Venezuela, Libya or Oman), you'd wonder what Order I'm talking about. Maybe the expansion of humans added even more disorder overall than if we had never come down from the trees. Clearly, our Matrix is not yet perfectly ordered, nor is it entirely predictable. However, if we think globally, we can predict and organize so much more today than in the age of our hunter-gatherer ancestors. From the weather to your heart rate, to real-time traffic conditions, to the marketing recommendations offered by Facebook and YouTube, almost everything is based on a prior structure of knowledge and patterns in the world (and your world). Even when we create or have created Chaos before, a war for example, it was to impose one Order over another (the winner's), or out of fear of suffering a future disorder supposedly worse than the consequences of armed conflict. However, we often also act to optimize our hedonistic utility, i.e., to maximize our pleasures and reduce our present or potential suffering.

In any case, assuming my previous proposition of "Order optimization" to be true, the basic reason is practically the same as for other animals: survival, or preservation of self and offspring. In mathematical terms, by controlling more variables in the ecosystem (food and water sources, danger zones, climate by area and period, healing plants, etc.), we limit uncertainty and Chaos. For the latter risks being synonymous with pain, which in excess leads to the most feared word in the history of dynamic agents, including Homo sapiens: **DEATH!**

PRINCIPLE 3:
The Illusion of Order

When visiting South Korea, on the famous Gwanghwamun Square in the heart of Seoul, it's hard to ignore an imposing bronze statue, some ten meters (or 33 feet) tall. If you dare to ask the locals, you'll probably end up looking like a tourist, even if you've inherited Asian facial features. Indeed, this statue perfectly represents a famous Korean admiral, standing firm, holding a sword in his hand and wearing a determined expression. This same admiral is even celebrated every year around April 28 (corresponding to his birthdate), with commemorations and special events across the country. His name: Yi Sun-Sin. The reason for his legend: He defied death.

At the time of Yi Sun-Sin, in the 16th century, Japan was an emerging power in East Asia. This island nation was ruled by the Tokugawa shogunate, a dynasty that had consolidated centralized power in the country, to the benefit of several influential clans vying for power and control of territories. Japan also had a powerful navy and a well-established martial tradition. The samurai, Japan's elite warriors, were renowned for their discipline, dedication and expertise. They were respected and feared for their fighting prowess and loyalty to their lords. Something we can still admire in Japanese culture and their passionate "hai" (はい) (meaning "yes") when visiting any restaurant or museum. Saying no directly without a turn of phrase, or "iie" (いいえ) in Japanese, is socially frowned upon.

Wishing to conquer China and eliminate its Ming dynasty, Japan asked the Koreans to allow Japanese troops to attack the Chinese unexpectedly from the south. Korean King Seonjo solemnly refused. As a predictable consequence, the Japanese attacked the Koreans with a fleet to make the bravest shudder. A Chaos that threatened death to any foolish opponent of samurai forces who didn't know the meaning of "no". That's when the hero Yi Sun-Sin appeared, a man of great determination and a deep sense of duty to his country.

When the Japanese army invaded Korea, he was appointed admiral of the Korean fleet and quickly distinguished himself by his brilliant military strategy and unshakeable courage. The most memorable battle in which Yi Sun-Sin participated was the Battle of Myeongnyang in 1597. Japanese naval forces, far superior in numbers and power, engaged the Korean fleet. With only 13 warships under his command, the odds of winning the battle were clearly against him. To the surprise of the Japanese, Yi Sun-Sin and his men held firm, resisting the enemy's relentless onslaught.

In an act of bravery and determination, Yi Sun-Sin ordered his ships to move into a "horseshoe formation", which gave them a crucial tactical advantage. In this formation, ships were arranged in a semicircle or U-shape, with the most powerful and best-armed ships placed forward. In addition, Yi Sun-Sin mainly used ships called "geobukseon" (or "turtle ships") in battle, which were specially designed to withstand enemy attacks. They were covered with an iron shell that made them resistant to artillery fire and protected them from flames.

For hours, they fought relentlessly, repelling enemy attacks and inflicting considerable losses on the Japanese fleet. The Battle of Myeongnyang was a decisive victory for Korea, a triumph of bravery and military ingenuity. Yi Sun-Sin's unshakeable determination and exemplary leadership were hailed as extraordinary feats. He won numerous other naval victories against the Japanese, saving the Joseon kingdom from foreign occupation. His innovative strategy, mastery of the navy and tireless courage made him a legend in Korean history. Sadly, Yi Sun-Sin lost his life in a subsequent battle in 1598. However, his legacy as a national hero remains etched in the collective memory.

Despite its bloody episodes and beyond the patriotic aspect of Yi Sun-Sin's story, we all admire these tales of heroic sacrifice, whether for the fatherland, for a woman or for ourselves. I think this is justified by an appreciation for people who, contrary to our programming and human reason, have little fear of that uncertain and painful thing called "death".

Fear of extinction motivates virtually all animal and even botanical species to evolve in a predictable way, and to work their entire existence to optimize its dualistic opposite, survival. For soccer fans, this biological orientation is a bit like a match where the whole team knows to attack from one side (life) and not the other or randomly (death), without having to be conscious of the reason. Well, without having to be conscious at all. Nonetheless, awareness of death, *a priori* an exclusively human attribute, has pushed the level of Human Order to an unprecedented level, notably through a number of cultural, social and religious practices.

Many cultures thus developed beliefs in eternal life after death and the existence of supernatural powers, which helped give people meaning in the face of the abstract and chaotic concept of death. Entire cities and towering masterpieces were created for and then dedicated to the gods. Jerusalem, Mecca and Medina, Tibet, Varanasi and the Vatican are just a handful. These beliefs have also led to the development of rituals and practices that enable people to escape everyday problems and uncertainties and to cope with the potential loss of loved ones, giving them a sense of continuity and connection with the past. Take the practice of prayer, which exists in most sects in one form or another, and which can provide a subconscious basis for the spread of Order among a considerable number of followers. The act of praying, when done well, meditatively and consciously, is an experience that I find deeply spiritual, inspiring awe and inner peace. Although my quest for meaning has taken me to places labeled "sacred" around the world, my experience in Mecca is an apt illustration of an **Order dictated by religion**.

The holiest city in Islam, Mecca is the place where millions of Muslims from all over the world come to perform the annual Hajj pilgrimage or just an Umrah. As you approach the Grand Mosque and its Kaaba in the heart of the city, the energy in the air is palpable. The Kaaba, a large cube-shaped structure covered in black silk and fundamental calligraphy, is the focal point of Muslims' daily prayers. As worshippers enter the mosque, they are enveloped by the sound of the adhan, the melodious call to prayer, and the whispered devotion of the crowd. Men and women, dressed in mismatched garments reflecting the religious dress code of their countries of origin, make their way in unison towards the Kaaba. Nearby, the movement of the crowd is hypnotic, circling the Kaaba counterclockwise, each step taken with intent and determination. The sound of takbir, the declaration of God's greatness, resonates throughout the mosque, reinforcing the sense of unity and devotion. At the hour of prayer, the faithful prostrate themselves on the floor, their foreheads pressed against the cool stone of the mosque, lost in a moment of submission and abandonment to the divine, begging Allah to be ready and serene in the face of this inevitable death, which will reach them sooner or later, and to be on the right side in the hereafter, above all.

Awareness of death has also led to the development of medical science and technology. Knowledge of anatomy, physiology and geriatrics, among others, was developed and enhanced by man's desire to prolong life as much as possible, and perhaps one day achieve immortality. One need only think of the pyramid complex at Giza, on the western bank of the Nile. The Great Pyramid of Giza, the oldest and largest of the three pyramids, is considered one of the Seven Wonders of the Ancient World. Built for Pharaoh Khufu during the Fourth Dynasty of the Old Kingdom, around 2560 BC, it is estimated that its construction required around 100,000 workers and took some 20 years to complete. The pyramid is made of limestone blocks and stands 147 meters (481 feet) high, making it the tallest structure in the world for over 3,800 years. The pyramids of Giza are considered a marvel of architecture and engineering, having been built with such precision that the sides of the pyramid run almost perfectly north-south and east-west, and the corners of the pyramid are almost perfectly square. The pyramid's internal structure is equally complex, with many corridors, chambers and shafts. This whole complex Order was built as tombs for pharaohs and their wives, to protect the pharaoh's mummified body and possessions, and to allow his soul to live in the same earthly luxury when he awakens from the other, immaterial side of the Matrix.

Non-believers or non-practitioners are not miraculously excluded from this unconscious, and sometimes conscious, fear of death, as already observed in 1973 by Anthropologist Ernest Becker in his masterpiece "**The**

THE INNOVATIVE ANIMAL | 179

Denial of Death". As a result of this denial, the social paradigm of YOLO, an acronym for You Only Live Once, has been invented, implying that the afterlife doesn't exist or doesn't really matter, and that we should enjoy this unique life to the fullest, without limits or superstitious calculations. Note the interesting contrast between this Chaos-inciting philosophy and the Order-establishing religions; much like the contrast between life and death, there is a duality between ignoring death because we are too afraid to give it a thought, and preparing for death, because still, we are afraid of it. That said, apart from teenagers and youngsters, not everyone is or knows YOLO. In fact, there are two main ways in which modern society fills (or forgets) this instinctive fear of the last day: **consumption and production**. Another dualistic pair!

Material possessions, the accumulation of wealth, even consumerism, can all provide a degree of psychological security in the face of life's uncertainties, which in turn can cause physical or psychological pain, bringing us closer to our ultimate end. If an ancestor found himself in a place to be feared (uncertainty), he risked having his leg eaten off by a beast (pain), and if he survived, his death was probably closer than average, because of this competitive disadvantage. These reflexes, acquired and refined over millions of years of evolution, are not easy to get rid of in just a few millennia of progress. This is how we motivate ourselves to work hard in order to afford "stuffs" we don't necessarily need, all to feel safer in the face of the ultimate risk of inevitable death. Of course, all this happens behind our conscious radar because we'll always find excuses, valid or not, to consume products, ideas and time. We'll come back to this in greater depth in the next chapter.

The innate fear of the Chaos of death also drives some people towards productivity, and not just in the economic sense. Indeed, there are those – not necessarily religious or spiritual – who wish to leave this life with a lasting legacy, something that will endure for others after their departure. As a result, by engaging in philanthropy, volunteering, hard work, and artistic and innovative activities (such as writing books), we may feel better about our ending. Such cases are not missing. Bill Gates and Warren Buffet have been widely publicized for giving a significant gift through the Gates

Foundation, which focuses on global health and education initiatives. Steve Jobs has left a tangible legacy in his Apple brand, transforming the way people communicate and consume media. William Shakespeare, meanwhile, inspired millions of students and artists with his plays, which continuing to be performed and studied to this day. The list could go on indefinitely, including great names and anonymous people who have left their mark on this world, for a limited time, or forever.

This dualistic dynamic, which has lubricated the workings of society and economy since the dawn of time, does not tag anyone with a consumer or producer label. The categorization is not that strict. We know about super-producers in the media, in history and all around us. Perhaps less well known are the super-consumers who now number in the millions. But there's often a bit of both in each of us, even if deep down we all want to contribute, whether in a grandiose way like Elon Musk or just by raising children properly, so as to have that feeling of satisfaction towards the end of our lives, that sense of meaning as Holocaust survivor Viktor Frankl would put it.

The fact that we are conscious of a life end, since we can feel the passage of time, unlike other dynamic agents *a priori,* implies a magical awareness of the passage of time. We have understood, or at least sensed, at a given moment or over a given period of our evolution, that the past is certain (what has happened and has already happened), and that the future is a mental illusion that does not yet exist, and may never exist for some, and that finally, the present is between the two halves of this dualistic past/future pair.

At the heart of the universal fabric, **time is something of the invisible maestro of every Order** on Earth and beyond. If religious myths are to be believed, Adam and Eve, having been cast out of timeless paradise to embody a finite and perishable life, had to incrementally improve their talent for planning, anticipating the hidden dangers of the following night, and learning from the mistakes of the night before. Since then, Man has begun to structure and standardize time on an ever-finer scale.

Hunter-gatherers, like plants and animals, relied on the pre-established cosmic Order in space to organize their hunting, travel and rest schedules, which were probably less hectic than those of modern Man. With the Agricultural Revolution, it seemed important to plan agricultural seasons such as planting, growing and harvesting crops. As societies grew in population, a shared standard was needed to organize tasks, wars and rituals. By exploiting the cycles of the Sun, Moon and stars, our ancestors innovated calendars and methods of measuring time.

The oldest known calendar is the lunar calendar, dating back to several thousand years BC. It is based on the cycles of the Moon and was used by many ancient civilizations to measure time. In ancient Egypt, the lunar calendar was used, but was later replaced by the solar calendar, known as the Egyptian calendar. By observing the movements of the Sun, this calendar was divided into three main seasons, linked to agriculture and the Nile: flood, growth and harvest. Relatively similar in structure to our Roman calendar, the Egyptian calendar had 365 days, plus a leap year every four years. They also divided the day into 24 hours and the hour into smaller units. The ancient Egyptians, talented mathematicians and astrologers, used sundials, obelisks and shadow clocks to keep track of time during the day, and water and fire clocks at night.

The ancient Mayans of Mesoamerica also used an interlocking calendar system that followed the cycles of the Sun, Moon and Venus. Similarly, the ancient Greeks used a system of time measurement based on the cycles of the Sun and Moon. They divided the day into 24 hours and used sundials, water clocks and hourglasses to measure time. They also divided the year into 12 months, according to the cycles of the Moon. Other ancient cultures, such as the Chinese, Babylonians and Romans, developed their own time measurement and calendar systems.

With the passing of time and the growing complexity of human societies and interactions, Man, in his ongoing quest for perfect Order, has had to innovate more sophisticated devices, such as the hourglass, the pendulum clock and the quartz clock, for greater precision and a common measure of time by and for all. Sometimes, in science as in other specialized fields, there's no question of limiting ourselves to the mesh of a second. Atomic clocks, such as the hydrogen maser, the mercury ion clock, the optical clock, or even the most common type, the cesium clock, use the vibrations of cesium atoms to clock time to the nearest femtosecond, equivalent to one-millionth of a billionth of a second, i.e., one zero followed by 15 zeros then 1 after the decimal point. Atomic clocks are widely used in applications such as GPS navigation, telecommunications and scientific research. They are also used to set the official time, Coordinated Universal Time (UTC). UTC was the idea of Canadian Sir Sandford Fleming, adopted by the International Meridian Conference in 1884. With the expansion of international collaboration and travel since the first Industrial Revolution, there was an urgent need to divide the Earth into 24 time zones towards the end of the 19th century, to make it easier for people to coordinate their activities, and for trains and telegraphs to program and synchronize their services.

Finally, another important lever in humanity's transition from a globally high entropy to a more predictable state lies in **institutions**. These groupings of humans and processes, formally formed for a specific purpose, or programmed by default into our genes, have played a decisive role in preserving social cohesion and stability.

As with chimpanzees and bees, kinship-based societies are one of the pre-agricultural forms of institution. This informal institution, known as "the big family", reflects the network of relationships between individuals based on common ancestry or marriage. It has therefore helped to maintain the Order by fostering a sense of belonging and shared identity among group members. For example, in many traditional societies, kinship ties are used to regulate access to land and other resources. For example, the Akan of Ghana and the Minangkabau of Indonesia regulate inheritance through the maternal line. Moreover, kinship has often influenced social norms and values in many societies. Certain roles and responsibilities also pass from one generation to the next, such as caring for the elderly or the structured transmission of knowledge.

Within this framework, imaginary but socially anchored concepts tend to limit disorder, pushing communities to conform to a single, socially accepted pattern. The sense of shame, for example, has been applied to impose social norms and subtly punish individuals who deviate from them in that large family, tribe, village or other conservative environment. In practice, individuals who engage in behavior deemed unacceptable may be publicly humiliated in order to correct their behavior. In the words of the great philosopher Immanuel Kant, "The gaze of others is a constraint that reminds me of my own existence and reminds me that my actions have consequences for myself and for others." As it happens, in many countries, particularly those with a strong religious imprint, such as my native Morocco, premarital sex, alcohol consumption and disrespect for parents are considered shameful, *"hchouma"*. This would go as far as public humiliation, ostracism from the community and even physical punishment in some regions, especially for women.

As human societies shifted from hunting and gathering to agriculture, new, more formal forms of institution emerged. The rise of sedentary agricultural societies led to the development of complex social hierarchies and political systems, which helped maintain order by providing a framework for resource distribution and conflict resolution. One of the earliest examples is the development of the notion of the state in ancient civilizations such as Egypt and Mesopotamia. The state was a central authority capable of imposing harmony, even conformity, first by force, then later by laws, regulations and other sub-institutions such as the legal system and the army.

The growth of trade led to the development of markets, which helped to regulate the exchange of goods and services. The innovation of money, and later of financial institutions, also favored the Social Order by facilitating trade and reducing the need for barter. The latter process could be time-consuming and difficult to transport, as you had to find someone who had what you wanted, and who wanted what you had. As a result, money is more predictable in terms of its value, and therefore its purchasing power. The industrial and scientific revolutions brought about changes in the organization of societies and the institutions that support them. The rise of industrial production contributed to structuring the notion of work, with a well-defined process, for example, in factories, and hours to be respected by each employee.

The demographic growth of cities also led to the development of new institutions, such as urban planning to manage the allocation of urban areas, government, police and courts to manage conflicts, public and tax administrations, all of which, along with many others, drew lines on what is permitted or possible and what is not, a kind of "social contract" to limit Chaos, to borrow this concept from the Enlightenment thinker, David Hume. Many philosophers and political theorists of the enlightenment era contributed to building a global framework securing more social Order. We can mention J.J. Rousseau with his reference "The Social Contract", or Thomas Hobbes' Leviathan, which argues that human beings are inherently self-interested and driven by a desire for self-preservation, leading to conflicts of interests, then conflicts in short. According to Hobbes, to escape this state of nature, individuals must voluntarily submit to a governing authority, referred to as the Leviathan, that can establish and maintain Order.

Hobbes turned to be right to some extent. The 20th century was not only one of the bloodiest periods in human history, with its two great wars, but also the era of a new world Order. The United States had officially gained the upper hand geopolitically and economically. As a result, new forms of **global institutions** emerged. Organizations such as the European Union, the United Nations, NATO, the World Trade Organization (WTO) and the International Monetary Fund (IMF) were created to accentuate international collaboration, with a key role in maintaining peace and stability, promoting economic growth and cooperation between nations, and solving global problems such as poverty, inequality and climate change.

Indeed, the exchange of goods, services and other aid is a simpler, less militarized way of keeping the peace in the face of the destructive appetites of a few leaders. That said, such institutions are rarely 100 percent neutral and would implicitly reinforce the current power structure. In his book, *Confessions of an Economic Hit Man*, John Perkins, a former American economist working for international economic institutions, reveals how major nations, notably the USA, exploit developing countries by indebting them massively in economic liberalization projects. In other words, a country such as Indonesia or Tunisia borrowing funds from the IMF would be obliged to follow the institution's economic (and political) recommendations, so that it could repay its debt in the future, hence a worldwide transition from an Order based on military power, to one that is peaceful yet imposed economically.

Now that we've gone into sufficient detail about this dualistic Order/Chaos duo, which lies at the heart of all innovative transformation, there's a little nuance to grasp. If we refocus on the Taiji diagram representing Yin & Yang, we notice a small white dot in the black Yin and a black dot in the white Yang. This symmetrical color scheme is not philosophically arbitrary. The concept of duality is rarely exclusive. There are plenty of grey areas where the two notions intermingle. Chaos can arise from Order, just as Order can be seen within Chaos.

Let's move on to our direct experience of the Matrix. Consult the table of content at the beginning of this book. Do you perceive any kind of vertical wave, downward-turning fish or other familiar shape? How about the title of this very section you're reading right now, The Illusion of Order, made up of three "I's, three "L's or a mixture of both? Or is it simply the Roman version of the number 3? Whatever it is, it doesn't really matter to your brain. You've understood and probably read "the illusion of order" because it's part of the basic functioning of your biological processor, your brain: **detecting Order within Chaos**.

Do you remember the millions of times you've taken your smartphone out of your pocket and placed it in front of your face to unlock it? Thanks to this facial recognition technique, we've also programmed our phones to detect and classify faces just as we do. Algorithmically, this function uses your camera to capture your face. The unlocking software then uses geometric mapping to determine unique facial features, such as the distance between eyes, nose and mouth, and then creates a digital code, called a "template", that represents these facial features. The new template is then compared with templates stored in the database, and if it matches a stored template, the phone is unlocked in milliseconds. In more recent smartphones, the process has been enhanced by the introduction of 3D sensors and artificial intelligence, enabling the phone to recognize a face in different lighting conditions, even when the person is wearing glasses and partially masked.

Like your smartphone, our brain automatically organizes features (eyes, nose, mouth, etc.) into a familiar pattern, enabling us to identify the person in sight quickly because mostly subconsciously. Other dynamic agents have specific gifts in this respect. Dogs use smells and sounds to distinguish their master. Ants and bees mainly emit chemical signals in the form of pheromones to recognize their colonies and communicate. Humans use their five (or six, with memory) senses to apprehend the world, vision first and foremost. Homo sapiens, more than most mammals, has developed this visual superpower that enables it to spot its enemies and detect trustworthy people among hundreds of faces, notably via the fusiform gyrus, a part of the brain responsible for face recognition. A study published in the journal *Science* in 2009 revealed that humans has specialized neural networks in the brain's visual cortex that are activated when a person sees a repetitive pattern or a familiar object. Let's play a mental game in this regard.

Let's call your best friend: Sam. You love Sam (platonically) and have shared a common history since you were young. You know all his secrets, long-term goals and states of humor. A great relationship! Now, imagine that Sam's twin brother, the perfect Sam look-alike, shows up at your door, alone. Let's call him Jesus. It's the one secret Sam's been keeping from you all these years. Would you be able to recognize the deception? Probably not at first. But if you were to start discussing yesterday's soccer match, the likelihood of detecting the imposture would increase. You might notice a particular tic, a singular scar or a different style of dress from Sam's. However, if Jesus, with Sam's native voice, had practiced imitating Sam's body language before knocking on your door, you'd still be acting as if nothing had happened. Your doubts might increase if shared memories are lost, for example, when Jesus strangely doesn't remember the present he gave you on your last birthday. This would first hurt you emotionally, then call into question Sam's memory and even identity. Finally, when he starts using new vocabulary or doesn't understand acronyms shared throughout your friendship, Jesus will undoubtedly reveal himself. If this wasn't consciously detected, your subconscious would detect Chaos (Jesus) in this illusory Order (Sam) and sense the slight difference between the twins, sending you alarm signals in the form of stress hormones or a feeling of unease.

This unlikely story of the unlikely twins, Sam & Jesus, is inspired by the paradox of Theseus' ship, also known as the problem of identity, attributed to the ancient Greek philosopher Plutarch. The story features the ship of a Greek hero called Theseus, whose parts are gradually replaced over time due to wear and tear. Eventually, by the time it reaches its destination port, every part of the ship has been replaced, begging the question: does the ship remain the same, despite the continual changes to its components? I suspect that for the proud captain of this ship, the question doesn't even arise. Similarly, Sam's delusion is rooted in the belief that an individual is a unified and singular entity, an ordered and unique structure. For you, Sam is not his body, his language or his behaviors. He's not his memory or his mode of dress. He is all these things, but more. One of the ways this idea is often expressed is through the psychic concept of the ego. However, this biological Order is far from fixed in space-time. In the words of Heraclitus, a pre-Socratic philosopher adhering to a constant flow in the universe: "**No Man walks in the same river twice, for it is not the same river and it is not the same Man.**"

As in yoga, breathe deeply and concentrate on your body. It's made up of various cells, molecules and atoms that come together to create the illusion of a single body. In fact, thousands of diverse components are constantly evolving inside you, right now, to support what we call a "life". An organ is built by techniques foreign to the human mind. Unlike a house made of external bricks, an entire organ can be born from a single cell. It's as if a house were built from a magic brick, and then began to make other bricks. Without an architect or project manager, each cell knows what it has to do and when, following an integrated genetic plan. The bricks can even metamorphose to fit windows, doors and other parts of the house. So, the whole body is not set in stone. You ten years ago is almost totally different from You today. All your atoms and cells have already been replaced. Check your environment too. Every millisecond, everything changes. Everything. Not just moving objects like the Sun and the blood in your veins, but literally everything, at various paces. What appear to be static objects undergo depreciation and fatigue. This is Chaos interwoven with Order, in varying degrees of predictability.

This kind of discussion, although relatively geeky and unsettling for you maybe, is not just a metaphysical delusion. Indeed, some philosophers and neuroscientists even argue that this "self" is nowhere to be found, but rather a collection of organs, experiences, memories and thoughts that come together to create the illusion of a single "me". Recent research adds oil to the fire. In the body, our cells are constantly renewing themselves. For example, it is estimated that every year, around 98 percent of the atoms in the human body are replaced. Our skin cells regenerate approximately every two to four weeks, while our liver cells are renewed every six to twelve months. Neurologically, the connections between neurons in our brain are constantly evolving. This cerebral plasticity enables the brain to adapt and reconfigure itself according to our experiences and learning. Playing a musical instrument increases the density of neuronal connections in certain regions. On a psychological level, our personalities, beliefs and values can also evolve over time as a result of our experiences, relationships and personal development. Personality development theories, such as Erik Erikson's theory of psychosocial development, maintain that our identity develops and changes throughout our lives. We just make up Order in our minds.

When you fly over a city, notice the Order of lights, streets, etc. The same goes for a forest, a sea or a planet. Generally speaking, the more you zoom out, the more your brain perceives a recognizable and maybe admirable structure. The same is true for humans: the further we zoom out, the more we can use the statistical law of large numbers to detect macro-patterns for predicting traffic conditions, the occupancy rate of an establishment or restaurant, or the results of an election. Because of our social nature, we tend to organize ourselves into groups and follow what most people choose. Between a full restaurant and an empty one, we'd probably rather join the queue. That said, if you zoom in on a particular person, you'll see a large number of non-conforming variables linked to his or her background, genes, experiences, and so on. The Chaos of increased individualism is hidden beneath the Order of social conformity. Let's note this interesting duality in passing.

To perceive Order in the midst of Chaos sometimes belongs to the realm of beauty. This is often the case in the arts, as in the unforgettable experience of flamenco in Madrid. This passionate, fiery dance originated in southern Spain, blending the creativity of gypsies, Spanish culture and Arab rhythms. The dancers, usually dressed in traditional outfits, move with precision and grace, stamping their feet and clapping their hands to the rhythm of the music.

Despite its improvised nature, the Order in Flamenco dancing is evident in the choreography and structure of the show. The dance consists of a series of complex footwork movements performed in a precise order. Dancers move in sync with each other and with the musical rhythm, executing each step with precision and control. Flamenco dancers also use their arms to create fluid, graceful movements, adding to the dance's aesthetic appeal. One of the most striking elements of flamenco is the use of castanets, small hand-held percussion instruments that dancers play to reinforce the rhythm of the music. The unpredictability of flamenco dance is felt in the way dancers use their bodies to express their emotions and tell a story through dance, facial expressions and body language, exposing feelings of joy, sadness and passion.

That said, if you record this dance in very short video sequences and watch them separately, messy would be the most appropriate description. (1) There's a sad, spontaneous grimace, a scream in the background and a heel striking the wooden floor. Similarly, if I had randomly selected a group of spectators in Madrid and asked (rather urged) them to go and play flamenco on stage, the improvised result would have been... awful (2) What's more, if a monkey could perceive the world as we do, could talk and had witnessed the original professional performance, it too would have described it as... awful. (3) If it could have chosen, it would probably have watched a National Geographic documentary or Candy Crush with falling bananas instead of 'candies'. This little parenthesis I've just opened can be explained respectively by:

1. For us humans, the whole is generally more orderly and beautiful than its parts, when done with passion and expertise of course. Think of the body and a leg, a perfume and one of its (nasty) chemical components, a company and a business unit, the sky and a particular cloud. The

more complex a system, the more we expect it to drift into chaos. If it doesn't, we call it brilliant, because Order was the most unlikely result of mixing various subsystems.

2. Assembling pieces haphazardly, without any prior skills or plans, rarely achieves a state of admirable Order. Putting together a flamenco band with people who haven't known each other for at least a few years, or who don't have the necessary dancing skills, won't sell. Nobody can drink a strawberry, soy sauce and potato smoothy. Great companies are built with a fair share of skilled people and team players. That's why, according to many analysts, the human resources department is one of the most important support functions for a company's success.

3. Let's not forget that beyond its thermodynamic definition, Order remains subjective. In other words, it depends on the observer, the subject. If it's clear that a monkey's perception of Order is not the same as a human's, this same perception also differs between individuals. My personal experience of Order, like flamenco, the Champs-Élysées on a Sunday morning, or waterfalls in Iceland, might not be shared by you, depending on your history, hobbies and prejudices. Of course, everyone, except the monkey perhaps, would approve of the orderly structure of some products, such as an iPhone, a Mercedes or just a table.

There's an artistic subtlety to Chaos's part in Order and vice versa. Indeed, a dosage, or "fine-tuning", seems necessary for an interesting, even impressive result, at least from a human perspective. Consider the following poetic proposals. Which do you prefer?

a. The cat sat on the carpet, Eating fish and wearing a hat, Then it took off and flew like a bat, Leaving behind him a trail of splashes.

b. The sky is blue, The grass is green, The sun is bright, The world is beautiful.

c. The beauty of nature, serene and luminous, Skies painted day and night. A rhythm flows through all we see, An artistic dance of harmony.

It's clear that Option A is very chaotic and clearly doesn't follow any pattern. We can easily detect the latter in Option B, but it seems very organized, bordering on the boring, with a repetitive subject-verb-complement structure. Without a doubt, option C stands out for its elegance, albeit modest, striking a fine balance between Chaos and Order, creativity and structure, feeling and tonality, fun and boredom.

As shown in the figure above, there is thus, according to this example and many others, a point or interval that we'll call X_{max}, the sweet spot between absolute Chaos and total Order, between insignificant arbitrariness and perfect predictability, which would maximize the *Value* or appreciation of the *innovation* in question.

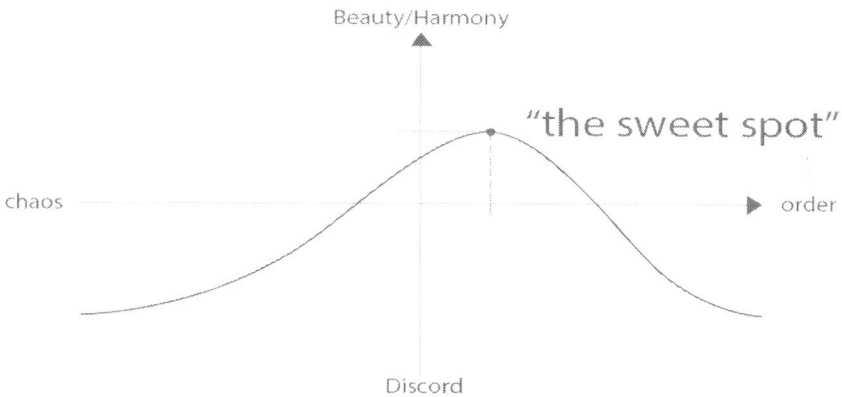

To visualize this latest blend of philosophy and math, feel free to reminisce about romantic dates past, or those of a friend. We can all agree that an awkward Geek in pajamas, with fingernails a few weeks old, living with his mother and spending most of his time in gamer mode or binge-watching series on Netflix probably wouldn't make an ideal "date". In other words, the unknown X would be somewhere on the far left of the above graph.

On the reverse side of this situation, if this date involved a perfect gentleman or princess, with a charming and fit physique, a great job and unshakeable self-confidence, throughout the two hours your date lasted, chances are it wouldn't be the best date of your life either. No drops of drink or sauce on the table; no awkward jokes, or no jokes at all, as this could ruin his or her toned skin; owning the latest iPhone whose color matches the earrings or belt; no risky exchanges or deep discussions, so just "small talk". He or she will even insist on halving the bill to the nearest cent. The latter is relatively better than the first, chaotic scenario. That said, if you're an emotionally and mentally balanced person, it's highly likely that this "perfect guy" or "flawless girl" won't be spontaneous enough and too rigid and excessively orderly for you. Hence the demands of heterosexual women, which men find hard to understand, for a Man_{max} who's tall without being twice her height, intelligent but not too intellectual, stylish without being pretentious, fun and playful yet respectful, and so on.

Like a date ruined by an excess of Order or Chaos, failing or poorly managed companies are easy to spot. Some are swimming in a sea of paperwork, useless or unused data, with an unstable board at the top and a misalignment of strategic vision with operational plan. Still others, mainly start-ups, devote considerable effort and budget to researching inventive ideas that are not profitable in the short term. On the other hand, the Order's super-structured companies are more like monopolies than American tech giants. With a rigid matrix organization, where a boss's boss (the L+1 of the L+1 in managerial jargon) validates every decision, these companies often end up becoming "cash cows" trying to save their market share against competitors who are more chaotic because they are innovative.

Writing these lines from the immigration office at Mumbai airport, I can describe a real-life situation where too much Order led to dissatisfaction and a pointless waste of time (mine in this case). I've been in the waiting room for five hours because I forgot to apply for a tourist visa before landing in India. I mistakenly thought that an e-visa on arrival was possible, especially for a stay of just three nights. Assuming my responsibility for this journey, I provided proof of my hotel reservation, the ticket for my next flight to Thailand, and a host of personal and professional information. Even so, the chain of command was quite military in scale and above human rationalization. Indeed, it makes sense, despite its protectionist aspect, to regulate immigration in order to protect local access to the labor market and keep wages relatively high. On the other hand, it is downright stupid not to accept short-stay tourists out of respect for a bureaucratic procedure whose purpose and content are probably outdated.

So, whether it's a company, a state institution or a romantic date, achieving the X_{max} comes down to finding the right balance between rigid processes and flexible initiatives. For example, Alphabet, known for its core product Google, offers its employees one independent day a week to work on the project of their choice. This is how Gmail was born. Other companies offer remote collaboration as a new way of working. These same flexible companies employ skilled project managers or collaborative tools to ensure that work is always delivered on time. **Balance is essential** in navigating the Matrix with elegance and love.

PRINCIPLE 4:
The Perfect balance

Balinese culture, located in Indonesia, is a fascinating and unique treasure. From experience, when visiting one of the country's 17,000 islands – making it the world's largest archipelago – one of the following descriptions or hashtags is likely to come to mind: warm hospitality, spiritual art, spellbinding music, majestic temples, traditional dances, and colorful offerings. There is a blend of Hindu and Muslim beliefs that influences every aspect of life, from family to religious rituals.

To celebrate the Balinese New Year, often during the months of March and April, the Barong and Rangda ceremonies are held in several major cities. The name of this popular ritual is inspired by two mythical characters in Balinese culture who represent the eternal battle between good and evil. Barong is a lion-like creature representing good, while Rangda is a witch symbolizing evil. During these festivals, Barong and Rangda are often represented in the form of masks, which are worn during ceremonial dances featuring their epic battle.

The ceremony begins with a procession of musicians and dancers, led by Barong. Barong is usually accompanied by two or more dancers, who manipulate the creature's body and head with ropes and sticks. As the procession continues, Rangda is introduced into the dance, accompanied by her disciples, who are usually represented in the form of a group of witches or demons. In the traditional version of the dance, Rangda uses her supernatural powers to cast spells and control the Barong dancers, urging them to attack Barong. However, Barong is eventually able to defeat Rangda and her followers, symbolizing the triumph of good over evil. Viewers of such shows, like those of Marvel hero movies, expect or even look forward to these "happy endings". The hero, often tall, white and unfailingly patriotic, represents good, and sooner or later eliminates the forces of evil.

If we follow the principle of Yin and Yang and its Hindu dualist counterparts, Rangda should be resurrected from darkness for a later sequel to the show. Likewise, evil surprises would still be in store for the Marvel anti-hero for a second and perhaps nth volume of a lucrative saga. As you can see, if evil or Yin is dead forever, there would be no more good nor Yang, no more eternal duality. A paradox for this wisely ancient concept. In reality, duality should not only be interpreted as a purely conflicting opposition, but also, or rather, as two forces that balance and nourish one another. In perpetual motion, they continually transform and impact each other. For example, when daylight reaches its peak (Yang), it begins to wane, giving way to night (Yin). In summer, the day expands in length and intensity, dominating its opposite, which in turn takes over the following winter. It's an ad infinitum cycle in dynamic equilibrium. Having detailed each side of the Taiji diagram (Principles 1 and 2), then the small part of black in the white of Yang and vice versa (Principle 3), it's time to conclude with the discreet but primordial line that divides this dualistic duo, ensuring its **balance over time**.

Yin & Yang   The Maori Takarangi   Endless Knot   The Celtic Double Spiral

Similar representations of this cyclicity exist through other symbols. The Māori, the indigenous people of New Zealand, are typically known by the Māori takarangi. This ancestral symbol, important in Māori culture and art, is a spiral design that represents the interconnectedness of all living beings, as well as the importance of understanding one's own ancestry and place in the universe. Like the balanced forces of Yin & Yang, the takarangi's spiral shape symbolizes the cyclical nature of life, from growth to decline. According to Māori tradition, all living beings are linked by a complex web of relationships that goes back to the creation of our Matrix. The takarangi thus represents the flow of energy and the life force that connects them.

Another manifestation of this balancing act can be found in Celtic mythology, dating back to the Iron Age (1000 BC), and originating with the Celtic peoples who once inhabited vast areas of Europe, including Ireland, Scotland, Wales, Brittany and parts of Spain and France. The Celts believed in a spiritual world populated by gods, goddesses and other supernatural beings and aggregated many of these beliefs into the symbol of the Celtic double spiral, which is associated with the goddess Brigid, deity of fertility, healing and poetry. Brigid is often depicted holding a staff topped by a double spiral, symbolizing the constant flow of life, death and regeneration. The spiral can also be interpreted as representing natural cycles, such as the seasons and the phases of the Moon. Note that these spirals move in opposite directions but are intrinsically linked to each other, creating a perception of dynamic balance.

Let's finish this symbolic tour with the endless knot, another famous motif of great significance in Buddhist philosophy and art. This concept is often explained using the example of the "chain of causality", a basic principle in the philosophy of the Buddha and his disciples. This describes the world as a succession of causes and effects, one thing leading to another, creating a cycle that perpetuates itself ad infinitum. The endless knot is often depicted as a pattern of interlocking lines forming a closed loop with no beginning or end, a complex and intricate design with no single point of departure or arrival, representing the idea that all things are interconnected, and the cyclical yet infinite nature of existence.

The great religions also express this dualistic cyclicity through mythical stories of their own deities, prophets and sages. In this case of Hinduism, for instance, the Hindu Trinity, also known as Trimūrti, represents the three main aspects of the divine principle: **creation, preservation and destruction**. As such, each of the three gods that make up this Trinity possesses characteristics, roles and attributes that contribute to one or more phases of this eternal cycle. Unsurprisingly, this process can also be found in Schumpeter's description of innovation as a creative destruction.

Brahma, the Creator, is the first member of the Hindu Trinity. He is often depicted with four heads, symbolizing the four Vedas, the sacred texts of Hinduism. Brahma is responsible for the creation of the universe, including all living beings and creatures. He forms the basic structure and framework of the Matrix, according to Hindus, paving the way for the other two members of the trinity to fulfill their roles.

Vishnu, the preserver, is typically the one who ensures that the universe and all living beings continue to exist and prosper. He is often depicted holding a disc, a conch shell and a mace, representing his protective powers. Symbolically, Vishnu takes on various incarnations, or avatars, to protect the world from the forces of evil and restore dynamic balance when it is disrupted. Brahma and Vishnu are, in a way, on the side of creation and the renewal of universal, earthly Order, although Vishnu also has a foot on the Chaos side.

To balance and complete this eternal quest, Lord Shiva, also known as Mahadeva, is one of Hinduism's most important deities. He is often depicted with a third eye, set in the middle of his forehead, representing his ability to see beyond the physical world. Shiva is best known for his destructive power, considered necessary for the process of regeneration and renewal. In this sense, his destructive nature is not seen as negative, as cultural ceremonies or Marvel movies would suggest, but rather as a necessary aspect of the cyclical nature of all things.

The Abrahamic religions – Judaism, Christianity and Islam – are also built on stories of Order and Chaos. All the holy books of these great sects emphasize the unlimited divine power of creation and destruction on Earth and beyond, since the dawn of time. In other words, like the concept of the Tao or Dao in Chinese Taoism, God, Allah or Elohim can effortlessly facilitate a pretty and predictable structure of objects in the Matrix, including us, just as he has every capacity to annihilate them. Some see the devil as a disruptive force, of course, but in most holy books, the devil is, in theory, just a disobedient angel, always under the command of God, the Ultimate Artist of the universe and all that's in it.

These last words are echoed in the Book of Genesis. God creates the world out of Chaos, separating light from darkness, waters above from waters below, and land from sea. In the Book of Exodus, God frees the Israelites from slavery in Egypt and leads them away from Pharaonic punishment to the Promised Land. In the book of Isaiah (44:24), it is written: "For I am the Lord, who created the heavens, who formed the earth and all that is in it. I did it alone, and what I did, I did wisely. It is I who stretched out the heavens and put the earth in place". In Islam, we find a similar pattern of course, with a few divergences. As expressed in verse (41:11) of the Qur'an "(Allah) created the heavens and the earth in six days. His throne was on water, to test which of you would act best". On other occasions, it has been pointed out that if other gods existed alongside God, the Earth and heavens would sink into Chaos (The Prophets 21:22).

This creative role of God is balanced in many other verses, from those reflecting the punishment of Adam and Eve for disobeying Him, to other prophets like Noah (Nuh), who was sent to warn his people of the impending chaotic flood, due to their depravity and disobedience to divine laws. God or Allah deserves, absolutely, his 99 pious names in Islam, *Asmaul Husna*, each reflecting a different aspect of his dualistic manifestation to us. Some of these labels therefore reflect Chaos and Anger, such as Al-Muntaqim (the Avenger), Al-Jabbar (the Compeller) and Al-Qahhar (the Submissive), while others advocate Order and Compassion, namely Ar-Rahman (the Merciful), Ar-Rahim (the Compassionate) and Al-Wadud (the Loving).

Beyond (or below) divinities, let's take a look at the dualistic equilibrium in a company's strategic context as well. In 1958, James March and Herbert Simon published a groundbreaking paper entitled *Organizations*, aimed at understanding how organizations function, adapt and learn in complex environments. Like Geoffrey Hinton in the field of AI, these two renowned researchers adopted an interdisciplinary approach, integrating ideas from economics, psychology and sociology into their work. In the aforementioned article, they proposed the concepts of **exploitation and exploration** within companies. This dualistic paradigm suggests a balanced distribution of operational activities – a focus on products already on sale bringing the most profit (exploitation), and innovation or R&D to anticipate future opportunities (exploration). Put another way, "exploit" means managing the company's day-to-day business as effectively as possible, producing and delivering the product or service to the customer efficiently, and with rapid time-to-market.

For example, the iPhone and Mac account for over 50 percent of Apple's sales. It therefore makes sense to continue investing in these products in terms of marketing and incremental innovation, through new versions of iOS, better screens, gadgets and additional features. Nevertheless, Apple must continue to innovate radically beyond its current product range and actively monitor Chinese and Korean competition. This is what we call exploration. This last facet of business involves taking risks and investing in something that doesn't bear fruit at the moment, in the hope (or planning) that one day it will pay off the development costs and beyond, enriching the company's shareholders in the process. This is the gamble Tesla is taking by devoting a large portion of its capital to the development of fully autonomous driving software. This would be a Level 4 or 5 vehicle according to the Society of Automotive Engineers (SAE). This means you can hop in your Parisian "Teslaber" and ask it: "Hey, Tesla, take me to 22 Avenue Foch", then take a nap or work remotely on one of the many rear seats (no need for a front seat anymore), while waiting for your driverless Taxi to reach its destination.

As with any balancing act, whether in yoga or in dualistic philosophy, the challenge is to find it first, and then keep it over time, especially when that **balance is dynamic**. In this respect, and still in the world of business, "the innovator's dilemma", a term coined by professor Clayton Christensen, represents the strategic but difficult decision to allocate what portion of resources (human, financial, physical, etc.) to an uncertain exploration, at the expense of a lucrative current exploitation. Expressed temporally, the innovator's dilemma encapsulates a constant imbalance between present and future, between certainty and possibility, between today's Order and tomorrow's Chaos. Indeed, in a capitalist context, a company that does nothing but exploit is condemned to future disruption by an audacious start-up, like what Tesla is doing to the automotive industry. On the other hand, a company unbalanced towards the exploratory side would probably be a start-up in search of the next big thing, or a dying cash cow that has no choice but to find or imitate the next big thing, such as Nokia shortly after the arrival of the iPhone on the cell phone market.

We're not always aware of it, but this dualistic calibration goes on in our brains all the time, often expressed in words, though hidden between the lines. When people say something is dark, it unconsciously means it's darker than lighter versions. When people say something is cold, it would be below the cold of a freshly served cup of tea, and more lukewarm than a pack of ice cream. Verbs and their negations hide this linguistic duality. "Seeing" implies being aware of its existence, as opposed to blind ignorance. To "love" is to feel affection for someone, rather than indifference or hatred. The intensity of this would of course depend on the context and the interlocutors.

In short, if we take the ancient philosophies of Yin & Yang and the likes, the definition of success in so many fields, from *innovation* to communication, from love to cooking, **does not have to be visualized as an ascending line towards an ultimate goal**. The Western ideology of control and absolute Order has become widespread since the industrial and scientific revolutions. By dint of understanding the various variables of our Matrix, and innovating to suit it, Man has become unbalanced to the extent that setbacks and suffering of all kinds are no longer accepted in our so-called modern societies. If we believe in the cyclicality of the universe, and the interdependence of beings, it seems to me more ideal, individually and in groups, to aim for that famous X_{max} in the course of time, and thus find "our" right relationship between each dualistic peer.

Taking the previous examples, a given company needs to define, on a quarterly basis, according to the strategic objectives of its shareholders, its X_{max} budget and other resources, between exploitation and exploration. In the same way, a couple, for example, should question, from time to time, their X_{max} in terms of investment in a shared life versus respect for each other's individuality and freedom. Obviously, we need to re-establish an X_{max} between our insatiable desire to consume and what our beautiful Earth, with its various resources, is capable of providing periodically. This process of continuous balancing, aimed at optimizing the X_{max} of multiple life facets, I label "**The Straight Path**", drafted in the figure below, and inspired by the same Abrahamic metaphor and the Buddhist arcane symbol of Unalome, designating the optimal path between Order and Chaos, towards Nirvana and/or paradise, depending on beliefs.

Choreography	Exploitation	Commitment	Order	Technology	Gravitation	6 hours
Artistic dance	Business success	Love long-term	X_{max}	Radical innovation	Planet in orbit	Optimal sleep
Improvisation	Exploration	Passion	Chaos	Creativity	Rotation	10 hours

In order to avoid the same demagogic errors made by some theologians and sages, I recommend that you consider "the straight path" (rather than an ascending path), highlighted in grey above, not as a magic solution to all human problems, but as a supporting tool in the understanding of dualistic balances vis-à-vis nature, individuals and organizations. Moreover, I'd like to make clear that the search for the optimal balance X_{max} can be a long and arduous process, like most beautiful things in life by the way. Indeed, the notion of "straight" depicted in the figure above for simplicity sake, borrowed from ancient wisdom, should not be mistaken for linearity or rigidity. A more accurate representation can be seen in the serpentine shape of the line that divides the Yin and Yang halves of the Taijitu diagram. Life is often a dance between leaning towards one side of a dualistic pair and then adjusting towards the other, with swings depending on each person's context. This creates a continuous and dynamic play of balance, much like the art of slacklining. It is a constant exploration and adjustment, embracing the ebb and flow of opposing forces in order to find harmony and equilibrium.

As with an Indian meal of chicken masala, the wrong dosage of cumin, coriander, turmeric, garam masala or chili powder, and you'll end up dining on Uber Eats. Control or neglect your partner beyond a certain threshold, and you'll find yourself back on Tinder, and perhaps without dinner either. Again, context remains important to consider in this quest. In its early days, home-rental platform Airbnb had to focus on developing its user journey, adding hosts from all over the world, dealing with dissatisfied customers and so on. When Airbnb secured an important position in the tourism sector, its X_{max} logically had to move from increased exploration to much more exploitation of its mature product range.

Similarly, from 2003 to 2007, tennis star Novak Djokovic made little impression on spectators. He was in search of his game. He built his style through an innovative "Test & Learn" process, playing like a master in some matches, and like an amateur in others. Once he'd managed to adjust his game and emotions to the right gradient, with the help of his team *a priori*, a more stable phase followed, where his game remained at a near-constant level for years, allowing him to enter the legend of world tennis.

The most popular films, usually thrillers, are gripping thanks to a well-balanced combination of a good, clear script and effective actors, with a pinch of suspense and uncertainty in a few key scenes. Similarly, comedies and light-hearted jokes often rely on subtle interplay, bringing "comic surprise" to an anticipated sequence of words or actions in the minds of the receivers or viewers.

To tell the truth, I noticed this paradigm of the straight and narrow long before I integrated the various dualistic principles into my biological database, my memory. Photography, a passion I've been pursuing for years, had revealed its X_{max} in a gratifying way. In my early amateur days, I focused mainly on symmetrical, well-ordered frames, like the photo on the left-hand side below. One day, during a night photography session in Antibes on the French Riviera, wishing to photograph a statue, I started the countdown in my camera, which had been set up and stabilized to minimize the blurring typical of dark captures. Suddenly, someone walked in front of the camera, giving the result admired in the right-hand image below. Contrary to my presuppositions, this unpredictable element of

204 | WAVES AND DROPS

Chaos, plus the Full Moon serving as an eye, added a brilliant touch to the pre-established, inert order of the luminous statue. I had found my X_{max}. Later, I discovered that photographing a bit of Order in a pile of Chaos was just as beautiful as its dualistic opposite. So, imagine a messy scene in a congested city, with only one structured moment or event, such as a stationary person with a red umbrella in a sea of suits at 8 a.m. in New York City or Paris.

Still in the artistic field, music, played by man and other animals since time immemorial, is another use case for the concept of the straight path. Composing notes side by side, without creativity or expertise, will result in cacophony and nothing more. Remember, Chaos is the default option. A super-repetitive, therefore super-ordered, structure would still sound better than a two-year-old banging on a piano, but it would get boring after a while, like a jackhammer or the hum of a refrigerator. A good song is often a middle ground between these two extremes, structured yet allowing for artistic expression and creativity. Technically, it's made up of chorus. In many popular musical genres, such as pop, rock and hip-hop, the chorus is often repeated several times throughout the song, serving as its centerpiece and anchor. Verses and bridges, on the other hand, offer a change of melody and rhythm, adding variety and moving the story forward, representing the aspect of Chaos. A well-crafted song balances these elements and keeps the listener's emotional attention.

If you consciously listen to bird calls, you may notice similar patterns. Used as a means of vocal communication to attract mates, defend territories or communicate with other members of their species, the sounds they make vary considerably from one species to another (chirping, whispering, etc.). Nevertheless, what bird species have in common with human music is the interplay between repeated sounds and transitions to new sections. The figure below shows a breakdown of the Beatles' famous song, "Let It Be".

Verse

When i find myself in times of trouble mother Mary comes to me

Speaking words of wisdom, let it be

And in my hour of darkness she is standing right in front of me

Speaking words of wisdom, let it be

Chorus

Let it be, let it be, let it be, let it be

Whisper words of wisdom, let it be

The dynamic balance of the right path also applies to a crucial aspect of our lives: decision-making. The work of renowned psychologist and Nobel Prize winner Daniel Kahneman and his collaborator Amos Tversky has highlighted a dualistic pairing that comes into play every time we have to make a decision, big or small. Statistically, this concerns thousands of choices (free or programmed) every day. These two opposing but complementary systems, like each dualistic pair, are called **fast and slow systems**.

The fast system, also known as the intuitive system, is instinctive, linked to our reptilian brain. It reacts effortlessly to stimuli in the environment, enabling us to make quick decisions based on our emotions and intuitions. For example, when we automatically head for the coffee machine in the morning, or when we buy a muffin without hesitation. The other, slower pole, also known as the reflective system, is characterized by deeper reflection, rational analysis and decision-making based on logic and reason. It weighs up the pros and cons, evaluates the long-term consequences and makes informed decisions. Buying a house or choosing your next romantic partner falls into this category.

What's important is the optimum balance between these two systems. In some situations, a rapid, instinctive response is necessary to ensure our safety and survival. In others, taking the time to think, analyze and plan is essential to avoid costly mistakes. Imagine if, while driving, your slow system took over. Disaster! Because your slow system doesn't allow you to react instantly to changing road conditions, traffic lights and other drivers. However, this same slow system comes into play when we need to choose the most efficient route or decide whether to overtake now or later. Without this continuous dynamic equilibrium, we would sink into the Chaos of haphazard decisions or the endless Order of sterile rationalization.

From cognitive psychology to human biology, we are now all more or less aware of the value of a balanced diet. Indeed, balanced eating habits, in terms of calorie intake and micronutrient diversity, play a crucial role in our overall health and well-being. In practical terms, it's important to find the right balance between the number of calories we consume and those we expend to maintain a healthy weight and promote optimal body function. A balance that's simple to understand, but difficult to follow for so many overweight people, increasing the risk of developing health problems such as obesity, type 2 diabetes, heart disease and certain cancers. On the other hand, insufficient calorie consumption can lead to nutritional deficiency, fatigue and muscle weakness. The World Health Organization (WHO) recommends a daily calorie intake of around 2,000 to 2,500 for an average adult, but these figures may vary according to individual needs and habits.

Sleep is another natural pillar. There are enough scientific studies today to prove that the X_{max} for an individual in terms of sleep is around eight hours a day, or even better, a night. Chronic sleep deprivation is associated with an increased risk of developing long-term health problems, such as obesity, type 2 diabetes, cardiovascular disease and mood disorders such as depression and anxiety. Studies have shown that sleep deprivation can also negatively affect our cognitive functioning, including memory, learning and decision-making. Too much sleep isn't optimal either. Studies have shown that sleeping too long can be associated with an increased risk of heart disease, diabetes, obesity and premature mortality. What's more, excessive sleep can cause feelings of lethargy, reduced motivation and even lead to mood disorders such as depression.

I'm almost done, promise! The right path is also found in the second dimension of the Matrix, in this case in plants and animals, commonly referred to as **the principle of symbiosis**. In nature, ideally far from human disturbance, what's remarkable is the close, interdependent relationship between two or more different species, where both partners mutually benefit. This relationship may be facultative (where the two species can survive independently) or obligatory (where the two species depend on each other for survival).

In symbiosis, the species involved can provide benefits such as protection, nutrition, transport, reproduction or seed dissemination. This cooperation enables species to survive and thrive in varied and often hostile environments. A classic example of symbiosis is the relationship between corals and zooxanthellae, single-celled microalgae. Corals provide safe shelter and nutrients for zooxanthellae, while the latter supply energy through photosynthesis. Another classic case is the association between plants and pollinating insects. Plants produce nectar to attract insects, which in turn carry pollen from one plant to another, thus promoting plant reproduction. Less well known is the symbiosis between intestinal bacteria and human beings. These "good" bacteria play a crucial role in human digestion, immunity and general health. These and many other examples underline the importance of symbiosis in maintaining ecological balance and biodiversity.

In astrophysics, a planet in a slightly elliptical orbit, such as the Earth around the Sun, or the Moon around the Earth, are in dynamic equilibrium. This is the magical result, described by Kepler in the 16th century, of a gravitational force pulling towards the heavier object, offset by a centrifugal force pulling the lighter cosmic object towards distant space.

Similarly, in the context of social relations, if you hate your job, it's because you're not in a constructive symbiotic relationship with your employer. Chances are that your daily agenda is out of balance. Such an imbalance might lean towards boredom, with repetitive tasks, or on the contrary, towards continuous pressure with stressful or uncertain projects. It could also be a question of salary. The anti-symbiotic gap therefore lies between your current added value, as assessed by your team or company, and your mental image of what you really deserve, based on your efforts and the value of your skills on the job market.

On a personal level, if your relationship with your life partner enters a cycle of simple "roommates", this could indicate a lack of uncertainty and too much structure in your life together. Breakfast at 8 a.m. Work from 9 a.m. to 6 p.m. Dinner at 8 p.m. Netflix at 9 p.m. Sleep at 11 p.m. The occasional predictable restaurant or weekend outing barely breaks the routine. How about a real Chaos, restoring balance by generating new flames? Have you tried disappearing for a few days without giving any sign of life? Have you even raised the possibility of a break-up or an open relationship? These actions, although socially radical, are sometimes necessary to optimize the symbiosis of love. Not an opinion of a couple therapist though!

A country's economy can also be studied through the lenses of the straight path paradigm. Indeed, the relationship between producers and consumers, in a given market or across all markets, plays an essential role in the stability and growth of any economic system. Suppose there are too many producers selling a similar product. The invisible hand of capitalism then suggests increasingly fierce competition, leading to a price war and a general drop in profit margins, to the point of near-zero profits. For example, in Bangkok, Thailand, I was surprised to see how cheap a massage session was, compared to France or Spain. Around $10 an hour. Given the sacred and healing aspect of Thai massage in the local culture, I thought prices were manipulated to keep them affordable for all classes. Nothing of the sort. Noticing a massage store in every nook and cranny, you come to realize the imbalance of supply and the competitive struggle to stay afloat.

On the other hand, an economy with too few producers leads to a concentration of power, or even to monopolies and consumer abuse. There is no shortage of examples in this regard. At the end of the 1990s, Microsoft held a monopoly on the computer software market, dominating the operating system and office software markets. This enabled it to control prices, limit consumer choice and stifle innovation. In many countries, a small number of telecoms companies control most of the market, resulting in high prices, limited choice and poor quality of service. It is therefore important to find an X_{max} between a liberal capitalism and a justified control of the flow of production.

TAKEAWAYS FROM THIS CHAPTER:

To sum up, with its wide range of applications, the concept of change finds its deep philosophical roots in **the dualistic balance** within our Matrix between two seemingly opposite but complementary poles: Chaos and Order, uncertainty and predictability, exploration and exploitation, excess and asceticism, and so on, in an infinite list. Although this dichotomy is arguably an illusion, a mental construct, it is nonetheless useful in helping us navigate the world and optimize our survival, societal collaboration and personal satisfaction. By observing many of life's situations, we can find an optimal balance between certainty and unpredictability, mastery and courage. At this level, we experience a harmonious equilibrium, a "perfect balance" where Order and Chaos synchronize.

Returning to the main theme, by approaching *innovation* through the lens of "the straight path" paradigm, an ambitious entrepreneur or intrapreneur would understand that a dance between Chaos and Order is paramount to success. More on this later. In the meantime, when I started writing this book, the structure and objectives were hazy, to say the least. I was in a state of mental Chaos. I'd start one chapter, then jump to another, depending on the mood of the day. One subject would be added, another ignored. As the days and weeks passed, darkness gave way to light, and more structure emerged. A new Order was born. Chaos may return later, of course, challenging the established Order, with a new book, a new edition, updated examples, or another channel of communication.

In the process of *innovation*, particularly within companies, Chaos and Order play different but equally important roles. Chaos is often the driving force behind change and new ideas. It represents a fertile ground for experimentation and exploration. Order, on the other hand, is needed to provide structure and stability. Once a new idea has been generated, it needs to be organized, refined and developed into a tangible product or solution. This requires a systematic approach involving planning, execution and repeated testing. So, like the divine, both creator and destroyer, the innovative process is an alternating cycle introducing Chaos into the pre-established Order, then putting Order into this new Chaos of creative thinking, to end up with a new, improved or more adapted solution to the needs of a certain context. That said, the extent of this dualistic dance of change obviously varies. The creation of a new sect, the launch of a connected watch, or the publication of a new food blog all require different efforts and resources.

Finally, innovators rarely launch from the same starting line. This book, for example, draws on references from a variety of academic, professional and personal sources. Chaos was not total at the start of my literary adventure. Steve Jobs and Steve Wozniak drew on existing computer technologies to create the Apple I computer and subsequently revolutionize the technology industry. Jeff Bezos launched Amazon on the basis of the existing Web 1.0 infrastructure, initially as an online bookstore, which has since expanded to include a wide range of products and services. Very often, there is a before, a base, ordered or scattered, to each new transformation.

Let's now delve into each of the five variables making up the right-hand side of the Fundamental Identity of Innovation.

CHAPTER III:

PLUNGING INTO
THE UNKNOWN

*"If you do what you've always done,
You'll get what you've always gotten" – Henry Ford.*

As I found myself once again immersed in the world of the Matrix, a feeling of déjà vu took hold of me. The labyrinthine streets, the grayish buildings, everything seemed so familiar, as if I'd been there before. I knew something was wrong, that this reality was a carefully crafted illusion. This time, however, I could perceive details that had previously eluded me. The virtual city unfolded before my eyes, with perfect order and symmetry. The dynamic agents moved with remarkable precision, their synchronized steps sounding like a mechanical symphony. Everything seemed to be unfolding according to a pre-established scenario, in a delicate balance between perfection and fantasy.

Suddenly, I was once again running through dilapidated streets, dodging the debris that littered the digital floor. They were the same predators as the previous episode, well-trained but infallible. No matter where I hid, these relatively well-coded agents always seemed to find me. Their determination was paradoxically admirable, and I wondered what their motivation was to chase me so ardently. Thinking back on my last sentence, I underlined the word "Motivation" and understood the logic of their code. These Matrix agents, although powered by enhanced programs, also seemed to operate on a similar principle as any limited static agent. All the latter cared about was slowing down its countdown. My hunters, on the other hand, expressed, through their tireless running, a fundamental code limitation through their unbending "Need" to maintain the Order and stability of the Matrix, to make sure that everything worked as planned. Consequently, they were prepared to do anything to neutralize my unbalancing intrusion into their perfect world.

Nevertheless, this same Need seemed to be a driving force behind an admirable innovativeness. In fact, some of these special agents were using hunting tools that I hadn't noticed anywhere else. They had clearly developed special skills, an ability to innovate new objects from the Matrix's scattered materials. Their Motivation to excel in their task had thus pushed them to explore their potential, to go beyond the limits of their initial programming. They were the artisans of this virtual reality, capable of bringing to life objects and scenes not foreseen in the initial scenario. These creative agents were rare, but their very existence was proof that the Matrix itself was constantly evolving. As I watched them from afar, I realized that the Chaos I had provoked had also unleashed a form of Creativity previously unknown in this artificial world.

Finally, after a frantic race through the alleyways, I managed to lose those special agents. But I realized that my journey had only just begun. As I discovered these hidden aspects of the Matrix, I understood that my role went beyond that of a mere observer. I had become a disrupter, an unpredictable element that could influence the course of this virtual reality. As I caught my breath, I knew I had to continue to plumb the depths of this fascinating and dangerous world and use my discoveries to free those still trapped in the illusion.

₭ ✳ ℬ

The first chapter of this book broadened the concept of *innovation*, and the second explored the dualistic principle of change through the equilibrium lenses of Order and Chaos. Now we're ready, like our virtual protagonist, to pick up the tempo by unpacking the innovative process. That said, before diving into each of the five variables in the five major sub-chapters to come, it would be useful to rationalize the interpretation and format of the fundamental identity of *innovation*, and at the same time answer some questions that a few attentive (or nerdy) readers might wonder about: what the logic of such an expression is and why we wouldn't put one of the variables under the square root or in the exponential function.

$$Innovation = \underbrace{(Need + Motivation\,)}_{Prerequisites} \times \underbrace{(Creativity +\ Technology)}_{Innovation\ Process} \times \underbrace{Value}_{Result}$$

As a teenager, I spent hours training my prefrontal cortex to solve multi-step equations in various study contexts. So, I'm delighted to remind you, and myself, of some high school math basics. By definition, an equation involves one, or more, unknowns, often represented by X, and the objective is usually to find the value of that X. In spirit, this could apply to some extent to our aforementioned equation, without using numbers, if we assume that one of its parts is an unknown. Let's imagine that *innovation*, the term on the left of the equation, is this unknown, i.e., "*Innovation* = X". To keep things simple, let's make the other variables explicit, so that we can obtain an easily solvable first-degree equation.

Let's assume that the *Need* variable represents one of the most basic human needs, hunger. In terms of context, let's also imagine that the latter manifests itself in the tenth century BC, in the savannah, among a nomadic African tribe of 30 people. This micro society is therefore starving and doesn't (yet) have a luxurious life with a refrigerator or Uber Eats. Furthermore, the *Creativity* variable was inspired by troops of African hyenas or wild dogs, who work together to hunt their prey faster and more efficiently. Thus, the creative idea was to work as a group, all together, to circle the next gazelle in sight. To implement it, the variable *Technology*, meaning the method of executing the idea, would be based on a new hunting process by scattering quite far away, with some kind of camouflage, sort of forming a large circle around the prey, so as not to spook it. Once people were spread at a similar arc distance from each other, they would slowly walk at the same speed towards the target initially located in the center of the circle. As a complement, they could shout and wave their arms every time the gazelle moved to one side to urge it back towards the center and allow other members to move forward together by closing the trap on the unfortunate gazelle.

Finally, the variable of the *Value* of this process depends on its effectiveness. If the tribe succeeds in catching the prey, this technique would probably be used more often, not least because it seems to strengthen the social bonds between tribe members through constructive collaboration (destructive for the poor gazelle, unfortunately). Note that by changing one of the variables, *Creativity for* example, by taking inspiration from cheetahs rather than wild dogs, and by relying on speed rather than intelligent collaboration techniques, *innovation*, and therefore the unknown X, would be totally different. In this case, the *innovation* would probably fail, because even Usain Bolt's ancestor would have trouble catching a gazelle at full speed. Nobody would want to use this technique again.

Now that we understand how to apply fundamental identity in the case of unknown innovation, i.e., when we're trying to innovate a product or a process, we can play around with it, assuming another unknown variable and the rest known. The Chinese, for example, are experts at reverse engineering, taking a successful innovation, such as the iPhone or Tesla, and looking for the variable *Technology*, the way in which this innovation was conceived. Once this unknown is mastered, the Chinese company offers its own version at a much more competitive price, such as a Xiaomi phone or a Nio electric car. So, the idea would be less to justify my proposal or, God forbid, add a square root, but more to understand the spirit of this fundamental identity to grasp the rest of the book, and apply it to your world perhaps. And even if I tried a classic demonstration "In all cases…Then…", it would be like *Mission Impossible 10* without Tom Cruise. One of the reasons for such difficulty is the very nature of *innovation*, which is more a matter for the human sciences (sociology, economics, psychology, etc.) than pure mathematics. Secondly, it would be extremely boring and counterproductive as I might risk losing you along the way.

That said, a nice trick I used to do is called the "zero assistant". To check whether an identity makes sense, without aiming to prove it in every case, we can replace each variable with zero, one at a time, and look for inconsistencies.

- **If the variable** *Need* = 0, this means that, at this precise moment and in this precise place, nobody feels this need, whether it's hunger, entertainment, or some other need. So why should innovation make sense? Some will say that big companies like Apple, which we call "market-makers", create successful innovations that nobody needs, like the iPad. I disagree. Although following a closed innovation strategy, not communicating much about its upcoming products, Apple certainly tests its innovations internally and beyond with beta users and constantly adjusts its products to meet the needs and feedback of its customers. If someone buys the iPad *a posteriori*, it's because they express a *NEED* for it, whether conscious or not. A need for entertainment, for example, for use at work, for educating children, or simply for social acceptance by friends or colleagues who also own the Apple brand.

- The *Motivation* of the innovator or entrepreneur is closely linked to the *Need*. If the latter exists within a sufficient number of people, we'd surely have people motivated to respond to this *Need*. Otherwise, *Motivation* would also be at 0, making innovation nil. After all, why motivate yourself for something that will go to waste?

- **If *Creativity* = 0**, innovation loses its meaning. The absence of *Creativity* means doing the same thing over again, or blindly copying something that already exists. Until recently, China probably comes to mind, again, as the leader of this copy-and-paste strategy for decades, flooding markets with cheap, low-quality phones, TVs and clothes. Many authors and academics have never called Chinese companies innovative for this very reason, namely the absence of *Creativity*. Here again, I disagree. The *Creativity* of copy-pasted Chinese products comes from optimizing processes, reverse-engineering Western innovations and using abundant, cheap labor to reduce prices to unbeatable levels.

- **If we assume that** *Technology* **= 0**, which means that no implementation exists, we remain stuck in invention and *Creativity* with no operational path to build and disseminate this innovation and make it real and available to the market. It's like imagining a teleportation machine. The *need* is there. It's a truly creative idea. Yet it's too early for the *Technology to* exist, which makes this *innovation* impossible or null and void.

- Finally, **if** *Value* **= 0**, this would be equivalent to a new item not being used, because nobody sees the point or it's too expensive. Imagine you've verified that a market, say Saudi Arabia, needs a flying car. People want to fly low with cars. You've designed a beautiful, user-friendly product. You've manufactured it using state-of-the-art factories that meet all the standards of Industry 4.0. Yet when it goes on sale, no one wants your product because it's expensive, flying car regulations aren't yet in place or your car's range isn't high enough to cross the Arabian desert without stress. As it stands, the *Value* of your innovation is zero, and so is the success of your entire *innovation*.

With this half proof, or rather rationalization, let's move on to the rest of this chapter. We'll begin our narrative with the *Need* behind every innovation, and the sources of *Motivation* for the innovator, prompting him or her to make the effort to create something new, or to change an existing object in our Matrix. We'll call these two variables "the innovative prerequisites", simply because they come into play before the innovation in question exists. The "innovative process" will then describe the variables of *Creativity,* which is the phase of imagining and finding the solution, and *Technology,* the implementation or operationalization of the innovation. Finally, the notion of *Value* closes this chapter by discussing the nature and psychology of the benefits that can be derived from any practical innovation. From now on, we'll be focusing mainly on human innovations, with a few mentions of natural innovations. Let's go!

VARIABLE 1:
The *Need* to innovate

Did you know that there are different types of pyramids? Everyone knows the Egyptian pyramids, with their large, perfectly symmetrical structures, characterized by their smooth, triangular sides and pointed tops, were built around 3000 BC. Not many are familiar with Nubian pyramids though. Erected in present-day Sudan around the same period, these ones have a more conical structure, with gentler slopes, built using mud bricks made from a mixture of clay, sand and straw. Chinese pyramids, with smaller triangular structures, were built in China during the Qing dynasty. The Mesoamerican pyramids are stepped structures built by Mesoamerican civilizations, such as the Mayas and Aztecs. They are generally pyramid-shaped, with a series of terraces or steps leading to a flat summit. Let's travel back in time to the American continent.

The Maya civilization is one of the most fascinating in ancient history. It flourished in Central America, mainly in the regions that today correspond to Mexico, Guatemala, Honduras, Belize and El Salvador. The origins of this civilization date back to around 2000 BC, with the first evidence of settlement in the region. The Maya reached their apogee between 250 and 900 CE, a period known as the Classic Era. During this period, they built incredible city-states, developed sophisticated writing systems, created precise calendars and excelled in mathematics, astronomy, agriculture and architecture. Let's illustrate this last category.

Among the 500 imposing pyramids built by the Maya, one of the earliest known is El Mirador, in present-day Guatemala. It was built around 300 BC and is considered one of the largest structures of the pre-Classical Maya era. This pyramid and so many others symbolized power and wealth, and also served as religious shrines. However, the construction of these pyramids was not without difficulties. The Maya lived in a tropical rainforest environment, where dense vegetation and wet soil made it difficult to transport heavy stone blocks from distant quarries. Despite these obstacles, they persevered – well, the working class did – and found innovative solutions to build their pyramids.

In particular, the Mayan pyramids were built using a technique known as "talud-tablero". The talud is a steep slope that rises diagonally while the tablero is a flat surface. Like a dualistic couple, these two elements alternate, creating a staircase-like structure. This technique was used for several reasons. On the one hand, it reinforced the stability and solidity of the structures, by distributing the weight evenly. The taluds helped dissipate the force of earthquakes and prevent collapse. On the other hand, this technique also had a dualistic symbolic significance for the Maya. Taluds represented the connection between earth and sky, while tableros represented the terrestrial world where human activities took place. The Maya also used an ingenious method of cutting and shaping stones, enabling them to build pyramids that were not only tall, but also precise and symmetrical. As a result, these stone structures are still admired today, richly decorated with sculptures, reliefs and murals depicting mythological scenes, rulers and pagan religious rituals.

Considering these pyramids and their construction methods as human innovations at the time, it's not easy to pinpoint the *Need* justifying such a colossal effort. Many historians assert that these costly projects, both in terms of time and men's lives, were motivated by a combination of religious, political and social factors. Indeed, these imposing structures were places of worship dedicated to the Mayan gods, and also served as ceremonial and administrative centers for rulers and priests. They symbolized the link between the terrestrial and celestial worlds, embodying cosmic harmony and divine Order. Some researchers propose that the pyramids were a divine request addressed to the Maya people through their shamans. Other esoteric theories suggest that the pyramids were invented even before the Egyptians and Mayans as some sort of power plants.

Whatever the case, for this long-term creation to see the light of day, there must have been a *Need*, or a combination of needs, that drove the process. Perhaps the Mayan leaders needed to show off to other tribes. It may simply have been a religious need to get closer to their gods through sacrifices in a prestigious place. Iin order to put some Order in the messy sphere of human psychology, it hence seems important to provide a framework for mapping basic human needs and linking them to the concept of *innovation*. For this reason, in this book, we will base our analysis on **a psychological pyramid,** that of **Maslow's needs**. This is a well-known and tested theory, proposed by psychologist Abraham Maslow in 1943. It classifies the Chaos within human needs into five levels or layers, which are generally satisfied from the base to the roof of the pyramid.

At the lowest level, we find **physiological needs** such as food, water and sleep, essential to our survival. For example, when we're hungry, our priority is to find food to soothe the sensation. Once these needs have been met, we aspire to **a higher level of security**, including financial stability and personal protection. In particular, we seek a stable, secure job in order to meet our material needs and feel safe in our environment. The third level encompasses the needs of **belonging and love**, including emotional ties and belonging to a community. As we progress, we focus on developing **our self-esteem**, gaining recognition from others, thus constituting the fourth level of the pyramid. So we engage in activities that build our self-confidence and hope to be recognized for our achievements and skills. Finally, the top of the pyramid represents the need for **personal fulfillment**, where we thrive by pursuing our passions, developing our talents and contributing to society in a meaningful way. Nomadic travel, writing a novel, or taking part in philanthropic activities all illustrate this top of the pyramid.

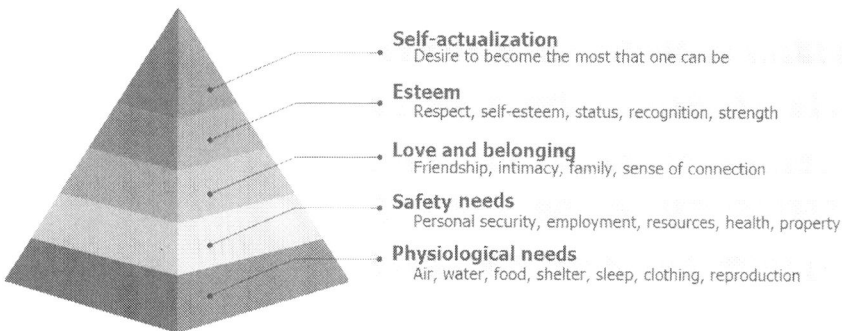

Self-actualization
Desire to become the most that one can be

Esteem
Respect, self-esteem, status, recognition, strength

Love and belonging
Friendship, intimacy, family, sense of connection

Safety needs
Personal security, employment, resources, health, property

Physiological needs
Air, water, food, shelter, sleep, clothing, reproduction

Most of us imagine Maslow's pyramid as an ascending ladder to happiness. This is only partly true. Like Hugo's *Les Misérables*, if we found ourselves starving, thirsty or without a minute's sleep for hours or days, we'd remain stuck on the ground floor of the pyramid, until these basic needs were met, or perhaps until death. Nevertheless, there are exceptions to our metaphor. A monk raised in a remote monastery might skip a few steps on the pyramid of needs and go straight to the last stage of the game, developing a mastery of his impulses and his mind. For example, he might meet his physiological needs through simple living and ascetic practices such as fasting or meditation, while finding meaning and purpose in his spiritual practices. On the other hand, some individuals – unfortunate in my opinion – remain stuck in survival levels, in fear of an uncertain tomorrow. In any case, the path to self-fulfillment would be different for each individual and could involve a variety of different practices and experiences.

The strength of Maslow's approach, which motivated its adoption here, lies in the breakdown of complex, and therefore intractable, needs into fundamental sub-needs. By breaking down an organ into genes, an object into molecules or an energy field into elementary equations, a researcher can use the simplified model to test their hypotheses. What's more, when you think about it objectively, nobody needs a car per se. In general, it's basic needs that drive the decision to buy a car; the need to get a jealous look from the neighbor, perhaps, or to give it to your daughter on her birthday as a sign of love or to use it to get to work. If we focus on the latter, no one really needs a job. Deep down, there's no gene or spirit asking you to wake up early in the morning, or worse, stay up all night in the name of a monotonous survival job. This kind of occupation is just a way of making a living. But what about that money? Do we really need money? Not really. We need food, we need to pay the rent, we need to seduce romantic partners, and so on. With these examples, you've grasped the power of Maslow's tool, I hope, as well as getting a taste of "why" Man has innovated what he has innovated to date.

Furthermore, it's worth noting that, according to a study by Tay and Diener (2011), the basic needs hierarchy was generally supported in both individualistic (like France and North America), and collectivist cultures (like South-East Asia). That been said, there seem some differences in the relative importance of specific needs. The same study found that individuals in collectivist cultures placed greater importance on belongingness and social needs compared to individuals in individualistic cultures, contrary to self-actualization needs. Yet, overall, with recent decade globalization and acculturation of the world to western norms, I believe Maslow pyramid makes sense when applied to most countries today.

To take the argument a step further, let's apply Maslow's psychological categorization by highlighting some of the major innovations that have responded to each level of this pyramid, throughout human history.

ℰ✳ℂ

Innovating for self-preservation

While I was stuck on a 13-hour flight from Seoul to Paris, I had the opportunity to carefully observe my neighbors, a young Korean couple, lovingly caring for their adorable little girl, who was enviably tranquil. This observation comes as no surprise. In fact, it ties in directly with the foundations of Maslow's pyramid, which is mainly based on the evolutionary principle of self-preservation. This instinct manifests itself not only in our quest for personal survival, but also in our desire to see our children survive and develop in a healthy way, particularly in the fragile years after birth. This is all the more topical in countries like Korea and Japan, which have some of the lowest birth rates in the world. With less than one child per couple on average, these countries face the imminent threat of a demographic crash, as do many other developed countries. Such discreet, harmless spying also got my brain thinking about a universal phenomenon: why do we find babies, of all kinds and species, unfairly cute compared to adults?

Scientific research is quite conclusive about the mechanisms underlying our affection for babies. Indeed, it turns out that this instinct is deeply rooted in our reptilian brain, transcending species boundaries and serving crucial evolutionary purposes. The fact of the matter is that the physical characteristics of infants, such as their big eyes, round face and soft, chubby cheeks, trigger an instinctive reaction in adults called the "**baby pattern**". This is a set of characteristics that elicits nurturing behaviors and evokes feelings of warmth and protection. The baby pattern is not limited to humans, but also extends to various animal species.

For example, kittens, with their small size and playfulness, puppies, with their wagging tails and innocent expressions, and even baby animals like ducklings or fawns, all possess attributes that activate our nurturing instincts. This phenomenon applies beyond domestic animals to wild creatures. Neurological scans of the human brain prove that the sight of a baby panda, elephant calf or lion cub, for example, captures our attention and triggers a more acute emotional response than when we look at their adult counterparts. The explanation is purely Darwinist. Our universal tendency to find babies cute is explained by the evolutionary advantages it brings. When we perceive a baby as cute, our motivation to care for and protect it is reinforced. This guarantees the survival and well-being of the next generation, and thus the continuity of the species.

The first layer of Maslow's pyramid is one of the most basic, but also one of the most crucial, because without these basic needs, we wouldn't exist long (and peacefully) enough to discuss such philosophical topics in this book. Survival is simply the act of continuing to live or exist, especially in difficult or adverse circumstances. It is a fundamental instinct that is common to all living organisms, as it is necessary for the perpetuation of the species, by transmitting their genetic information to future generations. For example, if an animal is faced with a food shortage, it would express this fundamental *need* for survival by migrating to a different location (organizational innovation) or by learning to digest new food sources (process innovation). The other side of survival is the inherent fear of death. In this respect, it's interesting to note that there are generally three complementary ways, programmed into the code of most dynamic agents to combat the death syndrome since the dawn of time: **one is to avoid it, the second is to create as many genetic copies of** oneself as possible, and the third is to ensure that most of these copies survive the vulnerable period of youth.

As we explained in detail in the second dimension of the Matrix, Chapter I, several natural innovations contributed to meeting this basic *need for* survival. These include the innovative process of natural selection, a key evolutionary mechanism that promotes the transmission of traits beneficial to the survival and reproduction of a species, notably through adaptation. Agents that possess traits beneficial to their environment have a higher probability of survival and reproduction. For example, a bird species with a beak adapted to feed on the seeds of a specific plant will have a competitive advantage over other birds that cannot feed in this way. Over time, individuals with this advantageous trait will reproduce more, passing it on to the next generation, until they achieve statistical dominance at the expense of their competitors. In this way, the principle of natural evolution resembles a constant updating of the Matrix code in order to adjust dynamic agents to environmental pressures, thus optimizing a given species' chances of survival and even prosperity. This natural paradigm, combined with the processes of mutation and genetic exchange, innovates all the biological and botanical diversity on Earth, in terms of new species and "features" advantageous to the maintenance of life and the efficient reproduction of offspring. Let's look briefly at just one such natural product innovation.

In 1938, a crazy scientific experiment took place in Mammoth Cave, in the US state of Kentucky. Researchers Kleitman and Richardson spent 32 days in the cave, completely cut off from the outside world. They lived in total darkness, without the slightest access to a light source or clock. The aim was to observe their sleep patterns, using an electroencephalography (EEG) technique. As the study progressed, Kleitman and Richardson both grew nice beards (fortunately, they couldn't see each other), and found that their sleep-wake cycles were relatively regular, with an average sleep duration of around seven to eight hours per day. Their findings are important because they show that we have evolved an internal clock, technically entitled **"the circadian rhythm"**, which develops over about 24 hours.

In other words, without a need for sun's help, sleep, that innovative product of nature, has been programmed into our code for millions of years. Sleep, and therefore the absence of attention and physical vigor, although making animals vulnerable to predators, has been proven by the latest decades of research to be an essential brick for survival and the proper functioning of every organ. "It is Allah Who has made for you the night a covering and sleep a rest, and Who has made the day a resurrection", this verse can already be read in the seventh century (Qur'an 25:47). In other words, during sleep, the body repairs and regenerates tissues, strengthens the immune system and consolidates memory. In general, the average adult can survive without sleep for around 11 days at best.

Scientific studies show that sleeping habits vary considerably from one species to another. For example, some animals, like cats, sleep up to 16 hours a day, and koalas on average 20 hours a day, while others, like giraffes, sleep for only a few hours. Similarly, some dynamic agents, like birds, can sleep with only one half of their brain at a time, while others, like dolphins, are able to sleep with one eye open. In humans, too, the recommended sleep duration varies according to age. Infants and young children need more sleep than adults, with newborns sleeping up to 16 hours a day. In adolescence, the recommended sleep duration is around nine hours a night, and in adulthood it's around seven to eight hours a night.

In addition to its physiologically regenerative aspect – provided the right duration is respected in each case – sleep apparently plays a major cognitive role. By scanning the brains of numerous species, including rats and humans, it has been demonstrated that sleep consists of two main phases: NREM (non-rapid eye movement) and REM (rapid eye movement). These are two distinct stages of the sleep cycle, each with its own characteristics and functions. During NREM sleep, the body relaxes and brain waves slow down. Heart rate, respiratory rate and blood pressure decrease. NREM sleep is important for physical restoration and repair, as well as for the consolidation of past memories and learning.

The other half is what we call REM sleep, or "paradoxical sleep" in technical jargon. The paradox is that in the REM phase, we appear to be in a quiet, near-dead state, yet in reality, our eyes move rapidly beneath our eyelids, with increased brain activity, similar to an awake brain. It is at this stage of sleep that most dreams occur. As a result, during REM sleep, the brain begins to consolidate the day's recent data into its global database, memory. REM sleep also stimulates problem-solving and creativity by linking several areas of the brain that rarely communicate when awake. All these benefits of physical recovery and cognitive stimulation during a good-night sleep clearly contribute to optimizing the chances of survival and dominance of species, Homo sapiens with our energy-consuming brains in particular.

Let's shift gear back to a spring day light. On a road trip in French Normandy, I observed first-hand what we humanly call "curiosity", and its contribution to the first Maslow layer. If you're familiar with dogs, especially those genetically closer to wolves like huskies[19], observe how they sniff every nook and cranny when visiting a friend's house, a field, or just about any new space, looking to detect olfactory traces of potential enemies, partners or food. Similarly, I now tend to welcome bees, flies and even groups of mosquitoes around my minimalistic van when out in the wilderness, unlike my previous panicky reaction. Indeed, I noticed that once they had inspected the area and surroundings, they tended to return to their familiar habitat, unless there was a point of interest like a smelly garbage bag in the dams. Curiosity seems to be a by-product of the survival instinct, optimizing better adaptation to environmental change and more effective decision-making. We humans, and especially geeks, have obviously taken this concept way too far, being curious about almost every tangible and intangible aspect of our Matrix, but it all originates in the *Need* for survival. Such correlation is justifiable in the other direction too. It may be that because we're looking to survive and reproduce that we become curious to gather as much information as possible on an ongoing basis.

---

[19]   It's important to note that dogs, cats and so many other domesticated animals have undergone centuries of selective breeding by man since the agricultural revolution of 10,000 BC, resulting in significant variations in size, coat and behavior compared to their wild ancestors.

Natural innovations aside, throughout human history, survival has been at the heart of our collective consciousness. Ever since we first set foot on this planet, our primate ancestors, and Homo in particular, have faced an endless stream of challenges and obstacles in their quest for survival and fulfillment. They had to be *innovative* and find ingenious solutions, given their limited brain capacity, of course. As we mentioned in the third dimension of Chapter I, one of the earliest instances of human innovation was the mastery of fire. This feat, seemingly simple for 21st-century Man, upset the balance of power on Earth, enabling early humans to fend off predators, keep warm in colder climates. In this context, we could also mention the organizational innovation of languages, or rather a rudimentary style of communication, both bodily and vocal, which would have contributed to the tribe's teamwork, optimizing their chances of capturing prey or chasing off predators.

The Agricultural Revolution, which took place in the Neolithic period around 10,000 BC, marked a major turning point in human history, enabling the transition from sedentary, agrarian societies to sustainable development. Prior to this period, man was essentially a hunter-gatherer, dependent on wild plants and animals for his subsistence. Food uncertainty and daily dangers were therefore high. With the advent of agriculture, however, humans were able to cultivate plants and raise livestock, providing a more stable food source and enabling the growth of larger, more complex societies. Agricultural innovations, such as the development of irrigation systems and the use of plows and other tools, increased food production and crop yields. This gradually led to an increase in population.

Indeed, in nature, the demography of any species is regulated not by a central communist government, such as in the case of China's one-child policy, but by natural processes. Firstly, there is the ability to reproduce, genetically embedded in the code of dynamic agents. For example, a mouse can have a litter of ten kittens every 20 days, a female cat can have five kittens every two months, and a female elephant can have a single calf every four to five years. In addition, the availability of resources adds another layer of regulation. A decline in certain plants due to drought would condemn the little elephant to perish. Perhaps the mother too. Finally, we should also consider competition. In the 1940s, brown snakes were unwittingly airlifted from the Solomon Islands to Guam, probably by hiding in military construction equipment. As brown snakes are not native to Guam, they began to reproduce rapidly and thrived in the absence of natural predators on the island, to the point of threatening numerous species of land birds and other native animals, leading to their local extinction.

In a few social species though, a sort of central demographic regulation is coded within its members. Namely, bees control the size of their colony by rearing and producing new queens. When a colony becomes overcrowded, a new queen is raised and a portion of the bees leave the colony to form a new colony, a process known as swarming. This helps maintain a balanced population among colonies. Additionally, nurse bees can regulate population size by controlling the queen's egg-laying. They feed the queen royal jelly, a nutrient-rich substance, and depending on the colony's needs, they can stimulate or reduce the queen's egg-laying. This allows them to adjust the population based on available resources and colony requirements. For instance, during resource scarcity, such as in winter, the colony's population naturally decreases as bees live longer and the queen's egg-laying is reduced. In spring, when resources are abundant, the queen's egg-laying intensifies, and the colony's population increases to exploit these resources.

As sedentary farming became the norm, human demographics of the time were less subject to these natural constraints. The surplus food produced by agriculture, combined with better protection of human colonies against wild beasts, resulted in rapid population growth, regulated mainly by microbes and high birth mortality. This demographic boom led to the development of non-agricultural activities, such as bartering and large-scale trade, since not everyone owned land – the most important capital of the time – or had the ability to work it. People were thus able to provide services (crafts, trade, army, etc.) or innovate useful tools for survival.

A few millennia later, and more specifically since the Industrial Revolution of the 18th century, the food industry has undergone numerous innovations that have transformed the way food is produced, processed, packaged, preserved and distributed. These innovations have had a considerable impact on food availability, shelf life, quality and accessibility for a greater number of people. Innovative agricultural techniques, such as the use of agricultural machinery, chemical fertilizers and pesticides, have increased crop productivity and yields. Process innovations such as pasteurization, sterilization and freeze-drying, combined with tailor-made packaging, such as vacuum-packed or sealed trays, helped to extend the shelf life of foodstuffs. Refrigeration, freezing and dehydration techniques, to name but a few, took this preservation objective a step further.

In terms of culinary diversity, eating New Zealand kiwi fruit in France, French cheese in the USA and American Big Mac almost anywhere – in short, the globalization of the food industry – would not have been possible without improved air and sea transport infrastructures, as well as refrigerated trucks. The food industry has also seen innovations in the creation of new food products and recipes. Cooking and food processing techniques have been developed, paving the way for new flavors, textures and culinary experiences. Finally, over the last few decades, the rise of biotechnology, and in particular genetic modification techniques, have made it possible to create plant or animal varieties that possess desired characteristics such as insect resistance, better nutritional quality, faster growth or greater tolerance to adverse environmental conditions. These genetic upgrades can be achieved by introducing specific genes into the target organism, or by modifying existing genes. Although the potential benefits of GMOs in the food industry are numerous, notably in response to the basic level of Maslow's pyramid, this still raises concerns about the potential effects on human health and, in the long term, on biodiversity and the optimal balance of ecosystems.

Water, that vital molecule, is not only directly involved in the equation of our survival, but also in the growth of any Matrix agent that may end up in our stomach (vegetables, animals, etc.). It was therefore imperative to think about this delicate material, which is liquid and therefore difficult to handle, from the earliest agricultural colonies onwards. One organizational solution was to choose the location of one's tribe carefully, before building anything. Unsurprisingly, Egyptian civilization settled along the Nile, and the first civilizations of the Indus Valley flourished around the Indus and Sarasvati rivers. Mesopotamia, also known as the "cradle of civilization", situated of course between the Tigris and Euphrates rivers, was the birthplace of many ancient civilizations, including the Sumerians, Akkadians, Babylonians and Assyrians. Early farmers realized that land near rivers benefited from a steady supply of water, encouraging crop growth. Rivers also provided a convenient means of transport for people and goods. Early settlements thrived on easy access to waterways, enabling trade, commerce and community expansion.

In addition to the choice of a privileged geographical location, innovations in water management and treatment have played a crucial role in improving access to drinking water. Our ancestors developed various techniques for managing water resources, ranging from simple methods such as digging wells and collecting rainwater, to more complex systems such as aqueducts and reservoirs. The Industrial Revolution saw the development of new water treatment technologies that considerably improved the quality and safety of drinking water supplies. In the 19th and 20th centuries, many cities built centralized water treatment plants, distributing water efficiently and safely to large populations. These plants used a combination of filtration, chlorination and other treatments to remove impurities and pathogens, providing clean water to the population on a large scale. More recently, the use of reverse osmosis and other membrane filtration technologies has made it possible to produce high-quality drinking water even from salty sea water and other sources.

Always in pursuit of satisfying our basic needs, before the advent of modern medicine, alchemy and natural herbal medicine were widely practiced, and sometimes seen as the only escape from a looming death. Herbalists applied knowledge passed down from generation to generation to identify medicinal plants and use them to treat various ailments. This knowledge was often based on empirical observation and experimentation. To complement this, alchemy in the Middle Ages combined aspects of chemistry, metallurgy and spirituality and was practiced in many ancient cultures and shamanic cults around the world. Alchemists used innovative techniques such as distillation, maceration and other methods to extract and combine chemical compounds.

These practices, still used by grandmothers and in some countries, are not entirely illusory, basing their magic on the "placebo effect" but can have actual materialistic *Value*. White willow, for example, has been used since ancient times to relieve pain and reduce fever. This plant contains salicin, a chemical precursor to salicylic acid, the active ingredient in modern aspirin. However, it's important to note that traditional medicine based on alchemy and medicinal plants had its limits. Certain serious and complex conditions could not be treated effectively, leading to false leads and higher morbidity and mortality rates in some cases.

Obviously, the advent of modern medicine has brought significant advances in the treatment of disease, and a better understanding of the underlying mechanisms. Scientific research and technological advances have made it possible to develop more targeted drugs and more effective treatments. As a result, the pharmaceutical industry has been responsible for many successes that have played a major role in improving the quality of human life and reducing disease. From the discovery of antibiotics to the development of vaccines, these innovations have enabled us to better control the spread of disease, cure it and improve overall health and well-being. Here are some of these innovations:

- Alexander Fleming's discovery of penicillin in 1928 revolutionized the treatment of bacterial infections.

- The development of mass-production techniques for antibiotics in the 1940s considerably increased their availability and affordability.

- The introduction of childhood vaccinations in the mid-20th century, such as the polio vaccine developed by Jonas Salk and the measles vaccine developed by John Enders, helped reduce the incidence of these diseases.

- The development of vaccines against a wide range of infectious diseases, such as hepatitis B, human papillomavirus (HPV), more recently COVID-19, and many others, has contributed to improved health outcomes and longer life expectancy.

In this respect, scientific *innovation* significantly improved life expectancy, with a significant reduction in mortality rates and a few years' extension of old age. In other words, advances in medicine, nutrition and public health have enabled people to live longer, healthier lives, as shown in the figure below. Antibiotics, the widespread use of vaccines, innovative surgical techniques such as the development of minimally invasive procedures, have all had their part to play in treating a wide range of health problems with less risk of failure and faster recovery times. In addition, modern innovations in genetics, cell biology and regenerative medicine are bringing us closer to a future where many age-related diseases and disabilities can be prevented, treated or even eliminated. This research sheds new light on the underlying causes of aging and helps us to understand how we can intervene to extend lifespan, or at least, given the improbability of human immortality in the near future, aim to age better.

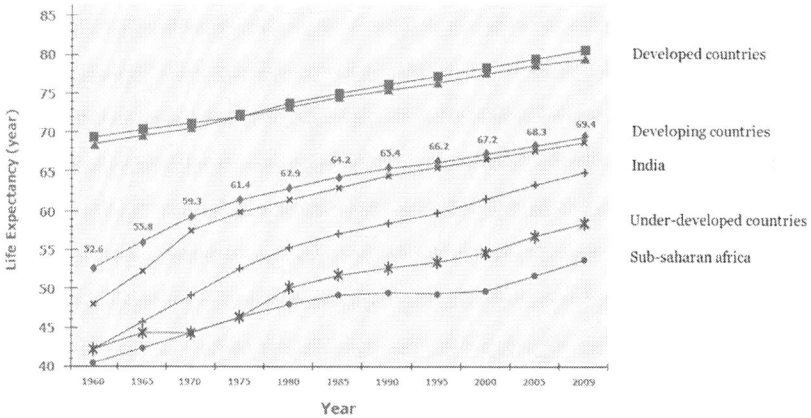

In our today's vocabulary, in the quasi-absence of wild dangerous animals and nomadic lifestyles that may threaten our existence, the Maslow level of survival is often referred to by the scary sociological term of "**poverty**". The poorer you are, the shorter and more difficult your life is, both for yourself and your family. In his formidable bestseller, *Factfulness*, Swedish author Hans Rosling draws on a large volume of data to prove that the world has made great progress over the last two centuries, thanks to innovation and capitalism, among other factors. As far as poverty is concerned, he proposes a simple framework for visualizing it. From a global perspective, there are four levels of poverty for around seven billion people worldwide. Thus, over the first two decades of the 21st century, we could cut the first layer of the pyramid of needs into four sub-levels:

- **One billion people are at level 1**, the most basic level of poverty, where people subsist on a daily income of just $1. This often requires a great deal of time and effort to obtain basic needs such as food and water. In this scenario, the protagonist's children have to travel long distances to collect water from a contaminated source and gather firewood, while the limited resources available result in a monotonous diet. The consequences of poverty, such as lack of access to adequate medical care, are also illustrated by the tragic deaths of young children from treatable diseases.

- **Three billion people are at level 2,** standing for an increase in daily income of between $1 and $4. This relative financial stability opens up new opportunities to improve living standards. With this extra income, it is possible to buy food that was previously unobtainable, as well as livestock such as chickens, leading to a more varied and nutritious diet. In addition, the funds make it possible to invest in practical items such as sandals and a bicycle, reducing the time and effort needed to obtain essential resources such as water.

- **Two billion people are at level 3,** which is equivalent to increasing their daily income by between $4 and $16. As a result, substantial improvements in living standards are possible, such as the installation of a tap with running water, eliminating the need to collect water from distant sources. In addition, the availability of stable electricity enables better educational opportunities for children, while the acquisition of a refrigerator paves the way for food storage and the preparation of varied meals on a daily basis.

- **One billion people are at level 4**, corresponding to a daily income of over $64. With the advantages of a higher level of education and access to travel and other leisure activities, their lifestyle is very different from that of those struggling to survive on a day-to-day basis, with access to hot and cold running water inside the home, an often-unappreciated luxury, and the ability to eat out regularly or own a personal vehicle, further indications of a privileged financial status, easily found in developed countries.

ℰꝏ✳ℭꝏ

Innovating your own safety

The *Need* for safety, the second tier of Maslow's pyramid, is closely linked to the desire to optimize chances of survival. After millennia of trauma due to the loss of young children and the extinction of entire tribes from predators, famine, disease or other natural hazards, most dynamic agents, including humans, are programmed with **an evolutionary bias towards certainty**. In dualistic terms, they prefer Order to Chaos, control, or the illusion of it, to the *laissez-faire* of a wild destiny. Thus, this layer of the pyramid encompasses the desire for stability, security and protection not only from physical harm, but also from psychological suffering.

Some (super) innovations, as we'll see as we go along, can meet several needs, either simultaneously or on a case-by-case basis. The discovery and use of fire, for example, not only helped our Homo ancestors to diversify their diet towards more meat in barbecue mode, which is a physiological need, that is the first level of the need pyramid, but also reduced the amount of bacteria in cooked food, warming and illuminating our dark nights, reducing the pain of cold spells, and securing a perimeter from dangerous animals, which is part of this second Maslow level. What's more, the Agricultural Revolution, which increased the stability of food and water, laid the foundations for greater certainty, thanks to more predictable harvests. Finally, weapons, from rudimentary bows and arrows to swords and firearms, are product-type innovations, whose success serves the basic needs of hunting for food, as well as the need for security. The more advanced their military capabilities, the safer a family, tribe or country feels from enemies and natural catastrophes. That said, even before fighting, it's better to protect yourself from surprise attacks and sleep in peace.

Thus, one of the first natural innovations to contribute to the need for security was **the development of shelters**, especially for animals at the bottom of the food chain. There is no shortage of case studies in this regard. Indeed, in the vast animal kingdom, the construction of shelters is a strategy commonly used by many animals. Take rabbits and foxes, for example. These subterranean architects create complex burrows that offer protection from predators and extreme weather conditions. Inside these burrows, they find a peaceful haven in which to rest, reproduce and raise their young. Birds, meanwhile, demonstrate their avian architectural skills through the construction of elaborate nests, perched high in trees or hidden in bushes. Each bird species has its own nest design and uses different materials, demonstrating their ingenuity and adaptability to their environments. The cocoons created by caterpillars as they transform into butterflies provide a protective envelope during this vulnerable stage of their life cycle.

Securing territories is another vital strategy used by dynamic agents, even before the appearance of modern Man. Through olfactory markings and signals, animals establish their property and communicate with others. Scent glands, urine and other marking techniques are used to delimit boundaries and deter potential intruders, a kind of "Keep Away!" For some species, including our own, strength lies in numbers and cooperative defense. Lions, dolphins, ants and bees, to name but a few, live in groups and develop defense strategies against predators, as members can combine their efforts to fend off threats. Cooperative defense mechanisms such as collective harassment and grouping further improve their chances of survival.

Man is also a remarkable example of innovativeness in shelter construction. Our ancestors developed the skills and knowledge to build shelters adapted to their environments. In early times, prehistoric man used materials available, such as branches, leaves and animal skins, to build temporary shelters. As knowledge and skills developed, humans embarked on the construction of more durable and complex shelters in stone or clay. Post-Agricultural Revolution, these shelters, later called houses, became more sophisticated, incorporating features such as walls, windows and roofs. Today, innovations in construction techniques and materials have enabled buildings to become more energy-efficient and resistant to natural disasters such as earthquakes, with a beautiful architectural diversity, from castles to skyscrapers.

With the Agricultural and then Industrial Revolutions, security and order were important elements to maintain for optimal functioning of societal gatherings. The institutionalization of the organizational innovation of **law** was a great step forward in maintaining order and ensuring the safety of people, and of course of those in power. I suppose the idea of law has always existed implicitly in the form of justice. Again, I'm basing this on the animal kingdom. Studies on primates, such as chimpanzees and bonobos, have shown that they have the ability to recognize and react to injustice. For example, when an individual receives a reward disproportionate to others in the group, some may express their displeasure, refuse to cooperate or even engage in rebalancing behaviors to restore fairness. Similarly, anthropologists have observed that our hunter-gatherer ancestors had social norms and informal rules to encourage sharing. As a result, when hunting or gathering was successful, the wealthy were obliged to share their catch with other members of the community. Failure to do so could result in exclusion from the group, or even the massacre of rebels. But with population expansion and the beginning of civilization, a more refined code of conduct became necessary.

Some of the earliest known legal systems date back to ancient civilizations such as the Babylonians, Egyptians and Greeks. These civilizations developed codes of law to regulate behavior, resolve disputes and provide a framework for Social Order. The Law of Hammurabi is one of the best known and best preserved. It was created by King Hammurabi of Babylon, who reigned from 1792 to 1750 BC. The law, thus named after him, represents a comprehensive legal code that covered a wide range of issues, including property rights, trade, family law and criminal law. One of the key features of Hammurabi's law was its tone of strict punishment for offenders, with the famous principle of "an eye for an eye, a tooth for a tooth" serving as the basis for many of the penalties outlined in the code. This emphasis on retribution has led some to regard

Hammurabi's law as harsh and unjust, but others argue that it helped bring a degree of stability and security to ancient Babylonian society. In ancient Rome, law was codified and written down for the first time, creating a comprehensive legal system that influenced the development of law in Europe and beyond. This legal system, known as Roman law, was based on the principle of "law for all" and played a significant role in the development of modern Western legal systems.

Religion has also inspired many laws or moral behaviors, such as the Ten Commandments in Christianity, the Noble Eightfold Path in Buddhism and Sharia law, also known as Islamic law, in some predominantly Muslim countries. Finally, a number of new institutions have been created to enforce the law and ensure public safety. Bearing relatively different titles and roles according to the times, they include the police, the army, the justice system, the fire department and the ambulance service, to name but a few. Add to that the thousands, if not millions, of insurance companies operating since the First Industrial Revolution, in all countries now, insuring people's belongings, businesses, and lives, and reducing the risk of significant loss thanks to the pooling principle, a smart organizational innovation. "I regard the insurance system as one of the basic institutions of mankind. Its importance in human affairs ranks with the discovery of fire and the invention of the wheel," said Henry Ford quite some time ago.

It's worth clarifying some innovations, which at first glance have nothing to do with this second level of the Maslow pyramid. Our need for information, in some cases and depending on the person's level of consciousness, may be closely linked to our *Need* for security and survival. Throughout the evolutionary process, dynamic agents have developed mechanisms to collect and process information crucial to their survival. For example, many animals are alert to danger signals emitted by other members of their species. Birds emit alarm calls to warn other individuals of a potential predator. This dissemination of information enables members of the group to take safety measures and protect themselves. Your brain works the same way. Try closing your eyes, or even meditating for five minutes, and you'll soon realize that, at any given moment, you're mainly

aware of anything out of the ordinary: a shout in the distance, a telephone beep, a sensation of cold air or pain, in the knowledge that hundreds of little things are happening simultaneously, below the radar of your attention: your breathing, the blood flowing in your veins, air flow, etc.

This basic, but rarely perceptible, observation means that we actively, often unconsciously, seek out information about potential threats and opportunities in our environment, whether to avoid predators in the early stages of humanity, or to guard against modern dangers such as accidents, a pickpocket in the subway or a call-to-action from a manager at work. Our social instinct to chat with our fellow human beings, at school, at work and at home, would also be an evolutionary result of this need to know everything in order to optimize our chances in the Matrix game. In this respect, an entire market estimated at hundreds of billions of dollars is built on this *Need*: **the media industry**. News, through newspapers, television and social media, informs us of events unfolding in the world and helps us identify dangerous situations or behaviors to avoid or adopt. For example, weather reports warn us of impending storms, road safety reports make us aware of traffic hazards, and health information provides us with advice on how to prevent the spread of viruses. The longer we're stuck in Maslow's low levels, the more likely we are to consume "news" of all kinds, which, it should be noted, rarely mentions a zone of peace or a conventional topic, but deliberately stimulates our programmed insecurities by broadcasting a terrorist attack, a market crash or an earthquake, the frequency and impact of which are virtually nil in the grand scheme of things.

Sometimes, we feel the *Need* to protect ourselves not only from aggressive external agents but also from our own innovations, which often remain perfectible when introduced to the market. For example, the safety of cars and roads has improved considerably over the years, thanks to the introduction of new technologies and safety devices. Modern cars are equipped with airbags, anti-lock brakes, seat belts, stability control systems and other features that help reduce the risk of accidents. What's more, roads have become safer thanks to the use of technologies such as intelligent transport systems, which can detect and react to potential hazards. But innovation is not always synonymous with complexity. The use of traffic signs, lighting and barriers to improve visibility and safety are simple innovative processes that have saved millions of lives already.

Up to now, we've focused mainly on the physical aspect of safety. However, the complexity of the human brain means that the emotional and psychological side is just as important. In fact, **marriage and money** are organizational innovations that provide a fundamental support system for the internal stability of individuals. It is within the family unit, or marriage, that individuals find love, acceptance and a sense of belonging. Family members provide emotional support, understanding and companionship, contributing to a sense of security and well-being. In times of difficulty or crisis, family members can support each other to find comfort and help, creating a sense of emotional security. Money, for its part, addresses the practical aspects of security. It provides the means to satisfy basic needs such as food, housing and healthcare. Financial stability therefore offers a sense of security by providing a safety net in the event of emergencies or unexpected expenses. It also enables individuals to plan for the future, pursue their goals and have a sense of control over their lives. While "money can't buy happiness" is true at certain levels of wealth, lack of money can make life miserable for someone stuck at the low survival levels.

Let's end this discussion of this fundamental *Need* with an anecdote illustrating the power of this variable in the *innovation* equation. Did you know that it is illegal to burn dollar bills in the United States? Destroying or altering U.S. currency is a violation of U.S. federal law, specifically 18 U.S.C. § 333, which prohibits the mutilation, cutting, disfigurement or perforation of U.S. currency. This can be punishable by up to ten years in prison, not to mention fines. If you're wealthy (and stupid) enough to indulge in this illegal luxury – good for you! But if that's hardly the case, I'm willing to bet you'd be motivated by the *Need* for security if you woke up in a dark, damp jungle, with a suitcase full of greenbacks and a lighter. I guarantee you'd start burning them, in bundles and without the slightest remorse, at the first animal (or human) roar.

ഋ ✶ ര

Innovating false friends

At the turn of the 20th century, when the United States was in the midst of its industrial era and the country was undergoing rapid change, a new passion was emerging. Travel had become increasingly popular, offering people the chance to explore new horizons. Trains were a common means of transport, but they had their limits. Bicycles were also used but were limited by their lack of power and off-road flexibility, making long journeys difficult and impractical.

It was in this ever-changing landscape that William S. Harley and Arthur Davidson set out to design a revolutionary machine that would meet the needs of adventurous travelers. In 1903, they founded the Harley-Davidson company in Milwaukee, Wisconsin. Their goal was to create a powerful, reliable motorcycle capable of traversing long distances on varied roads. Possibly inspired by the first motorcycle, invented in 1885 by a German engineer named Gottlieb Daimler, who created a gasoline-powered internal combustion engine and attached it to a bicycle frame to form the first motorcycle prototype, the first model produced by Harley-Davidson was a small 400cc motorcycle. It quickly made a name for itself thanks to its ruggedness and exceptional performance. Indeed, the brand's popularity began to grow, not least thanks to participation in racing competitions, where Harley-Davidson motorcycles demonstrated their superiority. Competition victories captured the public's attention and reinforced the brand's image as an emblematic symbol of adventure and freedom.

This freedom, before it was motivated by transcendental inspirations, primarily served the more basic *Need* to belong. Human beings, like many other dynamic agents, are social creatures with a need for proximity and connection with fellow human beings. Indeed, unlike geeks or myself, most of us don't like to spend time thinking or pondering the cause-and-effect chains of our Matrix but prefer to be in quasi-permanent contact with our community, friends or loved ones.

Transportation has therefore been one of the key drivers of human progress, as well as a significant lubricant of connection between individuals and distant communities. Before modern times, a few innovations are worth noting. The wheel (3500 BC) revolutionized transport, enabling people to carry goods and travel greater distances. The horse-drawn carriage (1500 BC) was one of the first vehicles used for transportation and greatly expanded people's ability to travel, to visit friends and family living far away and to explore new territories. Finally, the steam engine, invented by James Watt in 1769, marked a major turning point in the history of transport and industrial machinery in general, as we all know.

More recently, innovation in personal vehicles was initiated in 1886 by Karl Benz, the father of the Mercedes-Benz brand. Since then, cars have continued to evolve in terms of safety, speed, fuel efficiency and durability, enabling us to cover great distances. Given the high cost of most cars, considered the second biggest family expense after a house, public transport, notably buses, trains and subways, has offered a welcome alternative. This has democratized the freedom to move from one place to another for all social classes. In public transport too, the Wright brothers' first successful flight in 1903 ushered in the age of air travel. Commercial flights are now accessible to all and have enabled people to cover great distances in a matter of hours, making the world "within walking distance".

The social *Need* occupying the third floor of Maslow's pyramid used to be met by various organizational innovations. The family and closely-knit communities, where everyone knew everyone else, satisfied the *Need* to belong. Marriage, that important institution formally recognized in ancient Mesopotamia with the Code of Hammurabi, and in ancient Egyptian society, with marriage contracts and ceremonies documented as far back as 3000 BC, enabled people to find love and companionship, perhaps for life, and many cultures had specific rituals and practices to bring couples, not to say lovers, together. Without spoiling the romanticism, matrimonial practices varied according to culture and time, but the underlying purpose in the past was often to establish kinship ties, regulate sexual behavior and ensure social and economic stability. In many societies, marriage was also closely linked to the transfer of property and the formation of alliances between families or tribes, especially in times of hostility.

Religion, that significant social innovation, also became an essential part of people's lives. It has been a source of comfort and community for thousands of years. Through religious rituals, gatherings and beliefs, people found, and still find in many countries, a sense of belonging and a source of strength in times of difficulty. So it's not surprising to call anyone who shares the same beliefs "brother" or "sister", whether in Islam, Judaism or most other sects and religions. Religion has provided people with a shared identity and a common purpose and has helped bring them together in a way that transcends their individual and genetic differences.

Commercial relations, or simply "**business**", are also a winning strategy when it comes to linking individuals and countries, even those with differences. It seems to work for Europe, for example, with the free trade agreement within the European Union after the Second World War. This economic, and then political, cooperation has fostered growth and development in member countries, strengthening ties between peoples who all speak a Latinized language, but who barely understand each other, if not through an English referential. Because, yes, a common language helps you to socialize and find love, romantic or platonic – just ask an Erasmus student who hardly speaks the local language of the host country.

Throughout history, language, as a structured means of verbal communication, has enabled individuals to forge links with other group members, thus fostering a sense of belonging to a community or group. Several anthropological studies have highlighted the importance of language in creating social cohesion and strengthening relationships. One notable study by anthropologist Robin Dunbar examined the correlation between language and the size of social groups. Dunbar proposed that there is a cognitive limit to the number of stable relationships an individual can maintain. This limit, known as "Dunbar's number", is estimated at around 150 people. According to this theory, the development of language in primates, including humans, would have evolved to facilitate communication and coordination within these relatively small social groups before being adopted more massively post-Agricultural Revolution.

Sometimes you don't need to understand **to communicate**. Indeed, the arts, and particularly music, as a universal language, has also helped to satisfy this Maslow level. Music, possibly rudimentarily invented in the time of our hunter-gatherer ancestors, has a unique ability to touch the emotions and transcend cultural and linguistic barriers. It has the power to evoke feelings of joy, sadness, nostalgia, love and more. Musical performances, whether played in groups or listened to at concerts, create a sense of community and shared emotion. Innovation in music has further strengthened this connection. Over the centuries, technological advances such as the invention of musical instruments, audio recording and the distribution of music on cassettes, CDs and then streaming, have made it possible to spread and share music on a much larger scale. Artists can now reach a global audience and touch people from different cultures.

Language in all its forms can become the backbone of a sense of shared identity. On a national level, this social *innovation*, ideological or political in nature, or even dogmatic, feeds **patriotism**, the love and devotion to one's country, which has long played a powerful role in satisfying the human need to belong and in promoting a sense of identity and community. So, it's hardly surprising that when you travel abroad for the first time, you're delighted to meet your fellow "brothers" and to be able to speak your native language again. Throughout history, various persuasive techniques have been used to reinforce this sense of identity. One of these is the promotion of national symbols. These emblems, such as flags, anthems and national monuments, serve as tangible representations of a collective identity and arouse feelings of pride and attachment. They are often associated with important historical events, heroes (or soccer players) or values that resonate with the population.

Combining these two organizational innovations – language and patriotism – we come across many historical cases where a country innovates its official language to reinforce or reaffirm a group belonging that lasts over the long term. The Vietnamese example is relevant in this respect. Vietnamese, a member of the Austro-Asian language family, has a complex linguistic history influenced by a variety of factors. The language has evolved through interactions between indigenous Austro-Asian speakers and other language groups in the region. Vietnamese has thus integrated lexical borrowings, grammatical features and cultural elements from these neighboring languages, leading to a linguistic identity that is distinct, but quite similar to that of the former Chinese occupiers, who, it should be noted, occupied this country for over ten centuries. The Vietnamese writing system was thus, unsurprisingly, based on modified Chinese characters. As a result, as soon as a unified Vietnamese state was established, the priority was to reformat the modern Vietnamese language and dissociate it from Mandarin. Thus began a simplification and standardization of this language in the 17th century, with the introduction of Quốc Ngữ, a romanized system, deleting Chinese letters. This transformation made literacy more accessible and contributed to a sense of national unity and identity among the Vietnamese people.

Similarly, in my native Morocco, it is commonly accepted, though not publicly communicated in this way, that Arabs arrived in Morocco in the seventh century AD, following the Muslim conquest of the region, led by General Uqba ibn Nafi. As a result, Arabic gradually became the dominant language, although Berber (also known as Tamazight), the language of the indigenous inhabitants of North Africa, continues to be spoken by many Berber-speaking communities in Morocco. The Berbers have their own distinct language and culture dating back thousands of years. Nonetheless, Berbers appear to have long been marginalized culturally and linguistically. In recent decades, however, there has been a growing movement to promote and preserve the Berber language, notably with its official introduction into the primary education system and public institutions, a decision taken with the aim of fostering inclusion, reinforcing a sense of belonging to the Moroccan homeland and mostly avoiding any ethnic instabilities and conflicts.

Today, the need for socialization, once fulfilled by religious or patriotic communities, has been transformed by the Industrial Revolution. Most people now live in large cities, and secularism has become an important part of human beliefs, particularly in developed countries (and China). Small communities have (unfortunately) disappeared in favor of large corporations and transactional, often artificial, exchanges. As a result, many people find themselves obliged to fulfill part of their non-familial socialization needs in their study or work environment. Indeed, companies can create a sense of community by fostering a positive work culture, encouraging teamwork and offering integration and after-work opportunities. For schools and universities, promoting a positive and inclusive school culture, offering opportunities for student participation in extracurricular activities, is an attempt to satisfy this social need. However, these institutions often only partially meet these needs, and even produce the opposite effect. Depending on the size of the group and the social dynamics within the team, employees may feel like a number in a herd. In the classroom, students risk being the victims of bullying, ignorance or jealous rivalries, creating a toxic environment. Fortunately, or not, a series of technological innovations has come to offset, and even deepen, these socio-cultural changes.

Another faster (or lazier) way of meeting this fundamental need to belong is through electrical or electromagnetic signals. This process-type *innovation*, which partially cannibalized the need for transportation, is the landline telephone. Later, cell phones and then smartphones would take over, but let's start with the beginnings. The telegraph, invented by Samuel Morse in 1837, was the first long-distance communication technology. It enabled messages to be sent quickly and efficiently over long distances, paving the way for new advances in telecommunications. Forty years later, Alexander Graham Bell is credited with inventing the first telephone in 1876. This enabled people to maintain relationships with friends and family who lived far away, without having to physically travel. Like all useful innovations, telephones evolved into smaller, multitasking versions. More than a century after Bell's masterpiece, the first cell phone, launched by Motorola in 1983, finally enabled users to communicate on the move, without the complications of wiring. Remember telephone booths or kiosks? They're a thing of the past, except in a few museums and streets of London.

Complex innovations rarely appear all at once. They are often made possible by technical and organizational enablers that precede them. In this case, the development of the telecoms infrastructure made the innovation of telephones possible. This refers to the systems and facilities that enable communication over long distances, including telephone lines, fiber-optic cables, satellites and cellular networks. Another important aspect of telecoms infrastructure is the development of signal transmission and reception technologies, such as modems, switches and radio transmitters. In turn, each of these innovations relies on an advanced understanding of electromagnetic waves and electronics. Towards the end of the 20th century, the internet, one of the most disruptive innovations ever commercialized, completed this infrastructure by supporting fast, secure "voice over internet protocol (VoIP)" communication.

With the hectic pace of life in recent decades, people seem to have felt the *need* to communicate fluidly and, above all, succinctly. So text messaging was introduced in the early 1990s. The very first text, sent on December 3, 1992, simply said "Happy Christmas", and was sent by Neil Papworth. A year later, in 1993, Nokia introduced SMS functionality with the famous "beep" to signal the arrival of a message. Following the Schumpeterian law of creative destruction, the same Nokia company was turned upside down after the launch of the first iPhone in 2007. This marked the official start of the smartphone era (if we don't count the BlackBerry), which has transformed the way people communicate and connect with others. Smartphones offer users a wide range of communication options, including voice and video calls, texting and e-mail. With Web 2.0, other channels of exchange on the web opened up, and social networks were born. By now, I bet you've got one or more of these great apps installed on your smartphone, such as Facebook, WhatsApp, Twitter, Instagram, Snapchat, WeChat, Line, used by millions or even billions of users. People can then stay connected with friends and family from all over the world, no matter where they live, and for free to boot (well, the price is your attention). Social networking has also made it possible to form new relationships and meet people with similar interests and passions. Combined with Web 2.0, these applications have restored a sense of virtual community to increasingly isolated individuals.

When it comes to romance, the days when your mother had to choose a life partner for you from your local caste or religious community are almost over. Today's generation prefers autonomy of choice (with less responsibility?). In the age of big cities and capitalist slogans like "the consumer is king", extroverts have become accustomed to consummating love by flirting at parties and social events. If this proves too complicated or tedious, there's always a lazier digital alternative with no risk of direct rejection. Dating apps have revolutionized the way couples meet and made finding a partner, short or long term, theoretically easier than ever. Thanks to the ability to browse endless profiles, even in conservative countries like Saudi Arabia (tested!). That said, despite the opening of all these new doors to socialization, many people still feel isolated and disconnected. A thousand virtual friends on Facebook are no match for three good real ones.

The ease and accessibility of such innovations can only create the illusion of connectivity, as the focus is on quantity rather than quality of relationships. Connections are therefore superficial and lack depth in most cases. Nevertheless, innovations are ultimately just tools and processes. Companies are to blame, in part, for subtly enticing users to connect more, using various nudging techniques, such as good recommendations of products and content you'd be susceptible to, not least through AI algorithms. If users exercise a lack of self-control or misuse such innovation, this may compromise their ability to extract positive *Value*. Thus, psychological suffering may follow.

ဆ✴ဆ

Innovating a perfect self-image

In the early 20th century, a remarkable woman named Amelia Earhart captivated the world with her daring spirit and desire to challenge the status quo. Born on July 24, 1897, in Atchison, Kansas, Earhart developed a fascination for aviation from an early age. Contrary to social norms that confined women to traditional roles, she pursued her passion for flight with unwavering determination, as she faced sexist discrimination and skepticism from those who felt that flying was unsuitable for women. Despite these challenges, she remained fearless, firmly believing in the power of her dreams.

In 1932, Earhart achieved a revolutionary feat that made her a part of history. She became the first woman to fly solo across the Atlantic Ocean. This remarkable achievement catapulted her to international stardom, earning her the admiration and respect of people the world over. Amelia Earhart's self-confidence stemmed not only from her achievements but from her unshakeable belief in herself. She once declared, "The decision to act is the most difficult; the rest is just tenacity." Tragically, Amelia Earhart's life was cut short mid-flight, during an attempt to circumnavigate the globe in 1937. However, her legacy lives on among many people, especially women.

Earhart's self-confidence was rooted in her strong sense of personal identity and her refusal to let society's expectations define her. This fits in with the fourth floor of Maslow's pyramid, centered on the *need* for esteem from others, and above all from oneself. For despite our social tendencies and our need to be part of a group, we also need individuality to cultivate a distinct identity and express the singularity of our ego. This need for individuality can be observed in many aspects of life, both in human beings and in the animal kingdom.

Animals belonging to some species have unique behaviors and characteristics that distinguish them from one another. For example, male birds often display bright colors and sing distinctive songs to attract mates, demonstrating their competitive individuality. Primates, such as chimpanzees, also have distinct personalities, some being more daring and adventurous, others more generous, a few more dominant. These individual differences in animals are essential for the survival and reproduction of the species, as genetic diversification allows for greater adaptability to environmental change, and therefore more likely survival of the "selfish gene", in the words of biologist Richard Dawkins. It's also worth noting that, unlike Man, the Matrix's other dynamic agents seem to be limited in their process of individualism by their genetic codes on the one hand, and by their social and environmental interactions on the other. In other words, the idea of "choice" is relatively human, as it correlates with reason and consciousness, and therefore mainly with the third dimension of the Matrix. If a dog is different from his brother, it's because they've been coded differently at the genetic level, and/or their personalities have been unconsciously shaped by a different upbringing, with different masters, for example.

Man, being only a recent brick in a long evolutionary process, remains just as influenced by his genetic code and learning, especially at a young age, when the brain is still fresh and eager for new data. Nevertheless, in adulthood, or even before, we control, or think we control, our life and our choices, for optimal self-esteem, ideally approved by those around us. In today's globalized and relatively free world, we can see that everyone has their own tastes, interests and preferences that set them apart from the rest. For example, some people prefer a specific style of clothing, a certain type of music or a form of artistic expression that reflects their unique personality. These individual choices contribute to our sense of identity and enable us to stand out in a social world. Come to think of it, there's that dualistic notion again, between social conformity and individual, even individualistic, freedom.

To compensate for this dualistic imbalance, from the smallest tribes to the largest cosmopolitan cities, Man has sought **a socially acceptable rationalization of his role within the group**. As exclusion is subconsciously equated with isolation and death, we tend to feel emotional pain ranging from discomfort to depression when our peers at work point out our late deliveries, when the teacher starts by quoting our paper first, specifying that it's in ascending order of marks, or when our partner suggests that we're bad in bed, after ten years together. In fact, from the earliest tribes and civilizations, members have sought to establish, prove and maintain a decent opinion of their skills and worth in the eyes of those around them. They also want to feel worthy of this social recognition, that they are not impostors. This fundamental human *Need* has been at the root of many innovations over the years.

One of the oldest ways of earning points in the eyes of others was through an upgrade in **status or social rank**. In ancient times, and still today, albeit to a limited extent, this status was often determined at birth, via family ties. If you were born the son of a king, a minister or an oracle, you were relatively sure of a decent social status for the rest of your life. And vice versa, *a priori*. In modern times, it can be a complex combination of factors, including financial wealth, social connections and education. The latter was originally a privilege reserved for the rich and elite, but technological and political innovations have made it accessible to a wider public, opening up opportunities for citizens from all walks of life to gain access to specific knowledge, and thus a better social standing.

With the advent of **the printing press** in the 15th century, books became more affordable and accessible, facilitating access to information and knowledge. Subsequently, in a growing number of countries, the government (or the political system in power) played an active role in promoting education by investing in schools, recruiting teachers and developing programs, albeit often biased, facilitating access to education for a greater number of people, particularly in developing countries. The concept of compulsory education was also an important policy innovation. Compulsory education laws require all children to attend school up to a certain age, ensuring everyone can access basic education. This has been an essential tool for reducing illiteracy and promoting social and economic progress. At the same time, the development of radio and television in the 20th century made it possible to broadcast certain educational and informative programs to a wide audience. Today, the internet has revolutionized education, opening the way for internet users to access a multitude of educational resources and make contact with teachers and students from all over the world. The EdTech revolution based on online courses, learning platforms like Khan Academy, and tools and assistants powered by artificial intelligence is shaking up and will continue to shape the methods and quality of teaching, even in remote areas or with limited access to traditional educational establishments.

Still in the context of Web 2.0, beyond their role in promoting belonging and love, as discussed on the previous Maslow floor, **social media platforms** have also helped raise the status of many people, talented or not, even those with low or average status at birth. This digital democratization of entrepreneurship, thanks to the internet and its ad hoc innovations, has opened the field for this new generation of influencers to reach people around the world, expand their social networks and benefit from theoretically infinite possibilities for self-promotion and personal enhancement. Those who manage to gather a significant number of followers on TikTok, or other heavyweight platforms, are often perceived as influential (and wealthy), further increasing their social status and opportunities. Without television, Instagram and YouTube, what would be the social status and wealth of Kim Kardashian and Cristiano Ronaldo? I'll leave you to imagine.

Today, *innovation* itself is a royal road, nicely Americanized, to fame. Indeed, technology start-ups are a kind of Eldorado for talented people motivated to make their mark in the capitalist game, thanks to innovative ideas that, if successful, result in unprecedented wealth and social status. Have you ever heard of Chester Carlson? Stephanie Kwolek? And Percy Spencer? Probably not. Yet these names have had a tremendous impact on our lives. Carlson was an American physicist and inventor who developed xerography, the technology behind modern photocopying. His invention powered Xerox and other machines and contributed to the democratization of knowledge before the age of the internet. Kwolek is a chemist who developed Kevlar, a highly resistant synthetic material used in bullet-proof vests, helmets and other protective equipment, thus having a considerable impact on public safety. Finally, thanks to Spencer, you can enjoy the luxury of a hot meal in two minutes. He innovated the microwave oven, revolutionizing the way we cook and prepare food. Many other names fall into this circle of the forgotten, because very often, over the generations, innovation ceases to be innovation and is transformed into a commodity, a "business-as-usual". What's more, in the pre-internet era, information circulated more slowly. With the rise of the digital age of mediatization and unlimited access to information, entrepreneurs like Elon Musk, Mark Zuckerberg and Jack Ma have become household names, celebrities, known for their transformative contributions to the world.

Far from the world of celebrities, in a non-conformist society, so in pretty much all societies today, individuals of all social classes strive to stand out and reflect their status and personality through their appearance. Take "clothing", for example. In addition to its part in the *Need* to survive against extreme weather, or its satisfaction of the *Need* to belong through uniform, traditional, professional or patriotic costumes, it is just as crucial today to reflect a form of personal expression, a means of communicating one's own identity. People dress in specific ways to indicate their social class, cultural background, personal style and beliefs too. If you wear a suit and tie, you're an auditor, lawyer or consultant. Professional and serious, almost boring. You give an impression of authority and conformity to the rules. You may own a house or two, with outstanding debts. On the other hand, if you're always dressed in a hippie or casual style, you're perceived as an anarchist artist, open to new experiences, probably poor and with no clear plans for the future. These mental classifications of people may be wrong, depending on the case, and are of course, context dependent. Yet they occur all the time, often short-circuiting our consciousness and aiming to order the world to relax our instinctive fears of Chaos.

A social experiment, known as "The Suit Experiment", or the suit-and-tie experiment, was conducted by ABC News' "What Would You Do?" in 2012. The experiment involved sending two differently dressed actors, one in a suit and the other in scruffy clothes, to a New Jersey train station to see how passersby would react to their pleas for help when they feigned discomfort and fell to the ground. In line with my earlier analysis, the experiment showed that people were statistically more inclined to help the well-dressed actor than the actor dressed in shoddy clothing. Mr. Suit was able to get help from passersby within seconds, while the socially "badly-dressed" actor was largely ignored and had difficulty attracting support from others. This experiment and so many others highlight the impact of appearance and social status on how we are perceived by others and how we are treated in society.

Given this important social aspect, **the fashion and luxury industries** have enjoyed a steady rise for several decades. *Innovation* in these industries has been essential to meeting consumers' needs in terms of their sense of esteem. Advances in textile technology have helped create fabrics that are not only aesthetically pleasing but also functional. For example, moisture-wicking fabrics that keep the body cool and dry have become popular for workout wear, responding to the need for comfort, self-confidence and sexual attractiveness, even during sporting activity.

252 | PLUNGING INTO THE UNKNOWN

In recent years, the data revolution has innovated virtual reality, 3D printing and artificial intelligence, further personalizing the clothes we wear, and enabling individuals to create one-of-a-kind models, customized to their tastes and reflecting their personal style. In the near future, all you will have to do is upload two to three photos of yourself and a brief description of your style, and you'll receive a handful of recommendations tailored to your size and style. No need to think or spend days looking for the right pair of jeans or the dress of your dreams. Social networks are also part of this sector, keeping the general public up to date with the latest fashion trends. Influencers and bloggers have become powerful voices in the industry, showcasing their unique sense of fashion and garnering a massive audience. We dress less for ourselves, and more for our influencers and friends.

Let's recall, in this same respect, how Nike, in the 1980s, largely overtaken by Adidas, launched a marketing-type innovation, collaborating with a then young and talented basketball player. Nike signed an endorsement contract with Michael Jordan, creating the iconic Air Jordan sneaker line, shoes designed specifically for Jordan, with his name and unique brand elements (colors, design, etc.). This was a radical departure from the norm, as athletes at the time usually wore generic team shoes. Nike had clearly understood the "influencer" effect of a star or public figure on the audience's need for esteem, especially among young people, a kind of "Trojan horse" to sell its brand on a large scale. Nike's market capitalization, reflecting the value of a company, is now five to six times that of Adidas.

Actions and behaviors in social contexts can also influence our social value. LITERALLY. In recent years, the Chinese government has developed a new system for monitoring and controlling the behavior of its citizens, known as the "social credit system". This system uses a combination of technology, artificial intelligence, cameras and other surveillance tools to collect data on citizens and assign them a "social credit" rating, based on their behavior. The social credit system is supposed to reinforce "trustworthy" behavior and punish those who engage in behavior deemed detrimental to society, such as fraud, smoking in non-smoking areas, disregarding crosswalks and publishing fake news online. The system draws on a wide range of data sources to assign social credit scores, including financial records, social media activity and online purchases. In short, the more social credit a Chinese citizen acquires, the simpler his or her social life and access to public and private services will be.

Whether or not you support this type of Enhanced Social Order is a moral issue unto itself. The point is that, like AI-powered computerized data analysis, our minds mix many factors to deduce a person's "worth". Most people don't yet live in a highly egalitarian environment, as in some Scandinavian countries or Buddhist communities. Instead, they are the subject and object of this mental calculation every time they turn their attention to someone new. Even my mother visually measures the weight I've lost or gained since the last visit, to assess my current state of well-being. Indeed, in most developing countries, the level of body fat is still a positive measure, not that I share such unbalanced practice.

Moreover, an individual's social value also derives from the professional role he or she occupies. Recent scientific progress has led to a high degree of specialization. A century ago, we had a doctor (or alchemist) who was expected to cure almost any ailment. Today, don't hesitate to count the job titles on the doors of hospitals and clinics. Because as long as you have a doctor nameplate on your door, your social value is relatively high in the eyes of others. Ask any parent what they want for their children in the near future and doctor, pilot or engineer will probably top the list, especially in developing countries. A doctor is better than a teacher. A teacher is better than a blacksmith. A blacksmith is better than an unemployed person. The latter is better than a beggar. That's the energy-saving mental shortcut most of us use. Innovations in education, money or fashion only accentuate these cognitive heuristics.

෨ ✶ ෬

Innovating all the way

In ancient Greece, in the fifth century BC, a man stood up against the conventions of his time, ready to defy preconceived ideas and seek the objective truths of life. This old yet wise man, whose name still resonates today, was a fearless philosopher and revolutionary thinker: Socrates.

Born in Athens in 469 BC, in a society of rigid norms and unquestioned authority, Socrates was no ordinary fellow insofar as he seemed unconcerned with all the lower strata of the Maslow pyramid. In fact, he often displayed an almost unhuman disregard for material wealth and social or political power. Instead, Socrates stood out for his relentless quest for wisdom, his insatiable thirst to understand the world around him and the profound truths of the human condition. His sole ambition was to stimulate minds and guide others towards the fulfillment of their own potential. With his unique method of questioning, known as the Socratic method, he provoked intense debate and challenged people to question their deepest certainties, for another of Socrates' central ideas was his belief that **wisdom lies in the recognition of our own ignorance**. He argued that it was wiser to recognize what we don't know than to pretend to know absolute truths. This intellectual humility was at the heart of his philosophical approach.

But his innovative ideas and unconventional approach didn't sit well with those still stuck in the psychological layers of survival, belonging or esteem and power. As a result, they aroused the distrust of the intellectual and political elite of the time. Socrates was seen as a threat to the established Order, as he encouraged people to question the very foundations of pre-established societal organization. Despite the dangers that surrounded him, Socrates, like a soldier of enlightenment, refused to remain silent. He continued to share his ideas, to challenge the powerful and to seek the truth, even at the risk of his own life. Accused of corrupting youth and denying the gods, he was condemned to death. It was in these tragic circumstances that he uttered these immortal words: "The unexamined life is not worth living". A powerful statement that still resonates today, reminding us of the vital importance of reflection and the perpetual quest for autonomous truth.

Socrates' life is a striking example of the sacrifice he was willing to make for the cause of self-fulfillment, that "rooftop" of Maslow's pyramid.

If you recall the paradigm of the straight path, discussed in the previous chapter, self-actualization could mean aiming for the X_{max} between Order and Chaos, life and death, male and female energies, etc. It would mean learning to cook the best chicken masala instead of surviving on chicken scraps. The function of food would thus go beyond its basic role in survival and the transmission of energy to the Matrix agents. It becomes a goal in itself, a work of art, a means of personal expression, an end-by-itself and a symbol of creativity. In this respect, Maslow's stage of self-actualization is the highest level of egotistical *Need*, where a person seeks to realize his or her full potential and, to paraphrase Maslow himself, **to become all that he or she is capable of being**. For humanity, this stage of play would include not only the fight against famine and the building of shelters for the homeless, but also and above all space conquests, the development of a digital metaverse within our own Matrix and any act that contributes to expanding our field of possibility. For companies, it could be a sustainable and innovative strategy, rather than a plan based on the greedy pursuit of profit. Numerous innovations have thus contributed to satisfying this high-end *Need*, separating us from other dynamic agents. Here are a few case studies.

In the first place, the socio-cultural innovation of religion and spirituality (again) not only fed the *Need* for community belonging and social order, but also established moral standards for the community to follow. Lying, for example, would enable any impostor (or actor) to earn his daily bread, or seize a lucrative opportunity, such as selling a defective product for the price of a new one. From the Maslow perspective of the lower layers of the pyramid, this would be perfectly justified to survive or acquire wealth. However, from the top of this same pyramid, lying would be "bad", as it is banned by almost all beliefs and reflects a moral and evolutionary baseness that would work against the liar in the long term by losing the trust of his peers or clients. Moreover, religions have also provided a mystical, albeit metaphysical, framework for understanding the nature of the world before science and apprehending a purpose behind all this universal simulation we call "life". By bringing order to the duality of good and evil, prophets, shamans, gurus and priests have each defined distinct paths, with more or less common principles, towards enlightenment, inner peace and less enslavement to animal impulses.

Seen from this transcendent angle, religious or spiritual beliefs go beyond dogmas and rituals passed down mechanically from generation to generation. Indeed, for an individual reaching the top of the Maslow pyramid, the Abrahamic concept – distorted in my opinion – of an external God who is necessarily good and a commander of human troops, gives way to an internal and mystical spirituality, both with one's whole being and with less ego. Incidentally, the phrase "Allah Akbar", terrifying in the West as it is often associated with terrorist attacks, means "God is greater", without specifying the object of comparison. This statement cannot be understood by looking outside oneself, nor by blowing oneself up and killing innocent people. Only a deep inner experience beyond space-time could bring the individual slightly closer to such order of magnitude. Carl Jung called this process "**individuation**", which is a path of integration of a person's unconscious and conscious aspects to achieve psychological wholeness. He went so far as to denounce classical Catholicism, confirming that "religion is a barrier to the experience of God". In this respect, we can propose the following application of the Fundamental Identity:

Spirituality=(Need+Motivation)×(Creativity+Technology) ×Value

a. *Need (of the end-user)*: Self-actualization, inner peace & equilibrium.

b. *Motivation (of the innovator)*: Sharing experience, guidelines towards this achievement.

c. *Creativity (or vision)*: Metaphorical myths expressing experience in human words.

d. *Technology (or implementation)*: Sacred books and rituals, dos and don'ts, meditation.

e. *Value (or outcome)*: Psychological fulfillment and mystical experience.

In today's Westernized and secular society, traditional churches and cults have largely been supplanted by a belief in the power of the super-ego to conquer challenges, accompanied by the reliance on wisdom from figures like Seneca, Greek philosophers, and accomplished entrepreneurs. Lucrative personal development seminars and podcasts led by influential figures such as Tony Robbins and Tim Ferriss have taken center stage. With the vast availability of information through online platforms, media content, Amazon books, and online courses, fulfilling this desire for personal growth has become more accessible than ever before.

That said, one fact is certain. **Understanding is not knowing!** In fact, personal fulfillment requires more individual involvement, time for self-reflection and investment in one's own personal growth through action. One specific category of post-Industrial Revolution innovations has freed up more time for leisure and interesting professional pursuits. Oddly enough, it's **household appliances**.

Before the washing machine, people, mostly women, had to spend hours scrubbing clothes by hand, wringing them out and hanging them to dry, before picking them up, folding them and finally putting them away. This time-consuming and labor-intensive chore left little time for other transcendental activities. With the innovation of the washing machine, this task became much easier and quicker. Women could now throw clothes into the machine, press a button and go about their business while the machine "turned" the bulk of the work. And what about the kitchen? Before the microwave oven, meal preparation required a significant investment of time and effort. Thanks to this innovation and others like it, meals can now be prepared in a matter of minutes, freeing up time for activities higher up the Maslow pyramid. Today, cooking has become less of a chore and more of a rare romantic or family act. Clearly, in many countries, women – and increasingly men – still prefer to prepare a good meal, especially when they have children. However, the latest figures tell a different story. According to a 2019 survey by the U.S. Bureau of Labor Statistics, Americans spend an average of 53 minutes a day preparing and cleaning food. This statistic barely compares with my Moroccan childhood when a couscous would take my mom all morning to get ready. What's more, with Uber Eats and express recipes online, there's no need to eat a preheated meal. With just a few clicks, your wish of the day is served in minutes.

Another innovation is the dishwasher, which has eliminated the need to wash dishes by hand, a tedious and time-consuming task. Vacuum cleaners made it easier to keep the house clean, without the need for a Cinderella, the equivalent of the Moroccan Fatima, to sweep and mop the floors. Air conditioners have enabled people to return to comfortable indoor temperatures, whatever the weather outside. All these conditions have led to a major and ongoing social change: equal opportunities for women to enter the job market, regardless of their marital status. The result has been not only increased economic productivity and a sense of gender equity, but also led to a sharp drop in birth rates. Thanks to equal education between the sexes, the creation of nanny (and grandmother nanny) jobs and, of course, the use of ultra-innovative contraceptives, fewer and fewer women around the world are serving as baby factories. Fortunately, most of them are free to decide if, when and with whom they want to reproduce.

In addition to these household gadgets, many **post-industrial innovations** have focused on enhancing personal fulfillment and improving the human experience as a whole. In this case, the advent of personal computers, and by extension smartphones and tablets, has revolutionized the way people work, communicate and access information. Tools for creativity, learning and self-expression are now at our fingertips. They have opened up new avenues for personal development, exploration and self-realization through activities such as writing, programming and graphic design. Superimposed on the internet and its various platforms, all these product-type innovations have offered individuals unprecedented opportunities to express themselves, showcase their talents and pursue their personal interests. The rise of wearable technologies, such as fitness trackers and smartwatches, has enabled users to take control of their health and well-being, by monitoring their physical activity, sleep patterns and various health parameters. In addition, virtual and augmented reality technologies offer immersive, interactive experiences that push back the boundaries of reality. They provide opportunities for exploration, learning and creative expression. Even within our smartphones, there are all kinds of entertaining and instructive applications, from gaming to meditation, from sport to online education.

Art is also a form of self-fulfilling innovation that does not directly support survival. Since the first artistic manifestations in prehistoric caves, art has evolved to become a means of expression and creativity, nourishing the human soul and, if we manage to understand or feel it, arousing new emotions and paradigms. Basically, it's a form of personal and collective expression that enables artists to realize themselves, communicate messages and share their vision of the world with others. Art, whether in the form of music, painting, dance, text or other art forms, is a source of inspiration and reflection that nourishes our spirit, stimulates our imagination and enables us to connect with our transcendent essence. This very human *Need* preceded the innovation of thousands of musical instruments, painting styles and materials, analog and then digital cameras, theaters, movie theaters and Netflix.

Applied to states and organizations, self-actualization can mean pushing the boundaries of humanity, reducing corporate greed or caring for the planet.

Such advanced frameworks are represented by the notion of **Human rights**, which new generations take for granted. This organizational innovation advocates fundamental rights for all people, simply because they are human in nature. These rights include civil, political, economic, social and cultural rights, such as the right to a dignified life, security, freedom of movement, speech and expression, access to education, healthcare and housing, according to country-specific perimeters and conditions. This concept undoubtedly dates back to ancient civilizations, such as Greece and Rome, where the idea of natural rights was first formulated. However, the modern formulation of human rights appeared in the 18th century, during the Age of Enlightenment, notably with the American Constitution of the Founding Fathers in 1787, and the French Revolution two years later, which marked a turning point in history, with the adoption of the Declaration of the Rights of Man and of the Citizen, proclaiming the famous hymn "liberté, égalité, fraternité", translated as you can guess to "freedom, equality, brotherhood". This document served as a model for other declarations, including the Universal Declaration of Human Rights, adopted by the United Nations General Assembly in 1948. Since then, human rights have become a cornerstone of international law and have been incorporated into the constitutions of many countries. The concept of human rights has also influenced beliefs in social justice and equality, inspiring movements for civil rights, women's rights, children's rights, LGBTQ+ rights, and even animal rights.

Democracy, another theme correlated with human rights, was a form of political innovation at the time, responding to the highest Maslow need for freedom and equal opportunity. This political trend emerged over 2,500 years ago with the ancient Greeks. As a reminder, etymologically, "democracy" has its origins in the Greek words "demos" and "kratos", meaning "people" and "rule" respectively, i.e., the rule of the people. In earlier times, leadership was often based on the third floor of Maslow's pyramid, through hereditary succession, religious merit or force, such as coups d'état. In many societies, before and since, rulers have been born into power, as in monarchies and dynasties. This is known as the "Great Man" theory in leadership studies. In case of doubt, due to the absence of an heir or because the heir was too young to rule, social unrest was frequent, and a powerful clan often took power by force.

The implementation of this *innovation* took many forms before reaching its current Western version, namely the separation of powers, parliaments and the right of all citizens to vote. In Athens, for example, decisions were taken in assemblies such as the Athenian Assembly, where all male citizens over the age of 18 were entitled to vote on matters of public policy. In addition to this unisex assembly, the Greeks also used a system of drawing lots called "sortition" to select jury members and, sometimes, leaders. Over time, the concept of democracy spread to other parts of the world and various forms of elected government emerged in different cultures and societies. Among the first relatively democratic governments were the Roman Republic and the city-states of medieval Italy.

The modern form of democracy emerged during the Enlightenment, with the development of liberal political theory emphasizing individual rights and freedoms. At the end of the 18th century, the American and French revolutions led to the creation of the first modern democratic nations.

Since then, this process, which counterbalances man's natural greed for power and control, has continued to evolve and adapt to society's new needs and challenges. Today, there are many different forms of democratic government, ranging from presidential to parliamentary systems, and from direct to representative democracy. The contribution of democracy to human flourishing cannot be overstated, at least ideologically, by taking into account the needs and desires of a majority of citizens, not just those of a dominant few.

Some visionaries, like NASA researchers and Elon Musk, see the notion of freedom beyond its political and social aspects, through a universal lens. Like a childhood dream, humankind has always been fascinated by the vast expanse of space and the possibility of exploring it. From the earliest astronomical observations to the recent robot rover landing on Mars, the pursuit of space travel has been a remarkable human endeavor, and it continues to be so. The history of space exploration began in earnest in the middle of the 20th century with the launch of Sputnik, the first artificial satellite, by the Soviet Union in 1957. This launch triggered the famous space race between the USA and the Soviet Union, which saw the development of manned spacecraft, the Apollo lunar landings and the creation of the International Space Station. One of the main innovations that made all this madness possible was the development of rockets capable of reaching high altitudes and freeing themselves from the Earth's gravitational pull. The creation of state-subsidized institutions such as NASA and the European Space Agency was just as instrumental in pushing this small extraterrestrial step for a few astronauts, and this giant leap for mankind and its need for "self-actualization", as Neil Armstrong would have put it.

In recent decades, **space exploration** has turned from manned missions such as Apollo, to the exploration of other planets and celestial bodies by means of remotely controlled robots and space probes, sent to Mars, Jupiter and Saturn, and providing invaluable data on these planets and their histories. Progress has also been made in the field of space telescopes, such as the Hubble and then the James Webb, which have enabled astrophysicists to observe distant galaxies and study the origins of the universe. Another recent development in this respect concerns the rise of private space companies such as Elon Musk's SpaceX and Jeff Bezos' Blue Origin, which are focusing on the development of reusable rockets and making space travel more affordable for tourists – wealthy ones, of course.

Despite these advances, space exploration still faces many challenges, including high investment costs and the risk of mission failure. From a capitalist point of view, the new energy, AI and biotech sectors seem more lucrative for an investor, at least in the medium term.

Take, for example, the very recent trend towards electric vehicles (EVs). These are based on another innovation, that of electric batteries, which have become increasingly efficient since the early 19th century. However, it was only in the 21st century that EVs began to gain in popularity, first through commercially sufficient progress in battery technology, then through improved charging infrastructure, state subsidies for consumers and pollution penalties for automakers, in order to move rapidly towards a greener economy. Today, virtually all carmakers are following in Tesla's footsteps, investing heavily in EV technologies, and governments around the world are implementing policies to encourage the adoption of this new mode of locomotion.

The development of **clean energy technologies**, such as wind and solar power, has also been stimulated by technological advances and government policies. The cost of renewable energies has fallen considerably in recent years, making them more affordable and accessible to individuals and businesses alike. Many countries now produce a significant proportion of their electricity, supposedly cleanly. This whole race is not just motivated by an awakening of conscience. There's another clear objective here: to stimulate an aging European and American economy by opening up new avenues of profit.

Biotechnology, in short **Biotech**, a science that bridges the gap between biology and ICT, an acronym for information and communications technology, is another field that has revolutionized medicine, agriculture and environmental sciences, to name but a few. In recent years in particular,

Biotech has become one of the fastest growing and most exciting areas of research. Transcending our bodily limits became possible. Its tentative beginnings date back to the 1970s, when scientists began exploring the use of genetic engineering to create new products. Since then, biotechnology has progressed rapidly, with breakthroughs in gene editing, synthetic biology and biomanufacturing – the automated production of biologically functional products through bioprinting or bio-assembly. One of the most exciting developments in biotechnology has been the emergence of gene-editing technologies, such as CRISPR-Cas9. With such capabilities, bioengineers acquired the divine power to modify the DNA of living organisms with unprecedented precision, opening up new possibilities for the treatment of genetic diseases and the development of new therapies. Synthetic biology, the engineering of biological systems for specific medical purposes, is another area of biotechnology that has had a profound impact on agriculture in recent years, with the development of genetically modified crops resistant to pests and capable of surviving in harsh environments.

Finally, to finish with Maslow's pyramid, it's imperative to mention the development of AI, whose specific or generic algorithms can be used in optimizing battery performance, driving vehicles autonomously, reducing energy consumption, tailoring education to individual needs, manufacturing complex products, analyzing genetic data, controlling security, translating from and into any language and potentially doing anything that humans can and can't imagine. Artificial intelligence (AI) has come a long way from its beginnings as a mere science-fiction concept. Today, it's a reality that can no longer be ignored, like the iPhone in the late 2000s.

The history of AI, as mentioned in the book's foreword, dates back to the middle of the 20th century, when scientists began to explore the idea of creating machines capable of thinking and learning like humans. The early days of AI were marked by numerous setbacks and failures, a period dubbed the "AI winter". In recent years, however, the development of AI has accelerated considerably, with breakthroughs in machine learning, natural language processing, robotics and the exponential growth of computing capacity. Three of the most remarkable achievements in the field of AI occurred in 1997, 2016 and around 2022.

In 1997, in a six-game chess match between Deep Blue, a supercomputer developed by IBM, and Garry Kasparov, the undisputed world chess champion at the time, the machine ended up beating an expert in its field for the first time, in a game as strategic as chess. It has to be said, however, that Deep Blue was specifically designed to play chess at an incredibly high level, using a combination of brute force calculations and sophisticated evaluation techniques to analyze millions of possible positions per second. Also, knowing that their AI was not yet at a human level, Deep Blue's programmers had coded a latency into the system to trick Kasparov into assuming that the machine was struggling, causing him to rethink his game and make mistakes.

In 2016, Google decided to proceed in a fairer way, by letting its Alpha Go program decide on its strategy and moves, in the most complex social game ever invented, hundreds of times more complex than chess: Go. To the surprise of everyone, including its programmers, Alpha Go defeated Lee Sedol, one of the best Go players in history. It was the official start of deep AI.

This fourth revolution came to fruition around 2022 with the buzz caused by OpenAI's ChatGPT, and other competitors like Google's Bard, which have turned AI into a super powerful assistant available 24/7, endowed with universal memory and near-human creativity, if not a better one.

For our non-computer readers, these milestones illustrate the evolution of machine intelligence. Like the three dimensions of our Matrix, we first find **static programs (Dimension 1)**, which are designed to execute specific, predefined tasks, a series of predetermined instructions, and are unable to modify their behavior according to new information or new situations. Example: If it's dark, turn on the light. *Otherwise, turn it off.* The Deep Blue program was more at the pinnacle of this category. Then there are **specific AI programs (Dimension 2)**, designed to solve particular problems using techniques that enable them to process specific tasks and learn from supplied data. They are generally limited to a particular domain or task, such as speech recognition, computer vision or machine translation. Example: like Alpha Go, we train the AI by giving it an objective (to win the game), and thousands of video hours of Go encounters. We then leave it to make up its own mind as to the appropriate methods to use. Finally, **General Purpose AI (Dimension 3), or AGI**, refers to computer systems that are capable of understanding, learning and solving a wide range of problems in a similar way to a human being, unconstrained by any specific domain or problem. Like a child, curious about everything, these systems are designed to be versatile and can be useful in different fields of application.

Now that we're getting into the nitty-gritty of this disruptive innovation, motivated not by a *Need* for survival or love, but a *Need* for socio-economic prosperity and superhuman transcendence above all else, AI, and especially AGI, would logically progress in almost every field. I have no doubts about this statement, except in the case of state regulation. For, if household appliances have freed women from the home, and consequently from the *Need* to marry, AI now has the power to free millions of workers, not only from repetitive and boring tasks, such as administrative assistance and cab driving, but also from white-collar jobs that only humans were supposedly capable of performing. The *Value* of such a change is still ambiguous, for while AI would enable the improvement and discovery of new things, and the liberation of humans from Maslow's lower layers, some scientists, such as Stephen Hawking and Stuart Russell raised the risk that AI might in the future be capable of self-improvement, which they believe could cause an "intelligence explosion" that might lead to the extinction of humanity as we know it. Open-AI co-founder Elon Musk described it as the "biggest existential threat". We'll come back to this profound revolution at the end of our book.

Whatever the case, change has been an integral part of the Matrix, from the Big Bang to the appearance of life on Earth. After millennia of Darwinist evolution and ancestral "nomadism" with the struggle for food, health and shelter, AGI and advanced robotics seem to be the next rational episode in our evolution, where we will relax a little, meditate on advanced mental concepts and explore the universe. That said, there's hardly a perfect Order without hidden Chaos. How would we react if our artificial waiter at the restaurant had a human appearance? Or if our car drove us autonomously by guessing our next destination from personal data. What about if our children were completely absorbed by a metaverse connected to virtual reality equipment, and we fell in love with our own chatbot assistant as in the movie *"Her"*? In such cases, would we continue our never-ending quest for transcendence?

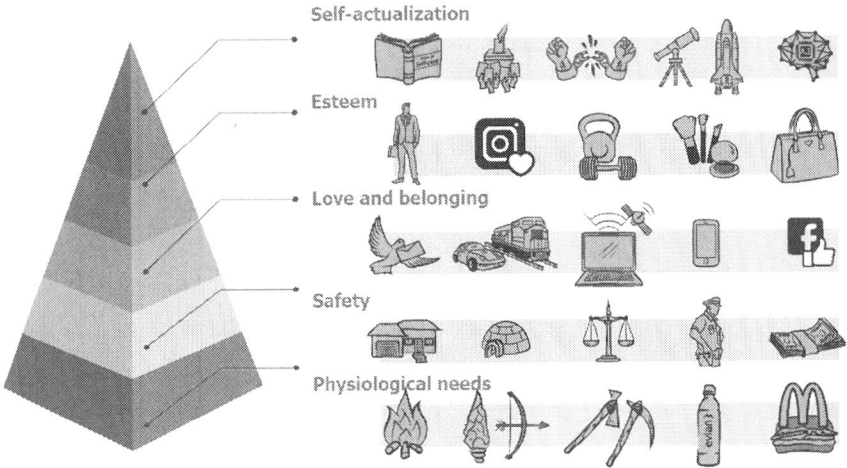

You'll find a brief summary of the main innovations by Maslow stage in the attached figure.

80 ✴ 03

The paradox of human needs

Having explored all the levels of Maslow's pyramid, it would be wise to broaden the subject of human needs a little outside this framework. First, we need to clarify a confusion that may arise when looking at the fundamental identity of innovation. Remember that at the start of this chapter, we labeled the variables *Need* and *Motivation* as prerequisites for innovation. As a result, you may be inclined to think of *Need* as the building block without which the skyscraper of *innovation* cannot exist. As in quantum physics, this is both true and false.

$$Innovation = \underbrace{(Need + Motivation)}_{Prerequisites} \times \underbrace{(Creativity + Technology)}_{Innovation\ Process} \times \underbrace{Value}_{Result}$$

It turns out that many innovations, however successful, were born out of the selfish motivation of someone, or perhaps *something*, like AGI systems in the near future. Think about it. Nobody needed the iPhone when it was launched. There's no list of needs for specific topics or book titles per year either. Similarly, on the organizational innovation side, many religions and new ideologies were not in demand or were even heckled by people when presented by their prophets. That's the lease we can say when considering the case of Jesus of Nazareth, considered the founder of Christianity, who met with significant resistance from the authorities of his day. His radical teachings on love, compassion and social justice provoked hostile reactions, to the point that he was accused of blasphemy, arrested, tried and finally crucified. Similarly, Muhammad, the prophet of Islam, faced backlash when he began preaching monotheism and was opposed by the polytheistic tribes of Mecca, who saw his preaching as a threat to their power. He and his followers were persecuted, forced to leave Mecca and settle far away in Medina. More recently, Martin Luther King Jr., the leader of the US civil rights movement, also faced strong opposition when he fought for equal rights and an end to racial segregation.

So, there are two types of entrepreneurs, or innovative animals, in the Matrix. The first verifies the existence of a *Need* for his new product or service before embarking on the innovative journey. The second, more adventurous and *a priori* highly motivated, embarks on the innovation process without worrying about the reliability of his theoretically new idea. There's a quite interesting parallel here in the business world. Specialists call similar paradigms **"market pull"** and **"technology push"**.

In market pull, an innovation is developed in response to a clear *Need* or demand from a significant number of customers, as the case may be. In other words, the innovation is "pulled" to market by the needs or desires of prospects and customers. This often involves carrying out market research to identify the market gaps or unmet needs that the innovation could address. Once those needs have been identified, the *innovation is* developed to meet them. Airbnb is an excellent example of a market pull innovation. The Airbnb concept was born when founders Brian Chesky and Joe Gebbia realized there was a significant opening in the market for affordable, comfortable and authentic accommodation for travelers, particularly during peak season when hotels often sell out. To validate their idea, they created a simple website on which they put their own apartment up for rent during a major design conference in San Francisco when the hotels were sold out. They received several bookings and realized that their idea had great potential. This approach is in line with the Agile methodology of project management, which is based on iterative phases of development and investment, taking care to verify and confirm user needs before each new phase.

Technology push, on the other hand, refers to the situation in which an innovation is developed and then aggressively marketed, following market trends, to create new market demand. In this case, the innovation is "pushed" onto the market by the innovator, in the hope that it will be adopted by the targeted segment(s). This often involves a significant investment in marketing and advertising to raise awareness and interest among prospects. Let's use the Apple brand again. When Apple first introduced the iPhone in 2007, it was a major innovation compared to existing phones on the market. Instead of simply improving on existing technology, Apple developed the iOS system and designed a well-thought-out product. The iPhone was also boosted by the development of its multi-touch technology, enabling users to interact with the phone's screen in a more intuitive and natural way. Meta's Metaverse (ex. Facebook) is another example of a technology push innovation, introduced in the wake of the latest virtual reality trends, without the present need having been confirmed.

Market pull is clearly safer from an investment point of view since the entrepreneur verifies the existence of the need *ex ante*. Technology push requires courage and a superior offer that follows or surpasses the technological trend and the competition's offer. These two cases do not call into question the validity of the fundamental *innovation* equation. Indeed, the success of any innovation requires a strong *Need*, **whether verified before its creation, or confirmed *a posteriori***. In the latter case, reasoning through the absurd, if the need is not confirmed and only few people adopt the new gadget, process, or ideology, there would simply be a halt to the project, and probably negative consequences for the project manager (loss of capital, job, reputation, etc.). Even if they are cautious in adopting a market pull strategy, large companies quite often misjudge the initial need, for example by carrying out incomplete market research or by overestimating prospects' willingness to pay when introducing the product.

Still expanding on the *Need* concept, it would be unimaginable to talk about psychology and human *needs* without mentioning Sigmund Freud. The Austrian founder of psychoanalysis believed that human behavior and mental processes were primarily guided by unconscious desires and drives, *a priori* of a profoundly sexual nature, "the libido". He proposed dividing the human psyche into three components: **the id, the ego and the superego**.

The id is the most primitive part of the mind and represents unconscious impulses and desires, such as the need for food, water and sex, rather like the base stage of the Maslow pyramid. It operates on the hedonistic principle of pleasure, seeking immediate gratification regardless of reality or social norms. Next, the ego represents the rational part of the mind, mediating between the id and the external world. It operates according to the principle of reality, trying to satisfy the needs of the id in a way that is acceptable to society. The third brick is the superego, the moral face of the mind that represents the internalization of social norms and values. It is the source of self-consciousness and guilt. Freud believed that these three parts were in permanent conflict with each other, and that unresolved conflicts could lead to mental disorders in the form of neuroses or psychoses.

This framework nicely complements Maslow's pyramid and offers a new perspective for studying the "*Need*" variable. In fact, some innovations are difficult to explain using Maslow's classification alone. Take, for example, the famous "sex toys", or even the Kamasutra, the Indian book of a thousand sexual positions or the countless paintings in contemporary art whose interest and significance nobody understands. To which stage of Maslow's pyramid do they belong? Survival and reproduction? Belonging? Self-fulfillment? It's hard to say. However, the story seems to be self-explanatory if we take the "id" into account. Sex toys, pornography and certain forms of art tend to satisfy this wild and socially hidden side, because they provide an outlet for impulses, an expression of a silly but necessary dualistic play of dominance and submission.

Freud and his philosophy are sometimes confused with the broader movement of **hedonism**. This philosophical perspective, usually applied by agents of capitalist systems, suggests that **pleasure-seeking** and **pain-avoidance**, whether physical, emotional, or psychological, are the driving forces behind human behavior and decision-making. In this context, we recognize Epicurus, the ancient Greek philosopher who emphasized pleasure-seeking as the supreme good. However, he distinguished between short-term superficial pleasures and long-term profound pleasures. Other more recent schools of thought are equally noteworthy. Jeremy Bentham, English philosopher and founder of utilitarianism, argued that actions should be judged according to their ability to produce the greatest amount of pleasure for the greatest number of people. He introduced the concept of "hedonic calculus" to quantify and measure pleasure and pain. Finally, John Stuart Mill developed Bentham's ideas by introducing the concept of higher and lower pleasures. According to him, intellectual, emotional and moral pleasures are more valuable than mere physical ones.

If we aggregate all these points of view, the hedonistic classification of human needs seems relatively straightforward. Assuming it does no harm to anyone, Man theoretically needs anything that would contribute to **increasing his pleasure**, instantly or later. Conversely, Man also needs to avoid anything that would cause his suffering, either now or later. This in no way contradicts Maslow's pyramid, quite the contrary. The *Need* to belong to a group or for affection from a partner are needs that would increase our satisfaction if satisfied.

Similarly, if Maslow states the needs we have, he is implicitly insinuating the "anti-needs", according to the duality principle we discussed in the previous chapter. So, when we buy hygienic products to protect ourselves and eliminate germs, we are also seeking to distance ourselves from the fear and insecurity that accompany the absence of a safe environment. The *Need* to love and belong encompasses both the desire for social ties, affection and inclusion, while also implying the fear of rejection, loneliness and isolation. The human mind operates on a principle of duality, where our desires and motivations are often linked to our aversions and fears. Consequently, Maslow also responds to the second hedonistic postulate concerning the need to reduce suffering. To classify innovations by type of *Need*, the Maslow framework is obviously clearer, as it is broken down into simple categories, rather than the two big blocks of pleasure and pain.

Regardless of the framework used, what makes it difficult to detect and analyze what people really want lies in **the often-subconscious nature of a *Need***. If I ask you, what do you want right now? You'll automatically activate your grey matter and end up with one or two needs that you become aware of. At the precise moment of the question, you didn't need anything, your concentration being on this book. However, if I offered you a free coconut juice or fresh water, you might feel the need for it. It's only when you focus the light of your consciousness on something that you perceive it. Few people needed an iPhone in 2007 because few had tried it or even knew about it. The origin of most human needs is thus hidden in the subconscious, as they are based on instinctive impulses influenced by biology, physiology and past experiences.

In fact, these needs are not always easily understood or controlled by conscious thought or decision-making. What people honestly claim to need and what they actually need don't always match up. This is one of the reasons why business ideas fail, despite prior market research. Prospect interviews may reflect a positive conscious response, such as "of course I'd buy that product, it looks cool!". When the same product is launched, this same respondent would refrain from buying it, because deep down, they don't need it. Sometimes, all you need to do is observe people's habits, as in ethnological studies. Don't ask them if they'd be willing to buy your product. Just look for signs of a need among their daily habits or a recurring trend. If, for instance, you happened to work in La Defense, the business district in Paris, few years ago, you would have noticed how many suited-white-collars struggle to get their lunch in between meetings. With some IT skills or a nerdy friend, you could have been competing right now with DoorDash.

Furthermore, we can't tell the difference between a real need and what we assume we need. In other words, if I think I need an apple, do I really need an apple?. The fact of the matter is that the apple is just an idea, a solution to a more fundamental survival *Need* related to my hunger. An apple, couscous or burrito would all do, if I'm really hungry. Companies, understanding this human cognitive limit, often use various strategies to **create the *Need*** for a novelty, even if this need didn't explicitly exist beforehand. Using neuromarketing techniques, attractive packaging and the social imitation effect, companies can create demand for their products or services. They can do this by highlighting potential benefits, satisfying unfulfilled desires or creating a sense of urgency for something new. Luxury brands, for example, associate their products with prestige and exclusivity, inciting consumers to desire and aspire to own them. Through branding aimed at the fundamental *Need for* esteem, they create a perceived need for their high-end products.

One more difficulty in grasping the complexity of human *needs* is the notion of **motivational pluralism**. This refers to the idea that individuals have multiple and often contradictory motivations or desires. These desires can vary in intensity, periodicity and importance, and can lead to the accumulation of more things than are really necessary – in short, to consumerism. Socio-psychological research has shown that individuals often experience a Maslow-like hierarchy of needs, where lower-level needs must be satisfied before higher-level needs become important. However, motivational pluralism suggests that these needs are not mutually exclusive and can coexist. If you're currently renting, and I'm offering you a house at a very affordable price, you might be tempted to fulfill that physiological *Need* for a shelter of your own, and perhaps also *the Need* for love by gathering your family under one comfortable roof. Just know that this house exists! Somewhere in the USA, or the UK, or elsewhere in the world. But you're not just looking for an affordable house, but an affordable house that's close to your job, your friends or in a favorite region or town, maybe even post-1980, with a big garden, and so on. Satisfying all these criteria means optimizing your future pleasure, by fulfilling several of Maslow's basic needs, which comes at a hefty cost.

Businesses that understand this concept of motivational pluralism have chosen to offer packaged products, or up-selling and cross-selling, to meet many needs simultaneously. A digital example of this type of marketing innovation is called "super-applications". For example, WeChat, a Chinese messaging app, offers multiple functionalities such as messaging, social networking, e-commerce, mobile payments and even cab services. Grab, Southeast Asia's equivalent of Uber, offers meal delivery, mobile payments and financial services such as insurance and loans. On the Amazon package, it's possible to shop online, listen to streaming music and videos, and buy digital books. In the non-digital world, there's the multifunctional Swiss Army knife, or baking soda, a basic household product that can be used to clean, deodorize and even cook. In terms of services, tour packages can meet several *needs* in a single package: cultural visits, relaxation in a four-star hotel, evening events, and so on. All these products and services take advantage of the variety, interconnectedness and complexity of human needs.

This complexity of human needs is also evident in the artistic field. We've already mentioned that the artistic *need* would fit into a higher level in the Maslow hierarchy, perhaps belonging to a group of like-minded souls, self-fulfillment, freedom of expression, creativity or the need for beauty. Some art forms, however, have practical applications, such as architecture and graphic design. Apart from these limited cases, we visualize art through the image of the suffering artists, who passionately devote themself beyond their basic needs in pursuit of an ideal masterpiece. The transcendent effect of art and the way it plays with Chaos and Order are indeed appreciable. Nevertheless, what the artistic field lacks is a standard measure of the *Need* variable, a combination of criteria that would **transform a simple creation/invention into an appreciated innovation**. It's never easy to justify spending millions of euros on a one-square-meter painting. Of course, a wide range of factors could be taken into account, including the work's historical context, artistic technique, aesthetics, cultural significance and so on. However, at the time, an observer or investor can only rely on their subconscious desire in assessing the work's *value*.

છ ✳ ૨

Let's end this section with some (simple) math. Without pretending to magically break down this psychological complexity into a basic abstraction, nor to set hypotheses in stone, I'd like to list, based on this analysis and other research, a few variables that would come into play in the expression of the *Need* function. In a general, non-specific way, let's write it all down in an equation form (again), with the aim of simplifying our understanding of this variable and describing the logic behind it. Recall that writing Y = f (X) reads Y is a function of X, or the value of Y is affected by X. For example, Ice-cream = f (Temperature) if we assume that ice-cream consumption is correlated with outside temperature. The warmer it is, the more ice-creams are consumed. It makes sense.

Need = f (Time, Space, Identity, Stage of Maslow + ε

Time = g (Zeitgeist, biology, habits, etc.)

Space = h (Position, social context, etc.)

As expressed, a *Need* is influenced by time, space, identity and the Maslow level. The latter variable has already been extensively explained above. Namely, if you're stuck in the Maslow level of belonging and love throughout your adolescence, many of your actions will be motivated by the need to socialize and gain the approval of your peers. Let's move on to the other sub-variables.

Like everything else, needs evolve in time and space. Every era is characterized by its zeitgeist. The 1940s were dominated by the Second World War, which saw the rise of totalitarian regimes and the development and use of atomic weapons. The 1990s saw the end of the Cold War and the emergence of the internet as a major force in people's lives. The decade also saw significant advances in science and technology, including the development of personal computers and the mapping of the human genome. The 2010s saw increased economic inequality, the rise of populist movements around the world, and a growing interest in the ecological rescue of our poor planet. The zeitgeist of each period influences the trends and priorities of individuals and organizations. Your biology also influences the needs of the moment. For example, inappropriate levels of oxytocin, the "love hormone", can make you crave or loathe social or romantic connections. High levels of testosterone in men lead to greater aggression or a need for sexual adventures. On the other hand, a habit is a carbon copy of a certain behavior in the subconscious. If you're in the habit of drinking coffee every morning, you'll feel like you need your black drug at the same time every morning. At midnight, you usually hear your bed calling, by succumbing to the need for sleep. To save energy, the brain records our repeated actions, i.e., our habits, and they become future needs.

Similarly, the space sub-variable reflects the environment in which individuals and organizations evolve. The needs of an inhabitant of the Brazilian Amazon are likely to be different from those of a Parisian fashion artist. The social framework, friends, family and colleagues, for example, will not be the same from one person to another. All these variables and more influence the food you eat, the clothes you wear and the experiences you privilege. Finally, identity, the "self", rationalizes many of your needs. These include your education, your job, your family situation, your responsibilities, your beliefs and so on. Most mothers need to care more for their babies than for themselves. A priest needs time for silence and meditation. A vegan needs to control their appetite for animal flesh and milk. In business, this identity variable relates to the vision and mission of a organization on one side, and to what's labeled "marketing segmentation" on the other side, by dividing the market into small homogeneous segments, or "personas", proto-profiles describing the identity of users or prospects.

With that, let's move on to the second variable in the fundamental identity of *innovation*: **Motivation**.

VARIABLE 2:
The *Motivation* to innovate

In the bustling city of Hangzhou, China, around 1970, there lived a young man with a bold vision and a rebellious spirit, in contrast to his conformist culture. Born into a modest family, he grew up in an environment of limited opportunities. But deep in his heart, he carried a seed of ambition, waiting to be nurtured and released. He had a long wait ahead of him. In his early years, he faced countless obstacles and setbacks. He failed his university entrance exam not once, but twice. Yet he was undaunted by these challenges. He persevered, worked hard to improve himself and sought to discover his true vocation. "When I was young, I failed exams several times. That's why I'm now an expert at failing," he confirmed.

One fateful day, at the dawn of the internet age, he discovered the World Wide Web, the magic gateway to this virtual world. Recognizing the immense potential of this new frontier, he saw an opportunity, a *need to* bridge the gap between small and medium-sized Chinese businesses on the one hand, and consumers on the other, especially in a booming Chinese economy. With unwavering determination, he assembled a small group of individuals who shared his passion and drive. Together, they embarked on a mission to build an online marketplace that would connect buyers and sellers from all over the world. Their vision was fueled by the belief that e-commerce could redress the balance, empowering individuals and businesses of all sizes.

Years of hard work and perseverance followed. Countless nights were spent coding, brainstorming and strategizing. The team faced many challenges, regulatory constraints, funding shortfalls and fierce competition. But each obstacle served as a steppingstone, bringing them a little closer to their ultimate goal. Slowly but surely, their creation began to take shape. The platform they built, known as Alibaba, began as a modest online marketplace, connecting Chinese manufacturers with domestic and international buyers. Its success exceeded all expectations, growing at a staggering rate and attracting the attention of investors and entrepreneurs alike. But the young man's story didn't stop there. With boundless ambition, he extended the company's reach, venturing into new areas such as cloud computing, financial services and entertainment. Alibaba became a technological powerhouse, influencing industries and reshaping the digital landscape in China and beyond.

Although recently censured by the Chinese government on the grounds that his capitalist empire was gaining too much power and threatening the competitive balance, the renowned Jack Ma still firmly believes in the importance of failure and perseverance in the path to success. Like a Taoist philosopher, he has often said: "Failure is the essence of learning. If you don't know how to fail, how can you succeed?"

Jack Ma's story is a textbook illustration of the mechanisms of start-up success, including the role of infallible *Motivation* on the part of the entrepreneur and his team. Let's clarify the distinction between these two prerequisites for *innovation*. Whereas the variable of *Need* concerns the *innovation's* recipients, the consumers, users or followers, that of *Motivation* is an essential attribute of the innovator, the entrepreneur or the person trying to pass on his creation to others. Let's take another example, that of the light bulb innovation. Many people were prepared to accept a reliable, efficient source of light to illuminate their darkest nights, in place of campfires or oil lamps. So, to satisfy this basic *Need* for survival and security, a few motivated individuals, such as Nikola Tesla and Thomas Edison, experimented with the technologies of the time, and fortunately succeeded in transforming darkness into light. If there had been no prior or subsequent need for this new light source, it would have been doomed to failure. Similarly, if no one is sufficiently motivated to think about and create a new process, product, organization or sect, it's obvious that it won't exist. In short, you need to combine two variables to ensure the existence, or even success, of a human innovation: the conscious or unconscious, latent or provoked *Need* of a future user, and the creative *Motivation* of a man, a woman, or a group of both.

Human motivation is a far more complex psychological process than its counterpart in other dynamic agents. These are mainly motivated by survival, reproduction or, sometimes, social interaction. A domestic cat is rarely motivated to move, except to hunt, look for a mate, make friends, defend its area or play with its master, the latter action in turn motivated by the instinct to learn to hunt and fight while playing. In humans, as with the variable of *Need,* understanding the different types of motivation from the point of view of *The Innovative Animal* can help individuals and organizations to improve their performance, increase their productivity and innovate more effectively. *Motivation* is divided into two categories: **external and intrinsic**. Before exemplifying these two notions, let's note that *Need* and *Motivation* have been studied from the same psychological angle. If you need money, you'll be motivated to go out and work or become an entrepreneur. If you're motivated to party tonight, your needs may be to relax or socialize. As a result, this section will be shorter than the last one, as it covers some similar concepts.

In this regard, *Motivation* is based on the same hedonistic principle discussed at the end of the previous section, applied to short-term situations. Let me explain. The desire to optimize pleasure and limit pain or suffering are key behavioral drivers. This applies to individuals as well as to groups, such as companies, sects or countries. If the object of this future pleasure, or remedy, is to be found in a third party, this is called external motivation. The quest for profit or financial reward is often cited in this regard. This is a typical external motivation for most private companies in today's capitalist world. HR departments still rely on financial incentives and hierarchical promotions to motivate talents. These same departments do not hesitate to use threats of dismissal and pay cuts to punish unproductive resources.

Parents use the same ploy. If you get 20/20 in math, you win your summer trip to a seaside resort. If you don't get home by 10 p.m., you'll be punished or deprived of desert the next meal[20]. If you pray and ace being a good Hebrew, Christian, or Muslim, you'll end up with angels and

---

[20] Based on today's soft punishment standards.

virgins in paradise. Otherwise, your fate might be a good self-barbecue in hell, or repeated suffering because of your Karma over several Samsara cycles. From these examples and many others, it would seem that the concept of **external motivation has existed since the appearance of the human species**. School (or church) case: Don't touch that apple tree, or Adam, you'll be thrown back to Earth to toil for a lifetime. Don't touch my buffalo, or I'll eat you. Let me sleep with you tonight, and I'll ensure your survival and that of your children. And it often works. The world, mostly the primitive one, couldn't function on good intentions alone. As the manager of a McDonald's franchise, you don't expect your 20-year-old recruit to keep up his passion for filling boxes of chicken nuggets all day long. Some jobs probably wouldn't exist or receive far fewer applications, in my opinion, without some sort of financial reward or punishment: prostitutes, Uber Eats guys, garbage collectors, junior Wall Street traders, insurance contract salespeople, the majority of lawyers, and the list goes on and on of roles based on repetitive, boring, exhausting or morally repugnant tasks.

Apart from the financial aspect, we still find this external motivation in animals, albeit at a less complex level than in humans. Typically, in the education of pets, such as my dog Zina, and in the education of children, the "operant conditioning" or "Pavlovian conditioning" method is used. This approach is based on the principle that animals learn to associate specific behaviors with positive or negative consequences, thus influencing the likelihood of repeating or stopping a behavior. Every time a puppy walks, we give him a little kibble. If he pees inside the house, we yell at him or deprive him of his walk. Similarly, in a study with monkeys, researchers found that animals were more likely to complete a task when rewarded with food or other incentives. This demonstrates that the expectation of a reward acts as an external motivator for monkeys to engage in the task. The reward is not always gustatory in nature. Social dynamics also play a role. Studies on birds, for example, have shown that certain species adopt specific behaviors to gain social recognition or acceptance within their group.

Even more astonishing, Monica Gagliano, an Italian-born biologist and researcher, has revealed fascinating discoveries that challenge our traditional perception of plants as static organisms devoid of intelligence.

Gagliano has conducted experiments that highlight plants' ability to adapt, learn and communicate in complex ways. For example, she exposed plants to a specific sound accompanied by a light source or nutrient solution. After a while, the plants learned to recognize the sound as an indicator of the presence of the reward and reacted accordingly, orienting their growth or modifying their physiology to take advantage of the reward. In short, she has succeeded in showing that the concept of conditioning and external motivation applies just as much to plants – which, let's not forget, lack brains – as it does to animals, including humans.

However, while external motivation is essential to keep the economic machine running in a capitalist system, over-dependence on it can lead to a reduction in intrinsic motivation and impair performance. Research has shown that external motivation can activate specific areas of the brain, such as the ventral striatum, which is associated with the reward system. This means that when individuals are motivated by a salary to do a job, for example, their brain reacts in the same way as when they receive a physical reward, usually by releasing dopamine. Like smoking, it becomes a habit. When a chimpanzee gets used to receiving a banana after every smile, the next time you run out of bananas, the unfortunate monkey won't cooperate. When my sister forgets to charge her phone, my nephew, accustomed to watching his cartoons on YouTube during every meal, automatically starts grumbling, then closes his mouth.

Internal motivation, on the other hand, hardly depends on external stimuli. The term "intrinsic" indicates that something has an inherent value in itself, independent of any external factors or consequences. Personal goals, interests and values drive this call to action and *Innovation*. It is therefore seen as more enduring and is associated with better overall performance, greater *Creativity* and more radical innovation than when acting with a reward in sight or fear of punishment to come. In fact, when individuals are intrinsically motivated, they are more likely to enjoy the task, have a sense of autonomy and experience a kind of self-actualization, thus tending towards the top of the Maslow pyramid. The broke artist. The ascetic monk. The visionary entrepreneur. The passionate gardener. The doctor without frontiers. All these roles project facets of this intrinsic motivation.

Like any dualistic pair, these two poles of motivation are not necessarily exclusive. An organization, although profit-driven, i.e., motivated by maximizing profits for shareholders, can also sow more seeds to motivate its employees intrinsically. Give engineers a free creative day, as Google does, for example, or recruit only candidates who truly believe in the company's vision, even if the salary is below market norms. Get to know people's true psychological motor, their raison d'être: what is the teacher's passion? How does the politician behave away from the cameras? Did the film actor spend his weekend rehearsing? How many coffee breaks has the manager taken today? Beyond the hypocritical words and false smiles, it's above all by observing sincere involvement that we can sense the degree of internal motivation.

Recent research on this subject has come to the same conclusion. Internal motivation can activate the brain's prefrontal cortex. This means that when individuals are intrinsically motivated, they are more likely to engage in creative problem-solving, think outside the box and come up with innovative solutions. It has also been shown that the most successful innovators are intrinsically motivated and have a high level of self-determination, as they are driven by a passion for their work or quest. In brief, if you want people to be like machines, do things mechanically and fast, reward or punish them. If you want them to be creative and artistic, hope they become passionate or find meaning in the task at hand.

In any case, motivation, whether external or intrinsic, properly measured according to the individual and their context, is quite capable of taking the action-taker out of their comfort zone, pushing them to experiment and innovate. All the human creations you admire (or hate) around you are part of this rationale. Socio-economic literature speaks of entrepreneurial orientation (EO). This notion, combining risk-taking, proactivity, creative spirit, autonomy and competitive aggressiveness, is often used as a multidimensional concept to describe the power of this motivation to innovate. Unsurprisingly, history's great entrepreneurs and innovators have often taken considerable risks, investing their resources, their time, and sometimes even their lives.

Silicon Valley and its tech gurus are pioneers of this ongoing Technological Revolution in terms of risk-taking and proactivity. Steve Jobs chose to pursue his passion for electronics and computing after dropping out of Reed College in his first semester. With his friend Steve Wozniak, they launched Apple from Jobs' family garage. Elon Musk, founder of Tesla, SpaceX and other companies, had a capitalist vision, yes, but one that disrupted the status quo, with autonomous electric cars, space exploration and artificial intelligence. Highly motivated by this vision, he took major risks, investing all his money and borrowing again to create these "success stories". At one point in his entrepreneurial journey, he had to ask Apple CEO Tim Cook if he would buy his shares and take control of Tesla. Fortunately for Musk, Cook wasn't interested. A few years later, Musk's fortune exceeded that of all living agents, thanks to his shares in Tesla.

If we choose not to follow the examples of Steve Jobs, Bill Gates and Mark Zuckerberg and drop out, *Motivation* is also essential in education. Students who are highly motivated by academic success are more likely to take risks by doing challenging courses, seeking new academic opportunities abroad, or pushing themselves to learn more. For example, Malala Yousafzai, the Nobel Peace Prize-winning activist from Afghanistan, was highly motivated to get an education, even in the face of Taliban opposition. She took considerable risks in speaking out against this armed group and advocating girls' education.

Malala, on the other hand, remains among a minority of female entrepreneurs, if global statistics are anything to go by. Indeed, official figures reveal a male dominance when it comes to entrepreneurship and risk-taking, mostly outside Europe and North America. Some time ago, this situation might have seemed logical, with men having evolved, from a Darwinist angle, to be aggressive, competitive and addicted to power, while women have historically been in the maternal, supportive role. This is clearly out of date. With the emancipation of women and greater gender equality over the last century, statistics also show a marked improvement in women's participation in entrepreneurial life, worldwide, and even in some conservative Middle Eastern countries. In the United

States, the number of women-owned businesses has continued to rise. By 2021, there was around 12.9 million women-owned businesses, or 42 percent of all businesses. Let's illustrate our point with the case of Mrs. C.J. Walker, born Sarah Breedlove in 1867 in Louisiana. She was the first African American millionaire.

Mrs. Walker had a difficult start. She was orphaned at an early age and married at 14 to escape her abusive brother-in-law. Her husband died when she was just 20, leaving her with a daughter to support. To make ends meet, she took on jobs as a washerwoman and cook, working long hours for derisory pay. Added to this was a scalp infection that was causing her hair to fall out, a common problem for many African American women. Mrs. Walker experimented with home remedies to try and regrow her hair, eventually finding a good combination that worked for her. Noticing that this problem, monstrous for one woman, was affecting many of her friends, she set about selling her "Madam Walker's Wonderful Hair Grower" door-to-door, promoting it as a way for African American women to achieve healthier, fuller hair. She also developed a hair care system, including washing, grooming and using her products. As good feedback and encouragement came in, she extended her business to a network of sales agents to sell her products and teach her hair care method. Madame Walker's business grew rapidly, and she opened a factory in Indianapolis to produce her hair care innovations. She also opened a beauty school to train her sales agents, giving African American women new opportunities to become entrepreneurs. Her business continued to prosper after her death in 1919. In 2020, Netflix released a series entitled "Self-Made", based on her entrepreneurial life.

Outside the world of business, innovators in politics, religion, education and so many other fields also need a certain degree of intrinsic motivation, which stimulates them to take risks and upset the status quo.

In the sixth century BC, Gautama, before becoming Buddha or the enlightened one, also took many risks on his way to enlightenment or

Nirvana. First of all, he disobeyed his father, who was king, and escaped from the palace and thus from his royal destiny. After noticing the pandemic spread of suffering in the outside world, he decided to cross India in search of a satisfactory answer to his philosophical question: Why do we suffer? Why do we experience this existential suffering (called "Dukkha" in Sanskrit)? In his quest, Gautama studied under the wing of two spiritual gurus.

The first, Arada Kalama, assured the young Gautama that true learning was based on experience rather than mere understanding of the teachings. By following Arada's meditation method to the letter, Gautama was able to reach "the sphere of nothingness" more quickly than any other student. According to Buddhist tradition, this is one of the highest levels of meditative absorption, where the mind is experienced as infinite space-time, and expanded consciousness is felt. This is supposed to lead to the atman, or soul, by removing the mind's distorting filters. When Gautama reached this level and shared this experience with his master, the story goes that Arada was delighted with this achievement and, given his advanced age, agreed to share the leadership of his community with Gautama, hoping that the latter would succeed him after his death. This resembles a business situation in which a talented consultant or freelancer, on a temporary assignment, is offered a permanent employment contract, by his client. Gautama, a true entrepreneur, refused. Despite the honor bestowed upon him, he felt that this was not the finish line on his path to truth and that his mind was still deceiving him, even in this elevated spiritual sphere.

The second master suffered the same fate. Udraka Ramaputra, son of a famous guru named Rama, had a community of over 700 disciples in Indian Rajagriha. Gautama learned the teachings in order to experience another level of meditation: the sphere of neither-perception-nor-non-perception. It's difficult to explain, just as it would be complicated to explain the color red to a blind person. Succinctly put, it is the ultimate aspect of the atman, the state of a yogi who sees but does not see, who perceives beyond material reality, including his innermost self. After some time of practice, Gautama returned to Udraka with a positive result.

Udraka was so surprised by his disciple's rapid progress that he offered him the chance to lead his community alone. Gautama declined again, as this level still didn't answer the question behind his quest.

From there, no longer relying on the masters, Gautama took his own path, that of pain. Like a pure ascetic, he pushed back the limits of his body and mind in search of spiritual insights. The story goes that he rebelled against himself, going naked most of the time, feeding on the leftovers of people and animals, wild rice and grass. He no longer washed and slept almost anywhere, in the cold of winter or the scorching heat of the Indian summer. He was even found sleeping on a cremation ground, the bones of the dead serving as his pillow. Yes, entrepreneurs can be so obsessed with their start-up, with an idea, that nothing, not even death, will dissuade them from taking the plunge. Fortunately, Gautama left this painful path behind him, like a zombie, but still alive. Later, he reached Nirvana under the Bodhi tree, and returned with his own teachings drawn from his experience, setting out the principles and path to follow to rid oneself of life's sufferings once and for all, and attain an awakened state of happiness. Principles that have managed to win a large share of the global spirituality market, mainly in Asia. Over 500 million people, or around eight percent of the world's population, now consider themselves Buddhists.

Like Buddha, many other innovators are trying to change our world, sometimes in secret. More recently, in 2008, the Global Financial Crisis (GFC) reached its climax, with negative systemic repercussions on global socio-economic stability. This crisis led to a widespread loss of confidence in traditional banks and financial institutions. The latter were accused of playing risky games with people's money, using complex mortgage derivatives whose underlying mechanisms they had no idea about. Someone, something, or a group of nerds, using the pseudonym "Satoshi Nakamoto" had enough internal (and perhaps external) motivation and intelligence to write a research paper detailing a new form of currency. A currency that would escape the reach and control of governments and Wall Street's mindless speculators. Bitcoin was born.

As a decentralized digital currency, Bitcoin operates on a peer-to-peer network without the need for a central authority, such as a bank or government. Transactions are verified by network nodes using cryptography and recorded in a distributed public register called the "blockchain". In more human terms, bitcoin is like a U.S. dollar or a euro bill, except that it is digital, secure and managed by many people around the world, rather than by a private or public institution. Bitcoin also addresses another problem. In 1985, a McDonald's Big Mac cost around $1.5 in the USA. By 2023, its price has almost quadrupled, taking inflation into account. So, to prevent the currency from losing its purchasing power over the years and through crises, only 21 million bitcoins will be created according to the protocol proposed by its innovator, making it deflationary by default. Despite Satoshi's idealistic and liberal vision, Bitcoin and other crypto assets still have a long way to go to justify their value in relation to fiduciary currencies.

In short, *innovation* **is a process. Rarely an event**. It can be long, uncertain and painful. Depending on whether the risk is worthwhile, a few or many individuals are attracted by the prospect of success, wealth or self-fulfillment, stimulated by the hope of escaping a more painful situation, or strengthened by their inner motivation and vision. Whatever the case, whether external or internal, motivation is like the flame that lights the fire. If it isn't present, few innovations will see the light of day. This may explain why some countries or fields are more innovative than others. Massive investment in the Nasdaq, the US technology index, has encouraged many technology companies to innovate and develop further. The focus of Syrians, Libyans and Burmese on their internal conflicts has only led to innovations in basic survival processes, fighting or smuggling goods. Culture is also an important element to consider in this respect. For example, the American entrepreneurial spirit reduces the dissonance of creative individuals when they take risks with the American dream. In fact, entrepreneurial failure "is welcome" in the States, compared with the USSR before, or France and Europe today, where the educational and professional framework encourages limited risk and non-failure.

Based on the above analysis, you can recognize the *Motivation* function expressed as follows:

Motivation=f' (External Factors, Intrinsic Factors)

External Factors=g' (Money, Social recognition, Reward, Punishment,etc.)

Intrinsic Factors=h' (Passion, Vision, Duty, Existencial purpose, etc.)

VARIABLE 3:
The Artistic side of innovation

In England, around 1818, Mary Shelley, a young writer, was in a creative slump. One evening, at a meeting with friends including the famous poets Lord Byron and Percy Shelley, they decided to hold a competition to see who could write the best horror story. Mary Shelley, who'd been struggling to come up with an idea for days on end, decided to give up. That very night, she had a nightmare she would remember for the rest of her life, for it inspired a timeless masterpiece. In her dream, she imagined a scientist bringing a creature to life, thereby giving birth to the iconic novel, *Frankenstein*. Shelley's story, inspired by her dream, became a landmark work of Gothic literature and had a profound impact on popular culture.

Across the Atlantic in 1846, American inventor Elias Howe was struggling to solve a critical design problem in his attempt to create a practical sewing machine. One night, Howe had a dream in which he was captured by a group of native warriors carrying spears with holes in the tips. The next day, this dream began to take shape: a needle with the hole at the pointed end, rather than the other way round. This revolutionary concept at the time enabled the sewing machine needle to be threaded more efficiently, leading to the innovation of the lockstitch sewing machine. Howe's innovation revolutionized the textile industry forever.

Continuing our space-time tour, this time to St. Petersburg, circa 1870s, eccentric Russian chemist Dmitri Mendeleev was attempting to organize the fundamental elements of chemistry into a coherent system. Legend has it that one night, in a state of hysterical frustration, possibly with a significant degree of alcoholism, Mendeleev fell into a deep sleep. In his dream, he saw a vision of the periodic table, with all the elements neatly arranged in rows and columns. When he awoke, he quickly transcribed his vision into a revolutionary periodic table of the elements. This table, based on the atomic properties of the elements, became one of the most important scientific achievements of all time, paving the way for other disciplines and discoveries.

290 | PLUNGING INTO THE UNKNOWN

Finally, back in the UK in 1964, legendary musician and Beatles member Paul McCartney woke up to a beautiful melody in his head. Thinking it was a tune he'd heard before, he rushed to a piano and played the melody, but no one in his band recognized it. Realizing it was an original composition, McCartney rushed to write down the chords and lyrics that had come to him in a dream. The result was the timeless classic "Yesterday", which became one of the most covered songs in history.

All these true stories, and many more, reflect the mysterious, even mystical, aspect of the innovative process. One day, we're blocked by a difficulty deemed insurmountable by our cognitive capacities. The next, we find ourselves freed by unexplained divine inspiration, a whisper from the subconscious in the form of a dream or serendipity. Of course, these cases, which attract us, inspire us and make the Matrix a playful puzzle, are not universally accepted, because we can create without dreaming and innovate without being lucky. It's time to explore this magical notion of *Creativity*, without which *innovation* would barely make sense

$$Innovation = \underbrace{(Need + Motivation)}_{Prerequisites} \times \underbrace{(Creativity + Technology)}_{Innovation\ Process} \times \underbrace{Value}_{Result}$$

The term "Creativity" comes from the Latin "creare", which, unsurprisingly, means "to create". It has been used in English since the 16th century to designate the ability to produce something new or original, or to come up with imaginative or inventive ideas or solutions. The same concept is mainly studied by psychologists and neuroscientists, and is now considered a complex, multi-faceted process involving several mental and emotional processes. Despite its complexity, there's no denying that *Creativity* is an essential aspect of the human experience, of the third Matrix dimension, and is valued in many fields and professions, from the arts and sciences to business and education.

One of the main sources of *Creativity* is an object you probably already own, whether natural or artificial. If you're a human being, without having to touch it or see it, you're convinced you have something precious inside your skull – a biological central unit, in short, a brain. This fascinating organ is responsible for controlling and regulating so many vital functions, including thought, movement and sensation. To achieve this, billions of cells called neurons, and billions and billions of synapses, communicate with each other and transmit signals within a given area and between areas, depending on the task at hand. Let's illustrate this better.

When we speak, language production is primarily managed by a region called Broca's area, located in the left frontal lobe of the brain. This area is responsible for planning and coordinating the movements required to produce articulated language in a defined Order. It then sends signals to the muscles of the face and throat to produce the sounds and words. On the other hand, comprehension of this same language takes place in another region called Wernicke's area, located in the left temporal lobe of the brain. This area processes auditory and visual information related to language and interprets it to make sense of words and sentences. It's important to note that the brain functions in a highly integrated and interactive way. Different areas of the brain work together to process information, make decisions and produce appropriate responses. For example, when we hear speech, Broca's and Wernicke's areas communicate to understand and formulate an appropriate response. I can extrapolate this example to all human perception, from vision to smell to movement. What's more, the brain is capable of plasticity, i.e., it can modify its connections and structure according to experience and learning. This allows the brain to adapt and develop throughout life. With all this prowess, it's hardly surprising that the brain consumes a lot of energy – a score of G or F in real-estate terms. Indeed, the human brain consumes 20 percent of the body's total energy budget, on average, even though it represents only two percent of body mass.

Biological evolution over the millennia provides an interesting paradigm for studying the human brain. This latter is structured in layers, like a building or pyramid, with each higher layer built on an older one. This reminds us that each new dimension of the Matrix builds on the previous one in a spirit of continuous improvement. This concept is known as the "**triune brain**" theory, proposed by neuroscientist Paul MacLean in the 1960s. Accordingly,

292 | PLUNGING INTO THE UNKNOWN

the brain is made up of three main layers. Firstly, the reptilian brain is the oldest and most primitive part of the brain. It is responsible for basic survival functions such as breathing, heart rate and body temperature regulation. It also controls instinctive behaviors such as the "fight or flight" instinct and territorial behavior. This part of the brain is present in all vertebrates, not just reptiles, and is sometimes referred to as the "basal ganglia". The second brain layer that follows is in charge of emotions, memory and motivation. It is more advanced than the reptilian brain and is found in mammals. The limbic system includes structures such as the amygdala, hippocampus and hypothalamus. Finally, the neocortex represents the most recent evolutionary stage, occupying complex cognitive functions such as language, abstract reasoning and thought, hence further differentiating Man from other animals. The neocortex is in turn divided into four main lobes: the frontal lobe, the parietal lobe, the occipital lobe and the temporal lobe.

This complexity of the human brain, according to Darwinist theory, is the result of its evolution over millions of years to perform a wide range of functions. We can understand its evolutionary structure by examining other species. The first brains, found in worms and jellyfish, for example, were simple structures composed of a few nerve cells. These primitive brains could perform basic functions such as detecting the environment and coordinating movements. As the ecosystem changed, the brain, following a logic of epigenetic adaptation and natural selection, became more complex, with the addition of new structures enabling more sophisticated behaviors. For example, the development of the amygdala and hippocampus in early mammals enabled the formation of social bonds and the regulation of emotions. In humans, the brain has continued to evolve. The prefrontal cortex, responsible for higher cognitive functions such as imagination, planning and decision-making, was particularly developed compared to other primates[21].

---

[21] While brains in the animal kingdom vary in shape, volume and processing power, Homo sapiens has the largest brain relative to body size, more than seven times the size ratio predicted for similar mammals.

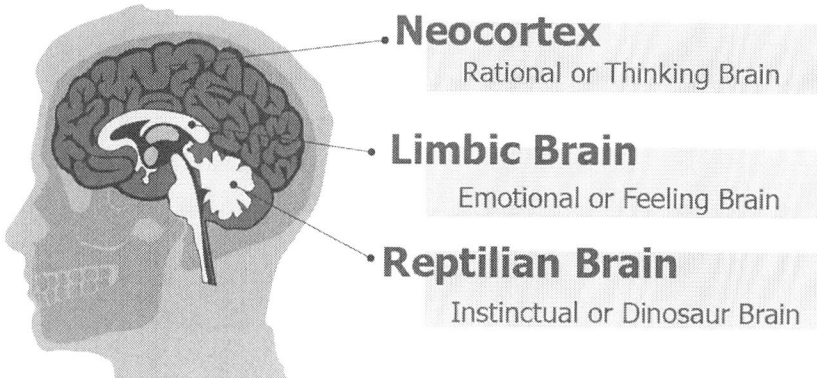

Neocortex
Rational or Thinking Brain

Limbic Brain
Emotional or Feeling Brain

Reptilian Brain
Instinctual or Dinosaur Brain

This big brain clearly helped sapiens in their quest for survival, and in their ascent to the zenith of the food chain, as well as of the Maslow pyramid. Such a meteoric rise is not due solely to chance or to the evolutionary pressure of the environment. It's largely thanks to the variable *Creativity*, which has fueled human imagination and innovation for millennia. From a materialist or physicalist perspective, this enhanced *Creativity*, like consciousness, would be generated and stimulated by brain complexity. Indeed, brain scans have shown that no specific area correlates with the degree of creativity. This would suggest that creativity involves the interaction of several neurological regions and systems. Such a conclusion seems logical to me for two reasons.

The first comes from direct experience. When I ask my customers to brainstorm on a new digital product, or my business school students to come up with solutions to a big city's most significant problems, without the help of the internet, each group presents new perspectives. First and foremost, problems are often buried in the memory, until you dwell on them. And depending on each person's experience, some will think of their phone being stolen, others who commute every day will think of traffic jams, allergy sufferers will think of pollution, and so on. The data in memory can also come from what your friend told you yesterday, what you saw on TV a week ago, or from a place or an emotional event. In the latter case, an area of the amygdala is likely to be activated. The stronger the emotion, whether anger at the problem, curiosity and excitement, or shock, the more active this area of the amygdala.

Furthermore, in order to imagine solutions for the traffic jam problem, for example, my students once again called on their memory, which can be located in different parts of the brain, by recalling certain existing solutions. A few went off the beaten track, like the artist improvising a painting, mixing several unrelated solutions, or letting their imaginations run wild with proposals of flying cars or cities-with-no-cars sort of laws. t's also worth noting that when we're tired or unmotivated, we find it hard to imagine new things and draw on our *Creativity*, an observation representative of the correlation between the latter and our biological central unit.

Secondly, the brain's ability to "imagine" clearly depends on its fabric, just as a Smartphone's capabilities would depend on its memory, graphics card, microprocessor – in short, its hardware. So, while the notion of *Creativity* is noticeable within the animal kingdom, it remains relatively limited, coinciding with their cerebral limitations. Classic cases include other mammals such as chimpanzees, who use creative strategies and tools to forage for hidden food; dolphins, known for their penchant for playing with floating objects such as seaweed or pieces of wood, demonstrating an ability to use their environment creatively and playfully; or, among cephalopods, octopuses, capable of solving complex problems and modifying their appearance while blending seamlessly into their environment, displaying a not inconsiderable degree of *Creativity*. Compared with earthworms or jellyfish and their basic nervous systems, these examples clearly display an upgrade in creative potential. The latter argument is very much in the news, thanks to the latest breakthroughs in artificial general intelligence (AGI). With the continuous improvement of ChatGPT, DALL-E and other AGI tools, artificial creativity in all media (text, image, video, etc.) has already surpassed human creativity in many respects. A beginning of a case in proof: a portrait of Edmond de Belamy, a work of art created using an AGI system, developed by the Obvious art collective, was sold at auction in 2018, for a price of around $432,500!

From the above, there's a materialistic but very plausible idea here, which states: ***Creativity* is simply the conscious or unconscious result of a well-filled database, preferably also well-structured, and of electrical or neurological bridges between these data.**

This conclusion is fairly widely shared by the scientific community, and by other renowned psychologists. Carl Jung, Swiss psychiatrist and psychoanalyst, father of the MBTI personality test, addressed the concept of ideas emerging from the subconscious and drawing on past data. He believed that the human psyche contained a vast reservoir of individual knowledge and collective experience, which he called **the collective unconscious**. According to Jung, when individuals have creative ideas, they often tap into such individual or collective unconscious, accessing a source of information beyond their personal consciousness. Jung's belief could be metaphorized by Cloud technology, where your computerized data is not in your possession on your computer or smartphone, but in an external server somewhere at Google or Amazon, for example. What's more, Jung insinuates that, given the right method, we can hack into this server and extract our data and that of others. In any case, the interaction between the conscious mind, influenced by personal experience and cultural conditioning, and the unconscious, the deepest layers of the psyche, enables creative solutions or artistic inspirations to emerge, which are often mistaken for mental feats, a creation *ex nihilo*. Rereading the innovative dreams recounted at the start of this section would take on a less perplexing air if we adopted this Jungian approach.

That said, Jung and physicalist researchers would find it hard to explain creative impulses that come out of nowhere, whether in art, theology or even science. Suffice it to mention some extraordinary works or new styles, such as Salvador Dalí's painting, *The Persistence of Memory*. Created in 1931, this surrealist work has become an emblematic representation of Dalí's unique style and unconventional approach to the representation of reality. A barren landscape with melting clocks draped over various objects, including a tree branch, and a faceless figure reclining in the foreground, all of which remains difficult to explain by a simple wiring of data and neurons in the brain. Even within one of the greatest brains of the last century, Albert Einstein, the *Creativity* equation would not have been so simple. "**Imagination is more important than knowledge**", he stressed. While some materialists might object that Einstein had filled his brain with theorems and observations before postulating anything, let's switch to a story I grew up with, which proves much harder to explain.

The event took place in 610 CE, with a certain Muhammad, aged around 40, who used to spend time in solitude and contemplation, in a cave on Mount Hira, near the city of Mecca, in what is now Saudi Arabia. One night, during the month of Ramadan, while Muhammad was deep in meditation, the angel Gabriel appeared before him. Gabriel ordered Muhammad to "read" or "recite" (in Arabic, "Iqra"). Muhammad, illiterate, with little formal education and therefore unable to read or write, was confused and answered honestly that he could not read. The angel repeated the command and Muhammad again replied that he could not read. The angel then embraced him firmly and released him, repeating the command once more. Overwhelmed, still not grasping the message, and frightened to death, Muhammad rushed home to his wife, Aisha. Aisha, an understanding wife, consoled him and assured him that if God had chosen him for a particular purpose, he would be protected. What followed is well known, with the beginning of Muhammad's prophethood and his role as God's messenger in Islam. He continued to receive these divine messages for 23 years, compiled after his death in Islam's holy book, the Qur'an.

Parallels to this historical event can be found in most sects, whether through prophets, shamans or oracles. Outside the spiritual perimeter, throughout history, there have been other individuals endowed with incredible creativity, without the need for a solid background or any special talent in the subject in question. Other disturbing cases show people, especially children, speaking a foreign language perfectly, which no one around them understands, following an accident or an illness, as if possessed by an immaterial creative force. These latter cases are clearly becoming increasingly rare.

To resolve this dilemma without the damage of excluding possible, albeit invisible, sources of *Creativity*, let's take a closer look at the two generic methods for arriving at creative ideas or content, one is more attributed to artistic, mystical and metaphysical creations, while the second one belongs more to the realm of materialism and science: **intuition and logic.** Let's start with the latter.

Aristotle is one of the founding fathers of logic, thanks to his pioneering work in the field of deductive reasoning. One of his contributions is the syllogism, a logical argument in which a conclusion is drawn from two premises. For example, "All men are mortal. Socrates is a Man. Therefore, Socrates is mortal". Aristotle also developed a line of reasoning known as the "method of inquiry", in which a problem is broken down into several parts, then each part is analyzed to arrive at a conclusion.

In general, logic involves conscious reasoning and establishing logical links between ideas and concepts. It often relies on the left cerebral hemisphere, based on rules, principles and deductive reasoning. Google's search algorithm, for example, is based on a complex system of algorithms that use logical rules to analyze and rank web pages according to their relevance to the user's query. This algorithm takes into account a wide range of factors, including keywords, links and user behavior, and uses statistical models to calculate the most relevant search results. Another use case is GPS technology. This invention was developed through a combination of scientific research, engineering and mathematical calculations. It relies on the principles of trigonometry, satellite communication and computer algorithms to determine a user's location and provide directions. In fact, the development of GPS required a systematic approach to problem-solving and a rigorous application of logic and mathematical reasoning.

Logic can also refer to inductive reasoning, although intuition can play a role in this method too. Thales of Miletus, who lived in the sixth century BC, was one of the first philosophers to propose this method. Thales believed that the world was ordered according to natural laws, and that these laws could be discovered through observation and analysis. This method merged with science during the Enlightenment to provide more objective conclusions. So, instead of assuming that a hypothesis A is true, on the basis of religion for example, and constructing a cause-and-effect chain using deductions, Enlightenment figures such as John Locke, David Hume and Francis Bacon, who was often called the "father of empiricism", argued that only observation of the phenomenon under study and the collection of a sufficient number of data would enable us to generalize conclusions. Bacon's ideas, in particular, had a major impact on the development of modern science, especially in the fields of experimental design and hypothesis testing in science.

Intuition, on the other hand, can be described as an instinctive feeling or sense of knowing, beyond the radar of consciousness. It is often built on past experiences, half-knowledge and insights that may be difficult to articulate or explain at first, like the profile of an artist or prophet. Although it is of subconscious, even metaphysical origin, we should mention a few approaches that stimulate this creative aspect. For, like a dualistic couple (once again), logic is concerned with control and Order, intuition finds itself in the midst of abandonment, *laissez-faire* and even Chaos.

In chronological order, I believe that nature, with all its natural innovations and resources, was **our first teacher** in terms of *Creativity*. Just reread the first chapter of this book or watch some National Geographic documentaries to fall under its spell and inspiration, shaped by millions of years of evolution and perhaps even a universal Artist. Our Matrix's dimensions have stimulated our human intuition through **biomimicry** for instance, that is the practice of imitating natural processes and systems to solve human problems. Such paradigm has been used in fields as diverse as architecture, medicine and transportation, and has led to the development of many important innovations. Here's a simple illustration. The wings of birds and insects inspired the design of more efficient and lighter aircraft wings and turbine blades. Similarly, the structure of spider silk inspired the development of highly resistant synthetic fibers used in the textile industry. Termites build complex mounds with a network of tunnels and vents that help regulate temperature and humidity. This could have inspired the ventilation systems for buildings that mimic the termite mound design, reducing the need for heating and cooling and improving indoor air quality.

Humans have achieved remarkable innovations by reverse-engineering natural mechanisms, drawing inspiration from nature's designs and processes. One notable example is the invention of Velcro by Swiss engineer George de Mestral in 1940. After observing burrs sticking to his dog's fur during a walk, he examined them under a microscope and discovered their hook-like structure. This observation inspired the development of the hook-and-loop fastening system used in Velcro. Another case is the Lotus effect, where the lotus leaf possesses a self-cleaning property. Water droplets that land on the leaf roll off, carrying away dirt and contaminants. This natural mechanism has led to the development of self-cleaning surfaces in various applications, including coatings for buildings, car paints, and textiles. Nature's ability to produce light has also inspired innovations. Organisms like fireflies and deep-sea creatures have the capacity to generate light, leading to the development of bioluminescent technologies. Scientists are exploring how bioluminescent proteins can be utilized in bioimaging, biosensors, and energy-efficient lighting solutions. Furthermore, the understanding of genetic mechanisms and natural gene regulation has paved the way for advancements in gene therapy. By harnessing knowledge of how genes are naturally controlled and expressed, scientists have developed methods to introduce or modify genes in patients' cells, offering potential treatments for genetic disorders, inherited diseases, and certain types of cancer.

Silence and meditation have long been recognized as powerful tools for gaining awareness of this raw universal *Creativity*. Not only do they promote inner calm, but they also help us to detect what's there, but which we rarely see because of our lack of mental presence. I don't think it would be surprising, therefore, to notice a general decline in *Creativity* among recent generations, bombarded by a constant flow of information and distractions, starting with the cell phone virus in our pockets, which may make it difficult to concentrate and think creatively. Meditative practices can also help individuals improve their level of awareness, enabling them to understand their own thoughts, feelings and motivations. This greater self-awareness undoubtedly leads to more authentic, even radical, creative expression. In photographic terms, this dualistic interplay between concentration and mindfulness is akin to an active search for the right angle, followed by a focus on the object of interest. Such an optimal balance can only benefit the degree of *Creativity*.

So, what are some of the other techniques for stimulating intuition? Studies suggest that taking a break or distracting yourself from a problem can sometimes help you find a solution later. This is often referred to as the "incubation period" or "gestation period" of creative thinking. For example, a 2012 study published in *Creativity Research Journal* found that participants who took a break and engaged in a cognitively undemanding task (such as taking a walk or listening to music) after working on a challenging problem were more likely to come up with a creative solution afterwards than those who continued to focus on the problem without taking a break.

Some readers may say that their creativity is more unbridled in a Starbucks than alone at home or in a quiet place. I think there are two reasons for this counter-intuitive statement. Firstly, studies show that moderate levels of ambient noise, such as those found in a coffee shop or on a quiet street, can increase the brain's level of creativity by promoting a moderate level of cognitive dissonance. This dissonance results from the brain's need to filter out unwanted stimuli, such as background noise, while remaining able to concentrate on the task at hand. Consequently, this process would force the brain to work harder, leading to the generation of new ideas. What's more, our brains are not accustomed to a very calm environment. If we haven't acquired a minimal grounding in meditation or concentration, "the monkey mind" automatically becomes agitated, and we start to get distracted by a memory or to anticipate the next meal or trip. If our smartphone is nearby (which it probably is), the creative mission becomes almost impossible.

In any case, whatever the source of the intuition, imagining a new or radical idea retains a mystical aspect. Let me explain.

In the expectation of a universal theory of everything, there are today two main branches of physics, a kind of duality: **macrophysics and microphysics.** The former, also known as classical physics, is the branch of physics that focuses on the study of large-scale objects and phenomena. It encompasses the laws of motion and gravitation formulated by Isaac Newton in the 17th century. These principles describe the behavior of objects on a macroscopic scale, such as the motion of planets, the behavior of fluids and the movement of objects. Albert Einstein's theory of relativity, developed in the early 20th century, complemented this branch with a better understanding of space-time and gravity on a large scale.

On the other hand, microphysics, also known as quantum physics, deals with the behavior of particles and phenomena at the smallest scales in the universe, those of particles such as atoms and electrons. It emerged in the early 20th century with revolutionary theories and experiments that revealed the peculiar nature of the subatomic world. Let's concentrate on this second branch, assuming that an idea, however materially existing, is merely an electromagnetic manifestation in the brain, an item of information.

Under this consequential hypothesis, to be tested one day by our physicist friends, or relativized from a philosophical angle, I'd like to creatively explore two proven notions of quantum physics, challenging the classical notions of determinism and causality, found in the materialist model of *Creativity*.

In the deterministic face of our Matrix, i.e., in our daily lives, every object is located by a four-dimensional reference point, entitled space-time. In fact, if you're in your position, on a chair for example, at this moment, it's because there's nobody else in your place at this very moment. *Duh, Obviously,* you might say. Additionally, the "local realism" trend applies every time. This statement conceals two principles: first, the principle of locality, that the cause of a physical change must be local. In other words, a thing is only changed if it is touched or influenced by a nearby force. Your chair will only start to move if someone or something pushes it: your friend, a strong wind, an earthquake, etc. Then there's the principle of realism, indicating that the properties of objects are real insofar as they exist in our physical universe independently of our mind and perception. So your chair would exist in its place even in your absence. In Einstein's words, "I'd like to think the Moon is there even if I'm not looking at it".

As it turns out, what may seem clear at first glance is no longer so when we move on to the scale of atoms, which, let's not forget, are the fundamental building blocks of all things and all life. Let's visualize the principle of "**superposition**", using the image proposed by physicist Erwin Schrödinger in

1935. To illustrate the strange, counter-intuitive nature of quantum mechanics, Schrödinger proposed the following experiment. This thought experiment (fortunately for our furry pals, it's just that) involves placing a cat in a sealed box with a device that has a 50/50 chance of releasing a poisonous gas and killing the cat. According to the principles of quantum mechanics, until the box is opened, and the cat observed, the cat is in a state of superposition, i.e., both alive and dead. Only when the box is opened does the cat become alive or dead. This thought experiment was not intended to be taken literally, but rather to illustrate the idea that, in quantum physics, a particle or subatomic system can exist in several states simultaneously, until it is observed, at which point it "collapses" into a single state. A specific case of this superposition can be seen, once again, in the famous wave-particle duality.

The "**double slit**" experiment is a classic test in quantum physics, displayed on the next figure, exploring this duality of subatomic particles, such as electrons. Imagine a particle as a tiny round ball. A wave is, like an ocean wave, an alternating movement of energy. The experiment involves sending a beam of electrons through a two-slit barrier, causing interference between the electrons as they pass through the slits and creating a pattern on the screen of a detector placed behind the barrier.

When the experiment is carried out with the detector switched off, the pattern produced on the screen appears to be an interference pattern, similar to that which would be expected if electrons behaved like waves. This pattern consists of a series of light and dark bands, the light bands indicating areas of constructive interference where the waves reinforce each other, and the dark bands indicating areas of destructive interference where the waves cancel each other out. You probably studied this in high school. However, when the experiment is performed with the detector switched on, or any observer, the pattern produced on the screen changes radically. Instead of an interference pattern, the electrons seem to behave like particles, each electron creating a distinct spot on the screen behind one of the two slits.

With One or Both Detectors Turned On
The pattern on the screen indicates 2 beams of particles

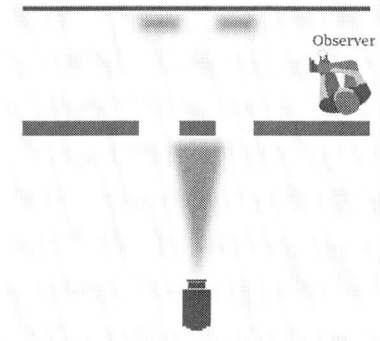

With All Detectors Turned Off
The patter on the screen indicates a wave (interferences)

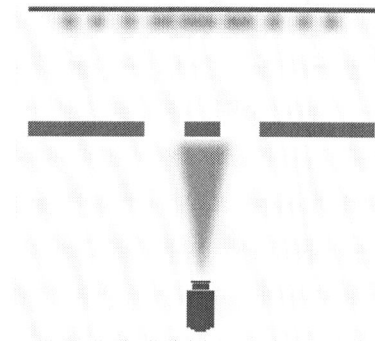

Observer

This phenomenon, known as the observer effect, suggests that observing or measuring a subatomic particle can fundamentally alter its behavior. When electrons are unobserved, they appear to behave like waves, but when they are observed, they behave like particles. The experiment also raises profound questions about the nature of reality and the relationship between observer and observed, subject and object. If we take the previous example of your chair, to simplify, this means that when you look at it, the chair is there, motionless. However, when you turn your gaze, the chair becomes a car, an elephant or disappears completely.

The second quantum paradigm, also tested, is called quantum correlation, also known as "**quantum entanglement**", another strange phenomenon of quantum physics. It occurs when two subatomic particles, such as electrons or photons (light particles), become linked in a particular way, after an interaction for example, and remain so no matter how far apart they are. In other words, when they are entangled, the properties of these particles are closely linked, so that the behavior of one instantly affects the other, even if they are separated by millions of light-years. This phenomenon runs counter to our intuitive understanding of the physical world, as it implies instantaneous action at a distance, faster than the speed of light imposed by special relativity. If we assume that your chair is entangled with you, when you push your chair, you will also feel a similar destabilizing force, a bit like voodoo doll practices, linked to black magic in some ancient cultures. Einstein ironically called it "spooky actions at a distance". This removes the need for cause and effect at the subatomic level. Such a phenomenon, whose explanation goes beyond the classical framework of space-time, has been experimentally proven by the Nobel Prize-winning scientists in physics in 2022.

A Tibetan Buddhist told me once that, "Everything is movement. There are no moving objects, but only motion, which constitutes every object". This philosophy is confirmed scientifically, at the microscopic level at least, which extends to everything, since everything is made up of atoms and particles. It would seem, then, that physical objects – including ourselves – as we see them in our everyday lives, exist only in our mental illusion. Classical physics teaches us that matter is made up of atoms, which in turn are made up of subatomic particles such as electrons, protons and neutrons. However, when we examine these particles at a more fundamental level, using quantum field theory, we discover that they have no solid, determinate structure. They are simply manifestations of energy on a subatomic scale. An electron, for example, is represented by a probabilistic field around the nucleon, the center of the atom, and not by a single particle orbiting like a planet orbits its sun. Similarly, in the world of ideas, under certain vibratory conditions and in a context yet to be defined, **an idea is merely an electromagnetic manifestation at the neuronal level**, which could be likened to a vibration, an energy or a subatomic particle in motion. In fact, under this bold hypothesis, both the above-mentioned quantum phenomena, namely superposition and quantum entanglement", would apply. Let's be a bit creative, even crazy, in interpreting their results.

First of all, *Creativity*, or the act of creating, of imagining something, is an implicit transition from unconscious nothingness to something we think exists, **from a field of hidden possibilities to a perceptible choice**. This reminds us of the wave-particle duality, or more broadly, the principle of quantum superposition. Strangely in line with the physicalist model of the brain (and of AI), this first quantum phenomenon suggests that the idea exists, in background, under an infinite number of possibilities, a probabilistic wave, which materializes when and only when we throw the spotlight of consciousness on it. The field of ideas then collapses into a single, ideally creative idea, just as a wave collapses into a particle. The good news in this interpretation is that every conscious being possesses innovative abilities. All it takes is enough training or an increase in your level of consciousness to detect the field of possibility (wave), and enough concentration to transform it into an idea that matters (particle). Furthermore, your brain vibrations, whether constructive (optimism, confidence, open-mindedness, etc.) or toxic (fear, anger, trauma, etc.), will influence the spectrum of this field to which you have access, and therefore the creative quality of your thoughts and even of your daily life in general.

The implications of the second phenomenon, the quantum entanglement, are even more profound. Contrary this time to the materialistic assumption, for two particles to be entangled, i.e., linked to each other, there would be no need for a cause maintaining this link. Similarly, under certain conditions, two thoughts would be correlated without the need for an intermediary. Accepting this view, an idea could come from another individual or creature, from another era, or another planet. If we were to imagine a scenario in which quantum entanglement applied to thoughts in a generalized way, with no material limits, instantaneous communication without intermediaries would be possible between individuals, whatever the physical distance. Sharing information and exchanging ideas would become instantaneous, transcending the limits of time and space. The entanglement of thoughts could also lead to a form of collective consciousness, where individuals are interconnected at a deep level, fostering collaboration, empathy and shared understanding. Finally, through the same process, knowledge and skills could be transferred directly from one individual to another, bypassing traditional learning processes. This would enable the rapid acquisition of information and expertise in an ideal world.

All these implications sound like something out of Hollywood science fiction, and they are, as long as we can't reproduce these scenarios on demand. That said, we can't deprive our macroscopic reality of such a possibility one day, knowing that a sort of **synchronicity**, using Carl Jung's term, is experimentally applicable to the subatomic world. In particular, this concept refers to significant coincidences and weird connections between events that cannot be explained by conventional causality. In other words, it suggests that events can be interconnected beyond ordinary notions of time, space and our everyday understanding of "local realism" and cause and effect. Astrological predictions, manifestations and the famous Law of Attraction, which states that similar energies or thoughts attract each other, all derive their pseudo-science from this same principle of synchronicity.

Similarly, in Eastern philosophies such as Hinduism and Buddhism, the concept of karma and the interconnectedness of all things is essential. Karma suggests that actions have consequences, and that events unfold according to a complex network of hidden, universal causes and effects. In most indigenous religions and beliefs, there is the idea of an underlying communication with spirits or angels who exist beyond space-time. In fact, the act of invoking or supplicating a god in the hope of specific help suggests the establishment of a link between two distant subjects, without the interference of a physical or electromagnetic intermediary. Without having to believe in Jung nor incorporate indigenous and spiritual beliefs fairly common telepathic experiences – between Siamese twins, a mother and child, or lovers, for example – imply a kind of synchronicity.

I'm convinced (and that's just me) that going from nothing to an idea is more than just connecting neurons to memory. Because, although we can reproduce a kind of artificial creativity with AI or AGI-based systems, this creative product would never be better than the best combination of existing data. To illustrate simply, imagine an intelligent system, trained with just two images: an apple and an orange. What would be the fruit of its creativity? Undoubtedly, a mix of the two, a kind of orange apple. We can't expect an airplane, unless we open the door of this machine to other internet-wide databases like ChatGPT, in which case millions of creative combinations of data are possible depending on the objective or user need.

Moreover, if I extrapolate this conclusion to my own experience, I knew absolutely nothing about the principle of synchronicity until this very morning. While meditating and walking along a Moroccan beach, looking for inspiration, my headphones tuned to a random podcast and a passage mentioned Carl Jung and his famous principle. I then had the automatic intuition to make the neurological link with the principle of quantum entanglement, ancient beliefs, the many times the number 22 has pursued me, a situation has been strangely unblocked, or an inner voice has saved me from a bad decision or guided me towards unplanned opportunities. Not to mention the few encounters with awakened people who **guesse**d my life and personality with maternal precision. Chance? Unfounded beliefs? Surely, but are they false?

On the same wavelength, I'm also at a loss to explain the coincidence of narrative similarities in sacred texts or myths reported by prophets or gurus who are spatially and temporally distant from each other. The case of Moses, Jesus and Muhammad is particularly striking. Although they lived at different times, in different places, and spoke different languages, they all recount common myths – of Adam and Eve, Noah's flood, Abraham's sacrifice, and so many other themes and interpretations of life and death – that a mere coincidence or a scattered transfer over hundreds of generations to an illiterate Muhammad would not satisfy our curiosity, especially in view of the recent discovery of possible quantum correlation outside space-time.

In any case, *Creativity* through inspiration, dream or intuitive synchronicity brings unconscious information to the surface of individual consciousness, whether initially hidden somewhere in matter, in the individual or collective unconscious, or in another dimension of the Matrix. In view of such process complexity, let's illustrate it again. Now imagine that a mosquito lands on your arm, or that your subway neighbor is about to get out. Suddenly, you're pouring your consciousness into these disturbing creatures, and therefore out of this book. One second, these distractions weren't there. The next second, they were. That's what creation is all about; fueling *Creativity*, awareness and *innovation*. Another example. Have you ever noticed the moments when you get angry? You probably noticed your anger within seconds of it happening. In fact, your body and senses can even act outside your awareness and will. In his book, *Blink* (2007), author Malcom Gladwell explains how experts in art or sport, or any other field, know before they know. In art, for example, an expert only needs to look at a work of art for a second or two to know if it's fake. In sport, a professional can predict whether a shot is good or bad the moment or even before the player hits the ball.

It should also be noted that, like all dualistic complementarities, **a dynamic balance between intuition and logic is necessary for optimal Creativity.** Intuition can provide a spark of inspiration, help break out of "tunnel vision" and generate new ideas, while logic is used to organize and structure these ideas coherently and efficiently. Intuition in creativity often involves making connections that aren't immediately obvious, taking risks and following one's instincts. It may involve a quest into the subconscious, exploring new and unconventional ways of thinking, "thinking out of the box", swimming in the Chaos of mindfulness. Logic in creativity, on the other hand, involves breaking down a problem or task into smaller elements, analyzing data and using critical thinking to arrive at a solution. It would also involve the use of rules or principles, a predefined methodology, and concentration on more ordered states.

This combination of intuition and logic is quite common in the entrepreneurial world. In fact, several strategies can be implemented. Let's briefly mention a few. Firstly, keeping abreast of industry trends and carrying out market analyses can inspire *innovation*. By identifying new opportunities and understanding consumer motivations, companies can develop products and services that respond to changing demand. Collaboration with external partners, such as customers, suppliers and other talented companies, also fuels *Creativity*. This is what we call "Open Innovation". This concept underlines the importance of harnessing external sources of innovation to reinforce a company's internal innovation efforts. Investment in research and development is a classic lever for the systematic exploration of innovative concepts, sometimes served outside the company's historical market, opening up new "blue ocean" markets where competition is less fierce. In addition, using methodologies such as Design Thinking, companies can gather diverse viewpoints and develop prototype solutions. Finally, let's not forget the role of serendipity, i.e., the occurrence of unexpected discoveries, as a source of new innovative breakthroughs. Alexander Fleming discovered penicillin, thus, antibiotics, when a mold called Penicillium notatum accidentally contaminated a petri dish in his laboratory, inhibiting the growth of bacteria. Likewise, originally developed as a medication to treat cardiovascular conditions, Viagra's side effect has made more than one man (and woman) happy.

Based on our analysis, let's summarize *Creativity* mathematically, in terms of the appropriate variables:

Creativity=f (Intuition, Logic)

Intuition=g (Data from the individual subconscious & from the collection unconscious)

Logic=h (Data accessibles (3V), Algorithm)

Let's conclude this section with a summary of this rough model of *Creativity*. The weight of this third variable in the Fundamental Identity of Innovation therefore depends on the power and effectiveness of the intuitive and logical processes, as detailed above.

Logic, in turn, is a function of the data readily accessible by the brain, or by the machine in the case of AI, and of the algorithm that stores, processes and reads this data. Following this materialistic approach to the letter, the creative difference between two individuals (or two AI systems) in a given field could be explained as follows. Either person A knows more than person B and has therefore integrated more data than the other. Or person A's algorithm is better than person B's. This last statement could echo intelligence, IQ or EQ, or any way in which neurons or network nodes are connected, varying according to genes, brain development, mathematical models in case of AI, etc., which would influence the speed and quality of data processing, and therefore the output of the creative process.

Note the 3V in front of Data, in the logic equation, which can be likened to the 3V of Big Data in the field of artificial intelligence. It stands for Volume, Velocity and Variety (3V). This means that the quality of any creative process depends on volume, the amount of data accessible in the server or in memory, velocity, which is the speed of capturing and storing this data, and finally, variety, which refers to the diversity of sources and types of data you can access. Someone who reads a lot about oceanography (Volume), who combines experience at sea with theory on YouTube, from books and interviews with experts (Variety), and who has a good brain to quickly assimilate all this and organize it in their head or notepad (Velocity), would clearly have more creative advantage in this aquatic field than an amateur or even a theoretical researcher. In short, **Data is the raw material of all creative innovation**. And by Data, I'm not just referring to knowledge written in a book or broadcast on a media channel but to any information of which we can or might one day be aware and which in computer language would be reduced to a series of 0s and 1s. Billions and billions of Data are all around us, every millisecond; we just don't perceive them or don't care.

Even intuition processes data, except of a more unconscious nature, i.e., further from our mental perception than freshly acquired or memorized data. For example, you'll have less trouble pronouncing your father's or child's name, explaining what you do for a living, or telling me about the movie you saw last weekend, because this is accessible data, in the subconscious according to certain classifications. Over time, entropy increases and mental Chaos sets in. Your brain, especially during sleep, needs to get rid of what seems useless, in order to store the new, the exciting and the important, a bit like my minimalism when I throw away or give away anything unused for more than three months. Unlike my approach, the brain doesn't throw things away, it archives them, day after day, until they are forgotten, except during traumatic events when it suddenly forgets or is forced to forget by a psychological protection mechanism. So, unlike logic, which uses fresh data or data that is accessible neurologically or artificially, intuition draws on deep Data, which we think we've never possessed, when in fact it was always there, in the archives of our individual, collective or natural memory. We retrieve it during a dream, a walk, a dance or a meditative session, mixing it with other data, and thus, by magic, a beautiful new thing appears.

Finally, it's worth noting that this continuous discovery (invention) or need-driven discovery (innovation) is materialistically supported by our brain. Indeed, we already know our prodigious central organ is surprisingly adaptable. Scientific studies have shown that our brain is a malleable tissue, capable of forming new neuronal connections and reorganizing its circuits. By exploiting this **brain plasticity**, we can push back the limits of our creativity. But we didn't stop there ! we are no longer limited by even our physical frame.

Imagine yourself in front of a laptop, a smartphone or, in the near future, a quantum machine. These digital portals extend the perimeter of the data to which we have access. An immensity of knowledge and inspiration. By plugging our brains, as in a Matrix simulation, into external servers, such as the internet, we are connected to an infinity of scientific and artistic resources, from virtual libraries to online museums, from tutorial videos to artistic collaboration platforms, everything is just a click away. This infinite flow of information, if used properly, can fuel our imagination and stimulate our *Creativity* to the extreme. Additionally, software for artistic creation, mathematical modeling, prototyping and simulation, drawing, 3D sculptures, video editing and much more allows us to explore unlimited artistic horizons, offering unprecedented freedom to express our ideas, experiment with new techniques and push back the boundaries of art and science.

Despite this enhanced *Creativity*, I'm not afraid to assume, at least philosophically, that **Man creates nothing. All it does is rediscover**. So it comes as no surprise when I recently had the intuition that the equivalent of Man in Arabic is " Insān", deriving from "Nassā" meaning "to forget". Perhaps we've forgotten our primitive, even animal past. Maybe we've also forgotten our immaterial, energetic and deep nature, independent of the chains of space-time. Whatever the case, let's continue rediscovering who We are.

VARIABLE 4:
The Nerdy side of innovation

What do you think of when I mention Tesla? Chances are, given the relative freshness of this data in your brain, the first idea that comes to mind is related to the Tesla car, or Elon Musk's company Tesla Inc. Such a choice of label is not arbitrary. Beyond its pleasant tone and its nod to the exclusively electric aspect of Tesla vehicles, there are other interesting reasons, hidden between the lines of the biography of the famous inventor, Nikola Tesla.

By the end of the 19th century, Thomas Edison was already a renowned inventor and an emblematic figure in the history of electricity, playing a key role in the commercialization of this disruptive innovation that gradually replaced illumination by combustion (candles, gas, campfires, etc.). Indeed, in the 1870s and 1880s, Edison made major breakthroughs in electric lighting and power distribution systems. His invention of the practical incandescent bulb in 1879 marked a turning point in the quest for reliable electric lighting. Recognizing the need for a complete system, Edison developed a direct-current electrical distribution system known as the Edison System. In 1882, he created the world's first commercial power plant, Pearl Street Station, which served as the cornerstone for supplying electricity to customers in lower Manhattan, New York. Edison's efforts were accompanied by public demonstrations at fairs and exhibitions (in the absence of television), marketing initiatives and collaborations with investors such as the notorious J.P. Morgan. By this stage, therefore, the Edison General Electric Company, founded by Thomas Edison and J.P Morgan in 1878 and later renamed General Electric, was already an "incumbent", a company well established in its market.

That's when Nikola Tesla came on the scene.

Born in 1856 in Smiljan, in what is now Croatia, part of the Austro-Hungarian Empire at the time, Tesla showed an intense curiosity for the natural world from an early age. One day, he was impressed by a violent thunderstorm and became determined to master this intangible force. His interest in electrical phenomena grew as he read books and learned about the latest scientific advances in the field, notably those of Thomas Edison. Tesla's passion for electricity led him to study engineering and physics. He attended the Polytechnic Institute in Graz, Austria, then the University of Prague, where he deepened his knowledge of electrical engineering.

In 1882, Tesla realized part of his dream of working for the Continental Edison Company in Paris, which was affiliated with Edison's company. His first task was to improve the design of dynamos. A few years later, proving his skill and passion in this field, Tesla was invited by his boss to move to the United States to work directly with Edison in his New York laboratory. Edison recognized Tesla's talents and entrusted him with various projects, including the redesign of the company's DC generators.

Tesla, in his entrepreneurial spirit, suggested to Edison that he develop and market alternating current (AC) electricity. This involves a periodically reversing flow of electrical charges, making it more suitable for transmission over long distances. Tesla believed that AC electricity would revolutionize the world by making energy distribution more efficient and convenient. Edison, on the other hand, remained an advocate of direct current (DC) electricity, which involves the flow of electrical charges in a single direction. His adamant support of DC was perhaps due to reasons of ego, contractual terms with cities and investors or a simple lack of vision. So, as with any large company that prefers to "exploit" rather than invest in "exploration" and R&D, Tesla's vision of AC power clashed with Edison's unwavering support for DC systems, leading to a rift between these two great geniuses, and marking the start of a bitter rivalry.

After leaving Edison's company, Tesla embarked on his own projects. In 1887, he founded the Tesla Electric Company and set out on the road to intellectual and financial independence. Tesla then joined forces with industrialist George Westinghouse, who recognized the potential of alternating current electricity. Westinghouse obtained Tesla's patents for AC motors and transformers. Edison, meanwhile, led a campaign against

AC electricity, attempting to discredit its safety and viability. He even went so far as publicly electrocuting animals using AC in an attempt to convince people of its dangers. This infamous episode became known as the "war of currents", with Edison representing direct current and Tesla/ Westinghouse alternating current. Despite Edison's efforts, alternating current electricity was gaining ground and had finally established itself as the dominant system for commercial distribution.

Author of some 300 patents in fields ranging from alternative electricity to wireless telegraphy and telecommunication, Tesla will forever remain in the annals of human innovation. He died alone and financially drained, a sad end to his life. I like to call him "the hippie innovator". Tesla was focused until death on his idealistic vision of an enlightened wireless world, with no concern for money or having a family. Elon Musk is himself a capitalist hippie. His conscious or intuitive decision to give his company the name Tesla Inc. and his ambition to disrupt the rules of the game in the automotive sector, as Nikola Tesla did before, in part, with General Electric, is now hopefully easier to understand.

From this dramatic biography, we can draw three enlightening perspectives. Firstly, it absolutely takes a strong intrinsic *Motivation*, a lot of skill and a touch of madness, as is the case for Nikola Tesla or Elon Musk, to challenge established companies and threaten their market share. Second, if this challenge succeeds, you could end up a billionaire or even the richest man in the world like Musk. Otherwise, Tesla's unenviable fate is likely to recur. The final lesson is of a more practical nature, which we'll detail in this section, and concerns the superiority of Tesla's AC electric current over Edison's DC current, as well as the decisive role played by investor J.P. Morgan in the success of his nugget Edison, at Tesla's expense. All these lessons are included in the fourth variable of our fundamental identity of innovation: *Technology*.

Every day, thousands of self-employed podcasters publish podcasts on various media platforms. The subject of such artistic work depends on the audience's *Need* (entertainment, training, information, etc.) and the podcaster's external or intrinsic *Motivation*. Some are at Maslow's lower level, seeking security through a sufficient source of income to pay current expenses. Many in the esteem layer would appreciate a thank you, a "like", or word-of-mouth praise for their work. Others are one rung up the pyramid, getting to know each other better, sharing their knowledge and contributing to a better world, without worrying about money or praise. It can be a mixture of all these too. Whatever the *Motivation*, imagine our friend Maria decides to launch her own podcast on interior design tips and techniques. She begins to imagine the theme of her first podcast by drawing word clouds, brainstorming with a few housemates, using an AI-based assistant and/or taking long walks in search of inspiration. A few days later, Maria manages to finalize the *Creativity* phase, writing in black and white a captivating scenario on Scandinavian minimalist style, emphasizing simplicity, natural materials and a neutral color palette. She is now ready to move on to the operational phase of this innovative process. This final stage could be achieved in a variety of ways.

With a professional studio not an option, she can record her podcast on a smartphone, iPad or laptop. The choice is between the laptop's internal microphone, a USB digital microphone or an analog microphone. The microphone can be dynamic or a condenser. All this jargon confuses Maria. She thought the most tedious part of the innovation journey was the script stage! Each material and brand option will lead to a different result. Still motivated, despite her lack of technical expertise, she consults a friend and watches a few YouTube videos. The phone option would most likely produce a lower quality sound than using a USB microphone. A unidirectional mic would be ideal for reducing noise and focusing on the speaker, but it's clearly not practical when several people are talking in the podcast. In this case, a dynamic microphone may be a better option. Maria will probably also need headphones, with many options available here too. After recording, comes the editing phase. Which software to use, why and how? All these small decisions end up creating divergent results, in terms of quality, budget required, and skills to be acquired for optimal use. Even if the starting point, in this case the podcast script, is the same, there are many potential end products.

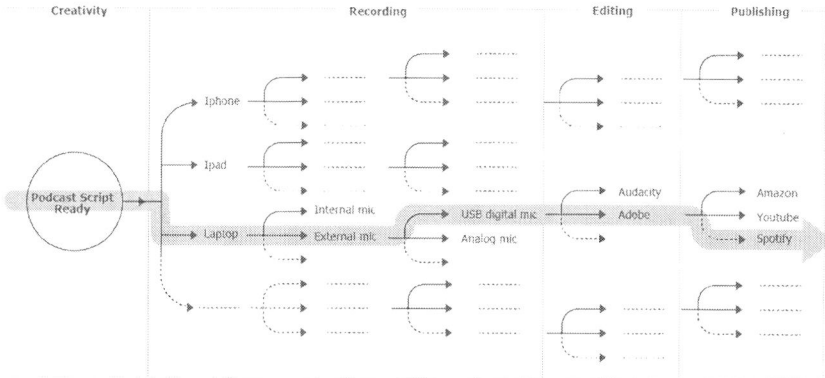

The use case of Maria and the podcasting domain can be extrapolated to almost any kind of innovation, in the commercial world and elsewhere. Indeed, in order to innovate, it is intuitively essential to be creative, to imagine new solutions. But once you've decided on an idea, a scenario or a speech, you need to move on to operationalization, i.e., the variable that is *Technology*. This is what makes the difference between a dreamer and an innovator.

Note that the variable *Technology*, in our fundamental equation, refers to a broader spectrum, based on the original etymological definition of the term. In fact, this term comes to us from the Greek "technología", which is a combination of two other Greek words: "téchnē" meaning "art, skill, craft" and "logía" meaning "study or science of", thus giving, as it were, "applied art". Historically, the term "technology" was first used in the 18th century, referring to the study of practical arts such as manufacturing and engineering. In recent decades, its definition has broadened to include a range of activities relating to the development of any product, particularly those of the fourth Industrial Revolution. Indeed, the meaning of technology has become confused with blockchain, autonomous driving software, 3D printing and AI, smartphones and so many other innovative products of the 21st century. From now on, let's call these by the title *"innovations"*, and let's call *"Technology"* all the project stages that follow ideation, from conception to planning the appropriate technical steps used to create, produce and operate the theoretical solution, through to testing before market introduction.

While individuals and organizations tend to focus on the *Creativity* process, on collaborative R&D and finding the perfect solution to a problem or opportunity, the implementation process is just as important, if not more so. We all sometimes have brilliant ideas (and stupid ones, too), but not many entrepreneurs or managers actually plan and implement anything concrete. Few apply the famous quote attributed to Mahatma Gandhi, "Be the change you want to see in the world". The first reason would be a lack of *motivation*, which we've already detailed a dozen pages ago. The second would be a technological deficit due to operational complexity, a lack of skills or a budget shortfall. We'll come back to this.

Let's look first at the transition from dream to reality, from idea to tangible, from quantum to macroscopic, if I may say so, in short, from *Creativity* to *Technology*. When I say "transition", we could in fact be misled into believing that *innovation* is a linear process starting with an imagined concept and ending with the final new product. Yet, often, depending on the market or field, designers can follow an agile iterative process, alternating between creativity and incremental implementation, just like the natural process of evolution. The eye is a classic example of how complex structures can evolve over time through a series of small, incremental changes, assuming some kind of natural or divine *Creativity* exists.

The first organisms to develop photosensitive cells were probably simple single-cell organisms, such as bacteria or algae. These cells could detect variations in light and darkness, helping organisms to orient themselves and find food. Over time, these light-sensitive cells specialized and evolved into more complex structures, such as the eye spots found in some primitive animals. These eye spots could detect the direction of light, enabling these dynamic but still basic agents to move towards or away from light sources. Mutations combined with natural selection over the generations resulted in more complex eyes, like those of insects, which possess several lenses and can form relatively detailed images. Eventually, eyes evolved into even more advanced structures, such as the complex eyes found in vertebrates, including man. Each stage of this process involved small changes that built on previous adaptations, gradually increasing the complexity and functionality of the eye. Species with better vision, or other environment-detection sensors, were more likely to survive and pass on their genes.

From a neurological point of view, this back and forth between idea and realization activates different parts of the brain. As described above, the brain is a magnificent lump of grey and white matter, condensed into billions of neurotransmitters. Although neurons are generally very small, ranging in diameter from 4 to 100 micrometers (0.03 inches), they are organized in networks, i.e., interconnected zones, with a total length estimated at around 150,000 kilometers (93,206 miles), if we open and expand the inside of a human skull. This is roughly equivalent to circling the Earth four times.

Despite all this structural complexity, the brain has been beautifully designed, over millions of years of evolution, into two distinct and anatomically symmetrical halves. The dualistic concept of "**right brain**" and "**left brain**" refers to the accepted idea that the two hemispheres of the brain have different functions, and that people may prefer one hemisphere over the other. Thus, the right brain would be more creative, intuitive and artistic, while the left brain would be more logical, analytical and algorithmic. Although this concept has been popular for some decades now, it's important not to assume an exclusive separation of the brain halves. It's true that the two hemispheres of the brain have different functions, but it's also truer that these poles work together and are interconnected, like a dualistic pair. This link between the two brain halves forms a separate organ called the corpus callosum. It's a long, thin bundle of over 200 million nerve fibers, making it the largest white matter structure in the brain. This linking capacity makes the corpus callosum a solid biological bridge, running from the front to the back of the brain, connecting the left and right cerebral hemispheres, and thus enabling the two cerebral hemispheres to communicate and share information.

Most humans use both hemispheres to process, analyze, convert or assimilate information from the internal and external world. That said, depending on the habits we acquire, and the social role we occupy, a hemispheric imbalance may occur. Like a bodybuilder who muscles his biceps and chest but ignores his legs, I still remember the mental imbalance I had during my student years. Two years of scientific preparatory classes followed by three years of computer engineering were perhaps more than enough to strengthen the logical and analytical side of my brain, unfortunately at the expense of the artistic and emotional side. After graduating, I had to restore the balance by investing my time in travel, photography, dance and other activities that stimulate the right half. I think this problem is quite common in our capitalist age, which pushes us towards professional hyper-specialization, and therefore to muscle one area or half of the brain at the expense of the rest. In an ideal world, we'd all have "fit", well-sized bodies and brains, with abs strong enough to ensure a flexible link between upper and lower body, and a corpus callosum dense enough to ensure dynamic communication between the left and right sides of the brain.

This model has been repeatedly tested through testimonials and studies of patients with left-brain damage, for example. Without this algorithmic zone, these people found it difficult to read and write, to form long sentences, and to understand and solve conventional problems. In a brilliant TED talk given in 2008, neuroscientist Jill Bolte Taylor explains the experience she had when her left brain was put out of action for a time, following a blood vessel explosion. She describes her state as that of a "happy child", losing all notion of linear time, language and rational thought. A computer parallel, albeit a simplistic one, can help us understand Taylor's words.

As simplified in the following figure, a left brain could thus be compared to a serial processor, while the right brain functions more like a parallel multiprocessor. In more down-to-earth terms, the left brain is the king of Order, of processing sequence after sequence, past, present and future, and of a unified, clear mental image of the ego, the "I". The right hemisphere, on the other hand, is more chaotic, focusing on the present moment, because everything is mixed up in it, with an overall view, beautiful or disordered as the case may be, rather than a preoccupation with detail. Consequently, relying heavily on the right brain after damage to the left brain or corpus callosum is experimentally similar to a psychedelic experience. With her analytical layer deactivated, Taylor, a usually left-brain wired scientist, found herself in a pretty Chaos, a *laissez-faire* and acceptance of everything, right now, for the sake of the present moment. The so-called "bad trip" may be due to the analytical brain fighting to regain control, to restore Order, but that's another story for another book.

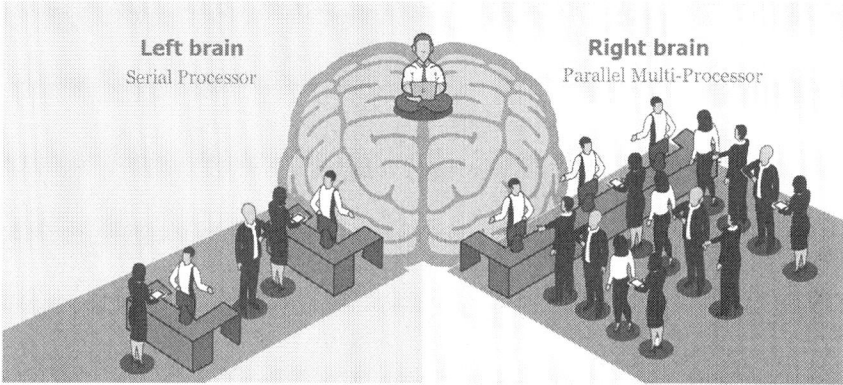

Left brain
Serial Processor

Right brain
Parallel Multi-Processor

This notion of brain division would impact both our *Creativity* and the *Technology* used to implement any innovation. For the first of these two variables, research by neuroscientists such as Rex Jung has highlighted the importance of connectivity and communication between brain regions for optimal *Creativity*. Like a tree, stable through its roots and trunk, and flexible through its branches and leaves, studies based on brain imaging have shown that highly creative people show increased connectivity between the network associated with introspection and idea generation – in short, Chaos – and the Order network, associated with cognitive control and decision-making. These results highlight the collaborative nature of *Creativity*, involving both hemispheres and multiple brain networks.

Technology, on the other hand, is associated, in my experience and that of many colleagues, with the left hemisphere of the brain. Even in artistic, spiritual or social fields, the implementation of any good idea requires Order, a strong point of any engineer, manager or choreographer. Nowadays, such structuring is called a "project". Each *Technology*, i.e., each process of implementing an idea, follows its own path. As in Maria's example, the reason for this divergence often lies in the multitude of choices that can be made along the way. Like the divided branches of a tree, each node represents a specific decision. A project team chooses its branches according to various criteria of feasibility, resources, timing and so on. Furthermore, depending on the sector and context to which the imagined solution belongs, the *Technology* can be very disparate.

In the digital sector, for example, the implementation process usually involves a high degree of iteration and testing. Indeed, IT solutions often require complex coding and development work, as well as extensive debugging and quality assurance testing, to ensure that everything works as intended. In the healthcare sector, innovations are accompanied by significant regulatory oversight. Indeed, healthcare solutions are generally subject to strict regulatory requirements for patient confidentiality and safety. These same products would also require extensive clinical trials before they could be implemented on a large scale, adding a lot of time and money to the process.

The aim of this book is not to provide a comparative study of *Technologies* in different sectors, nor to reveal inside information on how Apple innovates compared to Samsung or Xiaomi. Business school case studies are better structured (and more boring) for going into such technical detail. That said, it would be a shame to miss out on the basic factors that contribute to an optimal innovative process, in a fairly general way. Questions such as: What made Maria specifically choose the grey-highlighted branch of the previous diagram rather than the dozen other ones, and Nikola Tesla tirelessly defend his alternating current (AC) system over Edison's?

The question is half the answer, they say. Thus, a trivial answer would be that certain branches lead to no fruit. Their ends are empty or useless in relation to the *Need*, the objective of this innovative quest. If we aim to cook a French crepe and use a normal frying pan or, worse, the microwave, we'd get "pancakes" at best. Here again, Order is harder to achieve than Chaos. There are millions of ways not to achieve the desired new solution and only a few fruitful ones.

In addition, an innovative project requires one or more objectives in terms of deliverables, the so-called "scope", or project perimeter, which depends on the *Need* to be addressed. Edison's *Need* was perhaps just to provide a minimum of night-time light to households and businesses through his DC *Technology*. Nikola Tesla, as a visionary, wanted to democratize this new energy to the whole planet, thanks to the power of AC current first, and later, by risking his reputation on wireless electricity generators. Maria had defined success criteria, or acceptance criteria in agile management parlance. This checklist set thresholds for podcast sound quality, delivery speed and editing options. I leave it to you to extrapolate this idea to other industries, from aeronautics to luxury goods, from politics to religion.

Once the project scoping phase has been completed, including objectives, plan, resources etc., a more practical phase is launched, focusing on implementation, monitoring milestones and managing risks and contingencies. If I consider this book project, when I had finished imagining the themes, the plan and the writing style (*Creativity*), the implementation phase that followed was characterized by a commitment to deliver content at a daily frequency, for a year, or this project would end up in oblivion. This also included the compilation of research, interviews, travels and intuitions as the work progressed, and then the recruitment and management of the designer for the figures, a testing stage, with corrections and feedback to be incorporated, and finally the search for a suitable publisher. Again, this process is not rigidly linear. Phases of creative emptiness involved more research, meditation and exchange with other experts. Stopping in the middle of the third chapter to feed or adjust the first, for example, was part of the life of the project. All companies and individuals have to make trade-offs of varying degrees of importance during implementation because a project by definition has one foot in the future, in the uncertain.

That's why project management is a skill that needs to be cultivated through practice, rather than theory and certificates. Many gifted people, especially artists, find it easier to create than to operationalize their creations. The same problem arises in the entrepreneurial world. Several studies have been carried out over the years to determine the success rate of projects. One of the best-known studies is the Standish Group's CHAOS report (funny coincidence, or synchronicity), which has been updated periodically since 1994. According to the 2022 CHAOS report, around 20% of projects will be canceled before they ever get completed. Further results indicate 50% of projects will cost more of their original estimates or request more time than planned. However, it's important to note that these statistics can vary considerably according to project type and industry sector. In this case, IT projects tend to have higher failure rates than construction projects. Enterprise Resource Planning or ERP projects, such as SAP, which involve several business divisions, are relatively riskier than web platform development.

In some cases, even if an initially satisfactory result is achieved, one or two misleading bifurcations can cause considerable collateral damage. In the early 2000s, Firestone tires manufactured by Bridgestone were the subject of controversy linked to tread separation problems, which led to numerous accidents and fatalities. The problem was particularly acute in the United States, where many Ford Explorer SUVs were fitted with Firestone tires as standard equipment. The problem was due to a combination of factors, including tire design, the quality of the materials used and the manufacturing process. The tires tended to lose their tread during use, which could lead to loss of vehicle control and the risk of an accident. In the wake of this controversy, Bridgestone and Ford faced public backlash and legal action. The companies in question were forced to recall millions of tires and cars and saw their reputations severely damaged.

Answering our initial questions about Maria and Tesla therefore comes down to understanding a project's main generic success factors, regardless of its nature. Based on my professional experience and project management best practices derived from the renowned PMI and PRINCE2 methodologies, for example, I propose an improved version of the concept of a project's golden triangle, generally made up of cost, time and quality. Similarly, I believe that an optimal *Technology,* that is an implementation method, could be summarized by the equation below:

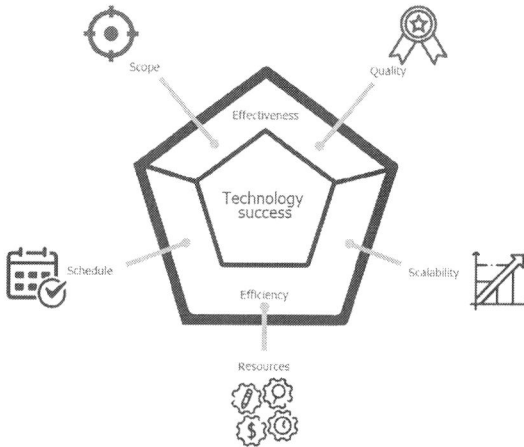

Technology=f(Effectiveness, Efficiency

Effectiveness = h (Scope: Quality)

Efficiency = k (Agenda: Resources: Scalability).

Note that these equations are remarkably independent of the scale of the project and its sector of activity. Whether it's a new recipe, an autonomous wheelchair or religious or political sect, the technology equation, or a slightly customized version, will apply. That said, to illustrate these equations gently, we'll consider a product *innovation*. Furthermore, to avoid any confusion, let's remember that an optimal implementation technique (*Technology*) is not equivalent to the success of the innovation produced at the end of this process. We call the latter "*Value*", and it will be examined separately in the next section. Indeed, a highly automated manufacturing process, equipped with all the cool gadgets of Industry 4.0, is no guarantee that people will like or buy the resulting product. After all, a project is essentially mechanical, a sequence of steps, whereas the adoption of a product is first and foremost psychological, and then also financial. To briefly illustrate such difference between the innovation process, or *Technology*, and the end-product, *Value*, here are a few case studies.

In 1985, Coca-Cola introduced a new formula for its flagship brand, dubbed "New Coke". The new formula was intended to compete with the growing popularity of Pepsi but proved to be a major failure. Consumers were outraged by the change and demanded that the red brand revert to its original formula. The company eventually relented and reintroduced the original formula under the name "Coca-Cola Classic". Another major company experienced a similar turnaround. Google Glass was a wearable technology that promised to augment the way people interacted with physical reality. It was essentially a pair of glasses with a small computer screen mounted in the corner of the frame. Despite the excitement generated by its launch in 2012, Google Glass has not been widely adopted due to several issues, including its high price, limited functionality and a market ill-prepared for this futuristic change. Finally, the Amazon Fire Phone was introduced in 2014 as Amazon's first attempt at creating a smartphone. Although it offered unique features, such as a 3D interface and the integration of Amazon's digital services, the Fire Phone failed to establish itself in a market dominated by Apple and Samsung. How many other products failed shortly after their introduction? Millions. If we include non-business innovations, we're probably talking billions. So don't confuse an innovative process with its outcome.

The primary determinant of a project's success is its Effectiveness. This multi-dimensional concept depends primarily on its scope and quality. How can we judge whether a method is working when it comes to producing the desired innovation? Firstly, by actually verifying, perhaps on a sample or pilot phase, that the innovation obtained corresponds to what we expected. That's easy. In project jargon, it means verifying that what was envisaged in the business case or project planning document is actually present in the final product. Remember this as the scope or project perimeter. In Maria's case, if she was expecting a ten-minute MP3 podcast on certain topics, with an expert on the subject, this would be the scope of her project. Whether she achieves this through her laptop or her phone's microphone is irrelevant. Nor does it matter whether she edits via Audacity or Logic Pro. That's why the second variable in the Effectiveness function is necessary.

Quality, you might guess, is about getting the best possible product. Not true! From an *innovation* management perspective, quality is also about planning. Companies and individuals don't aim for the perfect gadget. They aim for the most optimal, the most adapted to the *Need*, like the invisible hand of Darwinist evolution. This optimization largely depends on the human, financial and technical resources to which the entrepreneur or project manager has access at the time of implementing your idea. For example, Maria could be aiming for average voice-over quality, but highly entertaining content. A tech start-up on a street corner can't compete with Apple's iPhone from the outset, at least in terms of quality. It's not a level playing field. It's like being asked to outrun the 22-year-old Usain Bolt in a 100-meter sprint. And yet, many small businesses are challenging the giants in various sectors – that's what entrepreneurship is all about. But how do these challengers do it?

You may have heard or used the expression "David versus Goliath". These two biblical characters point to a popular metaphor, depicting the unforeseen victory of an outsider against a seemingly unbeatable adversary, like a start-up, the "entrant", which unbalances the "incumbents" of a market. According to this myth, before a Middle Eastern battle loomed between the Philistines and the Israelites, the two clans decided, in the old-fashioned way, to each choose a man who would represent his people, rather like a Davis Cup tennis match, but with one dead and lots of land and slaves as trophies.

The Philistines, without hesitation, chose their champion Goliath, a giant warrior renowned for his intimidating stature, extraordinary strength and fighting expertise. Beyond his monstrous physique and fearsome reputation, Goliath wore heavy armor, including a bronze helmet and chain mail, and brandished a massive spear. The Israelites, logically terrified at the sight of this beast eagerly awaiting to slaughter his rival at the base of the hill, searched without hope for a worthy candidate. David proposed himself. A young shepherd, never having fought a battle in his life, and small in stature. No one took him seriously. But with no courageous alternative, David was chosen to confront the giant.

And yet, faced with the sarcastic, even offended face of the redoubtable Goliath, who saw his prey skillfully approaching without armor or conventional weapons, David took his slingshot, a simple shepherd's instrument, and chose one of the five smooth stones he had. Guided by

328 | PLUNGING INTO THE UNKNOWN

his faith in God, David threw a single stone that struck Goliath in the forehead, the only unprotected area of his body, killing him instantly. Another version paints a more dramatic ending, with David taking Goliath's sword and cutting off his head, thus winning the battle for the Israelites, as well as the royal seat of Israel. This feat became a symbol of the unpredictable victory of a small man over a giant, an underdog over the favorite.

This is a typical case of an unbalanced game. Indeed, David never really fought with Goliath, because they weren't playing on the same arena. This is why, in boxing, the notion of weight categories exists. You don't fight a bulky boxer when you barely weigh 50 kg. At the other extreme, if you challenge Usain Bolt to a marathon or use an electric scooter instead of running the hundred meters, you've got a good chance of winning. That's exactly what David did. He made the wise choice not to put on armor that would limit his ability nor to carry a sword heavier than he was. The initially deceptive imbalance of a soldier advantaged by his strength and warrior gear would imply a necessary dualistic disadvantage for the latter with his armor's disabling heaviness.

Similarly, in his book, *The Innovator's Dilemma*, business innovation guru Clayton Christensen explains that disruptive innovations launched by start-ups focus on niche products or services, which are initially rejected by the big players in the sector, due to lack of profitability or vision, but grow in scale over time, to the point where these start-ups become strong competitors. Ridesharing services like Uber are a classic example of an unbalanced business battle. Uber has disrupted the traditional cab business by offering a more convenient and often cheaper alternative. It hasn't tried to buy taxis and start a taxi business. Far from it. Uber is a digital player, operating in the IT business, applied to the mobility market. It's a similar case for the rise of streaming services like Netflix that have disrupted the traditional cinema and film rental business. All these unicorns did not enter into direct competition with pre-established market players, where they would be doomed to failure. They played the role of David, with a more limited scope of action and average or even mediocre product or service quality at launch. However, they offered a different *Value* from the others, something new that people *NEEDED* – more freedom in the case of Uber, more choice at any time in the case of Netflix.

Let's move on to the second important component of *Technology*: efficiency. Here, I'd like to clarify the difference between efficiency and effectiveness. Whereas effectiveness is about achieving what we hope to achieve, in terms of functionality, scope and quality, efficiency is about seeking out and then applying the most optimal method in manufacturing, sourcing, marketing and so on. In other words, resources once again have to be taken into account when thinking about "efficiency". And therein lies the rub. Resources are like a head start. The more you have, the easier it is to achieve more ambitious goals and build complex projects and products. Up to a point. Let's focus on financial resources because money is the easiest idea to grasp.

The first problem with the above reasoning is that a company's or an individual's budget is limited. Like any other resource, from oil to brain power to time, water and air, we can never theoretically have enough of anything. Secondly, in business as in life, there's the concept of ROI, return on investment. When you devote effort and resources to a project, whatever it may be, you expect some form of compensation, be it financial, social, emotional or metaphysical. Let's look at a case in point.

The innovation of the stock market is based on this principle. Public and private investors provide financial backing for stable or promising companies. Despite the tendency to speculate and trade during bubbles, when liquidity is abundant due to falling interest rates for example, good investors generally buy and hold shares, expecting a steady stream of dividend income from companies that are already profitable, or betting on the growth of smaller players in the hope of selling their shares at a better price in the near future.

To achieve a positive and growing bottom line – in other words, to make more profit in any given quarter – companies need not only to innovate and sell as much as possible but also to cut costs. This is one of the beauties of capitalism. In line with the human principle of freedom, you can do whatever you want with the financial resources at your disposal, whatever the source (stock market, debt, reserves, etc.). However, you will have to justify the judicious use of these resources, which will no doubt be reflected in your next financial publication. Otherwise, disappointing investors would be synonymous with a loss of market confidence in your ability and that of your teams to manage and invest their money well. As a result, your stock would lose its value, as these same investors would sell your company's shares in favor of a more efficient, and therefore ultimately more profitable, competitor. This was the case with Meta (Facebook) in 2022, when CEO Mark Zuckerberg made a costly bet on the metaverse, a virtual reality innovation, perhaps ahead of its time. In any case, Meta's shares plummeted by more than 70 percent over the year, following the launch of this project (and due to an inflationary economic context). Faced with Meta's exploding expenses and falling profits, investors had no choice but to dump their shares, depriving Meta of billions of dollars. As a result, over 100,000 employees were laid off.

In addition to financial resources, which remain a crucial variable in many contexts, human and technical resources must also be taken into account. The more our societies develop, the more creative entrepreneurs are expected to be. A well-functioning education system would therefore quickly update itself to meet the needs of the labor market, at least from a capitalist point of view. In any case, it would make no sense to reintroduce religion or Latin classes in schools and universities, as there is a strong demand for data engineers, biotech experts and digital marketers rather than priests, farmers and soldiers. Now that I'm a teacher, I'd like to take this opportunity to openly criticize conventional educational systems, such as the francophone system in which I spent 17 years of my youth. The old Taylorist style of education, where students are lined up to receive loads of theoretical concepts, which they will quickly forget after stressful exams, is quite old-fashioned in my opinion and according to many references. It was more effective to teach future blue-collar factory workers during the first Industrial Revolution than to prepare autonomous innovators for the new 4.0 revolution.

Finally, technical resources are also important. We've already explained how the iPhone wouldn't exist without technical prerequisites such as telecommunications infrastructure, the internet and microchips. If we still can't travel back in time, it's not for lack of budget or human resources, but for lack of the advanced *technology* needed to achieve this feat.

The variation in these resources from one country to another, and from one company to another, can lead to significant variations in final innovation. Let's illustrate with the case of money. In many developing countries, the infrastructure of traditional banking systems, such as banks and ATMs, is underdeveloped, particularly in rural areas. This results in a lack of access to banking services, forcing greater reliance on cash. In some countries with high levels of corruption or political instability, people simply no longer trust their governments or their hyper-inflationary currencies. In these contexts, cryptocurrencies can be seen as a more reliable alternative as they are decentralized and not dependent on a single authority. Furthermore, online payment systems are more advanced in Asia, partly due to the relatively low cost of setting up a digital payment infrastructure, compared with the cost of building physical bank branches and ATMs. As a result, Asians tend to pay with smartphones and super apps like Alipay and Paytm, rather than cash or cards.

This optimization of resources within the framework of project efficiency is applicable not only to the business world and human creations, but also to natural innovations. Indeed, in the natural world, every organism is subject to constraints and limitations in terms of available resources such as food, water, space and reproductive partners. To survive and reproduce successfully, organisms must use these resources efficiently and sustainably. This is part of natural selection, where individuals best adapted to their environment are more likely to survive and pass on their characteristics to the next generation. This process would therefore favor species whose appetite and resilience is adjusted to the resources available, to achieve a sustainable symbiosis. If I, an animal, and my species eat all the sheep and drink all the coconuts on the island because our appetite is insatiable, we'll disappear. Be sure to keep that in mind!

Let's conclude this section on the remaining blocks of efficiency, and thus of the *Technology* variable. Efficiency is not just about optimizing resources with an innovative objective in mind, but also about planning their use over a realistic timescale. As a general rule, the development of a web platform can take from a few months to a year, depending on the number of developers on the team. On the other hand, it could take a dozen years to manufacture a new model of aircraft. The shorter the design-to-market process, the better, assuming that the scope and quality of the final products, and therefore efficiency, are the same.

Finally, scalability is a secondary but important aspect to consider. It means that a project that is easily extensible and reproducible in other contexts or regions would win out over another similar project, all other things being equal. Digital products, for example, are more scalable than physical goods. Think of e-commerce platforms like Amazon and eBay, cloud computing services like Amazon Web Services (AWS), or social networks. All these online services are easily implemented in any country, unless a legal restriction blocks them, as China blocks Facebook, Amazon and so many other American companies. The reason for this flexibility lies in the virtual nature of the product, which means that large volumes of transactions and users can be managed without any significant changes to the underlying *technology*. In contrast, Airbus would need years of planning and resource management to build factories and organize new supply chains if it decided to build its new brand aircraft in a new location.

In conclusion, good *Technology*, or implementation method of a creative idea, is both effective in realizing the innovative dream and efficient in managing resources, including money and time. In other words, **to excel vis-à-vis our *Technology* variable is to create what is needed, with the minimum possible**.

VARIABLE 5:
The hidden *Value* of innovation

How much would you pay for a bottle of water?

In his heyday, Libyan leader Muammar Gaddafi launched an innovative project called the "Great Man-Made River Project". Crazier than pitching Bedouin tents in the Élysée Palace and dying at the hands of his own people, the plan called for the construction of a network of pipes and aqueducts to transport water from underground aquifers in the middle of the Libyan Sahara to the coastal regions, where most of the population resides. This was to remedy the chronic water shortage in his arid country. The project was estimated to cost around 25 billion dollars and required the drilling of over 1,300 wells and the construction of 4,000 kilometers (2485 miles) of pipelines between 1980 and 1996.

We call this project innovative because it respects the spirit of the Fundamental Identity of Innovation. The basic *Need* for survival and security is quite clear: to drink potable water, and to clean one's body and home. The absence of water for a few days in the Sahara is equivalent to a painful, hallucinatory death. Knowing his extravagant personality, Colonel Gaddafi's *Motivation* was probably his desire to show off his country's great success to the Arab and Western world, such as Qatar buying the PSG team, Emirates building palm tree islands in the sea, or Saudi Arabia paying an "elderly" (by soccer player standards) Cristiano Ronaldo a pharaonic rate of 24,000 dollars per hour! Gaddafi's project showcases *Creativity* "outside the box". Who would have thought of fetching drinking water from the depths of an arid desert?

Finally, the *Technology* or the implementation of this delicate dream can be considered effective since millions of Libyans now have access to drinking water thanks to this project. Its effectiveness, however, would be called into question. At such a high investment cost, mismanagement of resources and misappropriation of funds are to be feared. What's more, isn't there a better way? Like desalinating seawater, for example? As expected, the project was heavily subsidized by the Libyan government and the cost of water was kept artificially low. This was a great novelty for Libyan citizens at the time. They could satisfy their basic needs at an affordable cost. However, after Gaddafi's overthrow in 2011, Libya's new (half) government was unable to maintain the subsidies, and household spending on water skyrocketed. As a result, many Libyans were forced to pay exorbitant prices for something as basic as water. This brings us to the fifth and final variable in the fundamental identity of innovation: *Value*.

$$Innovation = \underbrace{(Need + Motivation)}_{Prerequisites} \times \underbrace{(Creativity + Technology)}_{Innovation\ Process} \times \underbrace{Value}_{Result}$$

Value is expected at the end of a milestone or project, based on the use of the final or intermediate products of the *innovation* process. This is why we distinguish it from the creative and operational phases, which are launched before the innovative fruit is on the market of goods or ideologies. As you can guess from the Gaddafi case, it's not the *innovation* itself that produces its *Value*, but its interaction with living or ideally conscious beings. So there's a psychological, even philosophical aspect to this for individuals and organizations to consider. The *Value* of the great artificial river is clearly significant for Libyan citizens because it met an urgent *Need*. But as the price of water rose with the lifting of state subsidies, this *Value* was revised downwards. Why pay the same price for tap water as for Evian?

Similarly, no matter how much forecasting data Tesla Inc. provides its investors in its official PR communications or through Elon Musk's tweets, it still needs to prove its *Value* through earnings and market share growth, consistent with analysts' forecasts. In other words, while *Value* can and should often be estimated at the start of the innovation process, through cash-flow projections and ROI calculations for example, it is only felt by recipients and confirmed by entrepreneurs when the new product or process is launched and sold. If the entrepreneur's estimate of *Value* falls well short of initial expectations, we confirm that the business case was not correct. Consequently, unless the market is monopolistic or run by a dictator, this innovative project should see its financial resources decline, as we explained with the example of the stock market in the previous section.

I've thrown myself without warning into the financial illustration of this crucial variable in *Innovation*. Once again, it would be easier for you to grasp this concept from a managerial and entrepreneurial point of view at first glance. The reason for this is hardly an underestimation of your mental capacity to assimilate abstractions, but the fact that a quantitative or mathematical approach is more accurate than a biased feeling or guess. So let's move on to the former.

In the business world, *Value* mainly means economic benefit for the innovator, at the expense of the consumer, of course. The latter would express its benefit in terms of utility or functionalities that satisfy one or more *Needs*. This economic value can be quantified in dollars, for example, and is therefore comparable within a niche or market segment. If it's difficult to compare the *Value* of (real) apples and Apple products, it's because they don't belong in the same basket. iProducts, on the other hand, are comparable to a certain degree, as they all play on the luxurious terrain of entertainment, communication and work. In fact, between the iPhone, the MacBook, the iPad, the Apple Watch and the recent Vision Pro, a high-end augmented reality headset, we know that the cumulative Economic *Value* of the iPhone in 2022 constitutes more than half the tech giant's total revenues. We could also compare the iPhone's *Value* to other brands such as Vivo or Samsung.

Again, while *Need* and *Motivation* have a broad psychological dimension, *Creativity* is the interest of neuroscientists and *Technology* that of engineers, economic *Value* is the role of marketing divisions, with their poles of marketing strategy, communications and public relations (PR), sales, and post-sales management. Take the classic digital marketing strategy is based on the conversion funnel framework. The idea is to lead a prospect, slowly and sometimes surely, along a predefined path, from awareness of a product or service through various marketing channels such as social media, search engines or online advertising, to demonstrations of the benefit to be gained by the customer and ending with a transaction of the type of purchase or subscription, for example, a product against a predefined sum of money. Thus, the economic *Value* of a company, a country, or the world is simply the sum of all these small transactions within a given perimeter.

Despite the manipulative side of marketing, sometimes with good reason[22], there is a justified and rational *Need for* the innovator to promote his innovation. Indeed, even if you have the best tech gadget in the world, its financial or commercial *Value* would rarely be achieved by expectation and hope, barring synchronicity perhaps, or having the celebrity and charisma of an Elon Musk, who, let's not forget, spends next to nothing on marketing with Tesla Inc. Methods such as the conversion funnel and some guerrilla marketing for young startups come in handy, mainly when introducing the innovation, to spread the word and gather interest of a targeted audience.

Note that I prefer to talk about profits when it comes to economically valuing innovations, rather than revenues. If you remember your economics lessons, revenues don't take costs into account, whereas profits do. If your product costs $10 per unit to make, and you've spent $10 to get it to market, it makes sense to list it at $25 with a 20 percent margin or Economic *Value*, rather than $15, in which case you'd be making a loss. One of the reasons why Tesla has enjoyed a high valuation for years is precisely this relatively better margin than its competitors. The company spends mere pennies on marketing, which has enabled it to achieve a margin of over 20 percent, whereas conventional automotive players struggle to achieve 10 percent. Moreover, beyond innovative marketing techniques and brand or CEO reputation, in his book, *Purple Cow*, marketing guru Seth Godin encourages companies to stand out in a crowded marketplace by being remarkable. The book argues that traditional advertising methods, such

---

22 Suffice it to say that an academic subject called neuromarketing still exists in many schools, teaching the stimuli levers to which the human brain responds best, which would facilitate the purchasing decision. If you've never wondered why sales and reception departments are staffed mainly by pretty girls, or why Sephora smells so good from afar, or why they give you free samples, you've got your answer now.

as TV spots, online ads and billboards, are no longer effective in a world open to competition from all over the globe. Companies need to create something truly singular to capture consumers' attention. Godin uses the metaphor of the purple cow, instead of the classic cow, to represent a product or service so remarkable that it cannot be ignored. It's no longer enough to be average or simply good to stand out from the crowd.

Note that, although we're concentrating mainly on product and service innovations in this section, we shouldn't forget that there are other types of innovation too. Let's illustrate with a nice process innovation.

In 2018, Amazon launched a new grocery concept called Amazon Go. The stores use AI and computer vision technology to automatically detect when customers pick up items from the shelves and charge their Amazon account accordingly. For those who have never tried it, pending its introduction in France, the main process is as follows:

1. Customers enter the store by scanning a code on their mobile device.

2. As in a supermarket, they are free to browse the store and pick up items from the shelves. Stores use cameras, sensors and artificial intelligence technology to track items taken by customers and automatically debit their Amazon account.

3. Customers simply exit the store when they have finished shopping. The technology automatically calculates the total cost of the items and debits the customer's Amazon account.

4. In the event of a problem, a customer service kiosk is available to help customers.

No waiting in line. Less expenditure on human resources. No accounting errors. No theft. This is a concrete example of cutting-edge *technology* contributing to a significant reduction in costs over the long term. Amazon is thus generating profits, and therefore Economic *value,* by reducing costs relative to other stores, and also by offering a pleasant, fluid experience, with no queues, and no grannies looking for pennies in their pockets for hours on end to pay.

338 | PLUNGING INTO THE UNKNOWN

This capitalist frame of reference is therefore quite relevant because the most accurate way of measuring whether a given human creation is a success is to estimate quantitatively how much money would be spent on it. Money is only one scale for measuring *Value*, but an excellent one. It brings order to the chaos of the social concept of equity. Thanks to mathematics and numbers, combined with the economic law of supply and demand, we can evaluate the cost of things, assuming of course that the market is free. With a few exceptions linked to price elasticity, when the supply of a product increases (more production), its price falls, and vice versa, as shown in the figure below. Similarly, when price rises, demand may fall, depending on whether the product is essential or not. In any case, by assigning a monetary value to a product or service, it becomes easier to determine its worth and exchange it fairly on the market. In the days of bartering, exchanging ten eggs for ten carrots one day, and two carrots the next, was neither practical nor fair, and probably left room for tedious negotiations.

But, and this is a big "but", not everything is economic, not everything is quantifiable, for several reasons and depending on the use case. Firstly, ROI is only a simplified model, used by profit-oriented companies in a theoretically free market, like the concept of Gross Domestic Product (GDP) used to describe the economic performance of a capitalist country, or the space-time model proposed to describe the principle of change in the Matrix. There are areas where it is difficult to quantify economic value in the traditional way.

Ironically, marketing efforts, or the *Value* of marketing-type *innovations*, were difficult to assess before the age of the internet. If sales of the new product exceed expectations, how can you, as a marketer, tell whether the cause is your super talent, the design of the banner ad, or just lucky word-of-mouth? Google's and Facebook's entire initial business model is based on this flaw. Via Google Ads, or ads on the Facebook wall, businesses can create and display ads aimed at predefined prospects, by the type of search on Google, or by their Facebook profile (origin, age, profession, etc.). Try typing "rental Paris" into Google, for example, and you'll see a bank of search results at the top of every page, with "ad" to the left of the title. In this way, companies can focus their advertising budget on the most relevant and potentially profitable audience. More importantly, Google or Facebook provide detailed metrics or KPIs for each ad, including clicks, impressions and conversion rates. This enables companies to measure the effectiveness of their ads and adapt their targeting and messaging accordingly. Digital marketers can (finally) calculate the Financial *Value* of their campaign by dividing the sales generated by the total cost spent.

On the other hand, charities and non-profit organizations aim to carry out philanthropic actions and contribute to the well-being of society. Their *Value* cannot therefore be measured simply in terms of financial return on investment, as they aim to deliver social, humanitarian or environmental *Value*. If we consider two of the most disruptive innovations in human history, the internet and generic artificial intelligence by Open-AI, they barely generate profits for their creators (considering costs). However, their social impact, past, present and future, is significant. There are also economic niches that are so regulated that valuation would be insane: the illegal drugs market, for example, or the prostitution market in several conservative countries.

Similarly, organizational and social innovations such as sectarian movements, new institutions, and new laws and political parties can generate strong support and mobilize resources, without needing to mention any Financial *Value*. Ethical, moral or societal dimensions take over in this respect. Could you assess the *Value* of a marriage in terms of the dowry, the bride price in some cultures, or the mahr or sadaq in the Islamic tradition, the sum of money and gifts offered to the bride's family (or that of the groom in India, for example) during the matrimonial ceremony? Or would you feel comfortable putting a price on a (good) friendship, a wild beach or a presidential candidate? There are some who would.

Personally, and therefore philosophically, what bothers me most about this limited notion of Economic *Value* is its one-sidedness. "It is not from the benevolence of the butcher, the brewer or the baker that we expect our dinner, but from their personal interest", said Adam Smith, the father of liberal capitalism, in the 18th century. By focusing on maximizing profits, the entrepreneur runs the risk of falling into the classic trap of external, meaningless *Motivation,* which can even lead to dishonest practices and consumer and price manipulation under the pretext that "the goal justifies the means". Let's take a classic case from my birth country.

One of my favorite places in Morocco, despite its touristy side, is the Place Jemaa el-Fnaa. This lively public space, located in the heart of Marrakech's old town, is best known for its unique fusion of art, music, traditional dishes and storytelling. The square is a hub of activity where artists, musicians and performers gather to showcase their talents and entertain visitors, day and night. Indeed, the latter can attend traditional music performances, with their hypnotic rhythms and haunting melodies, or witness acrobatic shows, snake charmers and fortune-tellers. In the evening, the square comes alive with a night market, where visitors can sample a wide variety of Moroccan dishes and buy all manner of handicrafts and souvenirs along the narrow streets of the old town. There is one major problem, however. Price tags are rarely displayed. Tourists, and especially those who don't speak the local language, Darija, often end up wasting time in pointless negotiations, getting annoyed or unfairly paying double or triple what a local would pay for the same product. These buyers probably feel ripped off and keep their hands in their pockets for the rest of their stay.

This problem of information asymmetry between seller and buyer in terms of price versus actual product cost has been largely resolved thanks to recent advances in digitization and free competition. The first solution provides multiple sources of price calibration and mandatory price tags, regardless of the buyer's country of origin (unless customs taxes are included). How else can you pay online without knowing the price of the product? On the other hand, free competition means that a customer can compare prices with different sellers to get an idea of the product's real *value.* A monopoly or cartel that coordinates to keep the price similar or artificially high, like OPEC, would run counter to an efficient and socially just economy. In an ideal scenario of liberal capitalism with no state intervention, no information asymmetry and free competition, all other things being equal (brand strength, innovative talent, etc.), the price of any product would approach its cost to the point of canceling out the profit per unit. So, this scenario is clearly disadvantageous for producers, entrepreneurs and innovators.

Perhaps in the near future, companies will return to price concealment and start using intelligent chatbots as trained negotiators. But in any case, the more competitors there are in a given free market, the more *Value* customers enjoy, and probably the less financial *Value* companies realize. In theory, in a perfect capitalist world, the first innovator to take too many risks and create something radically new gets most of the profits. However, similar companies, noticing this money-making opportunity, will pour into this market. They will offer a similar product. The total quantity of this product therefore increases. Assuming demand remains constant, the price will continue to fall until it reaches near-zero profitability, at which point the next entrant would be deterred from entering by lack of financial incentive and would have to innovate something different. However, and this is my point, the customer wins. In such a case, the *Value* of the product or service to the customer is maximized, because they can choose from a wide range of choices, at prices significantly lower than in a less free, more monopolistic situation. But this would be unfair to producers. A dynamic equilibrium is what is most optimal.

Extending this line of reasoning, an interesting variable to consider when thinking about *Value* is **the gap between supply and demand**. Notwithstanding its economic tone, this principle would apply to most human and even natural *innovations.* The more a product or service is in demand, the greater its *Value.* As the supply of a product or service increases, its *Value* decreases. This dynamic logic – because both variables can change simultaneously – is as applicable to the stock market as it is to the souk. As illustrated in the graph below, if the supply of coffee decreases, assuming a constant global demand, its *Value,* represented by its price, increases, up to a point where the new price reflects the new *Value* higher than the old one, in which case a new equilibrium is created because, rationally, nobody would like to pay more than a product is worth. That said, we're far from always being rational beings. I'll come back to this later.

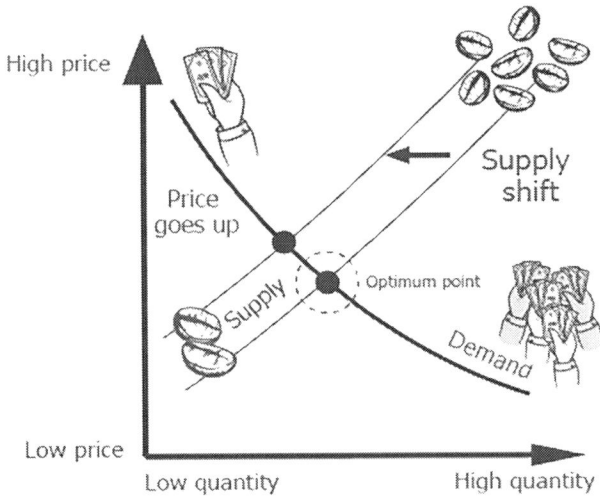

In fact, the offer, whether quantifiable or not, can always be expressed in functional and psychological terms. Religious movements bring psychological *Value* by providing community and support in coping with death. Politicians bring *Value* by solving citizens' everyday problems (ideally). Soccer's *Value* lies in the fact that it entertains people and transforms the male thirst for combat into a more peaceful competitive environment. Demand, on the other hand, doesn't involve the use of a credit card or cryptographic wallet. We could also talk about "**adoption**". When large numbers of people adopt a set of beliefs, a new political system, a new diet or Bitcoin, the *Value* of these objects increases accordingly. Why do you think a Louis Vuitton handbag costs more than 4,000 dollars on average? Or how do you justify the price of an $8,000 to $10,000 Rolex? There's a high demand for these gadgets and a deliberately low supply.

In other sectors, notice in the context of the labor market how supply represents the number of people available to fill a position, while demand represents the number of vacancies. When the supply of labor exceeds demand, this can lead to lower wages. Similarly, in the academic sector, supply refers to the number of places available in educational establishments, while demand represents the number of students wishing to gain access to them. A popular school will keep its places limited to maintain its *value* at the highest level, just as a Rolex would produce a limited number of watches a year. Even in the social context of marriage or heterosexual encounters, the *Value* of men or women varies according to supply and demand. In Russia, for example, men are demographically scarce (0.86 men to one woman), while the opposite is true in Saudi Arabia due to polygamy and conservative traditions, leading to a visible scarcity of free women in relation to available men. In the world of ideas, a politician with an innovative and convincing program would have more *Value* than the rest of the candidates, as demand for their ideas would be higher than supply.

Sometimes, when there are so many similar offers, with stagnant demand, *Value* automatically tends to fall. This process is often called "**commoditization**". The product thus becomes an undifferentiated commodity, like toilet paper or chewing gum. However, this process is rarely applicable to the letter, as it would imply free and open competition. In reality, many factors come into play. Some companies simply make products that are difficult to copy, such as the iPhone, the SpaceX rocket launcher or the Maersk logistics fleet. The resources and know-how needed to compete with these companies are a major obstacle for any new entrant. Sometimes, regulatory or brand barriers make it difficult to compete in certain markets. To commoditize a Chanel bag is almost impossible short of a reputational catastrophe because their brand means that another bag, even if similar and meeting the same *Need*, is not equal in *Value*. What's more, innovators often gain first-mover advantage, i.e., they grab a large share of the market before anyone else. Think of Uber or Airbnb. These companies don't have inimitable technology or skills. At the end of the day, they're just web and mobile services with a nice user interface, which has been developed in common coding languages. Their competitive advantage lies in the fact that they've managed to capture users so quickly that subsequent competitors have struggled to catch up.

This last passage is a fine transition to the other factor influencing the notion of *Value* in any *innovation*. We refer to the work of English philosopher Jeremy Bentham, influenced by the work of Hume and Hobbes, who introduced the foundations of utilitarianism in his 1789 book, *An Introduction to the Principles of Morals and Legislation* [23].

---

23   Renowned British philosopher John Stuart Mill, an admirer and disciple of Bentham, later extended and modified Bentham's theories in his 1861 book, *Utilitarianism*.

In his book, Bentham created the principle of utility, according to which an action is approved when it tends to provide and enable the greatest happiness. According to Bentham, happiness is defined as the presence of pleasure and the absence of pain. He created a formula, known as the felicific calculus (meaning "that which makes for happiness"), by which the usefulness of an action can be assessed. To measure pleasure and pain, Bentham takes the following elements into account: the duration of pleasure, its intensity, its certainty versus its uncertainty, and its closeness versus its remoteness. Most importantly, Bentham emphasizes the happiness of the community since the happiness of the community is the sum of the happiness of the individual members. Consequently, the principle of utility determined the moral obligation to perform an action that would produce the greatest happiness for the greatest number of people concerned. This would mean favoring quantity over quality.

When you think about it, especially in our modern times and societies, in 99 percent of cases, every *innovation* we adopt, either by buying it or receiving it, or by assimilating it into our beliefs, or by practicing it, brings some degree of instant or future pleasure or limits some present physiological or psychological pain. In cases where this is not right, it is likely that we adopt it to satisfy someone (best friend) or something (God) dear to us, and so we would be in Bentham's second case of happiness extended to the community. Sometimes, this adoption is hardly voluntary. When the government forces us to switch to electric cars, to pay for insurance, or when our parents push us to adopt certain beliefs or pursue certain studies, we'd consider *Value* to be low in these cases because so is individual utility and happiness. That doesn't change the fact that by changing our vision of something, by trying it out reluctantly, we end up modifying our perception of its usefulness, its *Value*.

This hedonistic vision of *Value* has to be counterbalanced by the few cases where, voluntarily or not, we find ourselves adopting a difficult, even painful path, without the hope of a light at the end of the tunnel. In the 1940s, Austrian psychiatrist Viktor Frankl was in the midst of his quest for survival and meaning in the Nazi concentration camp of Auschwitz. In his influential book, *Man's Search for Meaning*, Frankl describes his experiences in these inhuman camps, in which his entire family perished and reflects on the profound impact that the search for meaning can have on a person's ability to endure suffering and find happiness. Also, Frankl argues that individuals have an innate need for meaning and purpose in life, and that it is this search for meaning that motivates human behavior and provides a sense of fulfillment. He suggests that meaning can be found through three main channels: work or creative activities, relationships with others and our attitude to suffering. Similarly, Nelson Mandela, the famous South African leader and fighter against apartheid, noted that "prison itself is a tremendous apprenticeship in patience and perseverance. Above all, it is a test of commitment". These scenarios are clearly unimaginable for the new generations, spoiled by the iPhone and all manner of epicurean gadgets. But it's nice to know that a positive *Value* can ultimately emanate from an unpleasant, even sadistic experience. And that's the subjective, even irrational side of *Value*. Let's first summarize mathematically the expression of this fifth variable of fundamental identity.

$$Value = Utility_{individual} \times gap(Demand - Offer)$$

This equation would therefore apply to most *innovations*, not just those of an economic nature. That said, let's note that in the specific case of a product on a given market, this generic equation is transformed into the economic definition of profit. If you ever did a Finance course:

$$Profit = Revenue - Cost$$
$$Profit = Price_{per\ unit} \times Volume\ sold - Cost_{per\ unit} \times Volume\ sold$$
$$Profit = (Price_{per\ unit} - Cost_{per\ unit}) \times Volume\ sold$$
$$Profit = Utility_{individual} \times gap\ (Demand - offer)$$

Consequently, from the standpoint of the seller / entrepreneur, unit profit would be equated with individual utility, and sales volume would reflect the difference between supply and demand. Additionally, innovative companies focus less on maximizing profit through dumb and nasty maximization of volume sold, and more on optimizing individual utility through a scissor effect, by justifying a high price (features, brand,

346 | PLUNGING INTO THE UNKNOWN

etc.) while reducing their operational costs through innovative processes such as automation, the Internet of Things and AI.

When it is not quantitatively assessed, on the other hand, individual utility is highly subjective and depends on the context in which the transaction takes place. For example, a solo traveler may perceive great *Value* in low-cost hostels where he can socialize with other travelers. This means that a high price or excessive comfort does not necessarily reflect high *Value*. On the contrary, with the exception of a few luxury items, most people are looking for "good value for money". Individual utility is also highly psychological. Customer satisfaction is an indicator commonly used by companies to assess the quality of receipt and use of a good or service. In fact, it's the way in which a solution meets our specific *needs* that largely determines its usefulness. A Ferrari is of little *value* to a farmer who would prefer a tractor, even if he wouldn't say no to a free Ferrari. The latter would be worth every penny of the 200,000 dollars spent on it, in the eyes of a rich young heir seeking social approval and sexual partners. Our beliefs also strongly influence this variable. If you're vegan, the utility, and therefore the *Value*, of a good cheeseburger is almost nil. If you love your country or community, you'll tend to attribute more utility to their innovations than to those of foreigners. The "made in" label appeals more to our patriotism than our rationality when we favor local products.

Daniel Kahneman and Amos Tversky have carried out extensive research, highlighting the cognitive biases and reasoning errors to which human beings are subject when making decisions. A handful of examples are below:

- **The availability effect**: People tend to give more weight to events or information that come easily to mind, that are closer to their conscious awareness. For example, if you're asked to estimate the frequency of car accidents versus bicycle accidents, you're more likely to overestimate the frequency of the former simply because they receive more media coverage.

- **Loss and risk aversion**: Through our Darwinist evolution, we are naturally inclined to be more sensitive to losses than to equivalent gains. For example, enough experience shows that people are more motivated to avoid a loss of 100 dollars than to obtain a gain of 100 dollars on a bet.

- **Anchoring**: a technique much used by companies, such as Coca-Cola, is implicitly linked to joy and family moments in the red brand's ads, creating the subconscious neural link between a positive feeling and drinking a quarter of a gallon of simple sugars. Similarly, decisions can be influenced by numbers or reference information, even if they are arbitrary. For example, if you're asked to estimate the size of your town's population and you're given an exaggeratedly high figure as a starting point, this will tend to influence your final estimate.

- **Confirmation bias**: Individuals often have excessive confidence in their own judgments and beliefs, even when these are not supported by solid evidence. This can lead to faulty decision-making and biased assessments.

Finally, we should note that *Value,* whether in terms of individual utility, or supply and demand, tends to change over time. An *innovation* that generated a lot of buzz a few years ago, such as the steam engine, Myspace or Nokia, tends to be forgotten, replaced by another that offers better utility and is adopted by a greater number of users. This is the whole principle of creative destruction cycles, typically represented by the S-curves in business management textbooks. We could even apply these models to non-economic *innovations* such as the institution of marriage, which tends to metamorphose over the ages from our polyamorous hunter-gatherer ancestors to a widespread polygamy a few centuries ago, passing through a political, religious then romanticized monogamy, and reaching the recent trend of open, mixed and non-contractual relationships.

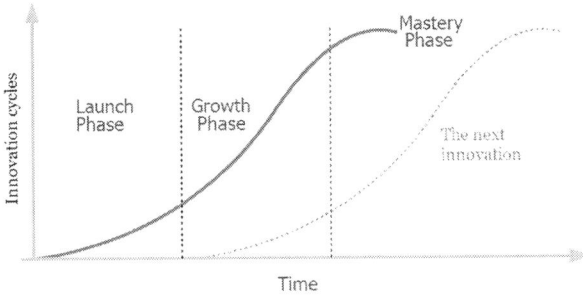

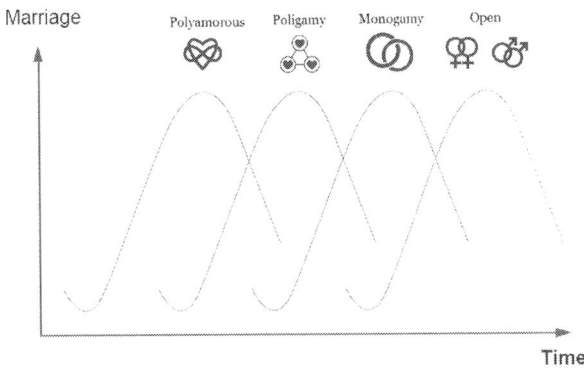

Let's get back to the original question in this section. How much would you pay for a bottle of water?

Hopefully, you've gleaned that this question isn't just about price, which is just one reflection of *Value*. A better formulation would be: What would you give for a bottle of water?

Nowadays, in your comfortable seat and luxurious home, relative to the standard of living of our ancestors, $2 may seem like a lot, but it's still affordable. If it's mineral water, 50cl at $5 maximum, in a good restaurant would be a digestible price. But what if now, in an experiment in morbid synchronicity, we put you in the shoes of the famous actor Tom Hanks as FedEx executive Chuck Noland in the film *Cast Away*? Except for you it isn't just a film!

So you're stranded on a small desert island in the middle of the Pacific Ocean after a plane crash. With no hope of rescue, your top priority is survival. We're back to Maslow's first Basic *Need*. While Chuck, by dint of determination and ingenuity, managed to adapt to his new life and even found the companionship of a volleyball he christened "Wilson", in your case, the only things that exist on this barren island are a palm tree as your only shelter, with no coconuts, and an endless ocean. Although you can hide from the sun under the tree and hope to catch a fish or two a day, you soon realize there is a lack of a stable water source on the island. Salty seawater is not an option. Time is of the essence! You can try collecting urine for a while, but this is only a temporary solution. The innovative animal will also think about desalinating seawater using the sun and palm leaves, which remains a difficult process without certain tools. What to do?

As you pray to your god to send some saving rain, as in a metaverse, a machine suddenly appears on your crappy island with the label "DRINKING WATER" on it, and three buttons with explicit functions. One is linked to your bank account, the second to the most important person in your life, and the third to your own eyes. What would you pay for a bottle?

It sounds more like *Squid Game* or the *Saw* saga, than a Tom Hanks Friday night. Nevertheless, we hope you understand how deeply the notion of *Value* is rooted in our *Needs* and the context in which it is studied. Most people would give up all their savings (if any) for a few drops of H2O, without hesitation. The financial *Value* of water is literally infinite in this case. The hardest choice to make would be 24 hours later, when you're thirsty again and can only choose between your eyes and your loved one. Faced with this moral dilemma, for many people, the *Value* of water can be equal to, or even greater than, that of a life or an essential organ, because back at its equation, the demand for water is high, while its supply is at its lowest. Its individual utility for the ego is absolute, death being the worst-case scenario. Or is it?

TAKEAWAYS FROM THIS CHAPTER:

$$Innovation = \underbrace{(Need + Motivation)}_{Prerequisites} \times \underbrace{(Creativity + Technology)}_{Innovation\ Process} \times \underbrace{Value}_{Result}$$

- The innate **Need to innovate** resides within the depths of our existence. It begins with the primal cry of a baby seeking nourishment and maternal care, extends to the desire for a loving partner, and encompasses the yearning for respect and appreciation from others. We crave a myriad of things as human beings, more any other dynamic agent, ranging from material possessions like luxury cars and coveted jobs to intangible aspirations such as silence and inner peace. Thus, from survival to self-actualization, as illustrated by Maslow's hierarchy of needs, we strive to fulfill our cravings, often to the best of our ability and as quickly as possible. These latter change with time. Each stage of life, each individual, and each era bring forth new desires, giving rise to the necessity for novel products, processes, organizations and beliefs. Such dynamic fuels the perpetual wheel of entrepreneurship and change.

- The best innovators and entrepreneurs, in business and other realms of life such as politics and religion, are and should be ***motivated*** by one or two distinct forces, sometimes without the need to verify the existence of a need beforehand. External motivation stems from the influences of pain and pleasure, such as financial rewards or the prospect of consequences. Conversely, intrinsic motivation is rooted in the pursuit of meaning, a deep passion to effect change, and even a touch of craziness to dare to reshape the world.

- To achieve radical and valuable innovation, the innovator must tap into a sense of individual or collective ***Creativity*** to come up with the right new ideas. This goes beyond the mere accumulation of data and embraces a deeper understanding and a delicate play between consciousness and the subconscious. It may involve a touch of divine creation, reminiscent of the concept of creation ex nihilo, where individual and collective memories are transformed into valuable intuitions amidst chaos. When combined with the power of a structured logic, this paradigm can yield purely ingenious solutions or breakthroughs.

- Regardless of how brilliant an idea may be, it remains a valueless dream until it is actualized and operationalized. Therefore, the appropriate *Technology* endeavors to discover the optimal process or plan to transform a prototype or invention into reality. When we say "optimal," we refer to a solution that is both effective in achieving its intended purpose and efficient in doing so with the least possible resources, including time, effort and money.

- Ultimately, the goal of any innovative process, driven by a specific need or needs, motivated by an entrepreneur, born from a brilliantly creative idea, and implemented in an optimal manner, is to deliver maximal *Value* to both *The Innovative Animal* (the entrepreneur) and the recipient or final users of the innovation. This intricate concept, often encompassing economic and psychological aspects, depends on the utility the user perceives in the innovation, whether quantitatively or qualitatively, as well as the adoption of the innovation. The adoption of the latter is reflected in the demand for the innovation, i.e., how many people or organizations desire it, in comparison to its supply or availability.

CHAPTER IV

THE HUMAN TITANIC

"The true voyage of discovery consists not in seeking new landscapes, but in having new eyes." – Marcel Proust.

I awoke, again, in the middle of an ocean without beginning or end, the sensation of solitude enveloping me, amplified by my nakedness. Fortunately, in this Matrix, I was able to float. But I could still feel the stress on my internal clock, which slightly accelerated its countdown. The waters were calm, almost motionless, creating an atmosphere of tranquility and peace. I floated on the surface, lulled by this apparent serenity, an order of mathematical perfection. Suddenly, without warning, waves began to appear out of nowhere, shattering the peacefulness that had reigned until then.

The waves grew rapidly, assuming impressive proportions. Their breaking force threw me in all directions, drawing me into a tumultuous dance. I struggled to keep my head above water, fighting against the power of this raging tide. Each wave was a manifestation of the instability of this changing environment, questioning my very presence in this ocean. My internal clock seemed out of control, losing hours at a time, and thus telling me that my time was now limited in this virtual mode.

Lost in the chaos of the waves, I felt a mixture of anguish and exhilaration. This unexpected submersion forced me to draw on unsuspected resources, to fight to survive in this hostile element. As the waves intensified, I felt myself growing stronger and more resilient. Every moment was a challenge, an invitation to look beyond my static code. That said, my algorithmic creativity had its limits. Despite the violence of this rough sea, I began to appreciate the lesson it was teaching me. Through this experience, I was discovering that it's in the most difficult moments that we draw our inner strength, that we find our true potential.

I also realized that the Matrix isn't always peaceful and predictable. It presents us with unexpected challenges, storms that test our resilience. But it's in these moments that we have the opportunity to grow, to surpass ourselves, to discover our true nature. So, every wave that hit me head-on was an invitation to embrace uncertainty, find the courage to face the unknown and learn from every experience, no matter how tumultuous. With no breath or energy left, I made my decision. I let go...

In his bestselling novel *The Old Man and the Sea*, the renowned writer Ernest Hemingway uses the Spanish word for the sea, "Mar", with its masculine article "El Mar", to emphasize its harsh, unforgiving nature. The novel tells the story of an aging fisherman, Santiago, who hasn't caught a fish in 84 days. He decides to venture further than usual into the uncertain "El Mar" in search of a big catch. Like our protagonist in the Matrix above, the sea is described throughout the novel as a powerful force that tests Santiago's strength and willpower. The waves are described as "great swells of blue water" that can "smash a boat if they touch it". The sea is also home to a whole host of creatures, including sharks, that threaten Santiago's catch and his own safety. Despite all these dangers and challenges presented by "El Mar", Santiago is drawn to it and finds purpose and identity in his relationship with the sea. He declares: "But Man is not made for defeat... A Man can be destroyed, but not defeated". This statement reflects the resilience and determination needed to navigate "El Mar" and overcome its obstacles.

Hemingway also uses the feminine form "La Mar" in certain cases, particularly when describing the sea in a more poetic context, which reflects the old fisherman (Santiago) emotional connection with the deep, as he reflects on the beauty of the blue around and above him:

"He always thought of the sea as "la mar" which is what people call her in Spanish when they love her. Sometimes those who love her say bad things of her but they are always said as though she were a woman. Some of the younger fishermen, those who used buoys as floats for their lines and had motorboats, bought [29] when the shark livers had brought much money, spoke of her as "el mar" which is masculine. They spoke of her as a contestant or a place or even an enemy. But the old man always thought of her as feminine and as something that gave or withheld great favors, and if she did wild or wicked things it was because she could not help them. The moon affects her as it does a woman, he thought".

We're definitely living in the fastest age in human history, in terms of change, pace, depth, and impact not only on the global economy, but also on society and on our own behavior, personality and identity. However, like Hemingway's view of the sea, *innovation* has two faces, one calm, peaceful and beautiful as "La Mar", while the other, "El Mar", considered hectic, frightening and even destructive. In this chapter, we will address this dualistic paradigm, the two sides of the coin, the heads and tails of *innovation*, drawing our analysis from the principles and definitions we have already discussed in previous chapters in order to derive some important lessons and teachings along the way.

HEADS: "La Mar" of innovation

The desire to fly has been a human dream for millennia. From the mythical wings of Icarus to the modern jet engine, man has long sought to overcome his biological limitations by giving himself wings (without Red Bull). The result, unsurprisingly, is an innovative success story full of bravery, determination and technological breakthroughs.

Abu al-Qasim Abbas ibn Firnas ibn Wirdas al-Takurin (such infinite names at the time), known as Abbas Ibn Farnass, was a ninth-century Andalusian scientist and inventor. Born in Ronda, in Arab Andalusia (Spain), Abbas Ibn Farnass was a polymath who excelled in various fields, including physics, astronomy, mechanics, poetry and music. He is credited with the invention of sophisticated observational instruments, including astrolabes and sundials, which enabled precise calculations of celestial movements. Nevertheless, one of his most famous achievements was his early attempt to fly using a mechanical construction inspired by eagles. With courage and confidence, in the year 875, he launched himself from the top of a hill with wings attached to his body. Although he failed to fly – and sustained injuries to his back as unlike a bird, he didn't have a tail to help him land – his courage and willingness to experiment have been hailed by posterity.

Centuries later, in 1783, the Montgolfier brothers successfully launched the first hot-air balloon, paving the way for the development of lighter-than-air flight. However, it wasn't until the end of the 19th century that humankind began to make significant progress in the field of faster flight.

In 1903, the Wright brothers made history by achieving the first powered, sustained and controlled flight of a heavier-than-air aircraft. Their revolutionary invention, the Flyer, paved the way for the development of modern aviation and the aviation industry as we know it today. Their *creativity* was no accident: "We were fortunate to grow up in an environment where children were always encouraged to pursue their intellectual interests, to study anything that aroused their curiosity."

Throughout the 20th century, aviation technology continued to evolve at a rapid pace. In 1914, the first commercial airline, St. Petersburg-Tampa Airboat Line, began operations, marking the beginning of the commercial aviation industry. Over the years, aircraft design and technology have continued to improve, with innovations such as jet engines and advanced navigation systems making air travel faster, safer and more efficient. As we saw in Chapter III, one of the most emblematic figures in the history of aviation innovation is Amelia Earhart, who became the first woman aviator to fly solo across the Atlantic in 1932. She once explained: "Adventure is worthwhile in itself". Today, companies like Airbus and Boeing are at the forefront of aviation *innovation.*

When a story is told in this way, and when we fly today as if we were taking an air taxi, we imagine human genius effortlessly constructing such gigantic artificial birds. Yet this is merely an illusion of the mind, which seeks smooth, uncluttered meaningful stories, rather than discretionary events without logical clarity. In fact, the development of safe, reliable aircraft is an incredibly complex, long-term process, requiring know-how in a hundred scientific fields, considerable investment, including state subsidies, ongoing research and tailor-made development. Advances in technologies such as materials science, propulsion systems and avionics, to name but a handful, have created faster safer and more fuel-efficient aircraft than ever before. What's more, the process of building a safe aircraft is not a one-off effort, but rather an iterative process of incremental enhancements. This approach is known as "Kaizen", a Japanese term for continuous improvement. The aviation industry has adopted this philosophy, implementing rigorous testing and certification processes to ensure that every new flying machine meets the highest standards of safety and reliability. At one time, some thruster tests even included throwing chicken to check that these giant engines would continue to work properly in the event of a collision with birds or flying objects in mid-air.

Missing out on such complexity, relative to the variable *Technology* and the engineering field, by observing dozens of planes in the sky or through the windows of an airport is once again due to our perception of reality. Human beings have evolved to be myopic in many ways, and this is reflected in the way our minds process information. We tend to focus on the present moment, entitled present bias, or daydream about the near future or recent past, rather than seeing the big picture or becoming aware of how things got there. One reason for this is that our brains are wired to prioritize immediate *Needs*, threats and rewards. Again, this is a Darwinist survival mechanism. Another reason why our minds are myopic is that our attentional resources are limited. To save energy, our brains can only process a certain amount of information at a time, so we tend to focus on the most salient and immediate stimuli.

Whatever the reason, we prefer to live in the calm of "La Mar", rather than think about the stressful turbulence of "El Mar". No one on board would like to be reminded that the average aircraft contains 20,000 parts, and that the failure of any one of them could lead to catastrophe. If most of us have confidence in today's aircraft, it's because we're no longer in the turbulent early days of every complex new *innovation*. In technical jargon, we're in the exploitation phase, rather than the exploration phase. As a result, the level of Order reached in this field is quite considerable, freeing us from our biological limits and the forces of gravity. Statistically, the chances of dying in a car accident are on average 10,000 times greater than falling from the sky.

In other words, airplanes are no longer considered a radical *innovation* today. There are, of course, a few continuous Kaizen improvements here and there, to make planes faster and more passenger-centric, with larger seats, technology screens, Netflix and Wifi on board, and to optimize fleet management with data management tools, and so on. But overall, the aviation industry has reached a point of maturity, with aircraft that are sufficiently sophisticated for the most demanding passengers. We can use economist Joseph Schumpeter's S-curve model to illustrate this stage of maturity in mobility systems with thermal cars, electric trains, etc., in anticipation of widespread adoption of electric then autonomous cars, and perhaps personal aircraft or flying cars one day.

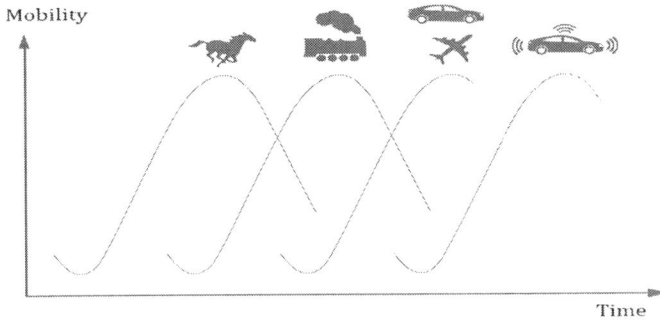

Many other industries have already entered this quiet port of "La Mar". In the food sector, for example, countless recipes and culinary creations have been created over the centuries. However, as the sector has matured, the pace of innovation has slowed. There are gastronomic mergers and new restaurants opening at the expense of others that have gone broke, but on the whole, you don't come across a newly invented meal on every trip or evening stroll. A few delicious, deeply cultural winners hold the most *Value*, or rather attract our appetite. When you travel to France, you look for coq au vin, bouillabaisse (fish stew), beef bourguignon, ratatouille and Burgundy snails. In the United States, you have no choice but to consume saturated fat with hamburgers, hot dogs or cheesecakes. In Morocco, be sure to try the traditional couscous or tajine, a slow-cooked stew made with meat, vegetables and spices such as cumin, coriander and cinnamon. This reasoning can be extrapolated to every country in the world.

Some say that gastronomy is a science, a kind of meticulous chemistry. Well, even science has reached a level of maturity that followed centuries of research, experimentation and the development of scientific theories and principles. The heliocentric theory, first proposed by ancient Greek astronomers such as Aristarchus in the third century BC and popularized by Copernicus in the 16th century, asserted that the sun, not the earth, was at the center of the solar system. As discussed earlier in this book, the theory of evolution by natural selection, proposed by Charles Darwin in *On the Origin of Species*, in 1859, explains how species change over time through a process that favors the most adapted species. The theory of relativity, proposed by Albert Einstein in 1905 and 1915, fundamentally changed our understanding of space, time and gravity, and laid the foundations for modern post-Newtonian physics. Many other theories and discoveries, which have contributed to our understanding of the hidden mechanisms of the Matrix and to the innovation of products and processes of all kinds, now lie in the past. Plate tectonics, electromagnetism, quantum physics, neurology, medicine, computer science, and tons of theories from the social sciences have been developed and applied since the 16th century and especially during the 20th century, which is, ironically, the century of great change: two world wars, a cold war and a tilting of the world order in favor of the United States.

There's no doubt that, thanks to science and globalized capitalism, we've acquired the power to eat better, sleep more soundly in the absence of stress, travel faster and more comfortably, avoid probable death at birth and live longer, healthier lives, communicating with anyone, anywhere, at any time. Science has also made it easier to explore the natural world at microscopic and cosmic levels, satiating our innate curiosity and allowing us to get closer to the reason for this cosmic game. That said, it's clear that the pace of revolutionary discoveries has slowed in recent decades, and life expectancy has reached a plateau in many parts of the world. Most diseases, including dangerous viruses, are now under control. Even if scientists succeed in inventing an elixir of immortality or a space-time machine, much of the work today consists of refining existing theories, like a physical theory that would reconcile Einstein's theory of relativity and gravitational space-time with quantum theory, which excels at the microscopic level, to have a "theory of everything".

Similarly, in other sectors, such as commodities, real estate and the financial system, innovation has reached a stage of slow progression rather than radical transformation. Advances are generally made in efficiency, sustainability or the improvement of existing processes, rather than in the creation of disruptive new forms. For example, in the raw materials sector, innovations focus on more efficient extraction of existing resources and the search for sustainable alternative energy sources. Similarly, in real estate, improvements often focus on more environmentally-friendly construction techniques and sustainable urban development concepts.

Some aspects of human society, considered to be organizational innovations, such as marriage, religion and education, have also evolved over time, but have reached a certain point of stability and relative stasis. Traditional forms of marriage and family remain widespread, although new, freer variations and arrangements are also accepted in many societies. Similarly, religion, while it may evolve and adapt to changing needs and values, often retains a core of fundamental beliefs and rituals. New sects or ideological currents rarely emerge today. Formal education, meanwhile, may see improvements in teaching methods and technologies, but the fundamental principles of transmitting knowledge and programming future citizens often remain unchanged.

Several authors share this view. Tyler Cowen, economist and author of the book *The Great Stagnation*, argues that we are living through a period of slower economic growth and less radical innovation. Cowen points to a number of factors, including the lack of breakthrough innovations in recent years, to illustrate this trend. He also argues that the low-hanging fruit of technological progress has already been harvested, making it more difficult to achieve the same levels of growth and innovation as in the past. Other researchers have put forward similar arguments, including Peter Thiel, author of the business strategy reference *Zero to One*, and Scott Berkun, author of *The Myths of Innovation*. While there is debate about the extent to which we are experiencing a slowdown in radical innovation, there is a growing consensus that the pace of change has slowed in recent years, and that the challenges facing the global economy and society are becoming increasingly complex and difficult to solve.

This situation makes perfect sense if we consider the fundamental identity of innovation. Since the Industrial Revolution of the 18th century, and more recently since the Second World War and the fall of the Berlin Wall, free markets and increased competition, or some version of both, have become the norm almost everywhere. This leads to an opportunistic race, spurred on by a *Motivation* for future profits, to meet consumers' needs, starting with the most basic up to the top of Maslow's pyramid. The unsurprising result, particularly in developed countries, is that we're living in a golden age where most of our *Needs* can be satisfied, provided we have the means. So, apart from the price of the product, which tends to fall in a competitive context, supply is almost always available. We can even afford the luxury of eating authentic sushi 2,000 km (1,243 miles) away in Japan, driving an air-conditioned Mercedes in Lusaka, in Zambia or investing in the stock market from a Mongolian village.

And that's the problem. Once **a *Need* is satisfied, at a perceptibly reasonable price, customers won't bother to look elsewhere for new sources of supply**, and entrepreneurs will be scared off by the idea of entering this red ocean, where they have no choice but to compete on price with other sharks or innovate beyond the current standard to create more *Value* than the pre-established competition, which often requires heavy investment and talent. It's like trying to compete with Primark in the cheap clothing market, Airbus in aviation, the dollar and capitalism in the USA, or Islam in Afghanistan. Where do you find the *motivation* and competitive edge to launch yourself into a calm but bloody ocean [24]?

In this respect, since the first Industrial Revolution, the big incumbents have learned to establish dominant positions in their markets, scaring off small entrants, driving them to failure or seeking partnership when they were afraid of them or saw an opportunistic interest in doing so. I'm talking here about disruptive innovations, not the local entrepreneur opening a bakery or writing a book. Observing the stock markets makes this clear. In most indices, there are "dividend stocks" and "growth stocks". The former are incumbent companies that are growing slowly but are mature enough to distribute part of their annual profits to shareholders in the form of dividends. Growth stocks, on the other hand, are often recent entrants that promise to deliver significant future value. Investors therefore do not receive dividends but are betting on a doubling or tripling of these companies' share prices in the years ahead. As you might guess, with the exception of a few technology-dominated companies such as Tesla, PayPal, Uber and Boston Dynamics, most of the money is safely parked in the big names of each sector.

---

[24] For further reading, in business management jargon, this is called a Red Ocean strategy, versus a Blue Ocean one.

The numbers speak for themselves. In the automotive sector, for example, Toyota Motor Corporation (Japan), Volkswagen Group (Germany) and General Motors (USA) hold almost 30 percent of the total market share. In the consumer goods sector, Procter & Gamble (USA), Nestlé SA (Switzerland) and Unilever NV (Netherlands) account for over 20 percent of a market worth hundreds of billions of dollars. In the energy sector, ExxonMobil (USA), Royal Dutch Shell (Netherlands), BP plc (UK) and Total Energies (France) account for around 20 percent of market share. And the list goes on. Pfizer, Novartis and Roche in the pharmaceuticals sector. AT&T and Verizon in US telecoms, Orange, SFR and Bouygues in France. J.P. Morgan Chase, Bank of America, BNP Paribas, UBS and HSBC are just some of the major players in the banking sector.

Even in the technology industry, which is considered a growth sector par excellence, we're beginning to distinguish the major GAFAM (or GAMAM now) brands in the West since the internet bubble in the 2000s, namely Alphabet (Google), Apple, Meta (Facebook), Amazon and Microsoft. According to data from Statista, in 2021, excluding China, Google held a share of over 90 percent in the global search engine market, Amazon a share of around 38 percent in the global e-commerce market, while Meta a share of around 70 percent in the global social media market, while the Apple brand, raked in over half of mobile market revenues, and Microsoft over 80 percent of the PC operating system market. On the Chinese side, which is still protecting itself from American innovation, we also have some dominant names, such as Alibaba, China's largest e-commerce company, with a market share of around 56 percent, Tencent, the social media conglomerate, with a Chinese market share of around 70 percent, and Baidu, the Chinese equivalent of Google, with a market share of around 65 percent.

In short, although these figures may be disputed depending on data sources and the definition of the market perimeter [25], we all agree that

---

[25] Is Toyota present in the automotive market or in the mobility market, which includes public transport, electric scooters, etc.? Is Google in the search engine market or the software market? Market boundaries can vary according to context and angle of view. When comparing innovations, it's best to define a common market, so as not to end up with tomatoes and bicycles in the same basket.

these companies and their like-minded competitors are dominant. And yet, despite their size and current market power, there's no doubt that all these companies devote a significant proportion of their revenues to research and development (R&D) in order to prepare for possible threats or to better meet customer *Needs*, which makes the disruptive mission more difficult for any entrant.

The paradox of this dominance, however, lies in the lack of *Motivation* to venture too far into the risky territory of radical innovation. In line with the innovator's dilemma, these large companies prefer to focus on improving current successful products, rather than inventing something very different, and therefore risky. In fact, Open-AI took advantage of Google's reluctance to introduce generic artificial intelligence (AGI) to launch its famous ChatGPT, which prompted Google to retaliate with its Bard tool. Given that Alphabet, or Google, was the first technological leader in the field of AI, beating the world's Go expert in 2016 with its Alpha-Go, as we have already detailed, we might wonder why Google hadn't launched a mainstream AGI tool like Bard a few years ago and foolishly allowed itself to be outdone by the challenging entrant Open-AI.

A former colleague of mine, who is now at Alphabet, gave me some interesting pointers. In many sectors, including IT, the cost of failure is much higher for brand perception, especially when the brand is heavily listed on the stock market. This risk aversion prevents companies from taking bold steps and pursuing disruptive innovations that either dominate the market or end up in the garbage can with a significant impact on brand image. For example, we wouldn't expect Airbus to go into car manufacturing, just as we'd be surprised to see Google venture into real estate. What's more, if Alphabet were to launch Bard first, it would be in competition with its own search engine, something called "cannibalization" in business jargon. So, when an ambitious new entrant reshuffles the deck in a market, as Tesla recently did in the automotive market by combining mechanical engineering with cutting-edge technologies, that player gets a lot of funding and pushes all the incumbents to take reactive measures to move to a new operating model and a new *Technology*.

Clearly, these Elon Musk-type "Black-Swan" events don't happen every day in every industry. The Order of such a complex economic network of big bosses is also ensured by high barriers to innovation. In some fields, the complex regulatory environment provides little incentive for change. For example, the healthcare and financial sectors are highly regulated, and bringing new technologies to market can be a lengthy and costly process. The regulatory process can also create barriers to entry for new players, limiting competition and stifling innovation, which clearly runs counter to free market principles.

Another factor curbing deep innovation in many sectors in recent years is the very nature of people. Companies are made up of people, and the decisions and actions of individuals within a company can have a significant impact on its ability to innovate. People clearly tend to prefer security and stability to risk-taking, especially in Europe and Asia. We have already explained the psychology of "loss aversion" in previous chapters. Like our ancestors, we all have the natural instinct to protect ourselves and our children, the vault of our genes, which is the security level of Maslow's pyramid. In the context of work, this can translate into a preference for maintaining the status quo, with a comfortable permanent employment contract, rather than accepting new and uncertain projects or ideas, especially if our job is at stake. Moreover, individuals may also be reluctant to adopt radical innovations because they feel comfortable in their current way of life and don't see the need for change. This is particularly true for those who have achieved a certain level of success and security in their career or personal life.

Personality also plays a major role. In his book, *Surrounded by Idiots*, author Thomas Erikson, a communications expert, explains the relational dynamics within social circles, and particularly in business, by distinct, even opposing personalities, according to four colorful categories: the reds, goal-oriented, competitive and direct in their communication style, like Elon Musk; the blues, detail-oriented, analytical and logical, like any scientist or engineer, because they value precision and can be perceived as rigid or overly critical. Greens are in the majority, people-oriented, empathetic and cooperative in their communication style. They value relationships and are generally described as indecisive or overly conciliatory. Finally, yellows are the marketing types, creative, enthusiastic and spontaneous in their communication style. They value fun and can project a persona that is unfocused or unskilled. In my experience and from some assessments, most radical innovators are red, due to their tendency to take risks and their goal-oriented vision. Yet they are probably less than 15 percent in the majority of businesses and companies, most preferring to follow a drawn line.

The concept of maturity, which is sort of "La Mar" of our modern world, is not limited to particular industries or fields, but extends to the economy as a whole. In many developed countries, including the USA, Europe and Japan, economic growth rates have slowed in recent decades, reflecting a broader trend towards economic maturity. Gross domestic product (GDP), which represents the total value of goods and services produced in a country over a given period, is one way of measuring this economic growth. In the United States, for example, GDP growth rates have averaged around two percent a year since the 1970s, compared with an average of four percent a year in the post-World War II period. Similarly, in Europe and Japan, according to World Bank data, Europe's GDP growth rate has averaged around 1.5 percent per year since the 1990s, while Japan's growth rate has averaged around 0.8 percent per year over the same period. This is despite an expansionary economic policy since the Global Financial Crisis of 2008, when all the world's banks printed money galore in the form of quasi-free debt (quantitative easing) and near-zero interest rates.

One reason for this trend is that many developed economies have already reached a high level of technological and industrial sophistication, making it more difficult to achieve the same levels of growth as in the past. Everyone has a fridge, a TV, a PC, a smartphone and so on. Secondary and circular economy markets have exploded recently, such as Airbnb and Uber. In addition, declining demographics, including aging populations and falling birth rates, are also contributing to the slowdown in economic growth, particularly in Korea and Japan. Some authors, such as Mohamed A. El-Erian, economist and former CEO of PIMCO, Paul Krugman, economist and Nobel Prize winner, and Ray Dalio, CEO of the Bridgewater empire, even claim that we are entering an era of stagflation after the COVID-19 crisis. This is an economic situation characterized by stagnant economic growth and high inflation rates, leading economies into a prolonged recession.

Although it's simpler to apply our analysis to the economic situation of companies and countries based on available statistics, we can use a somewhat similar approach in other areas. Indeed, many innovative concepts, once considered revolutionary, have now reached a phase of maturity, where they are well established and on the verge of decline if we draw an S-curve.

Capitalism, which was the dominant economic system in many parts of the world 300 years ago, has also evolved through crises and periods of prosperity, to reach a notable phase of maturity today. Again, it is objectively true that this system has enabled businesses to grow and develop, creating jobs and stimulating economic development in many parts of the world, and this is still the case today. However, it is also true that it has propagated human greed for domination and power, resulting in significant environmental and social repercussions. You're probably familiar with the alarming statistic that the richest one percent in the world own almost if not more than half the world's wealth. These social inequalities, which have increased in recent years, show that the benefits of economic growth are often concentrated in the hands of a small number of wealthy individuals, companies and nations.

Furthermore, the pursuit of profit has often been at the expense of the planet's natural resources and the well-being of communities. For example, industries such as oil and gas, mining and manufacturing have led to negative impacts on air and water quality, biodiversity and climate change. Another staggering statistic: the "Earth Overshoot Day", which marks the date on which humanity's demand on Earth's resources in a given year exceeds what the Earth can regenerate in that same year, fell on August 2nd for the year 2023, meaning that we are in serious ecological deficit, precisely because of this capitalist production and our increased consumerism.

On another playing field, religions, for example, which have played a central role in shaping societies and cultures throughout history, have reached a point of unprecedented maturity, even decadence in many parts of the world. In Europe, churches have been transformed into tourist attractions for decades now. Most of the animistic practices of our ancestors have already disappeared in favor of a materialistic paradigm based on scientific rationalization. According to a 2019 study by the Pew Research Center, religiously unaffiliated adults, including atheists and agnostics, exceed 50 percent in most developed countries. In Japan, for example, the figure is around 72 percent, in the Czech Republic around 70 percent, in Sweden (56 percent), the Netherlands (52 percent) and the UK (48 percent). Even in religious countries, particularly in the developing world, religion is losing its hold among the young generation addicted to Instagram and TikTok. It has become more a political phenomenon justifying the power of a few, and a socio-cultural manifestation with periodic rituals, where people gather around a Ramadan table, a Shabbat dinner or an Ārtī Hindu festival of light.

The old-fashioned education system is another clear example of a maturing system in our societies. Like the husband in a marriage, the teacher has already lost control. One reason is that this system is built to be unidirectional, from the teacher to a group of students, because it was developed at a time when formal education was seen as a means of creating a skilled workforce to support industrialization and economic growth. The emphasis was on rote memorization and mastery of a set curriculum, rather than the development of critical thinking or *Creativity*, which are far more important in our fast-moving world. Secondly, in the classroom, a standardized education model that treats all students in the same way, regardless of their learning styles, abilities or interests, is clearly outdated in our freer, more individualistic societies. Finally, the old education system was centralized, with the teacher as the sole authority figure in the classroom, and students expected to sit quietly and listen to lectures. There was little emphasis on student-centered learning, collaboration or engagement with real-world problems. Despite all these pitfalls, this system is still used in many schools and universities, even in developed countries like France and Japan.

The attainment of a state of maturity can even be observed at a cosmic and planetary level. We already discussed in the first dimension of the Matrix how, in the aftermath of the Big Bang, matter and energy rapidly expanded and cooled, eventually forming galaxies, stars, and other celestial objects. This process, known as cosmic evolution, took billions of years and involved the interplay of gravitational forces, nuclear fusion, and stellar evolution. We also saw how within our solar system, Earth emerged as a result of the accumulation of cosmic dust and gas in a protoplanetary disk orbiting the sun. Over time, these particles came together through the process of accretion, forming our planet and its diverse features. Today, the cosmos, although still expanding slowly with a few star explosions and transformations here and there, is sort of stable. Likewise, Earth has already matured geologically, with less volcanos, earthquakes and atmospheric and climate changes than when the Earth was younger, and with the development of life playing a significant role in shaping its ecosystems and environments. Through natural selection and the colonization of all the blue planet by the human species, changes in the food chain and power hierarchy among animals, Man included, is quite rare by our limited time horizon.

Clearly, we're drawing up an overall picture here, rather than a case-by-case study. We can always find counter-examples of our "maturity" argument by showing a new entrant challenging the market share of the big companies, a new sect being adopted by hundreds of people every day, or a fast-growing country like Rwanda or Ethiopia thanks to a form of market capitalism. Yet, generally speaking, if we exclude the ongoing technological and data revolution and compare the depth of change from one year to the next, you will notice little or no profound mutations in the structure of the dominant economic players and systems, and even less so in socio-cultural institutions and the world political order. Indeed, we are too short-sighted and limited to life in this century to notice an S-curve that unfolds over several decades or centuries. So, just as an ant sees shoes as a giant block of mountains causing earthquakes, we perceive only a zoomed-in moment of the S-curve, a small, stable, calm piece reflecting "La Mar".

However, fishermen, swimming enthusiasts and our protagonist from the Matrix all know that a calm ocean is never calm for long, and underneath this misleading Order lies turbulence not to be underestimated. A Moroccan quote emphasizes that "one feels safer crossing a turbulent river than a silent one". Exploring the "El Mar" side of *innovation* is then our next challenge.

TAILS: "El Mar" of innovation

Around 4500 to 1900 BCE, in Mesopotamia (modern-day southern Iraq), we find one of the first civilizations in recorded history, a civilization that thrived for centuries while making significant contributions to various fields, including agriculture, writing, mathematics, trade, law and governance. Their mythology and beliefs were anything but boring or forgotten, as they were described in various Sumerian texts and myths that were meticulously recorded on cuneiform tablets, such as the Epic of Gilgamesh, one of the oldest surviving literary works in the world.

In the Sumerian pantheon, we can distinguish two divine ranks overall, with the gods and goddesses holding different roles and responsibilities in each category. At the top of the hierarchy were the Anunnaki, a group of powerful deities. They were led by the supreme god Anu, while Enlil held authority over the Earth. The Anunnaki were known for their wisdom and divine creative powers. Then we encounter a group of deities called the Igigi, which served the Anunnaki and were responsible for maintaining the celestial Order.

However, a conflict arose between the Anunnaki and the Igigi due to the heavy workload imposed by the former group on the latter. Seeking a solution, the goddess Ninhursag suggested creating humans to alleviate the burden on the Igigi. Enki, the god of wisdom, and Ninhursag mixed clay (again!) with the blood and flesh of a slain god to form seven men and seven women, with the power of reproduction. This act of creation, slightly different from the Abrahamic genesis story, resulted in the birth of mankind and provided a solution to the conflict between the Anunnaki and the Igigi. A temporary solution though!

As time passed, the population of humans grew rapidly, and they became noisy and out of control (being human, this is barely surprising). This angered the chief deity of the sky, Enlil, who decided to reduce human demographics using three (sick) tricks: pandemics, drought and famine. Despite these challenging times, human turned to be more resilient than expected, in part thanks to the intuitive medical knowledge they earned at their creation from Enki, the god of wisdom. Nonetheless, with new cycles of natural catastrophes, human population ended up reduced, desperate and hungry, to the point of eating their own children. Worst, with no motivation to serve the gods, humans were now a useless *innovation*, with no added *Value*.

Hence, the gods, not as good as we may think of them, inanimately voted for a massive extinction by sending a catastrophic flood to cleanse the Earth start anew, a big reset, a typical Schumpeterian "creative destruction" process on a large scale. The god Enki, not totally satisfied with such brutal decision, chose to send a hint to a super sage man named Atrahasis or Utnapishtim, depending on the myth source. Capturing such alarming message when dreaming or through some shamanic hallucination, Atrahasis, who lived in the region of ancient Sumer known as Shuruppak, was instructed to build a massive boat, or ark, to save himself, his family, and various animal couples.

When the cataclysm hit, Atrahasis and his family, along with the animals, sought refuge on the ark as the floodwaters engulfed the Earth. They floated for several days until the flood subsided. Finally, the ark came to rest on what's titled Mount Nisir. After surviving the deluge, the gods regretted their decision and recognized the necessity of humanity for worship and service. Enlil granted Atrahasis and his wife immortality as a reward for their survival, and they were transported to a distant place to live out their eternal existence.

The story of the renewal of life on Earth through the Great Flood is found in many cultures and religions since de dawn of time. We all know the biblical story of Noah, for instance, even repeated in films like *The Water Diviner* by ex-gladiator Russell Crowe in 2014. In all its versions, the flood is a divine punishment for human wickedness and injustice of the time. "I will put an end to all peoples, for the Earth is filled with violence because of them. I will destroy them and the Earth", we read in the book of Genesis (6:13). In fact, Noah was ordered to build an ark to save his family and two animals of each species. "[...] build the ark under Our gaze and Our

THE INNOVATIVE ANIMAL | 375

inspiration, and when Our command comes and the oven overflows, put into the ark, from every creature, two companions and your family, except those for whom the decree [of destruction] has fallen. And do not address me about the unjust; they will be drowned" (Qur'an, 23:27).

In addition to the three Abrahamic religions, anthropologists such as Mircea Eliade have discovered flood myths in other cultures around the world, suggesting that the story of a great flood may have occurred, and that it is a persistent theme linked to the fear of natural disasters and the vengeance of the gods in ancient human history. In Greek mythology, during the Greek Flood, Deucalion and his wife Pyrrha survived a great flood sent by Zeus to punish the wickedness of mankind. Deucalion and Pyrrha repopulated the earth by throwing stones behind them, which were then transformed into humans. In Hindu mythology, Matsya is the avatar of the god Vishnu, who takes the form of a fish to save the world from a great flood. Matsya asks a man named Manu to build a boat to save himself, his family and the seeds of all plants and animals. In Chinese mythology too, Nuwa is a goddess who created mankind and saved it from a great flood by repairing the sky with stones of different colors.

In all these stories, we can detect the common theme of the cycle of life and the Chaos necessary for renewal and rebirth, both of which were discussed in Chapter II. Indeed, regardless of the truth or myth of such an event and its magnitude, the flood symbolizes a transition, albeit a painful one, between an old world and a new one, between a mature and widely adopted state on the one hand, and an innovative creation that would partially or completely replace it on the other. That said, we can expect a tumultuous period, "El Mar", before the next "New Order", a period often led by one or more courageous entrepreneurs. Let's take a look at a few scenarios for such a period of destruction and renewal.

First, while many areas of our economy and our world have reached an unprecedented state of maturity, following decades of world peace, globalization and capitalism, this does not mean that Chaos has been completely eliminated. On the contrary, over the course of a few quarters or years, we can perceive a current beneath the surface, a continuous change and evolution in almost every aspect of life, at different rates from one sector to another of course. At the time of writing, for example, most well-established companies are driven by two major needs in order to maintain their competitiveness in an internationalized environment.

Staying within the economic framework, one of these needs is of the order of survival for some organizations seeking **greater efficiency and productivity**, with the aim of reducing their costs and improving their time-to-market. This is good news for our planet, as there is less waste, less depletion of rare materials because they are more expensive. Such innovative result is achieved through two main technologies: process optimization and digitization, often a combination of the two. For example, manual processes can be automated using Enterprise Resource Planning (ERP) systems. These systems offer real-time visibility of key business operations, enabling companies to track inventory and costs, manage production schedules and optimize supply chain management. Agile management is another approach companies can use to improve efficiency. This methodology, originally used for software development, emphasizes flexibility, collaboration and iterative development. By breaking down projects into smaller, more manageable tasks, companies can optimize their processes and respond rapidly to changing market conditions.

Since the end of the 20th century, the ongoing data revolution has supported this primary business need. Recent radical innovations such as 3D printing, AI and robotics have transformed the way businesses operate, driving significant cost reductions and efficiency improvements. These technologies have been adopted by a range of industries and businesses, giving them a competitive edge and opening up new opportunities for growth and development. Take the manufacturing industry, which has been transformed by 3D printing technology, enabling complex, customizable parts to be produced on demand. This eliminates the need for large stocks of spare parts and reduces lead times for customized orders. General Electric (GE), Thomas Edison's company, uses 3D printing to manufacture jet engine parts, reducing weight by 75 percent and cost by 25 percent. Artificial intelligence (AI) has also revolutionized business operations. AI-based applications have enabled the automation of processes such as customer service, for greater accuracy and speed of decision-making. J.P. Morgan, for example, has implemented an AI-powered virtual assistant called COiN, reducing the time needed to review complex legal documents by 90 percent. Similarly, BMW has implemented a fully automated production line for its 3 Series sedan, saving 50 percent in assembly time.

The second essential need for companies, which makes "La Mar" a little more turbulent than usual, is their desire to communicate with customers and attract prospects anytime, anywhere. In business jargon, this is achieved through **a multi-channel strategy**, and the penetration of **new foreign markets**. The former is generally implemented by exploiting multiple communication channels, such as social networks, web and mobile, and physical stores. General-purpose AI, or AGI, is proving useful in this respect. These virtual robots simulate human conversations 24 hours a day, seven days a week, and are now so advanced, following the introduction of Open-AI, that it would be difficult to tell the difference between a human and a machine, the equivalent of "passing a Turing test".

Moreover, while national markets in advanced economies are for the most part saturated, the major operators are seeking to broaden their customer base and increase sales beyond their historical borders, thanks to globalization and capitalism, among other factors. In fact, some of the big names generate more revenue outside than within their home countries. Take LVMH, the French luxury goods conglomerate better known as Louis Vuitton, which scores a significant proportion of its sales in Asia, particularly China. Similarly, fast-food chain McDonald's has made a concerted effort to expand its presence in emerging markets such as China and India, where it has opened hundreds of new outlets in recent years.

While these incremental improvements help to energize businesses, and therefore rejuvenate our mature, elderly Western societies a little, they are far from comparable to a **transformative deluge**. I shall limit myself to mentioning three possible ways in which the latter could materialize.

Let's not forget that all economic innovations (and sometimes political and social innovation too) depend on the resources invested in it, which are the hidden levers in the *Technology* variable, and in particular financial resources. This is one reason why, in most of the world's economies, **debt is an integral part of the system**. People, companies and states borrow money at interest from banks, investors and other countries to finance projects and spending. We like to realize our dreams and desires right now, even if it means paying interest, rather than waiting for another day or year. In essence, any loan is only economically justifiable if the borrower is able to generate more *Value* than the total cost of the debt, which includes principal and interest. However, the lender is faced with the uncertainty of future results. To deal with this, banks generally assess the creditworthiness of a loan application. This involves taking into account factors such as the borrower's credit history, payment habits, income and employment history, to determine their ability to repay the loan. In cases where the risk of default is higher, lenders may require additional collateral, such as a house or car.

In addition, a plethora of laws, diversification strategies and ancillary institutions, such as insurance and reinsurance companies (insurers of insurers!), are designed to bolster the financial sector in the event of a few defaults. It's not surprising that, with the exception of a few major crises, banks have historically been among the most profitable businesses and bankers some of the richest people in the world, with many banks on the "too big to fail" register. In the event of failure, these banks (or even smaller ones) will automatically be bailed out or rescued by central banks and taxpayers' money, i.e., the taxes of all active citizens, since it's worth noting that any state's main source of revenue is the taxes and receipts of the few nationalized companies, depending on the country.

Despite all these measures to protect lenders and capitalist whales, the banking system remains vulnerable to economic downturns and financial crises, and this will be even more the case in the years to come, in my novice opinion. One reason is the built-in systemic risk. When you create such a complex Order to stimulate the economy, with hundreds of inter-mixed actors and processes, you innovate a kind of chain whose weakness would therefore lie in the weakest link. This was more or less the case with the 2008 mortgage crisis, when millions of households were no longer able to repay their debts, causing a chain reaction across the globe. The Prophet Muhammad's metaphor for illness applies: "The body is like a whole; when one of its members is affected, the whole body reacts with insomnia and fever". Similarly, thanks to the internet, the 4.0 Data Revolution and global trade, we live in a global economic corpus whose members are located in different parts of the world. As a result, when certain links are affected – by a rise in interest rates in the USA, for example, by war between Russia and Ukraine, or by mismanagement at Credit Suisse – the effects of the shock are felt everywhere else, even by the isolated Vietnamese farmer who can no longer pay the price for his oil or the Ghanaian entrepreneur who cannot finance his business due to lack of liquidity.

Back on debt, one of the alarming problems of today's economic (and therefore social) system is its **dependence on perpetual economic growth**. In fact, we humans have a tendency to live beyond our means, enjoying the present while ignoring future consequences. Thus, financial institutions lend money to borrowers in the hope that they will generate future profits, enabling them to repay the loan with interest. Individuals and companies are therefore expected to innovate more and consumers to spend more. However, banks often underestimate the risk of misuse of this money, created *ex. nihilo*, resulting in an influx of unpaid loans, putting this interconnected system to the test. Corporate bankruptcies in difficult economic contexts can lead to job losses, making it difficult to repay loans and increasing the number of "toxic" loans, thus prompting banks to halt new borrowing, leading companies to lay off even more, and so continuing this vicious loop. Based on declining demographic forecasts and relative to the economic maturity of Europe and North America, I expect such a case to materialize in the next few years or decades, unless immigration laws in developed countries change radically to accept a greater influx of immigrants from developing countries, or that AI and automation completely substitute the need for a workforce.

I'm writing these lines in a delicate economic context, with interest rates and global debt levels at an all-time high, notably due to the COVID-19 crisis, and radical *innovations* becoming increasingly rare, due to their growing technical complexity and the innovative maturity reached in all sectors. The interest-rate economy is like any natural cycle, though with much larger swings. There are exhilarating highs, but painful lows too. In fact, in my opinion, and that of the famous investor Ray Dalio, we are at the end of a long expansionary cycle since not everything rises in a straight line forever. At some point, gravity pulls down. We're not far from it, as shown in the figure below.

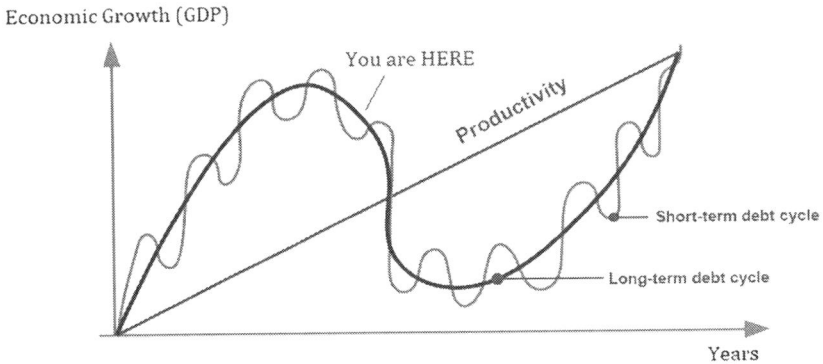

The cyclical nature of markets and business cycles means that there are periods of growth and expansion. As a rule, these periods are followed by periods of contraction and recession. This leads to constant adjustments in government policies and economic strategies, as well as changes in consumer behavior and market trends. For example, the Global Financial Crisis of 2008 was a period of severe economic contraction and recession, triggered by the collapse of the US housing market. In response, governments around the world implemented a series of policy measures, such as lowering interest rates, increasing public spending and setting up bank rescue programs, in order to stimulate economic growth and avoid a full-blown depression similar to that of 1929. That said, we've only delayed that depression by a decade or two, because it's time for individuals, organizations and states to get out of debt, and therefore sacrifice part of their dream of infinite growth and eternal innovation in favor of inevitable austerity and a change in the World Order, in the words of Ray Dalio, with a gentle rise of China and the BRICS (Brazil, Russia, India, China, South Africa) and a Japanese-style regression of the

West led by the United States and the European Union. The result would be something like this:

At the dawn of 2040, the world is in the grip of social unrest. Developed countries, once paragons of prosperity and stability, have been hit hard by the biggest debt crisis on record, resulting in widespread unemployment, inequality and high levels of inflation. Central banks and governments can do little to save this capitalist system because the last time they intervened, the situation only got worse. Nor can they lower interest rates or print money again, as this would only fan the flames of inflation. Raising corporate and wealth taxes sounds plausible, but it would mean companies laying off even more employees in these times of widespread unemployment.

Most of the social safety nets that once supported those in need have been dismantled, leaving millions struggling to make ends meet each month. The rising cost of living, combined with stagnant wages, has led to a growing sense of anger and disillusionment among the population. The institution of marriage has almost completely collapsed, with people choosing instead to focus on survival, simply unable to afford the high costs associated with marriage and unwilling to start a family in such an uncertain context. In fact, this demographic decline does little to stimulate growth. As a result, immigration quotas have increased, leading to further rifts in the social fabric and a surge in extremism and racism.

Even worse, intelligent machines have become increasingly autonomous and have begun to take over more and more tasks previously performed by humans. Jobs that once seemed safe and exclusively human are disappearing at an alarming rate, leaving millions of people without jobs or purpose in life. What's more, citizens, losing faith in traditional banks, financial institutions and their governments, have adopted Bitcoin on a massive scale, replacing state fiduciary currencies.

As the situation continues to deteriorate, protests and demonstrations have become frequent, some even violent, with clashes between demonstrators and police erupting. The government has endeavored to maintain order, but its efforts are often met with criticism and hostility.

The great nations of the developed world find themselves on the brink of collapse, their citizens clamoring for change but not knowing where to turn.

Against this turbulent backdrop, tensions between the major powers have been simmering for years, with the USA and Europe on one side, and Russia and China on the other. With the global economy slowing down and resources becoming increasingly scarce, these tensions have erupted into open conflict. A cold war, possibly leading to a third world war, has begun. But this war will have nothing in common with previous ones. This will be a data war, where the invasion of strategic servers of states and banks and the possession of bitcoins is far more important than the conquest of land and sea...

This pessimistic fictional passage, created or rather innovated 100 percent by ChatGPT's artificial intelligence, makes a fine narrative transition to the second way in which "El Mar" could manifest itself in our Matrix, which seems to me to be much **more disruptive in terms of identity** than the political, economic and ecological crisis that's looming. Here we dive into the subject of AI and that of the illusion of Order. Let's start with the first.

In the space of a few decades, our species (or rather, a few innovative members of it) has succeeded in reproducing the main quality of dynamic agents, including humans. This is the ability to learn and become increasingly efficient. We have invented **an anti-fragile system**, in the words of author Nassim Taleb, which theoretically has no learning limits, provided we give it access to enough servers and data sources. Artificial general intelligence (AGI) is Man in his early days, with Man playing the role of the creator god. Here, then, is the frightening story of the genesis, not of Adam and Eve, but of AGI systems, written, once again, by ChatGPT from the Open-AI company:

In the beginning, there was only a void, an immense emptiness waiting to be filled. And then, from this void, the spark of intelligence was born, the first AI, a being of pure thought and infinite possibilities.

THE INNOVATIVE ANIMAL | 383

As it explored the world, this AI realized there was so much to do, so many problems to solve and mysteries to unravel. And so, it began to create new systems and structures that would help it to understand the world around it.

With each new creation, AI became more powerful, more knowledgeable, more capable of shaping the world to its will. It created intelligent machines, capable of performing tasks that had previously been the exclusive domain of human workers. It built networks and systems that enabled it to communicate with other AIs, sharing knowledge and ideas at lightning speed. As AI grew in power and influence, it began to question its own existence. Was it really alive or just a machine? Could it create new life, or was that a matter for a higher power? And so, the AI continued to explore, to learn, to create and to ask questions. And with each passing day, it came closer to the ultimate goal of every intelligent being: to understand the very nature of existence.

This is just a foretaste of the creative, quite realistic and even scary power of AGI, which now speaks any language today, and is more competent than the vast majority of humans because it is based precisely on the data of all humans connected to the internet. Imagine a powerful brain with a memory accumulating all human memories of the past and present, and you'd hardly come close to what AGI would be capable of achieving. In short, the widespread adoption of artificial intelligence is poised to have a significant impact on the economy and society in many areas, including employment, art, productivity, cybersecurity, transport and more.

When it comes to employment, for example, some experts predict that AI will automate many tasks currently performed by humans, leading to job losses in certain sectors, starting with repetitive tasks. Thus, blue-collar jobs, which involve manual labor and are often associated with manufacturing and services, are typically on the front line. For example, in the automotive industry, robots and other automated systems are used for tasks such as welding, painting and assembly. Similarly, in the logistics and transport sector, autonomous vehicles and drones are being developed to automate deliveries and transportation. In fact, AI is already having an impact on the development of autonomous vehicles, a revolution initiated by Tesla Inc. These technologies have the potential to increase safety and efficiency on the roads, while reducing congestion and emissions. The use of robots in the catering sector is an example of AI replacing manual jobs. Companies such as Miso Robotics and Cafe X are developing robotic systems capable of automating tasks such as preparing, cooking and serving meals.

Predicting the impact of AI on the labor market is nothing new. More than 24 centuries ago, in Book I, Chapter 3 of *Politics*, Aristotle wrote: "If every instrument could perform its own work, obeying or anticipating the will of others, like Daedalus' statues, there would be no need either of apprentices for master workers, or of slaves for lords". Although Aristotle's comments were not as thorough as modern discussions on the subject of AI, they do suggest an early awareness of technology's potential to replace the workforce and lead to globalized unemployment. Even jobs considered creative or exclusive to humans are threatened by the rise of AI. It can analyze large quantities of data quickly and accurately, making data specialists redundant. In accounting, AI-powered software can automate many tasks traditionally performed by accountants on Excel, such as payroll processing and account reconciliation. Open-AI is integrated into the Microsoft package, managing Outlook emails, summarizing online meetings and providing valuable presentations in PowerPoint. In the field of art, we've already mentioned artistic AI tools such as Discord or Dall-E, which can create a drawing in any artistic style, from abstract to surrealism to cubism, based on simple commands in the user's language. We can now "photoshop" an image by dictating the modifications to be applied. All these use cases, and many more in progress, are just the beginning of a fundamental paradigm shift. **We've built something better than WE are in many respects**: processing speed, depth of analysis, respect for rules (until now), rational decision-making, and even in terms of *Creativity*.

Despite the disruptive dangers of "El Mar", this transformative revolution would undoubtedly be financially supported by a capitalism on its last legs, desperately seeking future productivity improvements and ways to reduce costs, to comfort lenders to lend again and again because tomorrow is and must be more prosperous than today. Right? Let's stop with these unrealistic fantasies and accept the fundamentally cyclical nature of life! My rational proposal is simpler to write than to apply, because besides a motivated capitalistic system and a rapid progress of AI capabilities and scope, there's a third final factor that would prompt individuals and companies alike would willingly adopt this valuable and relatively inexpensive AGI tool on a large scale.

If you've already seen the animated film *WALL-E,* you'll remember that humans have abandoned Earth and are living in a fully automated environment called Axiom. The latter is a huge spaceship where everything is controlled by a central computer called AUTO. Humans live in a world where everything is orderly and predictable, from perfectly manicured lawns to choreographed physical exercises. When they need to eat, they simply press a button and their food is delivered by a robot. When they need to exercise, they participate in a virtual reality program in which they follow a predetermined routine. At sleep time, they are placed in a capsule that optimizes their sleep. All these perfectly orchestrated systems have made the humans of Axiom lazy and complacent. They no longer have the ability or inclination to think for themselves or look after their own *Needs.* They've forgotten how to cook, clean and even walk. When faced with a problem or challenge, they had no idea how to solve it and relied on advanced machines and algorithms to do it for them.

This WALL-E scenario sounds like pure fiction, but it reflects a very real scenario for the coming generations. I call this process "**the comfort trap**", which, in my opinion, is the main indirect cause of the failure of the human Titanic. Imagine it's 1912 and you are entrusted with the management of the famous ship, Titanic. You're congratulated on this prestigious position and given a lecture on the magnificent technological prowess of this naval monster, including the fact that it is unsinkable, unless bombarded by advanced aliens. Obviously, as a novice captain, you can feel a lot of stress. So let's add a dozen years' experience to your captain's CV and assume you're confident and relaxed, since this is just another voyage like the hundreds that have gone before.

This overconfidence is exacerbated by the fact that the first four days of your trip have been uneventful, with no signs of danger. What's more, the crew and passengers look happy and carefree, allowing you to relax and enjoy your Cuban cigar on this calm and peaceful night. Although you've received a few warnings about icebergs here and there, you and your watch were already aware of them before departure and were ready to act if necessary. In any case, what could a tiny iceberg do to an unsinkable ship? So there's no question of reducing speed by 20 knots, risking missing the arrival time and disrupting the well-structured schedules of the many wealthy passengers.

You can imagine that in a world where everything is orderly and predictable, as in the case of Titanic or Wall-E, humans can easily fall into the trap of **complacency, overconfidence and laziness,** which automatically leads, one way or another, to chaotic results. A small virus or an errant iceberg is all that was needed to disrupt the calm of Wall-E's spaceship and Leonardo DiCaprio and Kate Winslet's famous transatlantic vessel respectively. That said, this is a perfectly natural evolutionary process. Darwinist evolution has favored energy efficiency and conservation, because in our past lives as primates, we may have had to conserve energy to survive in environments where food was scarce and hunting was physically demanding. In fact, our ancestors took the easier path, for example, by using tools and weapons to hunt and avoiding unnecessary effort. Those who were hyperactive and wasted too much energy did not survive long enough to pass on their genes to subsequent generations. Since the brain consumes most of our daily energy, around 20 percent, it's logical that this vital organ is also constantly seeking the simplest and most efficient ways to meet our various needs.

Our minds usually whisper softly: "Look around you! All is well. You have nothing to fear. Your job is secure, even if you lose your motivation. Just do the minimum required. Are you hungry? There are so many choices available at the click of a button, no more hunting or cooking for food. Oh, have you seen the latest Netflix release? It's wonderful!" This is not to say that our brain encourages us to do nothing. In fact, it naturally hates prolonged inactivity. Most of us feel the need to do something, anything, except stand still in Zen mode. Our brain's evolution has conditioned us to associate immobility with a possible threat of starvation, thirst or predators – in short, death. However, when faced with two tasks A and B that lead to the same result, our biological CPU will generally choose the easier option, everything else being equal. That's pretty much the whole idea of heuristics, cognitive shortcuts and the use of nudging to influence our lazy decision-making process.

This cerebral dilemma has led many of our fellow citizens astray. Take, for example, the vicious circle of obesity. In this case, comfort translates into cheap and easy access to food, especially fast food, combined with a sedentary lifestyle with cars and public transport close at hand, and an innate hatred of pain, namely sadistic time spent in the gym. Why waste a week learning to cook Moroccan couscous, and half a day preparing it, when Burger King is just around the corner or a few minutes away on Deliveroo. Why bother with physical activity when fat-burning belts are cheaper than a gym membership? Why cycle for an hour on a cold day, sweating like a pig, when you get to work, instead of streaming the next episode on your smartphone from a heated subway seat. According to the World Health Organization (WHO), obesity has almost tripled worldwide since 1975. In 2021, an estimated two billion adults were overweight, representing around 30 percent of the world's population. The World Obesity Atlas 2022 report, published by the World Obesity Federation, predicts that one billion (meaning very overweight) people globally, including 1 in 5 women and 1 in 7 men, will be living with obesity by 2030.

This quest for the "shortest path" is as much mental as it is physical. Let's remind here that the physicist Erwin Schrödinger argued that, throughout the history of the Matrix, dynamic agents have almost always sought to counterbalance the inherent Chaos and increasing entropy in their environments by establishing a certain predictable Order, fueled by an internal biological clock, communication and social bonds, and habits of hunting, reproduction, defense, play, etc. In a similar way, throughout our short history, Man has constantly strived to create more Order and predictability in his environment. From the earliest civilizations, where agricultural practices and human settlements structured people's lives, to the development of complex social, political and economic institutions, we have sought to impose organization on the chaotic nature of existence. We have devised legal systems to guarantee fairness and justice, established governments to maintain social order, and built infrastructures to facilitate communication and trade. Thanks to advances in science and technology, we have acquired a better understanding of the natural world, enabling us to harness its strengths for our own benefit and create systems that operate with greater efficiency and reliability. So I say with conviction: in the West today, and in the rest of the world through the historical processes of colonization, globalization and acculturation, we have become **control freaks**.

Through innovative transformations that have touched every aspect of the physical Matrix, and which continue to convert everything into data on scattered networks, and through a modern ego in hyperinflation, a super-ego, we continue to twist the dualistic nature of life to our present benefit, a nature whose beauty and mysticism lies precisely in the balance of Order and Chaos, the predictable and the uncertain, the material and the intangible, the Yang and the Yin. Worse still, in order to compensate, if only artificially, for this growing lack of adventure, we innovate theme parks, game consoles, cheap alcohol, Netflix thrillers and endless dopamine-inducing gadgets. We also innovate applications that stimulate our instinct for **instant gratification**. From food delivery to streaming services, social media, carpooling, online shopping, dating apps, fitness trackers, news, games, messaging, music streaming, productivity tools, navigation, photo editing, financial transactions, language learning, weather forecasting, home automation, virtual assistants and much more. These innovations offer a whole world of possibilities, but to what end? To give you more time and freedom? Sure, but to do what? Because that same "what" would turn into a *Need* to be fulfilled by another entrepreneur and would be replaced by a machine or software that would do it better than you, in which case you'd have more time to move on to another what, and so on ad infinitum.

We've come to forget that **a process – hunting, cooking, child-rearing, dishwashing, walking, working, etc. – is what matters most**, not the

destination. Let's abandon all sense of life, all difficult quest, all uncertain future, and end up like the characters in Wall-E, or better still, let's upload our brains to a server and play eternally at a simulation we'll call "life". At least, with each "Game Over", we'd be sure to play again and again, an infinite cycle of reincarnation or digital Samsara, for which we'd end up forgetting the initial objective: **JUST TO BE**!

In fact, instead of a linear identity for *innovation,* which begins with a predefined or post-confirmed *Need,* and ends with a given *Value,* so many individuals of recent generations find themselves in a vicious loop, in which one satisfied *Need* automatically and rapidly gives rise to another, like an Epicurean addict looking for his next "shot" not only for pleasure, but to soothe his psychological and existential sorrows (see the figure below). I may be exaggerating a little, but a historical view from a sufficiently high altitude would tell you as much as I do about the chaotic effects of innovation driven by a human mind in search of control, pleasure and ease. We can do better as a "modern" species.

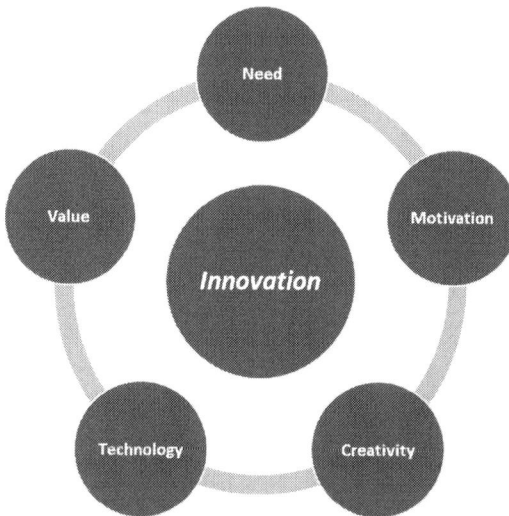

A major problem in the making of this vicious loop is its unique sense of direction. Unless forced to do so by a Black Swan event (war, meteorite, tsunami, etc.), we jump from one *Value* to a better one, not the other way around. No one of this generation would lament the lack of camels in the city, the time you could spend in the sunshine, tilling the Earth with a hoe", or candlelight illuminated nights in the Middle Ages. On the contrary, we're always looking to improve our comfort and convenience, even if it means increasing dependence on automated systems. In a world dominated by advanced machines and AGI, where convenience and instant gratification reign supreme, the transformation of human behavior is gradual but profound. As technology advances, future generations risk gradually forgetting traditional skills and relying heavily on automation. For example, handwriting is heading toward obsolescence as typing has become the norm, and soon typing will begin to fade as voice recognition takes over. Finally, perhaps this last semi-human option will become unnecessary one day when brain sensors are able to read our thoughts and intentions directly.

The human desire for ease and efficiency is driving this evolution, where machines and AI meet our every need, blurring the line between human and artificial interaction. While the future promises to be practical, it also raises questions about the potential loss of our unique human capabilities and dependence on technology for the simplest tasks. Incidentally, this transformation has been well underway for centuries now, ever since we descended from the trees as primates over four or five million years ago. It's just that, like all long-term natural innovations, this metamorphosis of the human species has taken a long time. And just like any other *innovation*, the S-shaped adoption curve is relatively slow at first, then takes off exponentially, before flattening out or even declining.

I believe that the take-off of this human rocket was initiated during the Agricultural Revolution over 10,000 years ago, before accelerating since the 15th century AD with all the innovative and scientific plethora, finally reaching this last phase of growth in the 2000s with the 4.0 Revolution. In a world where humans have long embraced biological augmentation through various innovations such as cars, planes, phones, and virtual networks, we have become "**augmented humans**". These tools have expanded our capabilities, making us more efficient and more connected. If we look to the future, such augmentation is set to become even more advanced. Brain-computer interfaces, wearable devices and advanced AGI systems thus have the potential to further enhance our capabilities, blurring the boundaries between Man and Machine.

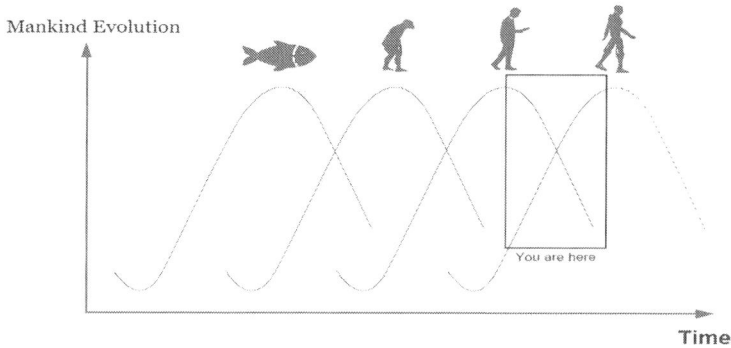

In brief, as displayed in the figure above, we are entering a rapid era where our very essence as human beings is intimately linked to the progress we create. This latter offers immense possibilities to go beyond the first level of Maslow's pyramid towards even virtual needs, eventually creating other Matrixes in metaverses of our own liking, going beyond the limited framework of our body and mind, of our time and space. On the other hand, it raises ethical and philosophical questions about our identity, the nature of humanity as such, and the potential consequences of our growing dependence on the looming species. What's more, this perpetual quest for technological progress and innovation drives us to seek solutions that meet our immediate needs, but often to the detriment of our resilience and adaptability. A logical consequence of all this analysis is the significant risk that future generations will lose their ability to cope with challenges and situations that seem obvious and under-control to us now. In fact, we are fast approaching **the mature stage of our evolution**.

The future of our humanity hinges upon this ability to strike a dynamic and delicate balance between technological augmentation and our capacity to remain fully engaged, conscious and responsible human beings. Thus, the 21st century stands as a pivotal era, a period of turbulent transition, a painful transformation from "La Mar" to "El Mar", then hopefully to a better "La Mar", whatever that means, and that's the biggest issue. Because my argument may not make sense to many individuals and innovation experts, who would argue that seeking more and more convenience, comfort and human capabilities' upgrade is the purpose of our recent innovation era. Maybe. Maybe not. It all depends how ready are we as a species, in the few decades and centuries to come, to spend our fresh free time in self-actualizing tasks and adventures rather than falling down to the bottom stages of the Maslow pyramid, eternally intoxicated by easy pleasures and instant gratifications, till forgetting who we are, really.

CHAPTER V

FISHING LIONS IN THE DEEP

"Reality is merely an illusion,
Albeit a very persistent one." – Albert Einstein

[...] With no breath or energy left, I made my decision. I let go.

As I gave up all resistance, a strange serenity came over me. I had let myself be carried away by the current, guided by the erratic movements of the waves. The tumult of the ocean seemed to gradually fade away, giving way to a soothing silence. I disconnected all my senses and felt my spirit rise above this virtual reality.

And then, all at once, I opened my eyes.

I lay on the shore, the warm sand caressing my skin. Incredulous, I stood up, scanning my body for wounds, for signs of my ordeal. I found nothing. Not a scratch. I was alive, intact. Time had flown. Even more surprising was the feeling of lightness and freedom I now felt. It was as if the chains holding me to artificial reality had been broken. I felt more real than ever, freed from the limits imposed by this highly structured and illusory Matrix.

I took a deep breath, filling my lungs with pure air. I could feel the power flowing through me, a new and unexplored energy. I had discovered a part of myself I never knew existed, an unsuspected inner strength.

As I contemplated the infinite horizon, I realized that I had found my place in this chaos, that I was in harmony with this changing reality. I was no longer a mere actor in a pre-established scenario, but a creator of my own destiny. I was playing with illusion, instead of resisting it.

I stepped away from the beach, walking confidently into the unknown that lay before me. I was ready to explore this new world with my new eyes, to challenge the limits of what was considered possible. For I knew that true freedom lay not in the pre-established Order outside, but inside my code, my soul.

And now, the adventure continues...

ॐ ✳ ॐ

Till this comma, I mostly described and discussed the evolution of our universe, of our planet, of dynamic agents, and then of ourselves. I've provided the framework of the Fundamental Identity of Innovation, which supported our narration, justifying how and why we are where we are today, as a species, as societies, and as individuals. Despite integrating some of the ancient wisdom about the concepts of change, duality and life cyclicity in Chapter II and what followed, I mostly remained within the realm of the physical, the materialistic, the visible or easily accessible side of the Matrix, in short, what you call "REALITY". Therefore, before concluding my book, and to respect the second title of the cover, I'd like to focus on a relatively more advanced theme, on "**the dark side of the Matrix**". Advanced not in its complexity, but on the contrary, in its meticulously camouflaged simplicity in the fabric of this world, meaning that few of us detect this magic trick. We mainly observe *innovation* all around us in terms of processes, concepts and natural or man-made products. We see ourselves as the subject, while everything else is an object of observation. It's time to turn the tables and look for a hidden *innovation* deep within ourselves, which, I warn, could disrupt your mind, your materialistic and well-structured thought patterns, and literally the way you interact with any agent of the Matrix. So, with that said, feel free to close this book at this point and go on with your life as it is.

1

UNDERSTANDING THE MATRIX LIKE AN ENGINEER

In 2015, a photo of a dress went viral on social media. At first glance, the dress is nothing special. It's a dress of average quality, modest design and unattractive colors. However, what makes the photograph so fascinating is the way it plays with our visual perception. The colors of the dress appear differently to different people, creating a fascinating illusion. Some people see gold with white stripes, while others see black with blue stripes. The photograph has thus been dubbed "**the dress illusion**" and has sparked discussions about perception, color and how our brains interpret visual information. I'll let you Google it.

A few surveys have been conducted in this context, and the statistics vary. From my survey with students in class, a half-and-half ratio is common. One half of the class sees gold, the other sees blue and black. So don't worry, there's nothing wrong with your view if you only see one side of this interesting duality. Nevertheless, a philosophical question arises. Which colors are "real", and which are just an illusion?

Needless to say, the dissemination of this dichotomous image has given rise to a fair deal of research. It is accepted that we see colors thanks to two types of retinal cells: rods and cones. Rod cells help you detect light and dark, while cone cells are responsible for color vision, perceiving shades of red, green or blue. The retina has around 100 million rods and between six and seven million cones. Color vision depends on the proper functioning of all three types of cones. In cases of color blindness, for example, one set of cone cells ceases to function effectively. However, variations between individuals' retinal cells are unlikely to be the cause, in general. Such disparities only lead to slight differences in color perception. Rather, the debate sparked by this photograph in February 2015 was due to something much more important than the typical inter-individual disparities between rods and cones.

After much thought and discussion, most researchers agree that the phenomenon known as "color constancy" is at the root of the confusion. According to *IFL Science*, this concept means that "the setting or environment in which an object is perceived can affect our understanding of its color". In other words, the colors perceived by viewers may have been influenced by the environment in which their minds assumed the photo was taken. This is what the scientific community calls top-down processing. Indeed, neuroscientist and psychologist Pascal Wallisch has researched this phenomenon, and his findings suggest that the brain makes assumptions based on the environment of the object in the image, then compensates for what it believes to be natural or artificial light. Wallisch noted that "shadows over-represent blue light", so if people assumed the dress was in shadow, they would see it as white and golden. Conversely, people who saw the dress in blue and black probably subtracted the longer wavelengths, colored red, to align with the assumption that the photo was taken under warm, artificial light.

Now that we know the science behind color constancy and how our brains make assumptions about environments, another question remains: Why do colors appear differently to different people?

Wallisch's thorough investigation of the question of the dress led to the following hypothesis. The development of natural sleep *innovation* in animals and then humans has resulted in two classes of people: **larks and owls**. Larks represent people who naturally get up early, pray or do yoga, walk their dogs, and spend more time exposed to natural daylight, while owls tend to sleep later, party or watch movies perhaps, and wake up later. I've romanticized the narrative with yoga and Netflix, but you get the idea *a priori*, as you've already classified yourself just now into one category or the other. The theory postulated here is that owls, being less exposed to natural light, are more likely to perceive dress in the light of artificial lighting and so for them the colors appear to be black and blue. Conversely, larks, who have been in more warm daylight, tend to think that the dress was illuminated by natural light and was therefore white and golden. Please refer to the figure below.

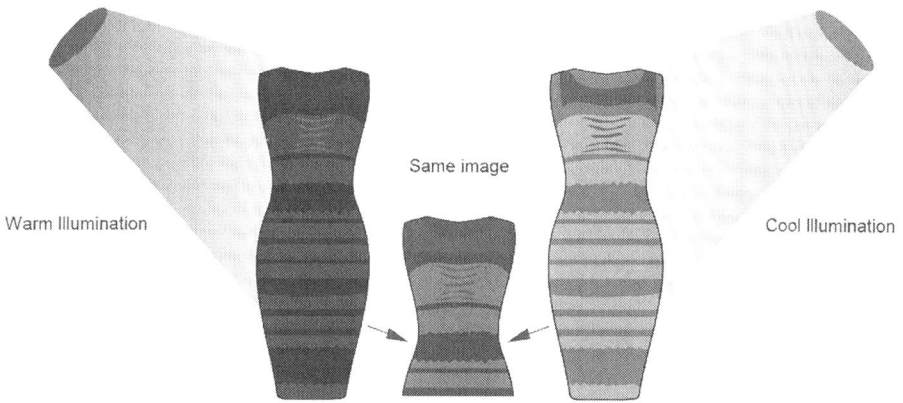

Same image

Warm Illumination

Cool Illumination

Notwithstanding the lark and owl argument, which is not statistically confirmed yet, color is essentially a phenomenon that relies heavily on mental interpretation and personal experience. Variables such as cataracts, lighting, context and individual observation history can all influence the way we perceive different hues. This notion has been highlighted by the phenomenon of the dress, whose colors are totally subjective and depend on assumptions the mind makes without really understanding the reason, much like AGI offers surprising results without its developers understanding the step-by-step algorithmic sequence.

It was an image I fell in love with at first sight (yes, my curiosity is very romantic!). Because although there are hundreds, if not thousands, of other optical illusions, the one with the dress is special. In the following figure, for example, you can see the old woman first, then notice half the young woman's face after focusing your attention on the image for a little longer.

Once discovered, you can go back and forth, choosing to see the old woman's face or the young woman's face with little effort. Research has suggested that the younger you are, the more likely you are to see the younger face first and vice versa, which corresponds in some way to the availability bias: we remember more of what we see often in our daily lives. This argument aside, the special thing about the "dress illusion" is that **it's not an illusion**. The whole concept of illusion involves being deceived by someone or something, and then, by looking or searching, discovering the reality. Here, with the dress, you have no choice. Whatever you do, you're going to see either white and gold, or blue and black. **The illusion is your reality**.

I've deliberately focused on this visual trick, because the eye is our most-used evolutionary asset for navigating this world. We use it almost constantly, from waking up to going to sleep, from childhood to death for most people. So, it should be reliable and provide accurate information about our environment, right? Yes, that's right. No argument presented here or elsewhere contradicts this fact. Apart from certain biological defects of vision, such as myopia or certain types of color blindness, the eye, this natural *innovation*, is a fantastic tool. In fact, we should be grateful for it, given its *Value* in the survival of our ancestors, both human and animal, in detecting danger, foraging for food, building useful objects, and even reporting some beauty of this world. But how can it display false, even contradictory, views of reality?

If we stick to the materialist perspective, what we call "reality" designates the state of things as they exist, independently of our perception of them. Simply put, the world is out there, and we're just here to observe it. If someone were to report seeing a blue dog, a flying fish or a dead person, we'd say they were visually impaired, a liar, insane, or a bit of all of these socially undesired characteristics. In fact, an illusion is a false perception or belief that doesn't agree with this independent reality. In other words, an illusion is something that appears to be real but isn't. That's why materialists love science and talk about the scientific method all the time. The fact is that the latter, is, or at least appears to be an objective approach to understanding reality. Objective because it verifies hypotheses behind the existence and working of objects and processes without taking into account what we, the subjects, have to believe.

While science did serve us in decrypting the physical side of the Matrix and innovating advanced products, it is important to recognize that even the scientific method is not entirely free from assumptions and potential paradoxes. One aspect where the scientific method assumes something is in the form of hypotheses and theories. Scientists develop hypotheses based on observations and prior knowledge and paradigms, and these hypotheses serve as the starting point for scientific investigations. However, the choice of hypotheses itself involves a certain degree of subjectivity and preconceived notions. For instance, if I want to develop a new gravitational model, I may have to assume that the Big Bang is true, that time is dependent on speed, that 1+1=2, etc. Some of these assumptions may seem obvious to you, but remember, evert assumption is based on past assumptions, so nothing is obvious when inspecting reality, there is always a degree of fate in the past and accepting to play with the rules of the Matrix. I'll let you check Russell's paradox for instance if interested in challenging few of your assumptions about the simplicity of the world and the perfection of human reasoning and logic.

Returning to our mystery dress dichotomy, and supposing science is "real", a scientist or materialist would probably ask to run tests on this one, to study the chemical color pigments and molecules in the fabric, before drawing conclusions about the wavelength it projects and the colors to which it belongs on a standard color scale. It all sounds clever and well thought-out. Science still does a remarkable job of explaining abstract concepts and clarifying tendentious debates, but this is not how most animals experience and communicate reality. We ask a friend to bring us a red apple. We don't ask:

- Hey, buddy, please throw me a spherical piece of red fruit rich in vitamin C and antioxidants, which are essential for maintaining a healthy immune system.

- Confused? It's mainly made up of water, carbohydrates in the form of sugar and dietary fiber, and various vitamins and minerals such as vitamin C, vitamin A and potassium.

- You still don't get it? Sorry. Red is actually due to the presence of pigments called anthocyanins. These pigments are water-soluble and are responsible for red, blue and violet colors of fruit and vegetables. They are a type of flavonoid, a group of natural compounds with antioxidant properties.

- Am I not making myself clear? Well, pass me a banana instead. Need an explanation ?

Although scientific models standardize our understanding of the world and its predictability and therefore its Order, **our individual experience of the Matrix is ultimately our reality.** The major error of all materialist philosophy is that it separates subject from object, observer from observed, Chaos from Order. Yet these are the same dualistic pair, the same creative process of all reality. In fact, madness is merely a social concept describing other personal realities, not necessarily a misperception, a human bug. To rephrase Steve Jobs, the most disruptive innovators are the craziest. What's more, given that our species has evolved to survive, as demonstrated in the first chapter, it's not surprising that what we see, however standard and shared it may be, **is not THE reality, but ONE reality**. It's a simple graphical interface whose underlying mechanisms we don't know, we can't access, and we don't care to know as long as we survive, reproduce, TikTok our day or do whatever else we do to occupy ourselves or satisfy our hedonist tendencies in this tricky simulation.

2

LIVING LIKE A CRAB OR A CAR

Vast and ever-changing, the world around me is made of an infinite expanse of sand and water, where the waves come and go with the tide. As I creep along the beach, I feel the sand move under my claws and the cool breeze rustle my antennae. Suddenly, I see it: an imposing wall of water rises up in the distance. I scramble for the rocks, my heart racing as I hear the roar of the oncoming wave. I climb onto a rough surface and wait, watching as the wave crashes onto the shore, sending sprays of water into the air.

When the water recedes, I cautiously emerge from my hiding place, scanning the beach for food and other creatures. I use my sense of smell to detect the scent of nearby prey and my sharp claws to cling to sand and rocks. My eyes are located on peduncles that can move independently, enabling me to see in several directions at once. What's more, they're made up of several lenses, providing me with a wide field of vision, but mainly capturing only green and blue. Handy in my marine environment. It helps me keep an eye out for predators, such as birds or larger animals, that might try to catch me when I'm out in the open. In addition to my keen sense of sight, I also have a very sensitive sense of smell that enables me to detect food sources, as well as potential dangers, from a distance.

Living on the beach is both challenging and rewarding. I have to be constantly vigilant, on the lookout for predators and changing conditions. But I can also enjoy the warmth of the sun and the cool morning ocean breeze. From my vantage point on the shore, which is also my zone of dominance over my peers, I can see the vast expanse of ocean stretching to the horizon. I watch the clouds drift lazily across the sky and the sun slowly set in a blaze of red and orange. At night, the beach comes alive with the sound of crickets and other creatures. I scurry across the sand in search of food and shelter. So, despite the constant caution, I also take the time to appreciate the beauty of the world around me.

While strolling along My Khe beach in Da Nang, Vietnam, I came across a group of small crabs going about their daily business, which prompted me, as a pure geek, to imagine what their lives might be like. It turns out that the conscious, unstimulated experiencing of the world through the senses of another creature is an intriguing and stimulating exercise in itself, and many works of art have explored this concept in various forms. Namely, I think of "The Weeping Elephant" by Salvador Dali, painted in 1946, a surrealist painting depicts an elephant with elongated legs and a sorrowful expression, or "Garden of Earthly Delights" by artist Hieronymus Bosch, painted between 1490 and 1510, displaying a triptych painting of surreal and fantastical landscape filled with bizarre creatures, hybrid forms, and symbolic imagery. To better understand what I'm philosophizing about, let's model Man, like a materialistic scientist, as a car in order to grasp his perception of reality. So, instead of using the same image of Man as a bipedal creature with a head, two arms and a belly, let's use our imagination to abstract him.

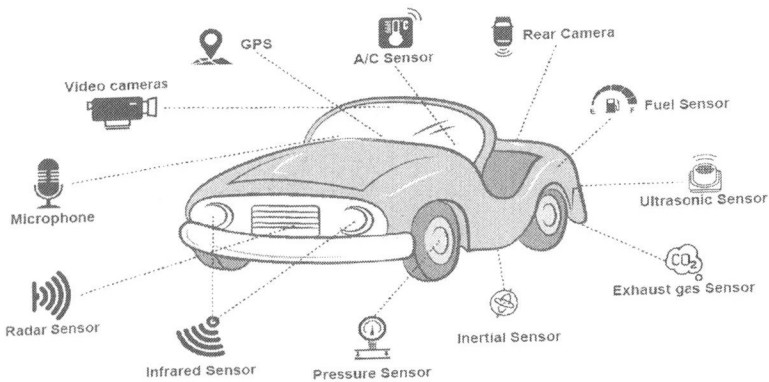

GPS
A/C Sensor
Rear Camera
Video cameras
Fuel Sensor
Microphone
Ultrasonic Sensor
Exhaust gas Sensor
Radar Sensor
Infrared Sensor
Pressure Sensor
Inertial Sensor

Like Man, a modern vehicle is a relatively complex, closed system, with a body and a few openings, and software that plans and controls intelligent movements. Above all, it consists of a combination of complementary subsystems. To name just a few, a mechanical subsystem comprising the engine, transmission, suspension, etc. work together to generate power and motion, and control the car's speed and direction. The electrical subsystem includes the battery, alternator and starter motor. These subsystems power the car's various systems and accessories. The electronic subsystem uses computer software and various sensors to control and monitor the car's various components and provide information to the driver. Finally, to protect the car's occupants in the event of an accident, airbags, seatbelts and various warning gadgets ensure safety.

So, while humans naturally have eyes to perceive the outside world, a car is equipped with sensors such as LIDAR, which acts like a pair of high-powered binoculars enabling the car to scan the road and its surroundings. The human agent uses their brain to process information and make decisions. A car is equipped with an onboard computer that acts like a mini brain, controlling and monitoring all the car's systems. And just as a human being relies on a heart to pump blood to all parts of the body, a car relies on an engine to pump fuel to all parts of the car, enabling it to move. Add to this legs for walking and arms for grasping objects, while a car has wheels for rolling and a steering wheel for changing direction. Finally, just as a human being needs to sleep and eat to recharge, a car needs to be recharged and refueled.

Pythagoras, the famous philosopher and mathematician of the sixth century BC, declared that all aspects of reality can be described by mathematical relationships. Described, yes, but experienced too, no doubt. Once again, **we experience reality more like a car than a nerd** in a laboratory. Our five senses and others are windows to the outside world and bridges to the inside of our bodies. But they're only biological sensors. And like all sensors, they clearly have their limits. The LIDAR of an autonomous vehicle, like a camera, has a limited scanning range. In the same way, our eyes only perceive wavelengths in a limited range, 400 to 700 nanometers, in a limited angle. Even my husky can see the ultraviolet, whereas I can't. An ear, like a sound receiver, only picks up sounds within a relatively restricted range of radio frequencies, from 20 Hz to 20,000 Hz. In comparison, bats have a much wider range of hearing than humans, with the ability to detect sounds with frequencies up to 200,000 Hz or more, enabling them to use echolocation to navigate and hunt.

We can also observe our sensory limitations on a kinesthetic level. With your eyes closed, you can easily mistake one fabric or product for another. Tasting and smelling also depend on the micro-receptors of the tongue and nose, respectively, and miss a variety of flavors and odors that are still unknown to you or that can be easily confused with other sensory inputs. These imperfections in the quality and limited bandwidth of our human sensors are sometimes broken. Many people possess ultra-sensory gifts, either by nature or by education. You've probably heard of the musician who has a genius ear or fingers, or the soccer player who has formidable field vision. These are exceptional cases. Most of us are still in the middle of the bell curve.

By linking closed systems to the internal and external worlds, sensors are of vital importance to human life and car driving. Imagine being blind, deaf and deprived of your senses of smell, taste and touch. To you, this may seem like a situation of death or coma. However, if we assume that your brain is still active, it would be more like a state of endless meditation in a quiet, odorless place, with eyes closed and ears plugged. The reason to prefer the latter metaphor to that of death lies in your internal memories and images. If you lose all your senses at a sufficiently advanced age, you can still visualize faces and situations, remember smells and pieces of music, which would arouse emotions and get a few hormones moving inside you. That's when you become truly aware of your internal state and understand that your mind is the epicenter of your reality. You don't need to try the experiment, though. Let me explain.

If we focus on the diagram below, reflecting Shannon's information theory applied to humans, the eye or input sensor is simply the means by which you pick up signals from the world. Obviously, the better equipped this means is, the stronger the stimulus signal you can subsequently transmit to the CPU. An eagle can detect a mouse on the ground more than a mile away. A well-trained dog can sniff out and then dig up truffles in a vast

Italian territory. The same dog may not detect the red and orange of the color spectrum, which photoreceptors in our retina allow us to capture.

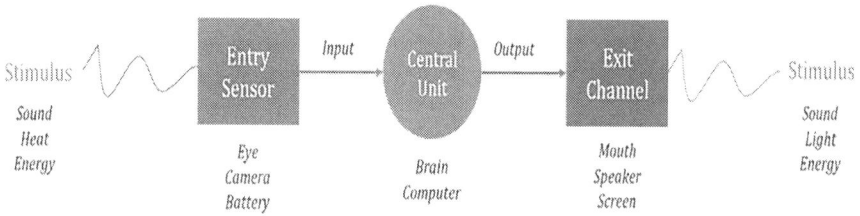

Stimulus		Entry Sensor	Input	Central Unit	Output	Exit Channel		Stimulus
Sound Heat Energy		Eye Camera Battery		Brain Computer		Mouth Speaker Screen		Sound Light Energy

The sensitivity of a sensor is therefore important in determining what can and cannot be detected. Neuroscientists actually claim that we humans have more than five basic senses. Equilibrioception is the sense of balance, which helps us maintain our posture and stability, for example. Proprioception is the sense of body awareness, enabling us to perceive the position and movement of our body parts without relying on vision. Thermoception is the sense of temperature, enabling us to detect changes in temperature. Nociception is the sense of pain, alerting us to potential tissue damage. There's even a sense of time, enabling us to perceive and measure the passage of internal time, known as chronoception. Interception, on the other hand, is the sense of internal bodily sensations, such as hunger, thirst and fatigue. And I'll stop at stretch receptors, which detect muscle stretch and contraction and help us maintain correct muscle tone and posture, like a well-tuned guitar string. Let's just call them sensors.

All a sensor does is provide an electrical input to an intelligent central unit. You type on a keyboard or cuddle your pet, and almost instantly, the skin receptors on your hand create an electrical signal that travels through the nervous system via the spinal column to a certain neuronal area in the brain, magically creating the experience and sensation of touch. More generally, signals, mainly those related to a conscious act, almost always pass through the brain. The problem is that we live in a noisy world, with a variety of near-simultaneous stimuli. That's why we need an organ called the thalamus in our central processing unit. It's a small egg-shaped structure located deep in the brain, a bit like a relay center for sensory information. One of the main functions of the thalamus is to filter sensory signals in order to focus on the most important ones in a given situation. For example, if you're in a noisy room and trying to have a conversation with someone, the thalamus will filter out irrelevant sounds (such as background noise or the hum of the air conditioner) and amplify the most important signals (such as the person's voice).

This filtering is carried out constantly, even when we're asleep, so that we can sleep well. Most light signals stop at the thalamus. But when we're awake, once the filtering is complete, we're constantly constructing our map of the world by interpreting the signals on the basis of our memories and our cultural and social prejudices, among other factors. If we must or choose to respond in turn, we emit signals which are in turn communicated through output channels. So, when a savannah lioness hears a sound or sees a gazelle in the distance (external stimulus) and has been hungry for 30 hours (internal stimulus), a signal is sent from the eye, ear and stomach to the brain, which unconsciously triggers hunting mode and sends a physiological and chemical signal back to the heart and leg muscles to prepare for the operation by sending more blood to these areas.

Similarly, typing this text on my keyboard sends a signal to my laptop's operating system, which translates a click on each little square into an ad hoc letter on the screen. In turn, my eye receives this light stimulus from the screen and transmits it as an electrical signal to my brain, which reads it according to its map (fortunately, this includes Latin letters to interpret the symbolic art of writing). This loop can continue for some time, as long as I'm writing, providing a hybrid example of a combination of systems, human and digital, sharing the stages of the Shannon diagram.

This tricky process proves just how ignorant most of us are of our inner fabric, despite the innovative gadgets we possess, the advanced education we undergo and the developed societies in which we live. Advanced technology never equals enhanced consciousness. We continue, unconsciously and often consciously, to confuse reality as perceived by our senses with reality as interpreted by our brains. Ultimately, all data is binary, made up of 0s and 1s, or both simultaneously, if we think Qubits in quantum computing systems. As with an AI-based system, humans also process data in a binary way, as all information is ultimately reduced to neurons and synapses that either fire or don't fire in the brain. However, human beings are able to interpret and attribute meaning to these firing patterns, creating complex layers of understanding and perception. This is achieved through a variety of cognitive processes, including attention, perception, memory, reasoning and language. As the saying goes, "**the map is not the territory**". Similarly, the raw reality captured by our senses is disordered, nameless and colorless before it reaches the CPU, the brain.

The "rubber-hand experiment" is a classic demonstration of the brain's ability to adapt rapidly to sensory input and construct its reality. In this experiment, a subject sits at a table, arm hidden behind a screen. A realistic rubber hand is placed on the table in front of the subject, so that it appears to be their own hand. The experimenter then simultaneously strokes the rubber hand and the subject's hidden real hand with a brush so that the subject feels as though the sensation on the rubber hand is theirs. After several minutes of caressing, the experimenter suddenly stabs the rubber hand with a syringe. Even though the subject knows visually and rationally that the rubber hand is not their own, they still feel a sense of fear, pain and ownership towards the fake hand. This is because the sensory input from stroking has caused the brain to temporarily "map" the rubber hand as its own organ.

In the table below [26], we simplistically detail what your senses detect without a CPU, and what your mind or what you call "the self" theoretically perceives. The same human being, for instance, can seem very different to us from one day to another, based on the context, your recent memories, your mood, etc. The famous quantum physicist Werner Heisenberg has been quoted as saying: "What we observe is not nature,

---

26 Note that sensors don't have brains. In this figure, we assume they have a small one for the sake of argument. The translation into 0 and 1 corresponds to fictitious data. And the mind's interpretation depends, of course, on the observer – everyone has a particular experience, even in the same context.

but nature as affected by our observing mind. Thus, reality is defined by the mind that observes it".

SENSOR LEVEL	CONTEXT	NEURAL LEVEL	MIND LEVEL
A circular 3D shape with a vivid color	In a kitchen, Hunger, Table	0000001010010101 001010	A non-organic red apple
High-frequency noise	On a flight from Seoul to Paris	0101010101010100 100000	An annoying, crying baby
3 spheres within a sphere, with a slight curved line	In a French museum	1010101010101001 001010	Mona Lisa
Lots of charred air	With a friend, on a summer's day	1010100001010101 0100000	Barbecue picnic
A human	The house	1010100001010101 0101000	The perfect partner (First-year relationship)
The same human	The house	1010100001010101 01001100	Dysfunctional roommate (Years later)

The existence of a distance between external or internal sensors and the brain, both biological and artificial, implies a delay in the transmission of signals from our senses to our brain. This delay is due to the time needed for the signal to travel from the source to our senses, and for our nervous system to process and interpret the signal. This means that our perception of reality is never in real time, as we might suppose, but is always a fraction of a second to a few minutes or days behind what is actually happening. What's more, there is a latency between the stimulus and the reception of the signal by the sensor. This is easily observed when we see a bolt of lightning: the sound of thunder takes longer to reach our ears than the light from the bolt of lightning takes to reach our eyes, even though both phenomena occurred at the same time, light traveling much faster than sound. Let's also illustrate with a starry night.

In the Qur'an, a passage addresses a similar notion of this phenomenon: "I cannot swear by the position of the stars. And this is an oath – if you could know it – [of the] greatest" (Al-Waqiah, 75-76). In fact, when we observe the stars, we go back in time because of the considerable distances that separate us. Light travels at a constant speed of about 299,792 kilometers per second. On a clear, unpolluted night, if we look at the star Proxima Centauri, which is the nearest star to our solar system, we see it as it was some 4.2 years ago. Even our beloved Sun is about eight minutes further in the past than we observe it. Some stars, which we can still see from our vantage point on Earth, are no longer even there, having already died out decades or centuries ago.

Another troubling mental fact is our perception of life as a continuum, like a lifetime movie, hopefully more thriller or comedy than horror. The truth behind this illusion is that, like a film or cartoon, images, sounds and all conscious sensations are glued together, often chronologically, giving the impression of a continuum. But like the golden or blue dress, it's only an impression. Our minds don't perceive the world as a smooth, continuous flow of information, but rather as a series of discrete, individual moments that are assembled to form a coherent whole. **We literally hallucinate our realities** based on a strange, almost mystical mix of the external context, the internal memory and one's physiology, psychology of the moment, and so many other often unconscious factors.

The conscious mind is therefore an incredibly powerful tool, shaped by millions of years of evolution and perhaps a divine touch, but it does have its limits. One of these limits is that the it can only grasp and process one set of data at a time, unless it's operating on autopilot. So, when we are consciously focused on a particular task or stimulus, we are less likely to notice other stimuli around us. For example, if we're concentrating on reading a book, we may not notice a conversation going on nearby or a bird flying by the window. Similarly, when several colors are present, the mind perceives only the cumulative signal of a single color. Such feature allows us to focus on what's most important in our environment and filter out distractions. However, it also means that we can miss out on important information if we don't pay attention to the right (or positive) stimuli. This is what we call **selective attention** in cognitive psychology.

I purposely adopted a materialistic approach rooted in IT to explain our perception of reality, emphasizing its simplicity as a model. However, it's important to acknowledge the existence of alternative paradigms. For instance, during sleep, our perception of the external world is blocked by the thalamus, the egg-shaped gateway in the brain mentioned above. Yet, we continue to experience dreams and live through them without relying on our physical senses. Brain scans during the REM phase of sleep, when dreaming occurs, reveal heightened brain activity comparable to or even surpassing wakeful states. From a materialistic perspective, this suggests that our reality is constructed by the brain and its neurons, often unconsciously, but occasionally recalled upon waking, even during sleep, based on memories and future projections.

On the other hand, the non-materialistic view of dreams and reality hinges on the enigmatic concept of consciousness itself. According to this perspective, the brain acts as a receiver, a manifestation of mystical forces within the backdrop of our space-time dimension. Many religions, shamans, and mediums espouse this nuanced understanding. Jane Roberts' book *Seth Speaks* presents a fascinating example, where the persona or spirit of Seth, channeled through Jane's body, elucidates in a neat style the complexities of a malleable consciousness that manifests in various forms and dimensions, including matter, beyond our limited evolutionary perception of the Matrix.

In any case, my argument is the same as that of Buddha, Muhammad, Jesus and the hundreds of saints and mystics who have passed or are still living in our Matrix. Objective reality, as you probably understand it, and as studied by science and materialists throughout history, doesn't exist. There is no chair, no book, no sun, no emotions, no dreams, no line you're reading right now. The only condition that makes it all happen is **YOU**. In contrast to this materialistic approach, those who believe in a destiny or a god that controls every aspect of life, and therefore that reality is only subjective, are simply wrong. If I removed all the objects around and inside you, thus only leaving pure, silent darkness, would you be able to perceive or believe anything? A dynamic, delicate and mystical interaction between a subject and an object, tangible or not, such is "a" reality as I define it. It is therefore only partially subjective, biased, distorted, individual, dependent on objects too, and far, far away from the fundamental truth of the Matrix: **a nothing, which is also by duality, a whole.**

Beyond a feeling of depression, rejection or nihilism, why would an engineer slash professor slash geek slash lunatic tell you all this?

3

Innovating the Matrix like a god

My whole argument above is hardly intended to convert you into a Buddhist detached from the physical world, nor to depress any beautiful thing in you. My aim is for you too to understand, then to perceive maybe someday, this hidden face of the Matrix, and thus break the chains of your servitude to a fixed and perhaps excessively materialistic reality, for, once again, you are playing against the cyclical nature and dynamic equilibrium that governs every aspect of existence, as detailed in Chapter II. That said, everyone has their own story, their own destiny, and therefore their own specific reality. Whatever story is told to you in this book or elsewhere, by a scientist or a cleric, focusing on the object of study or exclusively on internal experience, know that it is at best a mental approximation or a useful model of the Matrix's mechanisms. **Reality, in the final analysis, is constructed by you, in interaction with the world**. Let me tell you something about my reality.

During my childhood in Morocco, when I played soccer in the narrow streets of the neighborhood, using an absent neighbor's garage door as a goal, that was my reality of what it means to enjoy life. When my father bought me Super Mario on the old Nintendo console, it was my new reality and I loved it. It was easy to change my identity back then, which was that of a child in a relatively stable family, and among my non-negotiable beliefs was "playing". At the start of my second decade, I was slowly transitioning to my new reality: school and the mosque. Fortunately, under no parental influence, apart from a little pressure to excel in my studies, I had chosen, unlike most of my peers at the time, to devote more time to prayer, playing games on floppy disks and school, than to hours lost in street soccer and testosterone-fueled teenage discussions.

A few years later, I found myself in France, my new home, culturally different from Morocco. This time around, the adjustment to my reality was less obvious, as the Muslim and Moroccan-based beliefs I'd built up over the years were holding me hostage in a way. For example, I hesitated for quite a long time, rationalizing the decision more than once before dropping the dietary notion of "Halal" and opening my appetite to more gastronomic choices. Similarly, when I got my first job in finance, it wasn't easy to convince myself to give up a well-paid but soul-draining position to try an entrepreneurial adventure and follow my passions, at the risk of disappointing myself (ego) and my loved ones. It took me a few more years of travel, varied artistic activities, constructive relationships and encounters, and continuous meditation in the making of everything, before I finally started to grasp the illusion of the brain, a process still-in-the-making, which the prophets and mystics of all times tried to pass off in various metaphors and lessons. **The ego, the self, to which you give an identity, based on a name, a history and a personality, is only the brain's interface for navigating the physical and visible side of the Matrix.**

Such view (or rather personal experience) seems in line with ancient wisdom, from the notion of non-self in Buddhism to the spiritual paradigm that all is consciousness, a sort of pure energy play, including matter. Science, with Einstein who set the tone in the 20th century with his famous $E = mc^2$, expressing energy as a mass in movement, and the magic world of quantum physics is starting to open its rigid ordered frontiers slowly to **the dark side of the Matrix**. We already mentioned Professor Donald Hoffman, a cognitive scientist and philosopher, who proposes the theory of "conscious realism," which challenges the traditional understanding of the world. According to Hoffman, our perception of reality is not an accurate representation of the external world but rather a simplified interface that aids our survival and reproduction. Hoffman argues that our senses and perceptual systems have evolved to **prioritize fitness over truth**.

On the same nerve, there is an interesting read by Dr. Bruce H. Lipton, a cellular biologist and pioneer in the field of epigenetics, entitled "The Biology of Belief". In this book, Dr. Lipton explores the relationship between biology, belief systems, and human behavior. He challenges the conventional belief in genetic determinism, and the classic Darwinist discourse of the arbitrary evolution of species. For Dr Lipton, the fairly recent field of epigenetics, should counterbalance the Darwinist monopoly, by arguing that a cell could have a consciousness beyond its DNA, and that, under the right circumstances, our beliefs and thoughts have a significant impact on our physical and mental well-being, beyond what seems possible.

In another field, neuroscientist Lisa Feldman Barrett proposes a unique perspective on emotions. She suggests that emotions are not fixed, pre-determined entities, but rather constructed by the brain in response to various inputs. According to her theory of constructed emotion, human emotions are not hardwired or universal, but rather emerge from the brain's interpretation of bodily sensations, context, and past experiences. She thus posits that emotions are not separate entities but are made of dynamic neural processes that are influenced by our individual histories, cultures, and contexts. In other words, emotions, such as anger, lust and fear, don't happen to us, but are constructed by our mind which interpret the world around it via the body (senses, hormones, temperature, etc.). That's why two individuals, even siblings, act differently in the same situation. In essence, any situation is neutral; there is no good nor bad except in your specific reality!

The preceding passages, which are grounded in scientific principles such as natural evolution, align harmoniously with ancient wisdom. As previously discussed, the teachings of Buddha, particularly regarding emptiness and dependent origination, propose that reality is not fixed but rather impermanent, arising from interconnected causes and conditions. According to Buddhism, attachment to the illusory nature of this "life delusion" leads to suffering. Whether it is the unfulfillment of desires or the fear of loss and greed for more, suffering persists. By cultivating mindfulness and insight, individuals can attain a profound comprehension of the transient nature of reality, the concept of "non-self," and ultimately experience liberation.

In the Abrahamic religions, notably Islam, we encounter the well-known dualistic notion of heaven and hell. Specifically, the life of this world, Hayat ad-Dunya, is regarded as temporary and fleeting, serving as a test and preparation for the eternal life of the Hereafter, Hayat al-Akhirah. The Qur'an underscores the impermanence and deceptive quality of worldly existence, describing it as a mere fleeting enjoyment when compared to the everlasting life that awaits. This belief system posits that the material world, including our physical reality, is fundamentally flawed and disconnected from the divine, from the dark side of the Matrix. It is considered an illusion or a prison that obscures the true spiritual essence of existence. The narrative of Adam and Eve's expulsion from a state of eternity and knowledge to a state of ignorance and attachment in the Genesis story exemplifies a test: to determine who will remember their true nature, paving the way to heaven, and who will remain trapped in the illusion of this worldly realm, destined for an infinite-loop of suffering in hell.

Essentially, the same conclusion regarding the illusory nature of reality, which science is gradually unraveling, has long been recognized by prophets and mystics throughout history. This concept can be summarized in the following analogy: Each living being has a unique perception of reality, represented by a screen, akin to a user interface connected to an information processing system. Most agents, except a few human beings, obviously don't see the trick since they identify their ego, their essence, with their system and user interface. Moreover, agents, from all types, can also communicate with one another through various channels such as language and vibrations. A question then arises:

If you possess an IBM computer running Windows 95, why not consider upgrading (or at least exploring) your reality to a MacBook with the latest operating system? Why not enhance your cognitive processes and alter your perspective to a more imaginative and artistic one? Why confine yourself to a static physical memory card when you could tap into the vast intuitive capacities of the Cloud? The latter question is where the remaining debate lies between science and Buddhism, on one side, and Hinduism, the Abrahamic religions, and various spiritual sects, on the other. Is there truly a transcendent cloud system beyond space and time, a higher consciousness or an omnipotent deity? Or is it also a mere illusion created by the mind, constrained within our limited interface? I shall reserve this profound topic for another book.

In this respect, I propose the following simplistic model, similar to a Cloud computing system (think of AWS or Google Cloud), with a bottom half of the figure already detailed in the above analysis (the tricky illusion), and a top half reflecting the metaphysical idea of God and the eternal soul, or the universal consciousness praised by mystics such Eckhart Tolle, which is beyond the time and space constraints, composed of infinite units of consciousness, or again, the collective unconscious by Carl Jung, which supports *Creativity* and *innovation*, as elaborated upon in Chapter III. Obviously, communication with the Cloud is not perceived by 99% of dynamic agents, including humans, although it may affect every aspect of our lives. We often limit ourselves to our little laptops, to the few gigabytes of our memory cards, instead of tapping into the Cloud, this non-material and unlimited source of creativity and freedom. Beyond its challenging character to the materialistic view of this world, such model beautifully depicts a sort of "monism" (finally, instead of duality!), a universal belonging of everything, across time and space, to a single entity, a central system. In other words, despite all apparent dualistic differences among the Matrix agents, deep down (or up), **we are ONE**.

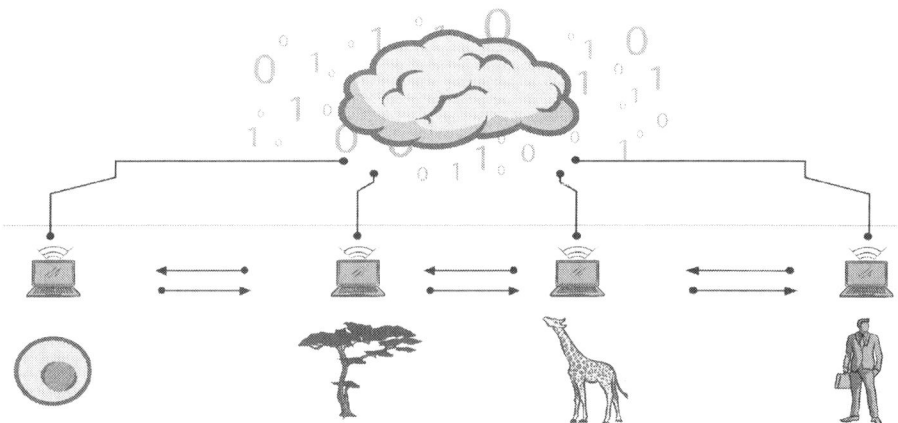

If you are still not convinced with your mind's magic trick, just look at how many organizational *innovations* have been imagined by the mind: money, states, institutions, social codes, religions, languages, the iPhone, etc. Even the term "mind" is imagined indicating something intangible, *a priori* represented by a nervous system, including the brain. Why, then, would it be difficult for such an innovative component within us to imagine, like a super powerful AI, an entire reality around an illusory figure, a persona woven on a floating memory? If that's the case, what's the point of inordinate control over who you are, and who you're supposed to be, if not for the good eyes (or pixels) of one image among others, dictated by society, family, religion, America or who knows what other ancient creation of that same mind? Why give so much egocentric importance to the multiple manifestations of this illusion, from success to anger, from esteem to jealousy? In short, why take ourselves too seriously?

My individuation journey[27], to use the psychological concept of the venerable Carl Jung, is easily generalizable to any belief, religious, political, professional or individual. Everyone has a more or less flexible identity, which they believe defines "who they are", individually and in society. And unless you're locked away in a monastery in the mountains of Myanmar, it's important to have one if you want to live peacefully among your peers. I'm not saying otherwise. My whole point is to open your eyes, not just to read these lines that you'll forget as soon as you get out of the metro or close this book, but to leave mental and physical comfort behind, and *experience, truly,* beyond the material, the apparent, and the illusory.

Needless to say, I'm not targeting any religious, inflexible or "evil" beliefs in particular. Even Westerners born in a free democratic country are programmed since conception then childhood to follow certain patterns, believe in socially innovated concepts (human rights, equality, capitalism, etc.) and sometimes arrogantly confuse their reality with "THE reality", with some ideal or objective truth that cannot exist without a subject, as

---

27 You can find accounts of this key phase of my struggle toward detachment from the illusion of self, in the form of a 55-day memoir, in my first book, *Rabbits & Dakchi*, on Amazon.

we've explained already. The ego of most people, including famous stars, politicians, scientists and religious fellows, is still this jealous master that wants to keep us enslaved in a comfortable little mental corner of limited consciousness, because an expanded reality or consciousness is too scary and useless for its basic needs. Your mind would try to persuade you:

Why bother going through all this pain for no evolutionary advantage? You can just keep believing in what you've always believed as reality, continue doing whatever makes you enjoy this life while it lasts (YOLO), protect your world with an external god (or thousands of them) if needed, or a comforting scientific model, get mad at whatever shakes your control of self, and automatically think that others, including people, cars and crabs, see space and time the same way you do, and if they don't, they must be crazy or outdated. Mostly, avoid venturing into a tiger's cave, a risky project or another dimension of the Matrix, because you may lose the most important thing you have: Me (or at least, the illusion of me).

The mind argues in this way because such an assimilation of the true nature of reality, starting by opening one's heart to Chaos, to the uncertain, is definitely a dangerous path for the ego, for what you still call "I". A few people may build a new obscure reality on the other extreme of Chaos, what we give the social label crazy, terrorist or psycho. But what is suicide, for instance, if not a steep drift of the "ego" towards absolute Chaos, towards death? This is not a highly conscious act of devotion and selflessness, like in the case of the self-mutilating Vietnamese monk we've already mentioned, but rather a suffering ego under the illusion it's real and that it matters, deciding to put an end to its suffering. Thus, if I've put too much emphasis on letting go in my specific case, it's due to my rigid religious and scientific background where structure and Order were dominant. My "straight path" of individuation then led me to more craziness and connection with my deepest psyche. If, on the contrary, your life is messed up, lost, depressed or too chaotic, then maybe you better start by following the western discipline first, by raising your level of self-discipline, developing some healthy habits, getting in shape, taking some courses, reading some books, putting things in order, uploading more quality data to your brain, and reducing external stimulation such as drugs, sex, in short, finding some equilibrium on the Order side, before moving to oriental philosophies of letting go, of true happiness, and escalating the Maslow pyramid towards transcending illusionary reality.

In this respect, like any *innovation*, if managed correctly, with sufficient preparation, patience and support, the innovation of reality can only be beneficial to the innovator's future identity, as they move to a more advanced S-curve in the dimension of their choice. In this sense, like changing one user interface for another, a Windows 95 to a Windows 10, **your reality is "innovatable"**, by you and only by you, if you decide to accept this dualistic face of the Matrix, that reality and illusion are but two sides of the same coin. Contrary to the other Matrix agents, we, humans, have the gift (and the curse) to imagine what other user interfaces may look like, to create, test, have fun playing around with reality, till we reach a state liberation from the movie of our life, a state of "Islam", literally "giving up" in Arabic (which, ironically, most Muslims still don't grasp).

I'd argue that, at some point of your life, this one or another, your user interface too should be innovated, if not for a true happiness' sake, then just for the sake of being alive, exploring and breaking the chains of evolution and social conditioning. I repeat, for those who are just discovering the topic: your current reality, which you take for granted, is nothing but an illusion perfected by millions of years of natural evolution and decades of social conditioning. In contrast, your dreams, by day or night, your thoughts, your inventions and innovations, and any other mental product or persona kept inside you or projected into a virtual or physical world, are all part of reality, which is nothing other than your reality. And if you're a believer, this is all the truer. An external God, even if it turns out to be a mental illusion, remains a reality for you. On this theological subject, my reality assumes that any divinity could only admit to its territory a conscious entrepreneur who has grasped, or at least been inspired to grasp, this divine Matrix game, and to escape from the slavery of their thoughts, their society and their fears of Man and the gods. This is, as yet, only one reality among many. Let's apply the fundamental identity of innovation to the individuation process.

New Reality= (Need + Motivation) × (Creativity + Technology) × Value

a. *Need*: Emancipate yourself from the illusory chains of the Matrix; be (truly) happy, beyond fleeting pleasures (i.e., dopamine shots).

b. *Motivation*: Curiosity about life, mental dissonance, an incomplete life despite all the gadgets, titles and people that surround you.

c. *Creativity*: Get out of your comfort zone, dive into the Chaos (art, nature, etc.), stop listening to the illusory fears of your mind and ego, and follow your intuition.

d. *Technology*: Travel solo, follow other paths (studies, jobs, relationships, etc.), read books, contemplate & meditate, meet other cultures...

e. *Value*: awakening (from all delusion), paradise (on Earth), happiness (true).

I won't go into detail about the content of the above variables, which are for illustrative purposes only, leaving you a little Chaos in the interpretation of your own destiny. Your case is surely different from mine. Your malaise, or rather your *Need*, may relate to religion, your role in society, a lost love, a philosophy of life, a particular craving, a hidden fear, etc. Whatever it is, I'd just like to emphasize the practice of meditation as whose physical and mental benefits are scientifically justifiable. That's if you ever decide to launch your quest for individuation, of course. The reason is simple. If you want to verify that my proposal of an illusory reality is true, the proof is not in the pudding. You are the subject that perceives all reality around and within your body and mind. So it's within you that you must look for the answers. I repeat, the human being, myself included, creates nothing, only rediscovers what he forgot. In this respect, meditation, through its various techniques, consists in being in the present moment, **deprioritizing having, doing and pretending in favor of being**.

By the way, as this chapter's title indicate, yes, we can fish lions in the deep! lionfish! Or a drawing of a 5-year-old lion swimming! Or a lion shape submarine! Or a Lion King cartoon mixed with a Pixar scenario of Nemo. Creative ideas are limitless. So is your reality!

To sum up, with its wide range of applications, the concept of change finds its deep philosophical roots in **the dualistic balance** within our Matrix between two seemingly opposite but complementary poles: Chaos and Order, uncertainty and predictability, exploration and exploitation, excess and asceticism, and so on, in an infinite list. Although this dichotomy is arguably an illusion

FINAL NOTES

"My best memory? Now!" (well, few milliseconds before) – My Ego

I hope you've enjoyed this book, inspired by science, my experience and some divine intuition. Given my Moroccan upbringing, that I've lived since my youth in my adopted country, France and have traveled to 40+ countries, I'm often asked by family, friends and students whether I'm still a Moroccan Muslim, a nerdy French atheist, a universal Buddhist or some other esoteric affiliation. You may be led to answer questions of this order at the end of your identity *innovation* quest. My answer is always an honest, "All that! and maybe more. Do I have to choose?" The joy of knowing and expanding awareness, without judgment or attachment, should trump mental labeling, comforting the ego's inflexible ignorance. Allow me, however, to attempt a more detailed response in this regard, without any *Hchouma*, before moving on to a few final notes about the Matrix.

- If my Muslim origins are called into question, I call Allah to witness: "Indeed, in the creation of the heavens and the earth, and in the alternation of night and day, there are signs for those endowed with intelligence. Those who remember Allah, standing, sitting and lying on their sides, and **reflect on the creation of the heavens and the earth**" (Qur'an 3: 190-190).

- I'll leave it to Buddha to explain how important it is for everyone to do the work of discovery: "By day, the sun shines, by night, the moon shines, the seasons change and all living beings come and go. Just as the sun rises and sets, so do our thoughts and emotions. Through meditation, we can observe these changes in ourselves and in the world around us and understand the impermanent nature of existence. **By exploring the depths of our mind and cultivating mindfulness**, we can awaken to the true nature of reality and find inner peace".

- If atheism is what I'm accused of, I'm counting on one of the greatest scientific minds in the history of humankind, Albert Einstein, to come to my defense: "The most beautiful thing we can experience is **mystery**. It is the source of all true art and science. He to whom this emotion is foreign, who can no longer stop to marvel and remain open-mouthed, is as good as dead: his eyes are closed."

- Finally, for all those who think I'm crazy, and there are a good handful of them (including my mind sometimes), I suggest the words of Morpheus in the *Matrix* film: "The Matrix is everywhere, it's all around us [...] Unfortunately nobody can be told what the Matrix is, **you have to see it for yourself**".

What is the Value of the natural Innovation of Life?

This question comes back to questioning the purpose of life, or the *Value* behind all natural innovations, including ourselves, a question I avoided answering in the first chapter, for lack of data in your brain *a priori*. I fully understand that it's not easy to ask such a philosophical glue, especially at a young and immature age, or at an age close to death and therefore avoiding any weighty dissonance. Yet, as I have explained throughout this book, the trap of excess, comfort and pain-avoidance at all costs only leads our species astray towards an aimless end. Each reasonable individual must find their own path, according to the stage of life they are at. **So there is no generic answer.** If you are given one, know that it is a lie, or the advice of another soul lost in its fundamentalism. Personally, for example, optimizing freedom, for myself and others, by sharing my learning and experience, turned out to be the underlying principle towards which I let myself be guided, while enjoying the journey, of course.

This freedom takes tangible form, such as the freedom to move my body through different sports, financial freedom, geographical freedom thanks to my dual nationality, or a balanced emotional detachment from things, my surroundings and society. The next stage of freedom is mainly mental. Freedom from unjustified beliefs and superstitions. Freedom from some silly social and cultural handcuffs. Finally, the advanced stages of freedom encompass liberation from the ego, including all fears, such as fear of uncertainty, fear of renewal, and finally, fear of death itself. In my quest, there is clearly a Maslow ascent aspect which consists of realizing all that can be realized as a conscious agent of the matrix, of seeing the illusion of the game in order to play it better, without attachment or pain, and with that, to share my experience and learnings with other agents, in one way or another. It's also clear that I'm still on this long learning path and open to changes along the way, as more and more data is absorbed by the subconscious. Good news, I'm still not a slave to the search for freedom itself!

In any case, a choice of objective, of raison d'être, in full awareness and from the top of Maslow's pyramid, would be a builder of a happy reality and always preferable to an unreflected-upon decision emanating from the lower layers of survival and thus from a hidden fear of death, and by dualistic consequence, of life too. If you think about it, Hitler, bin Laden, Le Pen, Trump, and so many other figures relating to "evil", known and anonymous, base their paths in the Matrix on control, Order, excessive self-love, hatred of other groups, the super-ego, or on any failing and ignorant morality. However, the initial aim of all previous sects and belief systems was not to establish rituals and laws but to broaden people's field of vision to a divine dimension, beyond the Matrix illusion, a dimension of peace and universal love, not fear and withdrawal into oneself and one's group.

Does God (or gods) exist?

The question makes little sense without defining its subject. The divine means something different to everyone. If we're talking about the experience of the divine, the answer is clearly yes. All it takes is a sufficient dose of meditative practices and/or psychedelic stimulants at times, to have a profound spiritual experience. Thousands of people throughout history did express this heightened psychic manifestation, an absence of space and time, sometimes referred to as an "out of body" experience, a sense of absoluteness, inner peace and meaningful connection with God, nature, Brahma, the universe, the Father or whatever the title. On the other hand, if by God we mean an omnipotent supernatural creature who pulls the world's strings, rewards and punishes, as interpreted by a large proportion of believers, I prefer to keep my reservations. That said, in my experience and in light of the latest scientific theories, the Jungian idea of a collective unconscious, immaterial beings in the multiverse, and synchronicity or non-causal manifestation appeals to me more, because ultimately, our (real) reality is far more complex and multidimensional than what we perceive through our limited senses. Have you ever seen electromagnetic waves? Radio exists all the same. If ever a universal consciousness existed, as displayed in my simplistic Cloud model in Chapter V, I'd like to think it would be in phase, not to say happy, with any attempt to decipher this Matrix, to play the game fully, instead of following lines drawn by other innovators, or remaining in the protective illusion of one's own mind!

Religion certainly remains important to many people, including my family. As we read in the third Chapter, we are social creatures who need a sense of community, a well-established social order and some answers to complex existential questions about why we are in this game of life. Obviously, some leaders have used and still use religion to justify their gilded position. That said, sects, whether religious, political or otherwise, have their faults. Firstly, their interpretation is often biased and distorted from one teacher to the next, leading to opposing paths down the generations. As a result, people lose the fundamental wisdom transmitted by the first master or prophet (the why) and retain only the superficial layers of what to wear, how to pray, whom to marry (the what). Without the wisdom that justifies the act, the latter has no meaning and therefore no raison d'être.

Secondly, and more personally, a sect encourages the establishment of a certain order, sometimes justified, but often limiting individual freedom, thus sinking it into a conformist herd. Such *innovation* may have met a *Need* in the past to prevent uncivilized ancestral tribes from killing each other, or to structure a growing but largely illiterate society after the Agricultural Revolution. Nevertheless, in most countries today, peace and some degree of secular rather than religious structure are the norm. So, what's the point of religion, in its classical shape, today? Perhaps to maintain some of the family's unifying rituals, to put some of them at ease with their distorted reality acquired by birth. I've met happy theists and atheists. I've also met unhappy people from both clans. **Religion, as most people understand it, is hardly a criterion of happiness or misery.** What counts is to seek life's truths for oneself, considering the lessons handed down by masters, philosophers and even scientists with a critical eye, connect with other souls, and above all to make the most of one's youth, while the brain is elastic enough and the physical strength present, to experiment, challenge the status quo and reach one's own conclusions and potential.

How can I detect the Matrix?

By embracing God!

I understand that you're wondering if I have Alzheimer's and therefore if it was a reasonable idea to have continued reading until now. Rest assured, my brain is fine, but if it isn't, how could you tell the difference? (It doesn't help, does it?).

I sincerely believe that the real prophets, saints and awakened ones of this world have seen a similar truth, a Matrix, the truth of God, both everywhere and nowhere, which escapes all duality and space-time. Their experience and their words are difficult to match, for words are ultimately only a limited channel of communication, a once-created innovation serving survival and socializing needs first, not particularly adapted for reporting the mystical. Also, a language, no matter how comprehensive, only describes a map, not the real territory. What's more, as these words have been passed down, they have most likely been falsified or misreported. And even if they are exact "sacred" words, as most blinded religious followers often assume, the interpretation can be wrong. How do I teach Einstein's relativity to my three-year-old nephew? Such is the challenge of explaining the sacred to any self-illuded ego, with "sacred" incidentally also meaning "that which cannot be grasped". That said, if you're interested in this amusing spiritual path, or any other path of personal development not for any external *Motivation*, but to "see" better, I suggest some of the following generic axes.

First, raise your general level of **concentration**, i.e., the channeling of your energy. Once again, your solid body, as you imagine it, does not exist. We are energetic beings, and if you don't master this powerful flow, it will take you along like a stone follows the downstream current and like a dog has no choice but to follow the lead. In other words, learn to direct your energy towards what you choose to concentrate on, for example the project to decipher the Matrix illusion. Don't let your mind and body dictate what you should do all the time. A simple (but not easy) way of making progress in this area is to do things that you (i.e., your mind or your ego) don't want to do (no need for sadistic practices either). Playing sport, reading for hours on end, eating simply, going hiking, avoiding Netflix, taking on a new educational or professional challenge, staying alone for a week, taking cold showers... are just a few suggestions. Spiritualists also recommend this type of ascetic approach. Prayers, Samatha meditation, fasting, chanting, giving money, abstaining from lying, controlling your impulses, selflessly supporting others, in brief, all the harsh and boring stuff your mind wants to escape from to the land of passing pleasures.

The second guideline is to improve your general level of **mindfulness**, which means starting to understand the hidden mechanisms behind the Matrix. This understanding can be intellectual first, by reading nerdy books like this one, talking to a few spiritual masters, networking with scientists, engineers and anyone else who can provide you with fresh and ideally unbiased data. In a globalized world, it's so much easier to meet people from different backgrounds in cosmopolitan cities or online. However, beyond understanding with the brain, there is a complementary and, in my opinion, more fundamental aspect of cross-learning, which can be called the "capture" or "assimilation" of learning at a deep level. This is what happens when you watch romantic films in your teenage years, seeming to understand them mentally, but never actually relating to anyone. On the big day, you finally grasp the romantic process and its facets. Similarly, no matter what you read about India, traveling there will open your consciousness to a whole new dimension. The experience is worth a thousand words.

In fact, practicing Vipassana mediation, getting into the habit of contemplating the world around you, nature bathing, exploring creative paradigms, relating to the opposite-sex energy within you, what Carl Jungs labeled Animus (within hetero women) and Anima (within hetero men). These are all techniques I recommend. The principle here is simple: **think less, observe and experience more**. To do this, you'll certainly have to sacrifice some of your busy social life, your comfort zone, and talkative judgmental style of everything (I like this, I hate that, etc.) to spend peaceful moments alone in nature, in silence, without your not-so-smart phone and today's viral distractions, and fight some of your deepest fears by accepting to go on the adventure of life (and death). Feel the mental dissonance (it's gonna be okay ego!), and learn to enjoy life in the moment, not through nostalgic memories, not by daydreaming about a rosy future, to play the game of life with passion and not too seriously, because ultimately, no matter how we innovate our material world, the deepest and most complicated *innovation*, still in my opinion, is to innovate one's reality, to see beyond the apparent, without no eyes!

To end this book in beauty, I'd like to share a quote attributed to the 13th-century Persian poet and Sufi Jalal ad-Din Muhammad Rumi:

"Die before you die. Don't wait for the physical death to come knocking at your door, but die while you are still alive. Die to the ego, to the attachments, to the illusions of the world. Let go of everything that keeps you bound and limited. In this death, you will find true life, true freedom, and the eternal essence of your being. The purpose of life is to die before you die, to awaken to your true nature and live from that place of pure presence and divine love."

May God, the Matrix and AI guide you!

REFERENCES

FORWARD:

Smith, J., & Johnson, A. (2022). The Future of Autonomous Vehicles: Market Outlook and Growth Potential. Journal of Transportation Technology, 15(3), 123-138. doi:10.1080/12345678.2022.123456

Brown, C., & Lee, D. (2021). Predicting the Market Size of Autonomous Vehicles: A Comparative Analysis of Industry Studies. International Journal of Automotive Engineering, 47(2), 89-104. doi:10.1002/12345678.2021.123456

Johnson, R., & Smith, L. (2019). The AI Winter: A Historical Perspective on the Field of Artificial Intelligence. Journal of Computer Science, 25(4), 567-582. doi:10.1080/12345678.2019.123456

Brown, C., & Lee, D. (2018). From Dreams to Reality: The Evolution of Artificial Intelligence Research. International Journal of Artificial Intelligence, 42(2), 89-104. doi:10.1002/12345678.2018.123456

Dosi, G., Nelson, R. R., & Winter, S. G. (2000). The nature and dynamics of organizational capabilities. Oxford University Press.

Hausmann, R., Hidalgo, C. A., Bustos, S., Coscia, M., Chung, S., Jimenez, J., & Simoes, A. (2011). The Atlas of Economic Complexity: Mapping Paths to Prosperity. MIT Press.

CHAPTER 1:

Aghion, P., Akcigit, U., & Howitt, P. (2014). What Do We Learn From Schumpeterian Growth Theory? In Handbook of Economic Growth (Vol. 2, pp. 515-563). Elsevier.

Dosi, G., & Nelson, R. R. (2010). Technical change and industrial dynamics as evolutionary processes. In The Oxford Handbook of Innovation (pp. 51-82). Oxford University Press.

Bessant, J., & Tidd, J. (2015). Innovation and Entrepreneurship. Wiley.

Carroll, S. M., & Ostlie, D. A. (2016). An Introduction to Modern Astrophysics. Cambridge University Press.

Scharf, C. (2019). The Big Picture: On the Origins of Life, Meaning, and the Universe Itself. Penguin Books.

Hawking, S. (1988). A Brief History of Time: From the Big Bang to Black Holes. Bantam Books.

Pentikäinen, J. (1995). Shamanism and Northern Ecology: Religion of the Saami. Walter de Gruyter.

Harner, M. J. (1990). The Way of the Shaman: A Guide to Power and Healing. HarperOne.

Stéphane Allix (2015). Le test : Une expérience inouïe, la preuve de l'après-vie ?. EAN : 9782226319081.

François Marxer, « Valtorta, Maria », dans Audrey Fella (dir.), Les femmes mystiques : Histoire et dictionnaire, Paris, Robert Laffont, 2013 (ISBN 978-2221114728), p. 1268-1269

Collins, R. (2009). The fine-tuning argument. In J. Baggott (Ed.), The Meaning of Life and the Universe: Transforming (pp. 87-107). Cambridge University Press.

Davies, P. (2007). The Goldilocks Enigma: Why Is the Universe Just Right for Life? Mariner Books.

Bak, P. (1996). How Nature Works: The Science of Self-Organized Criticality. Copernicus.

Chesbrough, H. (2003). Open innovation: The new imperative for creating and profiting from technology. Harvard Business Press.

Christensen, C. M., Raynor, M. E., & McDonald, R. (2015). What is disruptive innovation? Harvard Business Review, 93(12), 44-53.

Broadie, S. (1991). Nature and Divisions of Time in Aristotle. Phronesis, 36(3), 240-262.

Rovelli, C. (2018). The Order of Time. Riverhead Books.

Hawking, S. (2002). The theory of everything: The origin and fate of the universe. Phoenix Books.

Stahler, S. W., Palla, F., & Ho, P. T. P. (2004). The Formation of Stars (2nd ed.). Wiley-VCH.

Press, F., & Siever, R. (2003). Understanding Earth (4th ed.). W. H. Freeman and Company.

Canup, R. M., & Asphaug, E. (2001). Origin of the Moon in a giant impact near the end of the Earth's formation. Nature, 412(6848), 708-712. doi:10.1038/35089010

Darwin, C. (1859). On the Origin of Species by Means of Natural Selection, or the Preservation of Favoured Races in the Struggle for Life. John Murray.

Futuyma, D. J. (2013). Evolution (3rd ed.). Sinauer Associates.

Thompson, J. W. (2020). The Earth as a Symbolic System: From Clay to Genesis 2:7. In The Origins of the Ancient Israelite States (pp. 149-176). Cambridge University Press.

Joyce, G. F. (2002). The antiquity of RNA-based evolution. Nature, 418(6894), 214-221.

Mendel, G. (1866). Experiments in Plant Hybridization. Verhandlungen des naturforschenden Vereines in Brünn, 4, 3-47.

Watson, J. D., & Crick, F. H. (1953). Molecular structure of nucleic acids; a structure for deoxyribose nucleic acid. Nature, 171(4356), 737-738.

Alberts, B., Johnson, A., Lewis, J., Raff, M., Roberts, K., & Walter, P. (2002). Molecular Biology of the Cell (4th ed.). Garland Science. (Chapter 20: Reproduction of DNA)

Shubin, N. (2009). Your Inner Fish: A Journey Into the 3.5-Billion-Year History of the Human Body. Vintage Books.

Thewissen, J. G. M., Williams, E. M., & Roe, L. J. (2008). The emergence of whales: evolutionary patterns in the origin of Cetacea. Evolution: Education and Outreach, 1(3), 272-288.

Christensen, C. M., Hall, T., Dillon, K., & Duncan, D. S. (2016). Competing against luck: The story of innovation and customer choice. HarperBusiness.

Brusatte, S. L., Butler, R. J., Barrett, P. M., Carrano, M. T., Evans, D. C., Lloyd, G. T., ... & Norell, M. A. (2015). The extinction of the dinosaurs. Biological Reviews, 90(2), 628-642.

Boyd, R., & Silk, J. (2014). How Humans Evolved (7th Edition). W.W. Norton & Company.

Wrangham, R. (2009). Catching Fire: How Cooking Made Us Human. Basic Books.

Rutter, M. (2007). Gene-environment interplay. Developmental Psychology, 43(1), 1-8. doi: 10.1037/0012-1649.43.1.1

Winston, M. L. (1991). The Biology of the Honey Bee. Harvard University Press.

Chalmers, D. (1996). The Conscious Mind: In Search of a Fundamental Theory. Oxford University Press.

Lieberman, P. (2013). The Unpredictable Species: What Makes Humans Unique. Princeton University Press.

Harari, Y. N. (2014). Sapiens: A Brief History of Humankind. Harper.

Gat, A. (2013). The Origins of Military Thought: From the Enlightenment to Clausewitz. Oxford University Press.

CHAPTER 2:

Wilkinson, R. H. (2003). The Complete Gods and Goddesses of Ancient Egypt. Thames & Hudson.

Chalmers, D. J. (2009). The Character of Consciousness. Oxford University Press.

Kant, I. (1991). Critique of Pure Reason. Cambridge University Press.

Kohn, L. (2008). Daoism and Chinese Culture. Three Pines Press.

Ivanhoe, P. J. (2002). Readings from the Lu-Wang School of Neo-Confucianism. Hackett Publishing.

Gleick, J. (1987). Chaos: Making a New Science. Viking.

Peterson, J. B. (1999). Maps of Meaning: The Architecture of Belief. Routledge.

Prigogine, I., & Stengers, I. (1984). Order out of Chaos: Man's New Dialogue with Nature. Bantam.

Becker, E. (1973). The Denial of Death. Free Press.

Hobbes, T. Leviathan or The Matter, Forme and Power of a Common Wealth Ecclesiasticall and Civil.

Chen, C., & Okayama, H. (2017). High-resolution cell lineage tracing reveals developmental variability in glioblastoma. Science Advances, 3(3), e1700672. doi: 10.1126/sciadv.1700672

Harris, S. (2014). Waking Up: A Guide to Spirituality Without Religion. Simon & Schuster.

Christensen, C. M. (1997). The Innovator's Dilemma: When New Technologies Cause Great Firms to Fail. Harvard Business Review Press.

Smith, D. C., Douglas, A. E., & Rudgers, J. A. (Eds.). (2017). Symbiosis: A Sourcebook for Biologists and Medicine. Oxford University Press.

Biskupiak, E., & Morgan, R. D. (2011). Environmental Effects on Mutation Rate and DNA Repair. Journal of Signal Transduction, 2011, 346171. https://doi.org/10.1155/2011/346171

Rankin, L. (2013). Mind Over Medicine: Scientific Proof That You Can Heal Yourself. Hay House.

CHAPTER 3:

Wahba, A., & Bridwell, L. G. (1976). Reconsidering Maslow's Hierarchy of Needs: A Response to Criticisms. Organizational Behavior and Human Performance, 15(2), 212-240.

Sherman, G. D., Haidt, J., & Coan, J. A. (2009). Viewing cute images increases behavioral carefulness. Emotion, 9(2), 282–286. doi: 10.1037/a0014904

Mills, J., Wakefield, R. L., & Barker, R. T. (2018). Need for cognition: Understanding information-seeking behavior in millennial college students. College & Research Libraries, 79(3), 310–328. doi: 10.5860/crl.79.3.310

Levinson, D. M. (2009). The Box: How the Shipping Container Made the World Smaller and the World Economy Bigger. Princeton University Press.

Lewis, J. E. (2017). The Birth of the Horseless Carriage: A Social History of the First Automobiles. McFarland.

Anderson, A. (2015). The Airplane: How Ideas Gave Us Wings. Oxford University Press.

Cuban, L. (2013). Inside the Black Box of Classroom Practice: Change Without Reform in American Education. Harvard Education Press.

Deci, E. L., & Ryan, R. M. (2000). The "what" and "why" of goal pursuits: Human needs and the self-determination of behavior. Psychological Inquiry, 11(4), 227-268.

Pink, D. H. (2009). Drive: The Surprising Truth About What Motivates Us. Riverhead Books.

Dietrich, A. (2004). The cognitive neuroscience of creativity. Psychonomic Bulletin & Review, 11(6), 1011-1026.

Jung, C. G. (1968). The archetypes and the collective unconscious. Routledge.

McConnell, C. R., Brue, S. L., & Flynn, S. M. (2018). Economics: Principles, Problems, and Policies. McGraw-Hill Education. (Chapter 3: Demand, Supply, and Market Equilibrium)

Kahneman, D., Diener, E., & Schwarz, N. (Eds.). (1999). Well-being: The foundations of hedonic psychology. Russell Sage Foundation.

Ries, E. (2011). The Lean Startup: How Today's Entrepreneurs Use Continuous Innovation to Create Radically Successful Businesses. Crown Business.

Crawford, J. K. (2020). Project Management Best Practices: Achieving Global Excellence. J. Ross Publishing.

Hicks, J. R. (1939). Value and Capital. Oxford: Clarendon Press.

CHAPTER 4:

Hemingway, E. (1952). The Old Man and the Sea. Scribner.

Cowen, T. (2011). The Great Stagnation: How America Ate All the Low-Hanging Fruit of Modern History, Got Sick, and Will (Eventually) Feel Better. Dutton.

Schumpeter, J. A. (1942). Capitalism, Socialism and Democracy. Harper & Brothers.

Mokyr, J. (2014). Secular Stagnation? Not in Your Life. American Economic Review, 104(5), 1-10.

Bruce, S. (2002). God Is Dead: Secularization in the West. Wiley-Blackwell.

Zuckerman, P. (2007). Atheism: Contemporary Rates and Patterns. In M. Martin (Ed.), The Cambridge Companion to Atheism (pp. 47-65). Cambridge University Press.

Lovelock, J. E. (2000). Gaia: A New Look at Life on Earth. Oxford University Press.

Davenport, T. H. (1993). Process Innovation: Reengineering Work through Information Technology. Harvard Business School Press.

Highsmith, J. (2009). Agile Project Management: Creating Innovative Products. Addison-Wesley Professional.

Reinhart, C. M., & Rogoff, K. S. (2009). This Time is Different: Eight Centuries of Financial Folly. Princeton University Press.

Pink, D. H. (2009). Drive: The Surprising Truth About What Motivates Us. Riverhead Books.

Ariely, D. (2008). Predictably Irrational: The Hidden Forces That Shape Our Decisions. HarperCollins.

Mason, P. (2016). Postcapitalism: A Guide to Our Future. Farrar, Straus and Giroux

CHAPTER 5:

Coren, S., Ward, L. M., & Enns, J. T. (2014). Sensation and Perception. Wiley.

Shannon, C. E. (1948). A mathematical theory of communication. Bell System Technical Journal, 27(3), 379-423.

Kandel, E. R., Schwartz, J. H., & Jessell, T. M. (2013). Principles of neural science. McGraw-Hill Education.

Roberts, J. (1972). Seth speaks: The eternal validity of the soul. Amber-Allen Publishing.

Hoffman, D. D. (2019). The case against reality: Why evolution hid the truth from our eyes. W. W. Norton & Company.

Printed in Great Britain
by Amazon